BETWEEN TOKYO AND MOSCOW

JOACHIM GLAUBITZ

Between Tokyo and Moscow
The History of an Uneasy Relationship,
1972 to the 1990s

UNIVERSITY OF HAWAII PRESS
HONOLULU

© 1995 Joachim Glaubitz
All Rights Reserved

Published in North America by
University of Hawaii Press
2480 Kolowalu Street
Honolulu, Hawaii 96822

Published in the United Kingdom by
C. Hurst and Company (Publishers) Ltd., London

Printed in Hong Kong

Library of Congress Cataloging-in-Publication Data

Glaubitz, Joachim.
    Tokyo and Moscow : the history of an uneasy relationship,
1972–1990s / Joachim Glaubitz
    p.   cm.
    Includes bibliographical references and index.
    ISBN 0–8248–1674–9
    1. Japan—Foreign relations—Soviet Union. 2. Soviet Union—
Foreign relations—Japan. 3. Japan—Foreign relations—1945–1989.
4. Japan—Foreign relations—1989– 5. Soviet Union—Foreign
relations—1945–1991.   I. Title.
DS849.S65G53   1995
327.52047′09′045—dc20   94–11085

CONTENTS

Preface	page vii
List of Abbreviations	xi

Part I. EAST ASIA AT THE BEGINNING OF THE 1970s

1. The international framework: the United States, China and the Soviet Union — 3
2. Japan's policies and the changes in surrounding conditions — 10
3. Japan under pressure from the Sino-American rapprochement — 13

Part II. JAPAN'S RELATIONS WITH THE SOVIET UNION

4. Aims — 27
5. The territorial question — 32
   Historical background — 32
   The protagonists change positions 1956–1973 — 42
   The eve of Tanaka's visit to Moscow — 49
   Tanaka's visit to Moscow — 54
   Fundamental positions under fire: 1973–1985 — 63
   Signs of the 'New Thinking' — 75
   The territorial problem and public opinion — 85
6. Beginnings of economic cooperation — 96
   Projects in the Soviet Far East and Siberia — 96
   Difficulties with Tyumen — 102
   Economic relations within narrow limits — 107
   Oil and natural gas exploitation off Sakhalin — 116
   Tentative revival of economic relations — 123
7. Japan's entanglement in the Sino-Soviet conflict — 134
   China and the Japanese-Soviet territorial question — 136

Offers of competing treaties	143
Japan's armed forces and the Sino-Soviet conflict	157
8. Aspects of security policy	167
Historical background	167
Primary targets of Soviet criticism	171
Departure from traditional positions	174
The Soviet Union as a threat to Japan	181
The threat and its effect on public opinion	198

Part III. RECENT DEVELOPMENTS AND PERSPECTIVES

9. Expectations before Gorbachev's visit to Japan	205
10. Progress, results, reactions	217
11. Continuation of the dialogue: prospects for the future	231
Epilogue to the English edition	243

APPENDIXES

A. Joint Soviet-Japanese declarations	255
B. Draft of a treaty of good neighbourliness and cooperation between the USSR and Japan, 24 February 1978	269
C. Japanese-Soviet economic relations	272
D. Opinion polls	284
Select Bibliography	293
Names Index	301
Subject Index	304

MAPS

1. Overview of the region	28
2. The disputed South Kuriles	33
3. Borders in the 19th century	34
4. Borders in the 20th century	35
5. Oil and natural gas exploitation off Sakhalin	117

PREFACE

In the hundred years between the first Russo-Japanese treaty of 1855 and the 'Joint Declaration' of 1956 that marked the resumption of diplomatic relations after the Second World War, relations between Russia and Japan were always characterised by periods of tension. The same pattern can be seen in the three and a half decades which followed, up to the disintegration of the Soviet Union in 1991. Historical evidence has demonstrated that only a few years after diplomatic contact between the two countries had first been established, Yukichi Fukuzawa, a driving force behind Japan's modernisation programme, wrote after visiting Russia in 1861 that here was a force which was not to be trusted. Surveys show that even today this prejudice prevails among the majority of Japanese.

What was the reason for Fukuzawa's negative image of Russia at such an early stage? Its origins are worth reviewing. The man who later founded Keio University travelled to Europe in 1861 on a diplomatic mission that took him through England and the Netherlands to Berlin and St Petersburg. Describing a characteristic episode of his stay in the Czarist capital, he recounted how one day a member of the Russian reception committee took him into a side room and said:

> I do not know much about Japan. Possibly I am not qualified to speak. But from general reasoning I feel that Japan is not a country for an ambitious youth. It is a small country – little opportunity for doing big things. What would you say to settling yourself in Russia?

Fukuzawa declined, giving as his reason his position in the diplomatic service. The Russian persisted, proclaiming his willingness to hide Fukuzawa until the Japanese group had departed. Again Fukuzawa declined. His insistent Russian colleague tried again and again. In vain.

Fukuzawa noted:

> This incident made its impression on me. I had heard that

Russia was different from all the other countries of Europe. Now I understood it. For during my visits in England and France, and also in America the year before, nearly all the people I talked with were eager to come to Japan. In fact, I was often bored by having people ask me about jobs in Japan; some had even wanted me to take them along. But I had not met anyone in those lands who advised me to stay in his country.

He concluded, 'At any rate, I decided that Russia was a country in which we could not safely unburden our minds.'[1]

This opinion has not, of course, prevented the Japanese from occasionally joining political forces with Russia against other states, with such secret collaborations generally being directed against China and Korea. Four Russo-Japanese treaties, concluded between 1907 and 1916, deviated in their published form from what had been privately agreed. The division of Manchuria into spheres of influence, the reciprocal recognition of special rights in Korea and Mongolia, and an agreement on joint action in the event of an attack on China by another power were all the objects of secret agreements.

The purpose of the present study, however, is not to examine each stage in the history of Russo-Japanese relations: something that has been thoroughly covered in a number of monographs. It should be pointed out that in examining the most recent developments in relations between these two unequal neighbours — which is the subject of this volume — the history of the relationship must also be considered. This relationship is, for example, marked by China's latent mistrust of Japan and the Soviet Union. Since the Cultural Revolution, China has not only been an attentive observer of developments in Japan's relations with its Russian neighbour, but through its own policies has also played a crucial role in shaping the framework of their development, a role which began in the early 1970s and which is certain to continue into the foreseeable future. Indeed, the process of normalisation in Sino-Japanese relations featured a marked anti-Soviet bias and had as its aim the exploitation of Japan as an instrument in Chinese politics, an aim that reinforced the general immobility characterising post-war Soviet-Japanese

1. *The Autobiography of Fukuzawa Yukichi*, Tokyo 1960, pp. 137ff.

relations. Japan's attitude to China, however, was unaffected by the significant changes arising from the Sino-Soviet détente of the 1980s. At the same time, these changes allowed the Soviet Union to deny the idea of granting concessions to Japan the weight which Japan wished it to receive. Only when President Gorbachev's initiatives in policies on Asia brought about the revision of previous Soviet foreign policies were the conditions necessary for a reshaping of Soviet-Japanese relations created. Only time will tell whether Japan's weight as an economic power and Russia's interest in exploiting this power will be sufficient to reshape relations with Russia, and whether Japan will be able to gain the political leeway between China, Russia and the United States necessary to this process. Such questions are beyond the scope of this study, which is intended to furnish a basis for the evaluation of future political developments in East Asia.

The core of the book is an analysis of the development of relations between Japan and the Soviet Union, which is based, so to speak, on twofold foundations. The first part outlines the dramatic changes in the international situation in East Asia at the beginning of the 1970s. The *rapprochement* between the United States and China proved a decisive factor in Japan's policies concerning China, causing as it did a reshaping of the framework of Japanese foreign policy. A detailed description of the bilateral aspects of Soviet-Japanese relations is followed by a third section that is multilateral in approach, in which the 'triangle' of Japan–Soviet Union–China is examined, together with security issues within the network of relations in the Far East and the factors necessary for a fundamental turnaround in relations between the Soviet Union and Japan, which will certainly play a significant role in Russian politics as well.

The work has admittedly been written with specialists in mind; however, the style and presentation are directed at readers with a broad interest in politics. While specialists may wish for a more systematic analysis, preference has been given to a chronological treatment of the material based on diplomatic history, with the sources indicated. The book aims to enable those unfamiliar with the subject to form their own opinions.

The transcription of Japanese expressions and names follows the Hepburn System in the footnotes and source list, and current international orthography in the text. Russian terms are transcribed scientifically in the sources, and phonetically in all other cases. Chinese names are, apart from common spellings, given in pinyin transcriptions.

I should like to express my deepest thanks to Gisela Helms for her careful reading of the text, innumerable corrections and valuable suggestions concerning the form of the manuscript.

University of Munich JOACHIM GLAUBITZ
September 1994

ABBREVIATIONS

APEC	Asia Pacific Economic Cooperation
APR	Asia Pacific Region
ASEAN	Association of South-East Asian Nations
AWACS	Airborne Warning and Control System
BAM	Baikal-Amur Magistrale
BPA	Bundespresseamt (German Federal News Agency)
CIS	Commonwealth of Independent States
COMECON	Committee for Mutual Economic Assistance
CPJ	Communist Party of Japan
CPSU	Communist Party of the Soviet Union
CSCE	Conference on Security and Cooperation in Europe
DIW	Deutsches Institut für Wirtschaftsforschung (German Institute for Economic Research)
DSJP	*Daily Summary of Japanese Press*
DSP	Democratic Socialist Party (of Japan)
EC	European Community
Exim Bank	Export-Import Bank
FEA	*Far Eastern Affairs* (Moscow)
FRG	Federal Republic of Germany
G7	Group of Seven (industrialised nations)
IISS	International Institute for Strategic Studies
INF	Intermediate-Range Nuclear Forces
JJSEC	Joint Japanese-Soviet Economic Committee
JSJEC	Joint Soviet-Japanese Economic Committee
KGB	State Security Committee (Komitet Gosudarstvennych Bezopasnosti)
LDP	Liberal Democratic Party (of Japan)

MD	*Monitor-Dienst* (International Monitoring Service of German Federal Radio)
MITI	Ministry for International Trade and Industry (Japan)
NHK	Nihon Hoso Kyokai (Japanese broadcasting association)
NIC	newly industrialising country
NKBS	*Nisso-kihon-bunsho-shiryoshu* (Collection of Documents Fundamental to Japanese-Soviet Relations)
OECD	Organisation for Economic Cooperation and Development
PECC	Pacific Economic Cooperation Conference
RFE/RL	Radio Free Europe/Radio Liberty
RIPS	Research Institute for Peace and Security
RSFSR	Russian Socialist Federative Soviet Republic
SDF	Self-Defence Forces (Japan)
SLB	Siberia land bridge
SODECO	Sakhalin Oil Development Corporation
SPJ	Socialist Party of Japan
SSJM	*Summaries of Selected Japanese Magazines*
SSN	Nuclear-Fuelled Submarines
SWB/FE	*Summary of World Broadcasts/Far East*

Part I

EAST ASIA AT THE BEGINNING OF THE 1970s

1

THE INTERNATIONAL FRAMEWORK: THE UNITED STATES, CHINA AND THE SOVIET UNION

Relations between regional powers and superpowers in the Asia Pacific region have undergone radical alterations since the turn of the 1960s and '70s, when Indochina was the principal scene of international confrontation and cooperation in the area. The initial conviction that the United States would be able to win the war here had been succeeded, even within the US government itself, by the realisation that a political solution to the conflict was essential. After massive military intervention in North Vietnam and reiterations of willingness to begin talks, by May 1968 the United States succeeded in finally persuading North Vietnam to participate in talks on ending the war. Richard Nixon, elected President of the United States in November 1968, adopted as his primary aim the release of his country from its involvement in Indochina, for which a fundamental change in America's previous policies on Asia was necessary. Nixon gave the first signal of this change during an informal press conference in Guam on 25 July 1969. His statements, immediately dubbed 'the Nixon Doctrine', basically declared that the United States would in future expect Asian countries to resolve their own problems of internal security and external defence – with the exception of threats of nuclear attack.

This somewhat sketchy outline of a new policy of alliance was followed by a reformulation of the defence policy accompanying it, the strategy of 'one and a half wars'. This stated that in times of peace the United States would maintain sufficient defence forces to repel a large-scale Communist attack in either Europe or Asia, to provide allies with support in the case of non-Chinese threats in Asia and, in addition, to deal with any unexpected crisis in any other region.

This strategy signalled the abandonment of the previously held assumption that the Soviet Union and China formed a single working unit. From that time onwards, each Communist power was regarded as an independent agent. President Nixon, who presented this fundamental change in American policy to Congress in February 1970, evidently no longer regarded the assumption of a coordinated attack on Europe by Warsaw Pact countries and on Asia by China as feasible. This shift in attitude was founded on the armed clashes between China and the Soviet Union at the beginning of March 1969, first at Ussuri and later at other points on the border, which clearly showed the extent of Sino-Soviet hostility and at the same time provided American politics with the vital impetus to place relations with China on a new footing.[1] The change of strategy was certainly an important step in this direction. Nixon's security adviser, Henry Kissinger, referred to it as 'one of our most important signals to the People's Republic of China that we mean to improve our relations with it'.[2]

Further signals followed; the military presence in the streets of Taiwan was reduced, the trade embargo was relaxed and supply restrictions on trade with China were lifted. At first Peking reacted with extreme caution, indicating that it was able to take steps towards political détente without expressly demanding specific actions in return. Yet the Ninth Congress of the Chinese Communist Party in April 1969 reiterated that hostility towards both superpowers was part of current policy; however, analysis of the report of this Congress reveals that party leaders saw the Soviet Union as more of a threat than the United States.

Complicated internal debates preceded the approval of a policy whereby confrontation with the United States was reduced while the state of conflict with the Soviet Union was maintained.[3] The decision to move in this direction seems to have been made in the second half of 1970. From then on there were an increasing number of signs from Peking indicating interest in top-level contact with the USA.

1. See Henry Kissinger, *The White House Years*, London 1979, pp. 171ff.
2. *Ibid.*, p. 220.
3. See Marie-Luise Näth, *Die Entwicklung der amerikanisch-chinesischen Beziehungen seit 1972. Hintergründe, Probleme, Perspektiven* (Developments in Sino-American Relations since 1972: Background, Problems, Perspectives), Cologne 1979 (Berichte des Bundesinstituts für Internationale und Ostwissenschaftliche Studien, no. 36).

Secret arrangements were made for Kissinger to visit Peking, with cryptic messages sent via other countries, notably Pakistan and Romania. The visit, which took place in mid-July 1971, led to President Nixon announcing his intention to visit the People's Republic of China at the beginning of 1972. This news, published simultaneously in Washington and Peking on 15 July 1971, took the world's breath away. Zhou Enlai had predicted it. Japan, more directly affected but just as surprised as all the United States' allies at the move, spoke of a 'Nixon Shock'.

Within just a few years, Sino-American détente, initiated after more than twenty years of hostilities, radically altered the international situation in Eastern Asia. For China, this transformation had a decisive effect on its ominously deteriorating relations with the Soviet Union. Ideological disagreements between the two Communist-led countries swelled from the polemics of the 1960s into outpourings of vitriol. The most strident tones emanated from China during the Cultural Revolution — that is, between 1966 and 1969. Moscow's every decision, whether in national or foreign affairs, was attacked in polemical tones, and the leadership of the Soviet Union was accused of being nothing but a Soviet-revisionist band of renegades, and above all of 'collaborating with the US imperialists'.

The accusations from the Soviets were more reserved in tone, but more direct in content. Since the start of the Cultural Revolution in the summer of 1966, these attacks had focused on 'Mao Zedong and his group' — the standard expression used. It was noteworthy that the attacks on Mao gradually came to hinge on matters of principle, finally culminating in the claim that the Chinese party leader had never, even in the earliest years of the Chinese Communist Party, been a genuine Marxist. Another remarkable feature was that the men in the so-called 'group' or 'clique' around Mao Zedong were neither attacked by name nor identified by name. Moreover, Soviet polemics carefully differentiated between the 'great power chauvinist' Mao Zedong, the Communist Party of China, which he had misled, and the Chinese people. Evidently the Soviet leaders did not want to spoil the chances of normalising state and party relations after Mao had gone, and thus concentrated their attacks on Mao himself. In preparing for post-Mao China, they avoided direct attacks on other powerful leaders in the Chinese Communist

Party, probably assuming that when Mao was no longer in power those leaders would be the ones to negotiate with the Soviet Union.

The Soviet invasion of Czechoslovakia in August 1968 also had a far-reaching effect on China's relations with the Soviet Union. Brezhnev described the invasion as 'Military aid for a fraternal country' to 'remove a danger arising for the Socialist order'.[4] The Chinese leaders vehemently rejected the repeated use of this interpretation of 'proletarian internationalism', describing the Soviet Union and its policies as 'social-imperialist'; for China too was accused of 'deviating from the principles of Marxism-Leninism and from proletarian internationalism'.[5] Even before 1968, Brezhnev himself had already accused the 'Mao Zedong Group' of undermining the unity of the global community of socialism and the international Communist movement.[6] China too was apparently endangering the 'socialist order', for which it was also threatened — at least 'theoretically' — with the application of the 'Brezhnev Doctrine'. The Soviet Union's differing reaction in the case of China may have had to do with the latter's natural protection, its geographical and demographic situation. In any case Peking perceived the Soviet Union's invasion of Czechoslovakia as a threat. 'The Czech affair is not an isolated event', stated the Peking *People's Daily*.[7] And the Chinese leaders acted accordingly by playing the 'American card'.

Brezhnev's speech in Poznan reiterating the doctrine of the limited sovereignty of socialist states was all of two weeks old when the Chinese Foreign Ministry announced its willingness to continue talks at ambassadorial level with the United States in Warsaw. At the same time, the American government was reminded that for the past thirteen years it had been Washington which had refused to sign an agreement with China over withdrawal from Taiwan and the 'five principles of peaceful co-

---

4. Speech by Brezhnev in Poznan on 12 Nov. 1968, quoted in Boris Meissner, *Die 'Breshnew-Doktrin'*, Cologne 1969, p. 79.
5. See *Pravda*, 16 Aug. 1967.
6. *Ibid.*, 7 Nov. 1967.
7. *Renmin-ribao*, 24 Aug. 1968 and 3 Sept. 1968, quoted in *China News Analysis*, no. 752 (11 April 1969), p. 7.

existence'.[8] This was an unfamiliar note! The very reference to the five principles of peaceful coexistence, which had been taboo during the Cultural Revolution, proclaimed China's new approach to foreign – and, as it later turned out, American – policy. The Soviet invasion of Czechoslovakia provided a decisive impetus for this.

Further impetus came from an initiative in Asian policy taken by the Soviet Union. On 7 July 1969, at the International Conference of the Communist and Workers' Parties in Moscow, Brezhnev proposed the foundation of a system of collective security in Asia.[9] At first he declined to elaborate on the plan; details were only furnished months later in Tokyo by a Soviet specialist in international law, Georgi Sadorozhny. According to the proposal, the Soviet Union's intention was to found a universalistic institution modelled on the United Nations – whose members would include both China and Taiwan. It seemed that the Soviet Union was approving a policy of 'two Chinas'.[10] Later comments on the planned security system did little to clarify the picture. Possibly the vagueness was a deliberate move to ensure that any reaction could be dealt with flexibly. In any case, the proposal as the Soviets saw it was to include such principles as non-aggression, the inviolability of national borders and increased cooperation in economic and other areas. However, the idea met with little interest in Asia, probably because of the anti-Chinese tendency that coloured it from the start. Both the speech in which Brezhnev presented the proposal and the commentary on it that appeared in an official Soviet newspaper were accompanied by heavy criticism of China's politics.[11] Peking's immediate reaction was to reject the idea, perceiving Brezhnev's initiative as a policy aimed at isolating China and as 'an attempt to form a new anti-Chinese military bloc by coercion and cajolery'.[12]

From the Chinese point of view, the situation in Asia in 1969 was thus that the United States seemed determined to reduce its

8. See Xinhua News Agency, *Daily Bulletin*, no. 3952 (26 Nov. 1968).
9. See *Pravda*, 8 June 1969
10. See *Yomiuri*, 19 Nov. 1969, in *Daily Summary of Japanese Press (DSJP)*, 19 Nov. 1969, p. 28.
11. See *Izvestiya*, 29 May 1969.
12. See *Peking Review*, no. 27 (1969), pp. 22ff.

military commitments and to avoid involvement in future conflicts within Asia. The Soviet Union, on the other hand, planned to increase its presence in Asia, justifying such an increase by proposing a system of collective security. One superpower, then, was engaged in conducting a military withdrawal, while the other appeared to be preparing to step up its military strength in this area. In Peking's view, the Soviet Union had become the more dangerous of the two: 'It is even more deceitful than the old-line imperialist countries, and therefore more dangerous.'[13] Given this assessment of the situation, the only logical course of action was to reduce confrontation with the United States in order to increase national security. For the same reason, it seemed advisable not to break off all contact with the Soviet Union. The armed skirmishes along the common border had focused the attention of both sides on the risks involved in an escalation of conflict. Negotiation of the border question was essential. On 11 September 1969 Prime Ministers Kosygin and Zhou Enlai met for a surprise discussion in Peking in which they agreed to resume negotiations on the border question through their Deputy Foreign Ministers. Bilateral trade, which had previously sunk to a minimum, was somewhat revitalised by the news, totalling 42 million roubles in 1970 and 210 million roubles in 1972. In 1970 the ambassadors of both sides returned to their posts.[14]

In fact, the resumption of diplomatic activities and the expansion in trade were not an expression of improved relations, but rather part of a gradual normalisation of Chinese diplomacy after the Cultural Revolution. It is rewarding to trace China's tentative moves towards normalising foreign relations during the late 1960s and early 1970s after three years of self-imposed isolation: tentative, because the balance of power between the leaders had not been finally settled; rewarding, because the order in which embassies were reopened demonstrates a certain order of priorities in China's foreign policy, in which South-East Asia and Africa were focal points. The reopening of the Bucharest embassy as early as June 1969 is also remarkable; this, together

13. *Ibid.*, no. 40 (1972), p. 10.
14. See G.W. Astafyev and A.M. Dubinski (eds), *Aussenpolitik und internationale Beziehungen der Volksrepublik China* (Foreign Policy and International Relations in the People's Republic of China), Berlin 1976, p. 334.

with the representative in Albania, were China's only fully staffed foreign outposts in Eastern Europe until mid-1970.

Of China's neighbours, North Vietnam and North Korea were also given priority. Thus in 1970 Pyongyang was the destination of Zhou Enlai's first visit abroad after the Cultural Revolution. The situation in the Indochinese peninsula was complicated, as Peking considered the area to lie within its sphere of interests, for historical, geographical and ethnic reasons. During a trip abroad in March 1970, the Cambodian head of state, Prince Sihanouk, was deposed amid accusations of having promoted pro-Communist policies. After a spell in Moscow he formed a government-in-exile in Peking, the 'Royal Government of the National Union', which was recognised only by North Korea, North Vietnam and China itself. Soviet diplomats remained in Phnom Penh. Observers suspected that China's strong support for Sihanouk was aimed at creating a Cambodia which would be a counterweight to an all-too-independent North Vietnam after the conflict in Indochina was over.[15]

China's long-term aims could be readily determined from the redirection of its policies from the end of the 1960 onwards; Peking aimed at expanding and consolidating the independence gradually won from Moscow after the end of the 1950s in issues of ideology, economy and foreign and defence policies, in order to create a foundation for the status of non-allied third great power to which it aspired. The leading politicians in Peking, Mao Zedong and Zhou Enlai, believed that cautious, controlled cooperation with the United States would serve as an effective strategy of protection against what they perceived as expansionism on the part of the Soviet Union.

---

15. See *Far Eastern Economic Review* (Hong Kong), *Yearbook 1971*, p. 118.

2

JAPAN'S POLICIES AND THE CHANGES IN SURROUNDING CONDITIONS

Changes within the regional system of relations within the Asia Pacific area naturally led to changes in the conditions under which Japan had customarily made its foreign policy decisions up to the beginning of the 1970s. Four processes of development occurred more or less concurrently:

- the change in America's Asian policies announced in 1969 in the Nixon Doctrine;
- the willingness of China to adapt to this change;
- the escalation of the Sino-Soviet conflict;
- détente between the United States and the Soviet Union.

As a direct consequence of these developments worldwide, Japan was obliged to adapt its foreign relations in certain vital areas:

- Its relationship with the United States shifted from one of subordination to partnership, signalled by the return of Okinawa to Japan in May 1972. However, economic rivalry increased at the same time. In addition, Japan believed it should develop independent political initiatives against declared opponents of the USA, such as North Korea and North Vietnam.
- The safeguarding of stable sources of raw materials and energy took priority in Japan's foreign policy during and after the energy crisis of 1973.
- Recognition of the People's Republic of China and the normalisation of relations with that country, principally under conditions determined by Peking, also followed logically from global developments.
- At the same time, contacts with the Soviet Union were increased, mainly in economic areas but also to some extent in the political arena.

Despite such adjustments, Japan's foreign and defence policies were, are today and will in the foreseeable future be determined by the country's alliance with the United States. There are two reasons for this. First, this alliance, encompassing as it does shifting degrees of dependence in such areas as trade, supplies of raw materials and foodstuffs, and defence, is the only framework that enables Japan to survive and develop. Secondly, and this applies chiefly to the Japanese, there was and is simply no feasible alternative to an American-Japanese alliance. This also means that Japan's efforts to diversify its primary supply-sources in a conscious attempt to reduce dependence on the United States (for their relationship is frequently seen as purely one-sided) should not be interpreted as a search for alternatives to this alliance. Potential sources of raw materials and energy would be China and the Soviet Union, particularly because of the geographical proximity of, and the political rivalry between, these Communist neighbours. Exploitation of this rivalry featured largely in Japanese diplomacy until the end of the 1970s and was the chief factor, after the alliance with the United States, determining its foreign policy. In accordance with this alliance, the development of friendly relations with China was given priority. Japan's reasons for favouring China and turning away from the Soviet Union will be examined separately.

Generally, however, it is true to say that the unique nature of the triangle between Japan, China and the Soviet Union lies in the historically rooted asymmetry of Sino-Japanese and Soviet-Japanese relations. Japan's relationship with China is, in simplified terms, shaped by a compound of cultural solidarity and pangs of conscience; its relations with the Soviet Union, on the other hand, have always been founded on sentiments of cultural superiority, coloured by an enduring mistrust rooted in historical events.

The political consequences of this philosophy are manifest. China can reckon with Japan displaying a degree of readiness to make concessions that it has never bestowed on Soviet or Russian negotiators. The Kremlin, well aware of this disadvantage, has repeatedly informed Japan that too great a degree of Sino-Japanese understanding would cause displeasure in the Soviet Union and adversely affect relations with Japan. However, this attitude accelerated the very process the Soviet Union was attempting to prevent, namely *rapprochement* between China and Japan – one partner under-developed and over-populated; the other highly industrialised, a technological superpower allied with the United States.

Japan's foreign policy as such only came into existence in the second half of the nineteenth century, but from its inception China occupied a central position within this policy, and today a new element has been introduced in the form of China's undeniable status of a regional power with global interests. The latter's claim to a leading role within Asia is strengthened by its geographical and strategic characteristics: extensive territory with reserves of raw materials and energy sources; a largely self-supporting population of over 100 million; growing military strength, both conventional and nuclear; and a system of rule that is striving to achieve the modernisation of the country by applying a combination of moderate Stalinism and pragmatic economic reforms.

The fundamental differences between China and its neighbour Japan are plain to see. Some 120 million Japanese inhabit their tiny country, in a highly industrialised society which is dependent almost entirely on imports for its energy and raw material requirements, and which for over a decade has no longer been able to produce enough food to support itself. Japan's massive dependence on outsiders and China's still considerable independence from the outside world represent a fundamental difference between the two countries; a difference that, as well as exerting a profound effect on the course of their politics, has affected them both regionally and internationally, particularly since the end of China's self-imposed isolation.

When China opened its export trade to the capitalist countries after the progressive deterioration of Sino-Soviet relations at the start of the 1960s, Japan was among the chief exploiters of this process, and not only from an economic point of view. Relations between China and Japan began to achieve normalisation at the time of Prime Minister Tanaka's visit to Peking in September 1972 and the establishment of diplomatic relations that followed. However, if Japan had previously been only slightly affected by the Sino-Soviet conflict, it now found itself in the thick of tension between China and the Soviet Union. The altered Sino-Japanese relationship changed more than just the general framework of Japanese politics. More importantly, Japan was forced to learn how to deal with both Peking and Moscow, while simultaneously coping with its own national affairs and their repercussions, and safeguarding its own position.

3

JAPAN UNDER PRESSURE FROM THE SINO-AMERICAN RAPPROCHEMENT

Japan soon learned that maintaining a position within an international environment in the process of regrouping can be extremely difficult. One of the most powerful industrialised nations in the world was confronted with the arduousness of translating economic power into political action, and was forced to recognise that within the shifting pattern of its relationships with the United States, the Soviet Union and China, Japan was the weakest member. On 29 September 1972, the heads of government of China and Japan, Zhou Enlai and Kakuei Tanaka, put their signatures to a Joint Declaration in which Japan recognised the government of the People's Republic as the sole legal government of China. At the same time, both sides agreed to exchange diplomatic representatives, after a break of twenty-three years. Official relations with the Republic of China (Taiwan), which had begun in 1952 under American 'tuition', were broken off, and the peace treaty with Chiang Kaishek's government which had been concluded that same year was annulled by a unilateral declaration by the Japanese Foreign Minister, Ohira.[1]

Recognition of the People's Republic of China, a prerequisite for the normalisation of Sino-Japanese relations, was preceded in Japan by the complex process of forming a consensus. This began with a débâcle for the Japanese – the decision of the Chinese leaders to reduce confrontation with the United States and to normalise relations by calling upon the principles of peaceful coexistence. America's acceptance of this decision caught the government and people of Japan completely off guard. The Japanese people's criticism of their own government's foreign policies developed into national political pressure to follow the precedent set by America, drawing Tokyo into the slip-

1. See *China aktuell*, vol. 1, no. 8 (Sept. 1972), p. 31; *Peking Review*, no. 40 (1972), p. 15.

stream of dialogue between Washington and Peking. In addition, China, by skilfully exploiting the situation, was largely able to impose its own conditions for normalisation on Japan. This process requires more detailed examination.

It began on 15 July 1971 with the fanfare of announcements of Kissinger's hitherto secret trip and Nixon's planned trip to Peking. Analysing this sensational news, Tokyo came to the conclusion, as accurate as it was banal, that no Japanese foreign policy on China existed. Even Japanese observers who had been relatively reticent up till then could no longer accuse their government of lethargy and passivity in its policies concerning China.[2]

Public figures and the mass media became louder and louder in their demands for normalising relations with China. The Chinese Question soon came to dominate treatments of foreign policy in the country's press. The Chinese government could not have wished for anything better than increasing criticism of the Sato government's incompetence over policies concerning China, coupled with more and more urgent calls for the normalisation of relations with Peking, if possible to preempt the United States. The Member of Parliament of the Liberal Democratic Party (LDP) who carried out extensive preparations for Tanaka's first visit to China wrote in retrospect:

> Last year [1971], the atmosphere in Japan suddenly changed. The wind changed its direction completely. Because of the dramatic changes in the environment around us, such as the announcement of Nixon's China visit and China's recovery of its UN seat, all people began to turn their faces toward Peking at about the end of last year. I was filled with deep emotion at this drastic change.[3]

China cleverly exploited the Japanese reaction, on the one hand rejecting normalisation of relations with the Sato government and the negotiations that this process would involve, and

2. See Masataka Kôsaka, 'Shingaikô-jidai-no-kôsô' (Concept for a New Era of Foreign Policy), in *Shokun*, no. 12 (1971), pp. 23–44; Shunichi Matsumoto, 'Tenka-ni haji-wo sarasu Nihon gaikô' (Japan's Shameful Foreign Policy), in *Bungei Shunjû*, no. 12 (1971), pp. 124–32.
3. Yoshimi Furui, 'Inside Story of Normalization of Sino-Japanese Diplomatic Relations', in *Summaries of Selected Japanese Magazines* (*SSJM*), Tokyo, Jan. 1973, p. 47.

on the other issuing invitations to Sinophile delegations from all corners of Japan's political firmament – with the exception of the 'revisionist' Communists – and attempting to convince them of the justness of its own demands.

Peking presented the Japanese government with three conditions for the establishment of official contact, all three of which, typically enough, concerned the status of Taiwan:

- the recognition of the government of the People's Republic as the sole legal government of the Chinese people;
- the stipulation that Taiwan should be regarded as an inseparable part of the territory of the People's Republic;
- the annulment of the peace treaty concluded in 1952 between Japan and the government of Chiang Kaishek.

The Chinese leaders reiterated these conditions in all their meetings with Japanese visitors. It is noteworthy that the third demand, which posed the greatest problem of international law for Japan, only appeared from the summer of 1971 onwards, in joint communiqués issued when Japanese delegations made unofficial visits to or attended talks in China. This indicates that the Chinese increased their demands the moment they felt they could count on talks with the United States getting under way. China obviously believed that Japan would be prepared to concede the point, in order not to miss the opportunity of participating in this development.

The approach adopted by China clearly shows the difference in status between the United States and Japan from Peking's point of view. While holding talks with a high-ranking US government representative without setting preconditions, and even declaring its intention of receiving the President, Peking was also piling up obstacles in the path of a Japan eager to establish official contact. Only after fulfilling conditions which, if not unacceptable, were certainly on the verge of being humiliating, was Japan offered the prospect of talks at government level. At the same time, China was busily interfering in Japanese party politics. Too early a start to official talks with Tokyo would have improved Japan's political image, especially in Asia, which ran counter to Chinese intentions. As a consequence, priority was given to direct talks with the United States, while Japan was put on ice to increase its willingness to agree to concessions.

With these tactics, China succeeded in temporarily increasing the political distance between Japan and the United States, in influencing to its own advantage Japanese public and media opinion of Japanese policies on China, and in affecting Japan's domestic policy. Six weeks after the announcement of Nixon's visit to China, an opinion poll conducted in Japan revealed that the majority of those questioned (63%) regarded the visit of the American President as useful and a help towards achieving détente; an equal number of those questioned believed that Japan should immediately begin negotiations to open diplomatic relations with China. However, a relative majority of 36% – against a minority of 21% – believed that this latter alteration of policy would not be possible under Prime Minister Sato.[4]

Sato was placed under increasing pressure within both Parliament and the ruling party by China's strict rejection of official contact with his government (itself unable to accept the Chinese conditions) while agreeing in principle to normalisation. The mass media created a mood of normalisation euphoria, combining moral viewpoints with an emotional call for peace, which received widespread support. Carefully selected invitations to influential members helped the Chinese government to influence the formation of opinions within the governing party to its own advantage. Sato, increasingly regarded as an obstacle on the path to Sino-Japanese détente, was finally forced to concede to this pressure and resigned on 6 July 1972 after more than seven years in office.

China's methods were a classic example of the efficiency of its 'people's diplomacy', by-passing the Japanese government system and turning instead to more 'open-minded' groups and influential individuals with the aim of influencing governmental decisions in its favour by this seemingly roundabout route. The rash of invitations issued demonstrates the resolution of this people's diplomacy during the run-up to normalisation; 1969 saw 2,643 Japanese visiting China, while only seven(!) Chinese visited Japan.[5] In 1971 the figures were 5,718 and seventy-four, respectively.[6]

4. See *DSJP*, 23 Sept. 1971, p. 10.
5. Hideo Ueno, *Gendai Nitchû-kankei no tenkai* (Recent Developments in Sino-Japanese Relations), Tokyo/Osaka 1974, p. 271.
6. *Japan Times*, 17 Jan. 1972, p. 5.

The most promising candidates to succeed Sato were Takeo Fukuda and Kakuei Tanaka. Both men favoured the normalisation of Sino-Japanese relations, but with one difference: while Fukuda let it be known that he would only negotiate without the imposition of preconditions, Tanaka had repeatedly made clear that he was willing to accommodate Peking further. Zhou Enlai had already expressed his pessimism at the prospects of normalisation in the event of Fukuda becoming premier. The precise influence of this assessment on the election of the new premier is hard to estimate today; however, it was probably not ineffective.

On 5 July 1972, the day before Sato's formal resignation, the LDP elected Tanaka its new party leader and thus the new Prime Minister. At a press conference, he declared that the time was ripe for relations with China to be normalised. On 7 July Tanaka formed his first Cabinet, announcing afterwards that the process of normalisation of relations with the People's Republic would be accelerated.[7] This corresponded precisely to what the Japanese people expected of his foreign policy.

In an opinion poll carried out two weeks after Tanaka's election, 36.2% of people accorded the normalisation of relations with China top priority on the scale of foreign policy responsibilities; in second place, 13.9% deemed the harmonisation of economic relations with the United States most important. The settlement of territorial problems with the Soviet Union came only third, with 11.5% regarding this as the key issue. When in the autumn of 1972 the question was asked how normal relations with China should be restored, 56.2% were in favour of a gradual process and 26.1% were for immediate restoration.[8] Tanaka's election had evidently had a calming effect: in April 1972 (that is, after Nixon's visit to China) 66.9% had approved the establishment of diplomatic relations with Peking 'as quickly as possible', while only 21.9% had believed that excessive haste was inappropriate.[9]

7. See Gaimushô (ed.), *Waga gaikô-no kinkyô, Shôwa 48* (The Current State of our Foreign Relations, 1973), vol. 17, Tokyo 1973, p. 126.
8. Sôrifu kôhôshitsu (Information Department of the Office of the Prime Minister) (ed.), *Yoron-chôsa, gekkan* (Monthly Opinion Surveys), vol. 4, no. 10 (Oct. 1972), p. 38.
9. *Ibid.*, vol. 4, no. 7 (July 1972), p. 77.

On 9 July 1972, only two days after the formation of the new government, Zhou Enlai made a statement welcoming Tanaka's intention of normalising relations with his country.[10] The next day, a ballet troupe from Shanghai arrived in Japan for a tour of several weeks under the leadership of the deputy secretary-general of the Association for Sino-Japanese Friendship, Sun Pinghua. Sun brought Tanaka an invitation from Zhou Enlai to visit China – the use of seemingly non-political events, here the visit of a ballet troupe, for significant political actions was a typical method in Chinese diplomacy. Tanaka accepted the invitation on 11 August, at which Peking immediately reacted by officially reporting the Japanese Prime Minister's intention of visiting China, adding that Zhou Enlai welcomed him and invited him to visit.[11] This followed the same pattern as the announcement of the visit by the American President; in Tanaka's case too, it was important for China to announce publicly that the desire to visit originated not with the host, but with the guest.

At the beginning of the 1970s a mood of détente prevailed in Europe. Thus at the same time that Europe was increasingly coming to view areas of potential understanding and cooperation as more significant than areas of confrontation in East–West relations, tension in East Asia was also easing. In both cases, although in very different ways, the key issue was the limitation of Soviet power. In East Asia a partial conformity of interests transformed almost two decades of hostility between China, the United States and Japan into an atmosphere of accord.

There is a clear difference between the Atlantic-European and the Asia Pacific areas of détente: the Soviet Union was excluded from developments in East Asia, whereas the United States played a crucial role in reducing conflicts within both areas. This explains the Soviets' reaction; months before Kissinger's visit to Peking, Moscow had already expressed concern at America's 'diplomacy of smiles' regarding China. Suspicion that the Americans wanted to force China's break with the socialist camp was never far away, for such a development, if it occurred, would work against Soviet interests in East Asia and throughout the world. This fear can be traced in all contemporary Soviet state-

10. See Gaimushô, *Waga gaikô-no kinkyô*, vol. 17, p. 126.
11. See Xinhua News Agency, *Daily Bulletin*, no. 5383 (13 Aug. 1972).

ments and analyses of the situation; after the United States and China had taken the first steps towards improving relations, the implications of this began to sink into Soviet politics. The Soviets at first reacted with a half-hearted admittance that the normalisation of relations between two states was in itself a positive thing; critical remarks about the background to Sino-American *rapprochement* immediately followed, but they demonstrated no comprehension of the true consequences of the change in relations between Washington and Peking.

It is remarkable in this context that contemporary Soviet commentators barely noticed the so-called anti-hegemony clause of the communiqué agreed in Shanghai by Nixon and Zhou Enlai, which was to play a role in Soviet-Japanese relations a few years later. This clause stated that 'neither [state] should seek hegemony in the Asia Pacific area and each is opposed to efforts by any other country or group of countries to establish such hegemony',[12] a formulation clearly directed at containing Soviet interests in the Pacific. The first Soviet analyses completely passed over this.[13] Later examinations commented on this point only in general terms, interpreting the clause in a purely passive sense, as an attempt to divide the Pacific into Chinese and American spheres of influence.[14]

At the same time, the Soviets' concern was unmistakable; the accusation was levelled against China that its long-term aim after the Cultural Revolution[15] was first to exploit contacts with America as a means of gaining power in the region, and then

12. Text of the communiqué in *Peking Review*, no. 9 (1972), p. 5.
13. See Dimitri Volski, 'Nixons Pekinger Woche' (Nixon's Week in Peking), in *Neue Zeit*, no. 10 (March 1972), pp. 10ff; Boris Koloskov, 'Nach den chinesisch-amerikanischen Verhandlungen' (After Sino-American Negotiations), *ibid.*, no. 11 (March 1972), pp. 4–6.
14. See Akademija Nauk SSSR (Academy of Sciences of the USSR) (ed.), *Meždunarodnye otnošenija na Dal'nem Vostoke v poslevoennye gody* (Post-war International Relations in the Far East), vol. 2: *1958–1976*, Moscow 1978, p. 212; B. Koloskov, *Vnešnaja politika Kitaja* [China's Foreign Policy] *1969–1976*, Moscow 1977, p. 203.
15. The Cultural Revolution was declared officially over by the Chinese leaders in 1969, the date also taken here as a basis for its end. At the end of the 1970s Peking spread the opinion that the Cultural Revolution had lasted until 1976 and had only come to an end when the 'Gang of Four' had been removed.

to force the USA out of Asia by means of an artificially provoked discord between Washington and Tokyo.[16]

The Soviet Union responded to the challenge from China by concentrating more attention on its policies on Asia, aiming to gain partners and friends there as a counter to China's activities. The success of this policy should be neither under- nor overestimated. At the beginning of August 1971 the Soviet Union signed a treaty of peace, friendship and cooperation with India, with both states agreeing to consultations, in the event of attack by an outside country, to implement any measures necessary to safeguard the two countries. India expressly justified the treaty by referring to the rapid, dramatic changes in the international situation and the new constellations of world powers. China's reaction to the treaty differed from the Soviet Union's reaction to Sino-American *rapprochement*; Peking avoided any criticism of it, much to India's relief. Soviet policies on Asia continued with increased emphasis on propagating the proposal of a system of collective security in the region; a proposal intended chiefly to attract the countries of South-East Asia and Japan.[17]

An immediate consequence of the reorientation taking place in Chinese foreign policy was the Soviet public announcement of an increase in Sinological research. At the end of 1971 a national Sinologists' congress was held in Moscow, with the participation of government representatives. The intention of the congress, which surprisingly was also publicly announced, was the future subjection of all aspects of China's political, economic and cultural life to scientific investigation. Even before the congress had taken place, a new quarterly publication from Moscow's Institute of Far Eastern Studies, *Problemy Dal'nego Vostoka* (Problems of the Far East), had been announced.[18] The first edition appeared in the spring of 1972 and was sufficiently

---

16. Akademija Nauk SSSR. Institut Dal'nego Vostoka (Academy of Sciences of the USSR, Far Eastern Institute) (ed.), *Vnešnaja politika i meždunarodnye otnošenija Kitajskoj Narodnoj Respubliki* (Foreign Policy and International Relations of the People's Republic of China), vol. 2: *1963–1973*, Moscow 1974, p. 255.

17. See W. Pavlovski, 'Regionale Zusammenarbeit und kollektive Sicherheit für Asien' (Regional Cooperation and Collective Security for Asia), in *Neue Zeit*, no. 30 (July 1972), pp. 18–20.

18. See *New York Times*, 5 Dec. 1971.

highly regarded for a detailed review to appear in the theoretical organ of the Soviet Communist Party.[19] Did this constitute an admittance that Chinese politics had been misjudged, or was it an attempt to found a realistic basis for new policies on China? Both these interpretations may be true.

As with Sino-American *rapprochement*, initial Soviet reactions to the normalisation of relations between China and Japan were muted. The Communist Party newspaper published the most important parts of the Joint Declaration of the Chinese and Japanese governments concerning immediate establishment of full diplomatic relations – but without comment.[20] What the Kremlin heads thought as they followed the progress of Sino-Japanese *rapprochement* could only be judged from the numerous Soviet statements which appeared subsequently.

At the beginning of 1972, months before diplomatic relations between Peking and Tokyo were established, it was remarked that the arrangement of relations between 'these two greatest states in the Far East' would not be regarded with indifference by the world. The Soviet observer posed the question of whether the leaders of China and Japan were conscious that their claims to hegemony were untenable – untenable, that is, if their aims were to attain the racial exclusivity of their peoples and a leading role in Asia. If, however, hegemonistic claims were not the driving force behind the new policy, then the question arose whether both countries would establish relations under conditions of peaceful, neighbourly coexistence without affecting the interests of other nations.[21] It can be seen from this that at the time Soviet judgement was as yet suspended.

After the normalisation of Sino-Japanese relations had been completed in the autumn of 1972, Soviet assessments became generally critical, and in some cases extremely negative. The Soviet Union saw the Chinese leaders as the real driving force behind normalisation, motivated by anti-Soviet intent; in Moscow's view, China was attempting to involve Japan in its anti-Soviet policies and to convince Prime Minister Tanaka that the

19. See *Kommunist*, no. 9 (June 1972), pp. 112–17.
20. See *Pravda*, 30 Sept. 1972.
21. See M.I. Sladkovskij, 'Kitajsko-japonskie otnošenija [uroki istorii, sovremennost]' (Sino-Japanese Relations [Lessons from the Past and the Present]), in *Problemy Dal'nego Vostoka*, no. 1 (1972), p. 60.

Soviet Union posed a 'military threat'.[22] Moreover, China was showing solidarity with Japan by supporting the latter's territorial claims against the Soviet Union – the demand for the return of the Kurile Islands – while at the same time attempting to slow the development of economic relations between the Soviet Union and Japan and to halt Japan's participation in the exploitation of reserves in Siberia. The Soviet Union claimed that China's attempt to involve Japan in its anti-Soviet policy was founded on the mere pretext that the Soviet Union posed a threat to China's national security.[23]

Commentaries on China's evident shift in attitude towards the American-Japanese security pact and towards the Japanese armed forces were also heavily critical. Previously, Moscow had believed Peking to be opposed to this treaty and to militarisation in Tokyo, but this opposition vanished just before Prime Minister Tanaka's visit to Peking. This was not all; China began to express positive views on the Japanese-American alliance and on Japan's efforts at defence,[24] actually citing the threat posed by the Soviet Union as justification for this new position. Referring to an article in the *New York Times*, Soviet sources now reported that Zhou Enlai had declared during talks with Tanaka in Peking that it was possible Chinese forces would fight alongside Japanese forces in the event of a Soviet attack on Japan.[25] Soviet references to the normalisation of Sino-Japanese relations at this time are full of wishful thinking and conjecture, including the assumption that discord and conflicts of interest between China and Japan were bound to increase. In particular, it was stated that the two countries would fall out over each other's political influence in

22. See Akademija Nauk SSSR. Institut Vostokovedenija (Academy of Sciences of the USSR, Institute of Oriental Studies) (ed.), *Istorija Japonii* [History of Japan] *1945–1975*, Moscow 1978, p. 429.
23. See Akademija Nauk SSSR. Institut Dal'nego Vostoka (Academy of Sciences of the USSR. Institute of Far Eastern Studies) (ed.), *Kitajskaja Narodnaja Respublika, Političeskoe i ekonomičeskoe razvitie v 1973 godu* (The People's Republic of China, its Political and Economic Development, 1973), Moscow 1975, p. 323.
24. See Koloskov, *Vnešnaja politika Kitaja* [China's Foreign Policy] *1969–1976*, p. 215.
25. See M.G. Nosov, *Japano-kitajskie otnošenija* (Japanese-Chinese Relations), Moscow 1978, p. 149.

South-East Asia, while tensions would mount as a result of economic competition between them in this area.[26]

A summary of these statements reveals the following Soviet perception of Sino-Japanese *rapprochement*. Moscow believed it was China, not Japan, that posed the principal threat to the Soviet Union in the Far East. However, the normalisation and continuing improvement of relations between China, in the role of initiator, and Japan, playing a passive role, were perceived as a clear exacerbation of this threat. Cooperation between China and Japan could seriously hinder the progress of Soviet interests in East Asia.

Japan was confronted with the question of how to shape relations with the Soviet Union. Tokyo had indeed hardly played an active role in the rapid changes in relations between the United States, the Soviet Union, China and Japan at the beginning of the 1970s; Washington had reshaped its policy towards Asia without giving any consideration to its Japanese allies, an omission permitted by Japan's dependent role in matters concerning security.[27]

True, there were demands for greater independence from the United States. Economic success – in 1969 Japan had risen to the position of the world's third largest industrial power, based on GNP – had strengthened confidence and also evoked some signs of a new nationalism. On the other hand, the government in Tokyo evidently had no concrete ideas of how to forge a more independent political role within Asia, and indeed seemed to shy away from the responsibility such independence would involve. Its policies towards China demonstrated its political weakness: an all-too-great readiness to agree to normalisation coupled with docile acceptance of the conditions set by Peking, and this despite the new danger of becoming involved in the Sino-Soviet conflict. Few Japanese expressed concern. But how did this Japan – an impressive economic power, yet an ineffectual

---

26. See *Akademija Nauk SSSR* (Academy of Sciences of the USSR) (ed.), *Japonija 1972, Ežegodnik* (Japan, Yearbook), Moscow 1972, p. 63; *New Times*, no. 41 (Oct. 1972), pp. 13ff.

27. The security treaty was due for renewal in 1971; the Japanese government managed to renew it without major problems, disregarding protests from the opposition. Since then the treaty has included a clause that every year automatically extends it by one year.

24   East Asia at the Beginning of the 1970s

element in foreign affairs – intend to achieve its political aims concerning the Soviet Union, in the radically altered environment of the Asia Pacific powers at the beginning of the 1970s?

Part II

JAPAN'S RELATIONS WITH THE SOVIET UNION

4

AIMS

From the mid-1960s onwards, Japanese diplomacy focused on two aims in its relationship with the Soviet Union: a general improvement in relations, with especial emphasis on the possibility of economic cooperation; and the conclusion of a peace treaty that included a settlement of the territorial question, namely the return of four Soviet-occupied islands or groups of islands at the southern end of the Kurile archipelago.[1]

The motivation behind this was the growing realisation of Japan's political leaders that their country, dependent as it was on free trade, raw materials, energy and so on, needed a world as free from conflict as possible; and that an active role in foreign affairs, involving participation in the shaping of global politics and underpinned by the country's economic strength, was essential to safeguard its standards of living. This would involve Japan retaining an active role in world economic affairs, while being less passive in issues of politics. The need for independence in foreign affairs stemmed from growing uncertainty about the commitments of the United States, Japan's only ally in Asia, from 1969 onwards. While not questioning the alliance with the United States, Tokyo was forced to consider a more independent role.

Masayoshi Ohira, Foreign Minister in the Cabinets of Ikeda and Tanaka and later (1979) Prime Minister himself, demanded in 1972 that Japan should become an active participant in the international community of states. A few months before he was reappointed Foreign Minister in 1972, Ohira formulated some basic principles for his country's future foreign policy, maintaining that the role of passive cooperation adopted in the past would no longer suffice. Japan had actively to accept its responsibilities in the outside world in proportion to its capabilities. He called on Japan to participate as an independent protagonist in creating

---

1. These were the Habomai Islands, consisting of several small islands, and Shikotan, Kunashiri and Etorofu (see Maps 1 and 2).

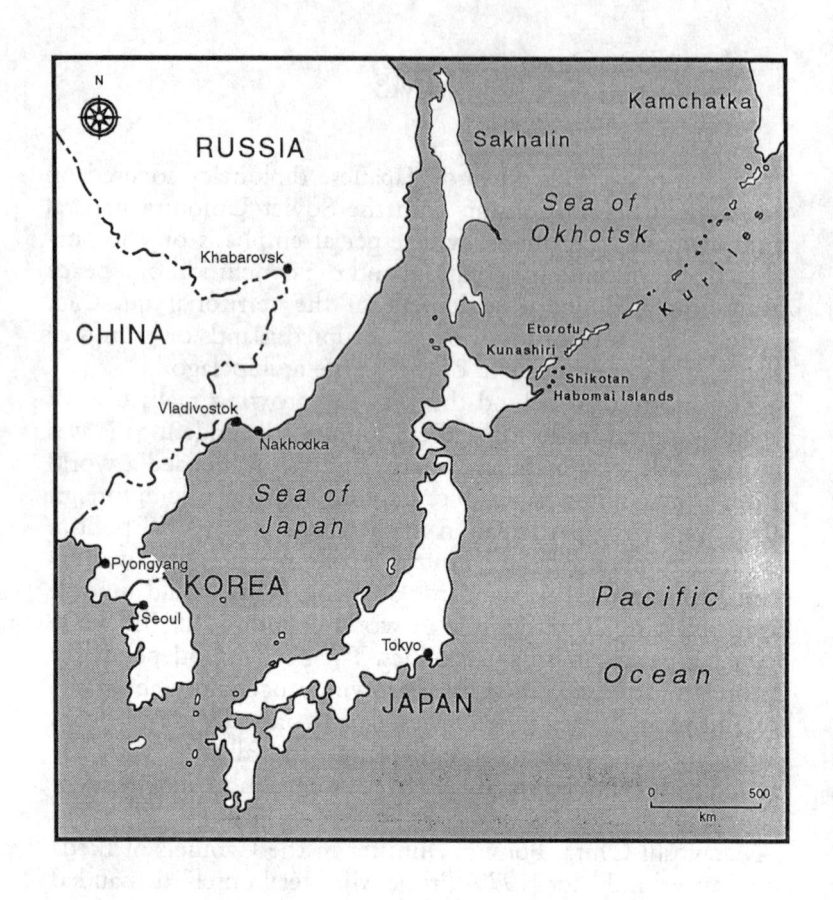

Map 1. OVERVIEW OF THE REGION

and keeping peace in Asia and the world.[2] When one considers that today, in the mid-1990s, Japan is still being challenged to take on increased responsibility in international politics, it is clear what difficulty the country is experiencing in freeing itself from its post-war political structures.

Ohira's view of the future envisaged a tripartite world centred

---

2. See Masayoshi Ohira, 'A New Foreign Policy for Japan', in *Pacific Community*, vol. 3, no. 3 (April 1972), p. 411.

around the United States, China and the Soviet Union, and excluded the European Community and Japan from the status of world powers because of their dissimilar status. In his view Japan's intention should be to maintain close and peaceful relations, both economic and political, with the three big powers; the government should not assume it could manoeuvre tactically between the three to gain short-term advantages. In this respect Ohira may be considered a realist; however, his idea that Tokyo's attitude towards the Soviet Union should echo its attitude towards the United States and China is harder to understand.[3]

Fortunately, this unrealistic concept of equidistance, albeit posited by a politician who had by then helped to shape Japan's foreign policy for more than a decade, was never put into practice. By August 1978 at the latest, with the conclusion of the treaty of peace and friendship between Japan and China, the foundation for this concept of foreign policy had dissolved. Japan had never kept equal political distance from the two superpowers and from China. Nonetheless, at the beginning of the 1970s the concept of equidistance represented a useful tool in foreign policy; it helped to present to the Japanese people the more active international commitment which Ohira and others demanded as a way of improving relations with China and the Soviet Union, while retaining existing close relations with the United States.

These considerations explained Japan's readiness to place a positive interpretation on the Soviets' efforts to improve relations, which were sparked off by the Sino-American *rapprochement*. It was only natural to investigate any chances of strengthening relations with the Soviet Union. However, Japan was forced to admit that while the Soviets urgently desired economic cooperation in the exploitation of natural resources in Siberia, they totally rejected any discussion of what was for the Japanese the central issue – the territorial question.

In 1973/4, around the time of this depressing realisation, a dramatic improvement in Sino-Japanese relations had already begun, bringing with it a change in focus. In a state of near-euphoria at this development, Tokyo turned to its Chinese neighbour, to which it was bound by historical and cultural

3. *Ibid.*, p. 417.

links, and began to consider closer political and economic cooperation with Peking as a priority of its foreign policy. The significance of relations with the Soviet Union receded before this goal. Responsibility for this development can be laid at Moscow's door: difficulties in carrying out large-scale projects in Siberia, crude attempts to disrupt Sino-Japanese *rapprochement* and demonstrations of military strength in Asia (including the invasion of Afghanistan in 1979) swiftly destroyed any illusions Tokyo had had of large-scale Japanese-Soviet cooperation. On the other hand, China courted Japan by offering attractive markets for Japanese products and setting more favourable conditions for the supply of raw materials than the Soviet Union did.

Japan's attitude to the two Communist powers was further complicated by their open hostility to each other. Tokyo vainly tried to avoid becoming caught up in the Sino-Soviet conflict. Peking, however, fully intended its involvement, and also succeeded in exploiting Japan as an element of its anti-Soviet policy between 1974 and 1984, thus reducing Tokyo's chances of persuading the Soviet Union to agree to compromises in negotiations over a peace treaty.

Since Japan's alliance with the United States continued to form the basis of its foreign and defence policies, Tokyo was hardly concerned about the permanently strained relations with Moscow. Throughout the period of East-West conflict, Japan's political leaders sometimes actually seemed to welcome the problem, in the shape of the unresolved territorial question, which enabled Japan to keep – and justify – its distance from Moscow; this position was in accordance with the interests of the United States and China, which for different reasons regarded Japanese-Soviet *rapprochement* as an undesirable development.

However, the end of the East-West conflict and the normalisation of Sino-Soviet relations have created difficulties for Japan over this policy. Its disagreement with the former Soviet Union has begun to prove an obstacle to Western policies, which are aimed at containing the dangers caused by the collapse of the Soviet empire and in which Japan's assistance is an essential element.

Thus, in the mid-1990s Japan is faced with the necessity of revising its policy towards the newly created state of Russia. Japan's principle of 'the inseparability of politics and economics' is irreconcilable with the new challenges. But Russia, too, must reassess its own position and show more flexibility towards Japanese demands, which it could demonstrate, for example, by returning two of the four occupied islands. The territorial question is the greatest obstacle facing both countries in their efforts to improve relations. It is one of the quirks of history that two such major powers as Japan and the Soviet Union/Russia have spent decades blocking the progress of mutual détente because of what amounts to a trivial question of territory.

5

THE TERRITORIAL QUESTION

Historical Background

The territorial problem has a long history, which has been described in detail elsewhere.[1] For this reason it is outlined here only as far as is necessary to understand further discussions of the issue since the beginning of the 1970s.

The Japanese, the Russians and the Dutch have all claimed to be the discoverers of the Kuriles. The Russian claim later led the Soviet Union to deem the archipelago part of its territory.[2] Early contacts between Russia and Japan, during which territorial claims began to be more precisely defined, led to the conclusion of the Treaty of Shimoda on 7 February 1855. This trade, shipping and frontier treaty established the position of the Japanese-Russian frontier between the islands of Iturup (Japanese: Etorofu) and Urup (Japanese: Uruppu) and also stated that Iturup belonged to Japan, while Urup, together with all islands to the north, was Russian territory (Article 2). Sakhalin was declared the joint property of both states.

The frontier decided in 1855, together with all further treaties

---

1. See John Stephan, *The Kuril Islands, Russo-Japanese Frontiers in the Pacific*, Oxford 1974; Hans-Jürgen Mayer, *Der japanisch-sowjetische Territorialstreit. Aussen- und sicherheitspolitische Aspekte, 1975–1978* (The Japanese-Soviet Territorial Conflict. Aspects of Foreign and Security Policy, 1975–1978), Hamburg 1980 (Mitteilungen des Instituts für Asienkunde, Hamburg, no. 111); David Rees, *The Soviet Seizure of the Kuriles*, New York 1985.

2. An example of the justification for this claim was given in the autumn of 1984 in the newspaper *Sovetskaya Rossiya* in a report of archaeological discoveries made during investigations in 'Kurile Russia' (Kurilorossiya). The archaeologists had begun their investigations in 1978, had established the location of Kurilorossiya on the island of Urup and, according to their report, had been able to prove the existence of early Russian inhabitants. It was also claimed that Ivan Kozyrevski was the first to describe the Kurile Islands, in 1713. See *Sovetskaya Rossiya*, 13 Sept. 1984. The Deputy Foreign Minister responsible for Asian affairs, I. Rogachov, drew on this work for his own arguments. See *Izvestiya*, 24 April 1989, p. 7.

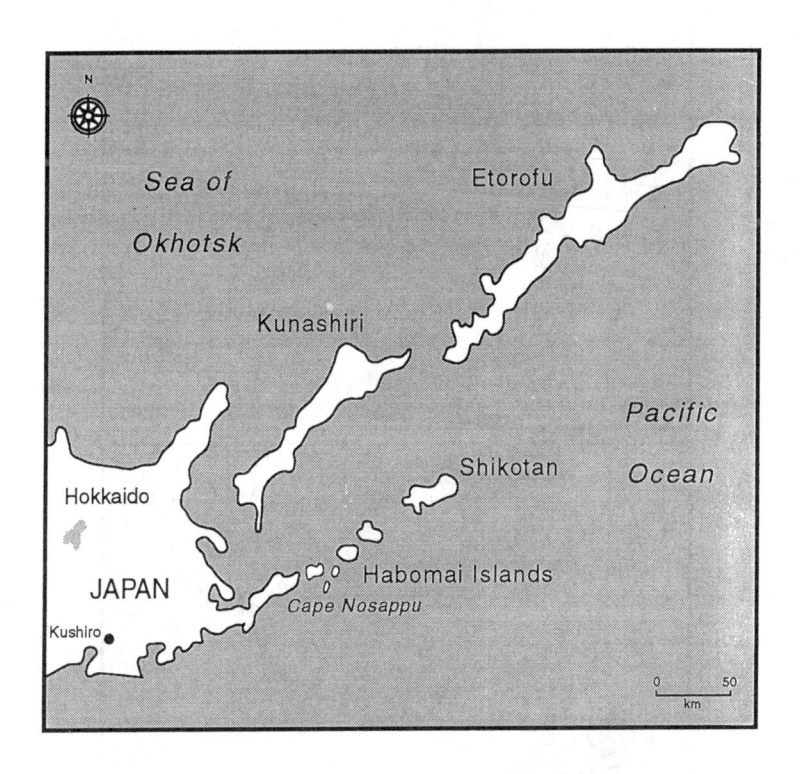

Map 2. THE DISPUTED SOUTH KURILES

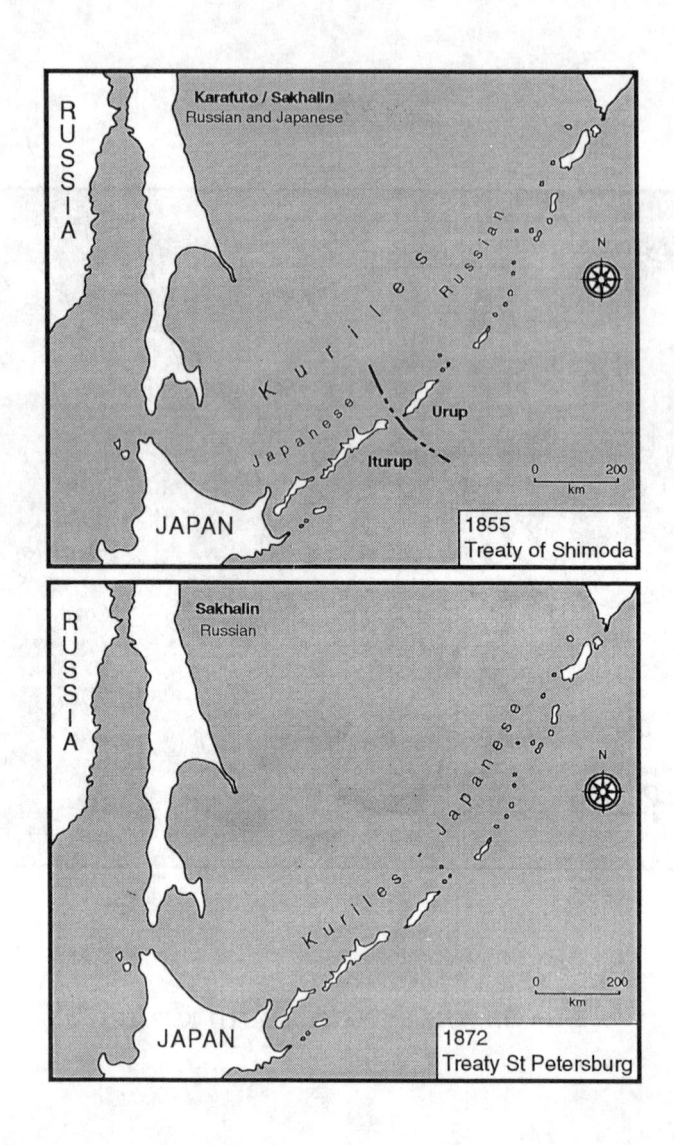

Map 3. BORDERS IN THE NINETEENTH CENTURY

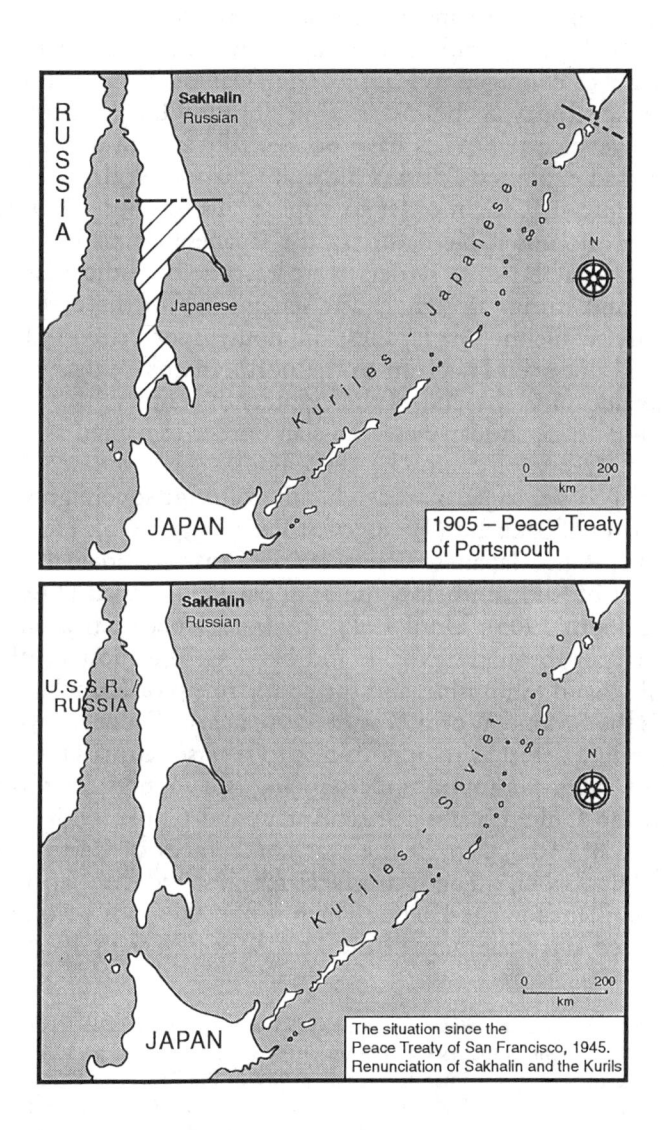

Map 4. BORDERS IN THE TWENTIETH CENTURY

(St Petersburg 1875; Portsmouth 1905), indisputably proves that since the initial agreement the islands at the southern end of the Kurile archipelago, although occupied by the Soviets since 1945, have never belonged to Russia. The Japanese government cites these facts today as the historical justification for its claim.

However, the Soviets have occasionally argued that in 1855 Japan had exploited Russia's difficult situation, in the middle of the Crimean War, in order to impose this frontier. They have asserted the untenable nature of the Japanese claims in view of the fact that Russian settlers were recorded on the islands of Urup and Iturup as early as the second half of the eighteenth century, while the first Japanese did not set foot there until 1786 and did not even lay claim to the northern and central parts of Hokkaido until the end of the eighteenth century.[3]

Until 1875, the Japanese-Russian border remained as agreed in the Treaty of Shimoda; then Russia gave the whole archipelago over to Japan, receiving in exchange sovereignty over the island of Sakhalin (Treaty of St Petersburg 1875). However, after the Russo-Japanese War of 1905 Russia was forced to return the part of Sakhalin below the 50th parallel to Japan (Treaty of Portsmouth 1905). Until 1945, the border between Japan and Russia ran through Sakhalin and between the most northerly Kurile island, Shumshu, and the southern tip of Kamchatka.[4]

As the Second World War drew to a close, Stalin saw Japan's impending defeat as an opportunity to reverse Russia's territorial loss of 1905. He found understanding and support for this aim from the United States, Great Britain and China, which were all at war with Japan, at the war conferences of Cairo (1943) and Yalta (1945). The Cairo Declaration stated that 'Japan shall lose all islands in the Pacific which it has taken possession of or occupied since the start of the First World War in 1914', and

---

3. See the Soviet edition of Shintarô Nakamura, *Nihonjin to Roshiyajin – Japontsy i Ruskije* (Japanese and Russians), Moscow 1983, p. 174. Earlier evidence of Soviet reference to the inequality of the Treaty of Shimoda can be found in Stephan, *The Kuril Islands*, p. 88. According to recent Soviet statements, the Treaty of St Petersburg (1875) can also be interpreted as the result of Russia's weakened state and its inability to defend its claims against Japan. See A.A. Gromyko et al. (eds), *Diplomatičeski slovar'* (Lexicon of Diplomacy), vol. 2, Moscow 1986, p. 495.

4. See Map 4.

that it 'shall be driven out of all other areas which it has taken possession of in violence and greed'.[5] Historically speaking, this declaration only applied to Sakhalin.

The Kurile Islands were not mentioned directly until the Yalta Conference, where Stalin summed up his claims against Japan in the demand: 'I only wish Russia to receive what the Japanese took away from my country.' President Roosevelt readily agreed.[6] Strictly speaking, Stalin's demand should have been restricted to Sakhalin, for Japan's sovereignty over the entire Kurile chain had been the result of negotiations which had ended with the Treaty of St Petersburg; however, at the end of 1944 Stalin had already named the price for his country's entry into the war against Japan, as the Western allies were demanding: the southern half of Sakhalin and the Kurile Islands in their entirety.[7]

In Yalta the US President was shown detailed Department of State briefing papers on the Kurile Islands, in which Soviet claims to the four islands at the south end of the archipelago were rejected as unfounded; however, Roosevelt, evidently assuming the Soviet claims to be justified, did not refer to them.[8] Accordingly, point 3 of the section of the Yalta Agreement on the Far East reads: 'The Kuril Islands are to be handed over to the Soviet Union.'[9] Carelessness is too lenient a word to describe Roosevelt's unquestioning acceptance of the Soviet claims.

The Kurile Islands were the scene of the last battle in the Second World War. On the morning of 18 August 1945, three days after Japan had surrendered, Soviet troops landed in Shumshu and engaged in bitter fighting with the Japanese, who agreed the next day to cease all hostilities.

A former officer of the Japanese Army, visiting island after

5. Helmut Stoecker and Adolf Rüger, *Handbuch der Verträge, 1871–1964. Verträge und andere Dokumente aus der Geschichte der internationalen Beziehungen* (Handbook of Treaties 1871–1964: Treaties and Other Documents from the History of International Relations), Berlin (East) 1968, p. 330.

6. Quoted in Stephan, *The Kuril Islands*, p. 155; see also Rees, *The Soviet Seizure of the Kuriles*, pp. 61ff.

7. See George Alexander Lensen, *The Strange Neutrality, Soviet-Japanese Relations during the Second World War, 1941–1945*, Tallahassee, Fla. 1972, pp. 258ff.

8. See Stephan, *The Kuril Islands*, pp. 154ff.

9. J.A.S. Greenville, *The Major International Treaties, 1914–1973: A History and Guide with Texts*, London 1974, p. 230.

island north to south in the company of the Soviet divisional commander, described the progress of demilitarisation on the archipelago. On 27 August off the island of Urup, the trip was halted for reconnaissance operations concerning the landing of American troops. Although this proved to be a false alarm, the expedition about-turned and returned northwards, claiming that the zone for which the United States was responsible extended southwards from the island of Etorofu. The Soviets, evidently exploiting the absence of American troops in these islands, then proceeded to take possession of the southerly Kuriles in the period between 29 August and 3 September.[10] The takeover was carried out by units of the Soviet Pacific fleet from Sovetskaya Gavan.[11] This procedure revealed that the traditional differentiation between north and south Kuriles, which still plays a role today, was retained.

When Japan's Foreign Minister, Shigemitsu, signed the treaty of surrender aboard the American warship *Missouri* on 2 September 1945, Stalin published a declaration in which he not only announced the return of southern Sakhalin and the Kuriles to Soviet hands but also emphasised the archipelago's strategic importance — the motive behind the Soviets' action. Stalin declared that from then on the Kuriles would serve neither to block the Soviet Union's access to the sea nor to offer a base for Japanese attacks on the Soviet Far East; instead, they were to form a link between the Soviet Union and the Pacific and act as an outpost against Japanese aggression.[12] This declaration left no doubt as to the interests of the Soviet Union and the intransigence with which this new possession would be defended.

The first document of the post-war period that was also recognised by Japan was the Potsdam Declaration of 26 July 1945, establishing in Article 8 of the section concerning Japan that the conditions of the Cairo Declaration (1943) were operative and that Japan's sovereignty was to be restricted to the islands of Honshu, Hokkaido, Kyushu, Shikoku and some smaller islands still to be named. The Kuriles were not mentioned, and

10. See Jinja Shimpô, 4 Jan. 1985. A detailed report of the entire military action may be found in Rees, *The Soviet Seizure of the Kuriles*, pp. 78–81.
11. See Stephan, *The Kuril Islands*, p. 166.
12. *Ibid.*, p. 170.

it remained undecided as to whether part of them was to be included in the unnamed islands.

The Peace Treaty of San Francisco between the United States and Japan, which was concluded in 1951 without the signature and against the will of the Soviet Union, concurred with the Soviet standpoint in an ambiguously formulated statement (Chapter II.c.): 'Japan renounces all rights, titles and claims to the Kurile Islands and the parts of Sakhalin and surrounding islands over which it gained sovereignty in the Treaty of Portsmouth of 5 September 1905.'[13] In whose favour Japan was to renounce the claim was not mentioned. Nonetheless, this relinquishment of sovereignty was binding under international law.[14]

At the Conference of San Francisco, Prime Minister Yoshida pointed out that Czarist Russia had formerly never protested about the allegiance to Japan of 'the two most southerly Kurile Islands, Etorofu and Kunashiri', that only the islands north of Urup had a mixed Japanese-Russian population and that Shikotan and the Habomai Islands, located directly off Hokkaido, were inseparably linked to their mother country.[15] However, Yoshida, as the representative from the conquered nation of Japan, was not given the opportunity to speak until the end of the conference, and his protests went unheeded. The Japanese delegation had assembled a wealth of details to support its arguments; however, the enterprise remained unsuccessful, especially as the American head of negotiations held the views of the Japanese in no particular esteem. The United States would have been the only power in a position to obtain a hearing for Japan over the territorial question, since Japan had given its unconditional surrender; however, the United States did not step in, and Japan was obliged to be satisfied that Yoshida's speech was recorded.[16] Remarkably, Yoshida described the is-

13. Stoecker and Rüger, *Handbuch der Verträge*, p. 520.
14. For a treatment of the problem as an aspect of international law, see Benita Langen, *Die Gebietsverluste Japans nach dem Zweiten Weltkrieg. Eine völkerrechtliche Studie* (Japan's Territorial Losses after the Second World War. A Study in International Law), Berlin 1971 (Schriften zum Völkerrecht, vol. 19), pp. 111ff.
15. See Hiroshi Shigeta and Shôji Shigeta (eds), *Nisso-kihon-bunsho-shiryôshû* (Collection of Documents Fundamental to Japanese-Soviet Relations, NKBS), Tokyo 1988, p. 121.
16. See Fuji Kamiya, 'The Northern Territories: 130 Years of Japanese

lands of Etorofu and Kunashiri as 'southern Kuriles' (*Minami-Chishima*); in other words, he regarded them as 'Kuriles', so they would therefore be included in the relinquishment stipulated in the peace treaty.[17]

The treaty was ratified unconditionally and without formal protest by the Japanese Parliament; Kumao Nishimura, the director of the Department of International Treaties of the Japanese Foreign Ministry, confirmed this interpretation of the relinquishment in a parliamentary enquiry concerning the peace treaty on 19 October 1951. According to Nishimura, the term 'Kuriles' as employed in the peace treaty referred to both the northern and the southern parts of the archipelago.[18] From the point of view of international law, this was absolutely correct, reflecting the opinion prevalent at the time that the Kurile archipelago as mentioned in the treaty included the southern Kuriles, that is Kunashiri and Etorofu. Moreover, a resolution of the Japanese Lower House of 31 July 1952 concerning territorial questions only listed in its demands the return of Okinawa and Ogasawara in the south, together with the Habomai group and Shikotan. Not until 1955 did a shift in the Japanese position occur, linked to negotiations over the resumption of diplomatic relations with the Soviet Union.[19]

The Japanese memorandum on the territorial question, presented as a basis for the London-based negotiations, described 'the Habomai Islands, Shikotan, the Kuriles and southern Sak-

---

Talks with Czarist Russia and the Soviet Union', in Donald S. Zagoria (ed.), *Soviet Policy in East Asia*, New Haven, Conn./London 1982, pp. 127ff. On this point see also Langen, *Die Gebietsverluste Japans*, pp. 129ff.

17. On 8 September 1956, the fifth anniversary of the Peace Treaty of San Francisco, Yoshida declared in an article for the *Sankei Shimbun* that he had emphasised in his speech at the conference that Kunashiri and Etorofu did not belong to the Kuriles but were Japanese territory by inalienable right. An outstanding expert on this material, Haruki Wada, describes Yoshida's claim as a 'downright lie'. See *Sekai Shûhô*, 15–22 Jan. 1991, p. 20.

18. See NKBS, p. 111; Kamiya, 'The Northern Territories', p. 128. The importance of the Soviet view of this definition is proved by the fact that the Deputy Foreign Minister, Rogachov, quoted Nishimura's statement word for word in one of the more recent public explanations of the Soviet territorial claim; see *Izvestiya*, 24 April 1989, p. 7.

19. See Haruki Wada, 'Yontô-henkanron wa kakute kimerareta' (The Creation of a Concept for the Return of the Four Islands) in *Sekai Shûhô*, 15–22 Jan. 1991, pp. 18–21.

halin as historically part of Japanese territory'.[20] Clearly, according to this formulation the islands of Kunashiri and Etorofu were regarded as part of the Kuriles, since they were not specifically named – a viewpoint that has since been revised by Tokyo. Kunashiri and Etorofu, no longer defined as belonging to the Kuriles, may thus be excluded from the relinquishment demanded in the Treaty of San Francisco. This is the weakest point in Japan's justification of its territorial claim, for this definition contradicts the accepted meaning of the geographical term 'Kuriles' as it has always been used, a term which includes the entire chain of islands between Hokkaido and Kamchatka and whose usage is verified by Japanese cartographical documents up to modern times. Only the Habomai Islands and Shikotan are not part of the Kuriles, but belong geographically to Hokkaido.[21]

On 5 August 1955, two months after the London negotiations had begun, the Soviets offered Japan the Habomai Islands and Shikotan and dropped their demands for the dissolution of the Japanese-American security pact. The Japanese negotiator, Ambassador Matsumoto, could hardly believe his ears; however, his government ordered him not to accept any compromises.[22] On 30 August, then, Matsumoto presented his own demands, which exceeded even the memorandum prepared for the negotiations, calling for the return not only of Shikotan and the Habomais but also of Kunashiri and Etorofu, and for an international conference to reach a decision on the remaining Kuriles and Sakhalin.

This more intransigent position had its roots in a compound of domestic events and pressure from the USA. The group of conservatives around former Prime Minister Yoshida had been as surprised as the USA at the Soviets' offer. Neither country wanted to make concessions to the Soviet Union. Foreign Minister Shigemitsu, on the other hand, made it clear during a

20. See Kamiya, 'The Northern Territories', p. 130.
21. See Langen, *Die Gebietsverluste Japans*, pp. 126–35. The 1961–4 edition of a 6-volume Japanese lexicon describes the islands of Kunashiri and Etorofu as southern Kuriles. See Heibonsha (ed.), *Kokumin-hyakka-jiten* (Lexicon), vol. 5, Tokyo 1962, heading 'Chishima-rettô' (Kurile Archipelago), p. 36.
22. See *Far Eastern Affairs* (*FEA*), no. 2 (1990), p. 144, in which the well-known Japanese diplomat Kinya Niizeki reports on the conference as a participant.

visit to Moscow in July 1956 that he was willing to accept a peace treaty on the condition that two islands (Habomai and Shikotan) were returned. He met with sharp resistance from Tokyo and abandoned his efforts. As we now know, the USA also opposed a compromise. In August 1956 Foreign Minister John Foster Dulles warned Shigemitsu against relinquishing the two other islands, with the comment that this action could give the USA grounds for retaining Okinawa – an incident dubbed 'Dulles' threat' in Japanese diplomatic history. A US government memorandum dated 7 September 1956 stated the USA's conclusion, after examination of the historical evidence, that Kunashiri and Etorofu had always been constituent parts of Japan;[23] from then on Japan was only able to demand the return of four islands. Pressure from Washington had limited Japan's leeway for negotiations on the territorial question. Probably in accordance with American interests, the problem was further from being resolved than ever. The Soviet Union remained intransigent. On the resumption of diplomatic relations in October 1956, Gromyko and Matsumoto could agree on no more than the continuation of negotiations on a peace treaty to include the territorial question.[24]

The Protagonists Change Positions, 1956–1973

In the period that followed, up to the time of Prime Minister Tanaka's visit to Moscow in 1973, distinct shifts could be detected in the positions of both Tokyo and Moscow, within the context of international relations in Eastern Asia and also within East–West relations.

23. See *Asahi Evening News*, 29 March 1991; *Sekai Shûhô*, 15–22 Jan. 1991, p. 20. Later, in a note addressed to the Soviet government and dated 27 May 1957, the United States referred to the unlawful nature of the Soviet claim to the Habomai Islands, Shikotan, Kunashiri and Etorofu, and explained that neither the Yalta Agreement nor the Treaty of San Francisco had included these islands in the term 'Kuriles'; they had always been part of Japanese territory. See 'The Note of the United States Government to the Soviet Government (Excerpt), 23.5.1957', in Northern Territories Issue Association (ed.), *A Border yet Unresolved – Japan's Northern Territories*, Tokyo 1981, pp. 106ff; *Asahi Evening News*, 29 March 1991; *Sekai Shûhô*, 15–22 Jan. 1991, p. 20; NKBS, p. 148.

24. See Kamiya, 'The Northern Territories', pp. 131–3.

In the Joint Declaration made by Japan and the Soviet Union on 19 October 1956, with which war between the two countries was officially declared at an end and diplomatic relations resumed, both sides agreed to begin negotiations over a peace treaty as soon as possible. Moreover, the Soviet Union repeated its offer to transfer (*peredacha*) the Habomai Islands and Shikotan – after the conclusion of a peace treaty – to Japan.[25] Even today, this Joint Declaration is the sole document on Soviet-Japanese relations to have been ratified by the Japanese Parliament since the end of the war.

Japanese governments have always adhered to the view that settlement of the territorial problem is essential to the conclusion of a peace treaty. However, a few years later the Soviet Union dissociated itself from the linkage it had accepted in the Joint Declaration. The cause of this shift in attitude was the revision of the Japanese-American security pact on 15 January 1960. Almost two weeks later, on 27 January, the Soviet leaders adopted the argument that the transfer of the Habomai Islands and Shikotan agreed in the Joint Declaration was rendered impossible by this revised pact; it could only be completed after all foreign troops had been withdrawn from Japanese territory and after Japan and the Soviet Union had signed a peace treaty.[26] More than thirty years were to pass before President Gorbachev's visit to Japan in 1991 would result in the Soviets' willingness to acknowledge the link between the territorial question and the conclusion of a peace treaty.[27]

The Japanese government pointed out in its protest on 5 February that the renewal of its security pact with the United States was of a purely defensive nature and in full accordance with the Charter of the United Nations. Moreover, the treaty had been in existence at the time of the Joint Declaration, when foreign troops had also been stationed in Japan; the Joint Declaration had been founded on this basis.[28]

The Soviet memorandum of 27 January 1960 belatedly tried

---

25. See *Pravda*, 20 Oct. 1956; text in Northern Territories Issue Association, *A Border yet Unresolved*, pp. 102–5.
26. See NKBS, p. 162. English text (excerpts) in Rajendra Kumar Jain, *The USSR and Japan 1945–1980*, Atlantic Highlands, NJ 1981, pp. 259ff.
27. See Chapter 10, pp. 223–4, and Appendix A, pp. 258ff.
28. NKBS, p. 163. English text in Jain, *The USSR and Japan*, pp. 261ff.

to alter the basis of the transaction agreed in 1956, while implicitly acknowledging the existence of the territorial problem. This would soon change. Four months after the implementation of the revised Japanese-American security pact, the Soviet government declared: 'Japan's territorial claims are unfounded; the territorial question has already been solved.'[29] But even this position did not appear to be immutable. On 4 September 1964 Khrushchev, Communist Party leader and head of government in Moscow, declared to a group of Japanese parliamentarians, led by Kenji Fukunaga, with reference to the American bases on Japanese territory:

> Under these circumstances if we returned Habomai and Shikotan, there is a possibility that these islands, too, would be strategic bases against the Soviet Union. If the US forces withdraw from Japan and the Okinawa issue is settled, the Soviet Union . . . would return them.'[30]

Immediately before Khrushchev's overthrow in October 1964, he reiterated to the former Japanese Foreign Minister, Aiichiro Fujiyama, and others that the Soviet Union would agree to the immediate return of the islands when Okinawa was returned to Japan.[31]

The Soviet Union's subsequent actions indicate that from the second half of the 1960s onwards it became determined to disentangle the territorial question from the issue of a peace settlement and to establish its territorial assets. Japan resisted this strategy, rejecting proposals from Prime Minister Kosygin in July 1967 (a feasibility study on an interim peace treaty) and from President of State Podgorny in January 1972 (to conclude a formal peace treaty without reference to the territorial question).

The Japanese government's answer to an 'interim document', suggested by Prime Minister Kosygin, to exclude the territorial question, preceded a visit by Foreign Minister Aichi to Moscow in September 1969. The argument was:

- Legally and historically, Kunashiri and Etorofu belonged [as did the Habomais and Shikotan] to Japan.

29. *Izvestiya*, 19 Oct. 1960.
30. Northern Territories Issue Association, *A Border yet Unresolved*, p. 42.
31. *Ibid.*

- The correspondence between Matsumoto and Gromyko in 1956, before the Joint Declaration had been signed, included the Soviet Union's agreement to the continuation of negotiations over the conclusion of a peace treaty, to include the territorial question, after normal diplomatic relations had been resumed.
- Without settlement of the territorial question, no truly peaceful relations could exist between Japan and the Soviet Union.[32]

Much as expected, the Foreign Minister's visit to Moscow brought no headway in the sense Japan desired; however, a new line of Soviet argument was uncovered when Kosygin rejected demands for the return of the islands with the sole comment, 'The post-Second World War status quo in the territorial question must be retained; changes in *one* area will affect the whole'.[33]

Further developments in the Soviet stance showed that Kosygin's answer was to be seen within the context of a series of events: the question of Sino-Soviet borders, an especially delicate issue in 1969; and the proposal, formulated with a distinct anti-Chinese bias by Brezhnev, of founding a system of collective security for Asia, in which securing the *status quo* of existing frontiers played a central role.[34] Finally, 1969 saw the start of a process in which the Federal Republic of Germany concluded treaties of recognition of post-war borders with the Soviet Union and Poland.

In autumn 1970 Prime Minister Sato declared before the United Nations General Assembly that no peace treaty could be concluded between Japan and the Soviet Union without a settlement of the territorial question, and that until the conclusion of such a treaty the post-war period could not be considered over. Moscow reacted with a formal protest to the Japanese government.[35] This diplomatic action was accompanied by a huge wave of publicity; a short intervals, both party and

32. See *Tokyo Shimbun*, 14 Aug. 1969, in *DSJP*, 14 Aug. 1969. p. 21.
33. *Sankei*, 27 Sept. 1969, in *DSJP*, 27–29 Sept. 1969, pp. 44ff.
34. See Leonid Brezhnev, *For the Consolidation of an Amalgamation of Communist Countries for New Dynamism in the Anti-imperialist Struggle*, Moscow 1969, p. 59.
35. See Jiji Press (Tokyo), 1 Nov. 1979, in *Deutsche Welle, Monitor-Dienst [MD] Asien* [Asian Monitoring Service], 12 Nov. 1970, p. 4.

government organs published extensive commentaries on the Japanese stance on the territorial question, reiterating the principal aspects of the official Soviet position.[36] In addition to accusations of revanchism, references to the San Francisco peace treaty signed by Japan and the historical argument crediting Russia with the discovery of the Kuriles, these statements had a further element in common: namely ,references to recent developments in Europe, which were held up, in contrast to the Japanese demands, as 'new directions' in international relations:

> The conclusion of treaties between the USSR and the FRG [Federal Republic of Germany] and between Poland and the FRG establishing the permanence of post-war borders in Europe reflects a new tendency in the development of the international situation in accordance with the interests of peace and security.

The statement went on to add that, in their brutally revanchist character, the Japanese territorial claims on the Soviet Union sounded a note of sharp dissonance against the striving of nations to achieve a reduction in international tension.[37]

Kudryavtsev linked developments in Europe and Asia even more emphatically:

> Any attempts to revise the borders created as a result of the Second World War are in direct contradiction to current tendencies in international relations, which were manifested so clearly in the treaty recently concluded between the USSR and the FRG. The revanchist campaign in Japan is doomed to failure, and the faster it is abandoned by Japan's leaders, the better will Japan's national interests and the cause of peace and security in Asia and the Far East be served.[38]

Although the Japanese Foreign Ministry adopted a fundamentally positive attitude to the Moscow treaty, it naturally issued a denial that the treaty would have the slightest effect on Japan's own

36. See for example V. Kudryavtsev, 'Dvojnaja igra' (Double Game), in *Izvestiya*, 29 Oct. 1970; V. Kudryavtsev, 'Vopreki nacional'nym interesam' (Against National Interests), in *Izvestiya*, 13 Nov. 1970; V. Mayevski, 'Revanšistskij zud' (Revanchist Twitchings), in *Pravda*, 26 Nov. 1970.
37. See Mayevski, 'Revanšistskij zud'.
38. *Izvestiya*, 13 Nov. 1970.

territorial problem with the Soviet Union, and took the view that the issue of national frontiers within Europe was quite a different matter from the problem of the northern territories.[39]

This aside, since 1969 the Japanese government had been pursuing the idea of giving demands for a settlement of the territorial issue with the Soviet Union heavier weight by citing Okinawa as an example. However, the formulation used by Prime Minister Sato to extrapolate from the 'case' of Okinawa to the problem of the northern territories had not been given adequate consideration. President Nixon and Prime Minister Sato had agreed in November 1969 that Okinawa should be returned to full Japanese sovereignty in 1972. During an election campaign in Osaka, Sato stated that his first wish for the northern territories was that the Soviet Union should recognise Japan's 'residual sovereignty' – a term introduced by the United States to describe Okinawa's complex status in international law.

The Foreign Ministry in Tokyo reacted to this with undisguised criticism. The use of the term 'residual sovereignty', it contended, was not compatible with the standpoint that the northern territories rightfully belonged to Japan. 'If we are to have residual sovereignty recognised by the Soviet side, that will consequently mean our recognition of the present unlawful occupation by the Soviet Union.'[40]

Sato stuck to his guns. His Foreign Minister was obliged to fall in with him and stated that:

– In consideration of Foreign Minister Gromyko's visit to Japan for regular consultations, planned for the beginning of 1970, new possibilities were being considered for Japan to lead negotiations on the return of the northern territories. The simple reiteration of demands for their return served no purpose.
– It was the Prime Minister's wish under all circumstances that the Soviet Union should recognise Japan's residual sovereignty over Kunashiri and Etorofu, a wish shared by the Foreign Ministry. There was a possibility that the Soviet Union could be persuaded to take this direction. The view that both islands

---

39. Jiji Press (Tokyo), 12 Aug. 1970, in *MD Asien*, 13 Aug. 1970, p. 8.
40. *Tokyo Shimbun*, 12 Dec. 1969, in *DSJP*, 12 Dec. 1969, pp. 16ff.

rightfully belonged to Japan remained unchanged. Insistence on residual sovereignty would be a method of negotiation with the Soviet Union. The aim of regaining the northern territories would be pursued with as much commitment as ever.[41]

The Japanese press enquired whether this announcement indicated a change in the government's position, or whether the idea had occurred spontaneously after the negotiations on the return of Okinawa. The government's previous standpoint had been that 'the southern Kuriles belong rightfully and historically to our nation, and the Soviet occupation is illegal, wrong and devoid of any lawful foundation.'[42] Since the beginning of the 1960s, it was stated, the Soviet Union's response had been that the problem had already been settled by a series of international treaties; however, recognition of Japan's residual sovereignty meant recognition, albeit temporary, of Soviet rights of administration over the northern territories. 'This would include recognition of the armed Soviet occupation which has been the object of our protests.'[43] If the Japanese government were to adopt a position contradicting its previous views, this would have negative consequences internationally. If Sato's statement had only been the product of a spontaneous idea, then the thoughtlessness of its expression had resulted in national confusion.[44]

The head of Japan's government had not considered the consequences of his initiative in terms of international law and politics; his actions had been marked by electioneering rhetoric and inadequate preparation, compounded by the obscurity of the concept in negotiating a fundamental issue of Japanese politics. Sato's idea sank with hardly a trace, ignored by the Soviet Union. Instead, Moscow rejected any connections with the return of Okinawa, declaring that the transfer of administrative rights to the Japanese government altered nothing in terms of the existence of this important US Pacific military base. In other words, the US military presence on Japanese territory would not be

41. See *Asahi* (evening edn), 17 Dec. 1969, in *DSJP*, 17 Dec. 1969, p. 10.
42. *Mainichi*, 13 Dec. 1969, in *DSJP*, 16 Dec. 1969, pp. 3ff.
43. *Ibid.*
44. *Ibid.*

reduced by the transfer of administrative rights. The remaining American military bases in Japan – Mayevski, the *Pravda* commentator, spoke of 245 – with over 100,000 members of staff, were also introduced into the argument. 'This military apparatus is directed against the Soviet Union and other socialist countries.'[45]

The Eve of Tanaka's Visit to Moscow

Prime Minister Tanaka's visit to Moscow in the autumn of 1973 represented the peak of diplomatic progress between both countries, from the time official relations were resumed up to the year 1991. Japan would wait more than seventeen years for a return visit from a Soviet party leader and head of state.[46] Neither side altered its position significantly prior to Tanaka's visit; however, the Soviet leaders reacted by beginning to refer to 'questions remaining from the Second World War', observing the new shift in relations with China on the one hand, and with Japan and the USA on the other.

Tanaka's visit was preceded by an exchange of visits by both nations' Foreign Ministers. In January 1972 Gromyko, outwardly flexible, travelled to Tokyo; in October of the same year Ohira paid a return visit to Moscow. With Gromyko's visit the Foreign Ministers' talks, abandoned more than four years previously, were resumed. The communiqué issued at the conclusion of the visit stated, among other points, that:

– the talks between the Foreign Ministers of both nations, abandoned years previously, would be resumed on an annual basis;
– the governments of both sides would make efforts to plan exchange visits of their Prime Ministers;

---

45. *Pravda*, 26 Nov. 1970.
46. At the end of September 1989 Foreign Minister Shevardnadze informed his Japanese colleagues that Gorbachev planned to visit Japan in 1991. It was the first time the Soviets had announced a visit by a party leader and head of state for a specific time. See *Asahi Evening News* 28 Sept. 1989. At the Foreign Ministers' conference in Tokyo in September 1990, the Soviets said the visit would take place 'around April 1991'. See *Summary of World Broadcasts/Far East (SWB/FE)*, 0864/C1/1, 8 Sept. 1990.

– negotiations were to begin soon over the conclusion of a peace treaty.[47]

The Japanese delegation attempted to introduce the term 'territorial question' into the communiqué, but this was rejected unequivocally by Gromyko. Eventually, the formulation 'conclusion of a peace treaty' was agreed.[48] This was understood by the Japanese to include the territorial question.

Gromyko's visit was presented in the conservative Japanese press as a significant change in Soviet policies on Japan. A twofold motive was attributed to the visit. The first was the fact that general developments in international relations had created a multi-polar world focusing on the United States, the Soviet Union and China as the chief protagonists – a development which forced the Soviet Union to re-examine its Asian policies. In this, it was said, the *rapprochement* of China and Japan played an important role, for this was something the Soviet Union wanted to preempt.[49] The second motive was believed to be an attempt to impose another dimension on relations which up to then had concentrated on economic aspects; after all, Japan, whose annual volume of trade totalled US$800 million, was still the Soviet Union's most important non-socialist trade partner.[50]

The official aim of Foreign Minister Ohira's return visit in October was to brief the Soviet government on Japan's new policies on China, introduced after Prime Minister Tanaka's visit to China a few weeks previously and after the subsequent resumption of diplomatic relations between Tokyo and Peking. The brusque communiqué accompanying Ohira's visit explicitly stated this intention, emphasising that the normalisation of Sino-Japanese relations was not directed against third parties. Mention was also made of the initiation of talks on a peace treaty and the

---

47. *Pravda*, 28 Jan. 1972.
48. See *Sankei*, 28 Jan. 1972, in *DSJP*, 29–31 Jan. 1972, p. 23.
49. Kinya Niizeki, Ambassador to Moscow from 1971 to 1974, expressed the opinion that Gromyko made the trip to Japan on the advice of M. Kapitsa, an expert on China who was at that time director of the first Far Eastern Department of the Soviet Foreign Ministry and who accompanied Gromyko to Tokyo. See *FEA*, no. 2 (1990), p. 150.
50. *Sankei*, 12 Jan. 1972, in *DSJP*, 13 Jan. 1972, pp. 27ff.

agreement that these talks were to continue.[51] As expected, the term 'territorial problem' was absent.

The Japanese Foreign Minister announced on his return from Moscow that negotiations with the Soviets would be 'a long business requiring a lot of patience'.[52] In reply to Ohira's reiteration of Japan's usual bracketing of a peace treaty with the territorial question, the Soviet Union warned the Japanese government in its party newspaper against 'backsliding into revanchist positions', and went on to make repeated references to the recognition of post-war borders in Europe: 'International life is proving to mean plotting a course which in our times will not win any laurels for politicians if they adopt a position contrary to the principle of the immovability of post-war frontiers.'[53]

Japan's Foreign Minister had set out hoping for talks with the Soviet party leader; however, this meeting never took place. Ohira was received by Prime Minister Kosygin, who persistently asked him whether Japan had made any military pact with China,[54] and brushed aside the fact that the Japanese guest was not given the opportunity to speak to the Soviet party leader. However, the Japanese were well aware that the American Secretary of State, Rogers, the Foreign Minister of the Federal Republic of Germany, Scheel, and the French Foreign Minister, Schumann, had all been received by Brezhnev.[55]

What was the reason behind such different treatment? It was obvious that the Soviet Union was disturbed by the swift and far-reaching normalisation of relations between Japan and China, especially as China had pledged support for its neighbour over the territorial question, should diplomatic relations be resumed.[56] So these actions may have been intended as an expression of the Kremlin's displeasure at this.[57]

51. *Pravda*, 25 Oct. 1972.
52. *Daily Yomiuri*, 10 Nov. 1972.
53. *Pravda*, 24 Nov. 1972.
54. See *FEA*, no. 2 (1990), p. 151.
55. See *Daily Yomiuri*, 25 Oct. 1972, in *DSJP*, 26 Oct. 1972, p. 38.
56. This was reported by the chairman of the Komei Party, Takeiri, at the beginning of August 1972 after his return from a visit to China during which he had also been received by President Zhou Enlai. See *Nihon Keizai*, 9 Aug. 1972, in *DSJP*, 11 Aug. 1972, p. 9.
57. A well-known Soviet observer posed the meaningful question, 'Have

The Soviet Union's fears that its influence in Asian matters would be limited by this *rapprochement* led to its attempts to extinguish all hopes of compliance in the territorial question. Four weeks after Ohira's return from Moscow, the following statement appeared in the official Soviet party newspaper: 'Equally illusory are speculations that these or similar foreign policy actions noted in recent times would make it easier for Japan to exert pressure on the USSR.'[58] There were no signs of any compliance here. Despite this attitude, and the lack of perceptible success of Ohira's visit to Moscow, Tanaka's government continued its attempts to sort out relations with the Soviet Union by emphasising its express interest in negotiations on a peace treaty. Today, Ambassador Niizeki admits that Prime Minister Tanaka had been over-hasty in pursuing normal relations with China.[59]

Tanaka may have become aware that he had overestimated the effect of his Chinese policy on his Soviet neighbour. His status in domestic politics also fell rapidly, and he was forced to face the fact that Washington understood very well how to go about normalising relations with Peking faster than had been expected, and – unlike Japan – how to do this without dropping Taiwan.

In March 1973 the Japanese Prime Minister sent a letter to the Soviet party head.[60] The letter proposed resuming negotiations on a peace treaty, announced Japan's 'great interest' in the development of Siberian resources and in other questions of economic cooperation, and promised the Japanese government's support for these projects. Finally, Tanaka expressed his desire

---

the leaders of both countries reckoned with the historical lessons of the past, with the lack of foundation of their hegemonist claims to a leading role in Asia on the basis of the so-called "racial exclusiveness of their people" or the "infallibility of the ideas of a leader and of the past greatness of the country"? Or are these relations commencing under the condition of peaceful, neighbourly co-existence without infringement of the interests of other peoples?' (Sladkovskij, *Kitajsko-japonskie otnošenija*, p. 60).

58. *Pravda*, 24 Nov. 1972.
59. See *FEA*, no. 2 (1990), p. 152.
60. Prompted by this, Brezhnev received Ambassador Niizeki for two and a half hours of talks, the first he had granted to a high-ranking Japanese diplomat since taking office in 1964.

to continue talks at government level and declared his willingness to visit the Soviet Union in the same year.[61]

In Tokyo, Tanaka's letter was explained as an answer to the passage referring to Japan in Brezhnev's speech of 21 December 1972, in which he had signalled the Soviet Union's willingness to enter into peace treaty negotiations.[62] The Soviet party leader had used a formulation which was later to increase in significance: he spoke of 'questions remaining from the time of the Second World War'.

A spokesman for the Japanese government denied the growing speculation that under certain circumstances Japan might modify its claims to the Kurile Islands, and continued to describe the territorial question as 'the most important unresolved problem' facing possible peace treaty negotiations.[63] However, international reports on Japan's reaction are contradictory; at least one source refers to an ambiguous answer given by the spokesman of the Japanese Foreign Ministry, Tsutomu Wada, to journalists' questions on whether Japan would sign a peace treaty. Wada, it was reported, avoided giving a direct answer, leaving the impression that his government might be prepared to sign such a treaty even without a settlement of the territorial question. He admitted that this was 'conceivable', while emphasising that Japan hoped for a solution.[64]

Tokyo's unusually positive and optimistic reaction to the talks between the Soviet party head and Ambassador Niizeki on 6 March 1973 was echoed in the Soviet press. Samyatin, the director of the Soviet news agency TASS, emphasised Moscow's desire to achieve friendly relations between the two nations and recalled the positive development of the bartering system, which by 1972 had reached a level equivalent to 800 million roubles. It would be reasonable, he stated, to assume that Soviet-Japanese trade showed favourable prospects for continued growth. 'In many respects, our country is a natural partner for Japan.' There were excellent prospects for trade with Japan for many years to come, he predicted. 'At the same time, people in our country

---

61. See *Japan Times*, 7–8 March 1973.
62. See *Pravda*, 22 Dec. 1972, in *New Times*, no. 1 (1972), p. 16.
63. *Süddeutsche Zeitung*, 8 March 1973.
64. *International Herald Tribune*, 8 March 1973.

are familiar with high-quality products from Japan.' With his reference to a possible settlement of the 'questions remaining from the Second World War', Samyatin adopted Brezhnev's formulation, which could be interpreted as an indirect reference to the territorial problem. In Japan this remark, in the same way as the oft-repeated hope of improved relations 'in political issues too', could hardly be interpreted in any other way. Without naming China directly, Samyatin criticised 'those powers, not just within Japan, obstructing Soviet-Japanese cooperation'.[65]

In the government newspaper, the commentator Kudryavtsev referred optimistically to the long-term converging of both countries' interests, and the logical consistency of Soviet policies on Japan, which remained uninfluenced by economic viewpoints. He recalled the goal of bilateral talks mentioned by the party leader – the settlement of questions remaining after the Second World War. The familiar ambiguity of phrase recurs. Kudryavtsev also took up Samyatin's reference in an indirect criticism of China, referring to forces that would like to turn Japan's relations with the Soviet Union 'into an object in the game of diplomacy on the international stage'.[66] However, no mention was made of the territorial problem.

Tanaka's Visit to Moscow

The visit of the Japanese Prime Minister was marked by actions intended to demonstrate the Soviets' firmness and superiority. Because of the linguistic ambiguity of a formulation in the final communiqué, the visit led to an irresolvable controversy. Each side interpreted the controversial formulation to suit itself. In the end, the Soviets could be satisfied with what they had achieved, for they had not yielded an inch in their basic position. The Japanese, on the other hand, had not come any closer to realising their aim. An analysis of this visit is primarily important for its exemplary presentation of the main features of contemporary Soviet policies on Japan: the abundance of natural resources used as a lure; the uncompromising stance on the territorial question; the exploitation of Japan's every political weakness.

65. *Sovetskaja Rossija*, 13 March 1973.
66. *Izvestiya*, 13 March 1973.

The preparations for the visit had clearly indicated who would set the tone. A few weeks after the optimistic prelude came the surprising news that the Soviet-Japanese negotiations over joint exploitation of the Tyumen oilfields in western Siberia had been indefinitely postponed at Moscow's behest.[67] Barely two weeks later, the Soviets also requested a postponement of Tanaka's proposed visit. Tanaka was placed in an embarrassing position; he had already announced that the visit would take place in August, but it was explained to the public in Moscow that August was not a favourable time for the Soviet leaders.[68]

Tanaka found himself in this position because he had not waited for *official* confirmation of his visit. Moscow exploited his undiplomatic haste by giving a public snub, following it up with another when a party of Japanese ministers was invited to Moscow for that same August, with the promise they would meet representatives of the Soviet leaders.

Tanaka's growing problems in domestic politics – he was involved in a bribery scandal involving the Lockheed company – had evidently not been overlooked in Moscow and were regarded as an opportunity to put him under pressure in foreign affairs. Two aims may have influenced the Soviets' actions:

- Moscow sought Japan's financial and technological participation in exploiting the Tyumen oilfields, but wanted more favourable conditions than those proposed by the Japanese.
- The Soviets intended to emphasise their concern at the speed at which Sino-Japanese normalisation was proceeding.

Tokyo returned the ball. Both Foreign Minister Ohira and the Prime Minister reaffirmed the Japanese standpoint on the territorial problem at the end of July, to applause from Peking.[69] Shortly afterwards, the Japanese withdrew from participation in the Japanese-Soviet Mayoral Conference, held annually since 1968, while the Sixth Meeting of the Joint Japanese-Soviet Economic Committee (JJSEC), planned for the end of July 1973 in Moscow, was postponed.

Tanaka's visit was finally fixed for 7–10 October 1973. During

---

67. See *Deutsche Presseagentur*, 26 May 1973.
68. See *Japan Times* 7 and 11 June 1973.
69. See Xinhua News Agency, *Daily Bulletin*, no. 5590, 24 June 1973.

preparations for the visit, even official sources in Tokyo attempted to play down public discussion of the territorial problem. Accordingly, there was no reference to Japanese territorial demands in an interview with the Japanese Prime Minister published in *Pravda* in August.[70] The Japanese Foreign Minister reiterated the importance of returning the islands,[71] but Tokyo was ostentatiously reticent.

Soviet tactics now seemed to be aimed at separating talks on the territorial question from the problems accompanying economic cooperation and the signing of a peace treaty. Before Tanaka's visit, Moscow had managed to fix an agreement in principle with *Keidanren*, the Association of Japanese Businesses, on Soviet-Japanese cooperation in the exploitation of natural resources in Siberia;[72] however, this agreement never progressed beyond a declaration of intent. Japan's foreign policy took precedence over business interests.

On 7 October 1973 Prime Minister Tanaka finally arrived in Moscow, the first visit by a Japanese head of government to the Soviet Union in seventeen years. Moscow did a U-turn: the status accorded to the visit by the Soviet government was evident in the special attention paid to its Japanese guest. Tanaka was even allocated accommodation in the Kremlin itself, a privilege normally only conferred on heads of state such as the US President, or on the leaders of Communist parties.[73] In addition, the day before Tanaka's arrival the party organ printed a detailed article on Soviet-Japanese relations. The economies of the two countries were portrayed as complementary – Japan, with its limited reserves of raw materials; the Soviet Union, with its abundant resources – while any aspect of Soviet-Japanese relations which could be placed in a positive light was also described.[74]

70. See *Pravda*, 19 Aug. 1973.
71. See *Japan Times*, 29 Aug. 1973.
72. See *SWB/FE*/4387, 1 Sept. 1973.
73. Government heads were usually accommodated in guest-houses in the Lenin Hills. Japanese sources report that the guest-house accommodation originally planned was changed only two days before Tanaka's arrival.
74. For instance, the visit of 25,000 Japanese to the Soviet Union in 1972, or the information that the book company NAUKA (with just one shop in Tokyo) had sold 130,000 books the previous year. The number of Japanese

According to *Pravda*'s Japanese correspondent, the foundation in February 1973 of a league of parliamentarians in favour of Soviet-Japanese friendship was a graphic example of the dramatic changes occurring in Japanese political life, which the large number of parliamentary visitors to the Soviet Union also unexpectedly confirmed. The league was composed of almost all the representatives of the opposition party, as well as the majority of parliamentary members from the ruling party, including representatives from both houses. The article did not conceal the criticism and opposition voiced in Japan against improvements in Japanese-Soviet relations by those attempting to capitalise on 'anti-Sovietism'. Since at that time this term was a standard feature of Soviet accusations against China, the reference was probably to Chinese attempts to influence Japan.[75]

The political talks, led on the Soviet side by Leonid Brezhnev, Prime Minister Kosygin and Foreign Minister Gromyko, began on 8 October. The Soviet delegation also included Baibakov, deputy chairman of the Council of Ministers, and Patolichev and Ishkov, the Ministers of Overseas Trade and Fisheries respectively. The choice of members included in the delegation indicated that economic considerations were to have priority in the talks; as the Japanese side later confirmed, this was indeed the case. The Soviets' desire, often expressed during preparations for the visit, for Japanese support for their proposed system of collective security in Asia, was not discussed in the summit talks; this omission had been stipulated by the Japanese during the preparatory talks concerning the final communiqué.

In one of the speeches published, the Soviet party leader emphasised hopes for a permanent improvement in relations and for the development of neighbourly cooperation between both nations. The overall tenor of his statements was optimistic, in accordance with his estimation of the possibilities of development in Japanese-Soviet relations.[76] Brezhnev said not a word

---

learning Russian, it was reported, had also risen. Since April 1973 the radio and TV station NHK had been broadcasting a Russian course, for which reason the Soviet speaker Shatylov had received an invitation to Tokyo. The number of members of the Japan-Soviet Union Association, with branches in a hundred cities across the country, was said to be 11,000.

75. See *Pravda*, 6 Oct. 1973.
76. *Ibid.*, 9 Oct. 1973.

about the territorial problem, the decisive obstacle to the conclusion of a peace treaty; only one reference to 'complications' could have been an allusion to it.

In his response, Tanaka likewise took the desire for further improvements in relations between both sides as his starting-point. Japan and the Soviet Union, he declared, were not only neighbours, they also complemented each other in their economic relations 'in a way which is seldom to be observed in the world'. On the subject of concluding a peace treaty, he touched on the necessity of settling those questions that had remained open since the Second World War: an indirect reference to the territorial problem.

In conclusion, Tanaka emphasised that a peace treaty between both countries would not only be in their mutual interests, it would also contribute to the achievement of peace in the Far East and in the whole world.[77] This, as far as may be deduced from the published versions of the speeches, was the prelude to Soviet-Japanese summit talks. At a further meeting with the highest echelons of the Soviet leadership on 9 October – those present being Kosygin, Masurov and Gromyko – Tanaka spoke of the problem of concluding a peace treaty 'on the basis of the settlement of the territorial question, which appears to be the greatest unsolved problem in relations between our countries'.[78] Remarkably enough for that time, *Pravda* printed the entire passage.

Kosygin avoided the issue, instead referring in his answer to Brezhnev's allusion to the necessity of consolidating peace and security in Asia and the world as a whole, and challenging Japan to contribute in a similar way towards solving international problems. The euphemistic statement followed that problems had been touched on in which 'the views of the two sides did not concur'.[79]

At the end of the visit both sides published a Joint Communiqué, whose most important points were:

– Both sides judged 'the settlement of the unsolved questions in existence since the Second World War, and the conclusion

77. *Ibid.*, 9 Oct. 1973.
78. *Ibid.*, 10 Oct. 1973.
79. *Ibid.*

of a peace treaty' to be a contribution to the creation of neighbourly relations.
- Both sides underlined the necessity of consolidating economic cooperation, and placed special emphasis on 'the exploitation of Siberia's natural resources', while not ruling out participation by other countries.
- Both sides pledged the initiation of 'consultations between the appropriate ministries of both countries as soon as possible' to deal with fishing questions, in order to 'safeguard the long-term stability of catches in the Northern Pacific'.
- Both sides recognised the necessity of broader cooperation in peaceful uses of atomic power and in the exchange of scientists, technological expertise and information.
- It was reiterated that the consultations between the two nations' Foreign Ministers agreed to in 1966 were to be regularly continued. Moreover, the party leader Brezhnev, President of State Podgorny and Prime Minister Kosygin accepted an invitation from Tanaka to make a state visit to Japan.[80]

Overall, Tanaka's visit achieved little. Indeed, in the central political question, the territorial problem, the Soviet leaders had made no concessions whatsoever. The formulation interpreted by the Japanese as a victory – 'the settlement of the unsolved questions in existence since the Second World War' – was unclear. It was based on the formulation of 'questions remaining since the Second World War' employed by Brezhnev in his speech of December 1972, and had been used time and again, with apparent casualness, since that occasion. Now it appeared in slightly modified form in the concluding document issued at the end of the visit – but how could Tanaka interpret this as a success? The Prime Minister stated at a press conference immediately after his return from Moscow that there were not *several* unsettled questions; that is, in addition to the territorial problem. However, it must be noted that the Soviets had not agreed to a *direct* reference to this question in the text of the joint communiqué.[81]

80. *Ibid.*, 11 Oct. 1973. English texts (excerpts) in Jain, *The USSR and Japan*, pp. 307–11.
81. See *Asahi* (evening edn.), 11 Oct. 1973, in *DSJP*, 12 Oct. 1973, p. 32.

While Tanaka spoke of the success of his visit, the statements of his Foreign Minister were couched in more reserved terms. Ohira expressed his regret that it had not been possible to resolve the territorial question; he had assumed he would receive a firm promise from the Soviets on a solution to this problem within a definite period. Japan's sole achievement, he continued, had been to persuade the Soviet Union to sit down at the conference table and discuss the issue; however, it encompassed so many considerations that it could not be settled in one or two discussions. Ohira admitted that Tanaka had done his best, but had failed on this point. The Soviets held the opinion that there were several unsettled questions between the two countries; namely the fundamental rules for economic cooperation, a non-aggression pact and the territorial question – Ohira pointed out that Moscow had carefully avoided using the term 'territory'.

Tanaka's opinion that he had achieved a major success with the reference to the territorial question in the joint communiqué – albeit formulated as an abstraction – read too much into the evidence. The Soviets evidently reserved the right to their own definition of what was meant by 'unsettled questions from the time of the Second World War'. Since in Moscow's opinion there were several problems as yet unsettled, the Soviets could continue to state that the territorial question had been resolved.

Hirokazu Arai, leader of the Eastern European Department of the Foreign Ministry and a member of the Japanese team of negotiators, reported that Brezhnev had given a clear affirmative to Tanaka's query on whether the 'unsettled questions' included the territorial problem,[82] although this was naturally of no import for the interpretation of this formulation. The Soviet interpreter of the talks between Brezhnev and Tanaka claimed afterwards that he had heard no such thing.[83]

The Soviet Ambassador to Japan, Oleg Troyanovski, remarked in reference to this that Brezhnev had 'lifted his hand in a gesture of rejection'; if Japan saw this gesture in a positive light, then that was a purely arbitrary interpretation.[84] In the Japanese Parliament, however, the leader of the European De-

82. See *Mainichi*, 18 Aug. 1986, in *DSJP*, 29 Aug. 1986, p. 16.
83. *Ibid.*
84. *Sankei* (evening edn.), 7 March 1978, in *DSJP*, 15 March 1978, p. 16.

partment of the Foreign Ministry stated publicly for the first time in April 1977 that the positive response of the Soviet party leader was included in the Japanese delegation's notes of the talks, but could not be published as such.[85]

Afterwards Japan held to the opinion that the formulation 'questions unsettled since the Second World War' included the territorial question, and noted in the Blue Book of the Foreign Ministry of 1974 that 'the highest leaders of both countries' had 'confirmed' (*kakunin*) this fact.[86] It was said among the Japanese delegates that an attempt had been made to adopt the formulation 'the unsettled question'; however, the Soviets had insisted on the use of the plural.[87]

The scope for interpretation that was offered, according to the Japanese, by the Joint Communiqué of October 1973 was later reintroduced in attempts to move the Soviet Union to resume dialogue after years of Moscow's rejection of visits and talks. The fact that Foreign Minister Shevardnadze actually visited Tokyo in January 1986 seemed to signal a new departure in Soviet policies on Japan. However, the communiqué that followed revealed that nothing had changed. The phrase 'territorial problem' was unmentioned, just as it had been in the joint communiqué more than twelve years earlier.

Tanaka's optimistic interpretation of the achievements of his visit to Moscow was shaken not only by the fact that the Soviets seemed immovable on the territorial question, as the subsequent Foreign Ministers' meetings showed. The interpretation of 'suc-

---

85. See *Asahi*, 14 April 1977, in *DSJP*, 16–18 April 1977, p. 8.
86. See Gaimushô (ed.), *Waga gaikô-no kinkyô, Shôwa 49* (The Current State of our Foreign Relations, 1974), vol. 18, Tokyo 1974, p. 20.
87. Only in this context does the rather stilted formulation used by Prime Minister Nakasone in East Berlin in January 1987 to Erich Honecker, the head of state of the German Democratic Republic, become clear: 'Japan above all, with its unsettled question with the Soviet Union . . . , cannot agree to such a concept [Gorbachev's proposal of an Asian-Pacific security conference]' (*Neues Deutschland*, 14 Jan. 1987). It is remarkable that Nakasone – perhaps out of consideration to his host? – preferred the indirect formulation to a direct use of the term 'territorial problem'. Since the Japanese side always understood the formulation used at that time, 'the settlement of unsolved questions in existence since the Second World War', to be a reference to the territorial problem, it had evidently set itself the minimum target of maintaining the position it had stated in 1973.

cess' was also called into question by the divergences which emerged between the Russian and Japanese versions of the joint communiqué, betraying carelessness in the final editing of the text. In the Japanese version of the text the key sentence in the communiqué reads: 'Both sides exchanged opinions on negotiations they had previously initiated concerning the operations of Japanese fishing fleets in sea areas about which a separate settlement is to be reached, *and agreed to continue negotiations about this question.*'[88] In the Russian version the italicised clause is missing.[89]

The Japanese explanation for this oversight shows an astonishing amount of carelessness, combined with naiveté, in view of Tokyo's later request that it be corrected. The Foreign Ministry declared that because of the territorial question talks had been exceptionally fraught; a situation had arisen where even the formulation of a communiqué did not seem straightforward. The difference in the texts, it was claimed, had been noticed before signing, but since Prime Minister Tanaka and his delegation had had to leave, time had been short and they had therefore signed with the intention of resolving the problem later.[90]

The Soviet Union expressed regret at the 'oversight' and apologised, while at the same time rejecting all efforts to revise the Russian — that is, the shortened — text and insisting on clarification through an exchange of notes. On 28 October the Soviets confirmed in writing that 'both Japan and the Soviet Union have reached an agreement on the point of continuing negotiations on this problem [the safeguarding of fishing operations]'.[91]

The whole affair was somewhat embarrassing, for Tanaka and other government representatives had presented precisely this point as the greatest success they had achieved in Moscow: the Soviets' willingness to continue negotiations on safe fishing operations, coupled with negotiations on the territorial question.[92]

88. See Gaimushô (ed.), *Waga gaikô-no kinkyô*, vol. 18, section 2 (Documents), p. 45.
89. See *Pravda*, 11 Oct. 1973.
90. See *Tokyo Shimbun*, 25 Oct. 1973, in *DSJP*, 25 Oct. 1973, p. 36.
91. See *Yomiuri* (evening edn.), 29 Oct. 1973, in *DSJP*, 1 Nov. 1973, p. 3.
92. See *Tokyo Shimbun*, 25 Oct. 1973, in *DSJP*, 25 Oct. 1973, p. 6. As a consequence of this error the diplomats responsible for the negotiations and drawing up of the Joint Declaration, Tsurumi (Foreign Affairs councillor),

The Territorial Question

Fundamental Positions under Fire, 1973–1985

After Prime Minister Tanaka's visit to Moscow, there were no significant improvements in the relations between Japan and the Soviet Union for the next fifteen years. Even after Gorbachev came to power in 1985, some four years were to pass before it became possible to speak of an improved atmosphere in relations. The intervening period was one of stagnation, during which both sides held fast to the *status quo*. During this time every attempt at least to relativise the fundamental position of the opposing side failed. It was a phase which tested the protagonists' intransigence, and it is important to trace the events of the period in order to understand the resistance that blocked any improvement in relations beyond a merely cosmetic one. The causes of this long stagnation may be found in the following factors which arose during the 1970s and continued into the 1980s:

- the steady deterioration in Soviet-American relations, which drastically accelerated with the Soviet invasion of Afghanistan in 1979;
- Japan's shift towards approval of China;
- the expansion of the Soviet military presence in the Soviet Far East and in East and South-east Asia;
- the fact that Gorbachev's new Asian policies concentrated on China and consequently neglected Japan;
- the uncompromising adherence of the Japanese government and public to their demands for a settlement of the territorial question.

The last of these factors plays an essential role in our examination of the situation.

While the talks in Moscow in which Tanaka took part permitted the beginnings of economic cooperation – in which the main interest came from the Soviets – they were countered by the lengthy negotiations over fishing rights, resulting in loss of ground for the Japanese. Immediately after Tanaka's visit the

---

Owada (director of the European Department, Africa-Near East and Oceania), Arai (leader of the Council for Eastern Europe) and Kuriyama (leader of the Treaties Department) were given official warnings. Action against Secretary of State Hôgen, with whom the highest responsibility rested, was deferred. See *Yomiuri*, 1 Nov. 1973, in *DSJP*, 1 Nov. 1973, p. 26.

Japanese were confronted with the Soviet Union's uncompromising stance over the question of safe fishing operations, the agreement of catch quotas and fishing limits.[93] The Japanese government was interested in settling this issue for two reasons:

- First, the sea has always been a vitally important source of food for the Japanese. Moreover, the collecting and processing of various sea products provides employment for a not inconsiderable proportion of the total working population, on whose behalf the government was obliged to raise the issue and attempt to win the most favourable conditions possible.
- Secondly, questions of fishing were directly linked to the territorial question, for the traditional Japanese fishing grounds extended to the coastlines of the islands at issue, and were thus no longer available to Japan after the Soviet occupation. In addition, Soviet territorial water limits extended to up to 12 nautical miles, whereas Japanese limits only extended up to 3. With the declaration by the Soviets (and the United States) of an economic zone of 200 nautical miles with effect from 1 March 1977, the Japanese government was placed in a difficult position in fishing negotiations with Moscow, and the possibility of carrying through Japanese territorial claims was further weakened.[94]

After 1973, Soviet policy on the territorial question focused on the gradual consolidation of advantages already won. It seemed as if Moscow wanted once and for all to shatter the exaggerated hopes developed and nurtured by the Japanese since Brezhnev's much-discussed gesture.

When Foreign Minister Miyazawa visited Moscow in January 1975 to negotiate a peace treaty, the Japanese side intended to include a formulation in the planned communiqué that was more precise than the 'certain problems unsettled since the end of the

---

93. From 1946 to 31 March 1973, the Soviet Union had seized 1,400 fishing vessels in the waters of the north-west Pacific and had arrested a total of 11,827 people. In these operations 23 ships sank, 861 were returned to Japan, and 32 fishermen lost their lives; see Gaimushô, *Waga gaikô-no kinkyô*, vol. 17, p. 211.

94. The complex fishing negotiations of 1974–8 have been thoroughly documented and evaluated individually; see Mayer, *Der japanisch-sowjetische Territorialstreit*, pp. 61–107.

war' used in the text of 10 October 1973. The Foreign Ministry decided on the expression 'territories', including the two islands Kunashiri and Etorofu,[95] but all attempts to introduce it foundered on the Soviets' unyielding stance. The communiqué following Miyazawa's visit is uninformative on this issue; the delegations merely referred to the communiqué text of October 1973 and agreed on continuing talks with the aim of concluding a peace treaty. The Soviets also promised that Foreign Minister Gromyko would visit Japan that year.[96]

This visit was not to take place until 1976. According to statements from the Japanese Foreign Ministry, Gromyko was not prepared to enter into a discussion of the territorial question.[97] Characteristically, he postulated a link with post-war frontiers in Europe, declaring to Prime Minister Miki, 'If we bring up the question of the northern territories, we cannot avoid touching on the territorial question in Europe.'[98] The Soviet Union used this justification subsequently to reject Japanese calls for territorial revision even more uncompromisingly than before, referring to the confirmation of European post-war borders achieved by Germany's treaties with the countries of the Eastern bloc and by the Conference for Security and Cooperation in Europe (CSCE).

Gromyko's position was not new to the Japanese; a few months before, in an article published in the theoretical organ of the CPSU, he had described Japan's claims to the islands as 'unfounded' (*neobosnovannye*).[99] The Japanese government had promptly registered its protest to Moscow. In February 1976, shortly after Gromyko's visit, the party leader Brezhnev himself had reiterated this view at the Twenty-fifth Party Conference of the Soviet Communist Party. Japanese territorial claims, he said, were 'unfounded and illegitimate'. He warned Japan against the temptation of accepting 'outside' support in this question.[100]

95. See *Yomiuri*, 11 Jan. 1975, in *DSJP*, 11–13 Jan. 1975, p. 34.
96. See *Asahi*, 19 Jan. 1975, in *DSJP*, 21 Jan. 1975, p. 32.
97. See *SWB/FE*/5107, 14 Jan. 1976.
98. *Yomiuri* (evening edn.), 13 Jan. 1976, in *DSJP*, 15–16 Jan. 1976, p. 20.
99. See *Kommunist*, no. 14 (Sept. 1975), p. 16; *Mainichi*, 9 Oct. 1975, in *DSJP*, 18–20 Oct. 1975, p. 4.
100. *Pravda*, 25 Feb. 1976. The last remark was an allusion to the unsolicited

The statement of the Soviet party leader led to consternation in the *Gaimusho* and was held to be a further departure of the Soviet Union from the formulation of the 'various as yet unsettled questions'[101] fixed on by Tanaka and Brezhnev in October 1973. This reaction arose because the Japanese, as explained above, had interpreted this formulation solely according to their own ideas, in other words as a reference to the territorial question.

In 1976 while Foreign Ministers from around the world were gathering for the UN General Assembly meeting in New York, the Soviet Foreign Minister took a further step towards confirming the *status quo* with his Japanese counterpart, while simultaneously excluding the territorial question from the agenda of future negotiations. Gromyko declared that the Soviet Union wanted a peace treaty: 'But we are not thinking of the problem of the four islands at all. We are not thinking of a treaty linked with [reversion of] the four islands at all.'[102]

One feature of the Soviets' strategy consisted of causing difficulties for visitors to graves in the Habomai Islands and Shikotan. Since 1954 around fifty Japanese a year had visited the graves of their relatives in the islands near the coast. The Soviets had stopped these visits in 1968, 1971 and 1972; when he was in Moscow in 1973, Prime Minister Tanaka succeeded in having the ban lifted. Soviet officials had always accepted the travel documents issued by the Foreign Ministry in Tokyo; however, in May 1976 Moscow informed the *Gaimusho* that while the graves could be visited, the type of travel documents previously issued were now insufficient – visitors would from now on require Japanese passports, just as they would for any other trip abroad. In the subsequent negotiations over details of the round of visits planned for August 1976, the Soviets finally insisted that visitors would have to obtain visas. The *Gaimusho* demanded that this condition be rescinded, arguing that the islands were Japanese territory and should not be categorised in the same way

---

but massive verbal support which China had given its neighbour Japan over the territorial question for years.

101. See *Tokyo Shimbun*, 25 Feb. 1976, in *DSJP*, 28 Feb.–1 March 1976, p. 8.

102. *Nihon Keizai*, 30 Sept. 1976, in *DSJP*, 2–4 Oct. 1976, p. 8.

as foreign territory.[103] The Soviet Union called this demand 'futile ambitions' and pointed out that visas were required of any traveller visiting another country. It was to be made quite clear that the islands in question were an integral part of Soviet territory. The Japanese rejected the ruling and abandoned the possibility of visiting the graves.

These intransigent positions did not begin to soften until a decade later. On the occasion of Foreign Minister Shevardnadze's visit to Tokyo at the beginning of 1986, the Soviet Union announced that 'on humanitarian grounds' it was prepared in principle to allow Japanese citizens visiting rights to the graves of their relatives.[104] Foreign Minister Abe and the Soviet Ambassador accordingly came to an agreement in Japan on 1 July 1986. Japanese citizens with specially issued identity documents — that is, without Soviet visas — were permitted to visit the islands.

At first sight it may be thought that the Soviet Union had made a concession with the lifting of the visa regulation, but Tokyo was forced to return the favour. Thus from then on Soviet citizens were to be permitted to visit the graves of their relatives in Japan, chiefly war graves from the Russo-Japanese war of 1905, under similar conditions. The Soviets had gained a position whereby the access granted to a limited number of Japanese citizens to visit the islands claimed by the Soviet Union and actually annexed to the Soviet Union was accorded exactly the same status as the access granted to a limited number of Soviet citizens to visit Japanese sovereign territory. With this ruling Moscow had not only held firm to its standpoint that the islands at stake had become Soviet territory, but had even had Japan confirm this viewpoint by a roundabout method. This may also be concluded from the fact that Foreign Minister Abe found it necessary to explain, in the context of visiting regulations, that Japanese territorial claims to the islands were in no way affected.[105]

The publications in which the Kuriles are described as part of the Soviet Union and their inhabitants as Soviet citizens, and

103. See *Asahi Evening News*, 3–4 Sept. 1976.
104. See *Pravda*, 2 June 1986.
105. See *MD Asien*, 2 July 1986, pp. 6ff.

in which the economic expansion of the previous decades is presented in a favourable light, were additional features of Moscow's strategy of consolidation, intended to communicate the idea that the islands belonged to the Soviet Union as a matter of course. One such publication from 1975 contained the information that Kunashiri and Shikotan had been included in the Soviet Union's internal tourism programme.[106] Statements such as 'Life in Kunashiri and the other islands is in general no different from life in other parts of the Soviet Union', or 'all the others I met love their islands and do everything they can to make them more pleasant', were intended to underline the islands' closeness to the Soviet Union and the commitment of their inhabitants.[107] The same bias may be found in a detailed discussion of Sakhalin and the Kuriles, whose author was listed as P. Leonov, first secretary of the Sakhalin Regional Committee of the Communist Party of the Soviet Union.[108]

The Sovietising of the islands described in these articles – the Soviets called them the South Kuriles – appeared to be progressing apace. Today the islands have between 20,000 and 30,000 inhabitants, excluding military personnel – nearly twice the number of Japanese living there at the end of the war. A large proportion of the employable population, especially in Shikotan, works in fishing and the fish-processing industry.[109] The gradual 'militarisation' of the islands, which began in mid-1978, is also a significant step towards confirming the *status quo*.[110]

In addition, attention should be drawn to the process within the Soviet strategy of consolidating acquired rights whereby textual alterations were carried out in an officious reference work, among whose editors' names is listed that of the Soviet Foreign Minister, Gromyko. The *Diplomatic Lexicon*, published in three editions (1960–4, 1971–3, 1984–6), contains brief reference articles on personalities and events in Soviet foreign affairs and diplomatic history, including Russian and Soviet-Japanese relations. In the first two editions of this work, the Treaty of St Petersburg (1875), under which Japan exchanged

106. See 'In the Kurils', in *New Times*, no. 46 (1975), pp. 24ff.
107. *Ibid.*
108. See *FEA*, no. 1 (1978), pp. 14–30.
109. See *Mainichi*, 16 Oct. 1985, in *DSJP*, 23 Oct. 1985, p. 16.
110. For this process see pp. 191ff.

its claim to the island of Sakhalin for the possession of the entire chain of the Kuriles, is described in these words: 'Czarist Russia agreed to this concession and transferred territory which had originally been Russian – the Kurile Islands – into the hands of the Japanese, in exchange for Japan's official relinquishment of its absolutely unfounded claims to the island of Sakhalin.'[111] In the most recent edition, this passage was formulated rather differently:

> Just as Russia was at that time unable simultaneously to defend its rights to the Kuriles and southern Sakhalin, it was forced in accordance with the Treaty [of St Petersburg] to transfer territory which had originally been Russian – namely eighteen Kurile Islands – into the hands of Japan, in exchange for Japan's official relinquishment of its unfounded claims to Sakhalin.[112]

Historical accuracy is left open. It is interesting that the Soviet Union returned to the construct of the 'unequal treaty' as justification for transferring the Kuriles to Japan; in other words Moscow adopted an argument it had vehemently refused to countenance when Peking had used it in the conflict over the Chinese-Russian border.

A further example can be found in the *Lexicon*'s entry on the Joint Soviet-Japanese Declaration of 1956, which stipulated in Article 9 that the Habomai Islands and Shikotan would be transferred to Japan upon the conclusion of a peace treaty. This article, a vital part of Japan's claim to the islands, was reproduced correctly in the first edition of the *Lexicon*, but was deleted from the following two edition, which contained no reference whatsoever to this agreement.[113]

The joint communiqué which came about as a result of Prime Minister Tanaka's visit to Moscow in 1973 was treated in a similar fashion. The agreement valued so highly by the Japanese, that negotiations on 'the settlement of unsolved questions in existence since the Second World War' would be continued,

---

111. Gromyko *et al.*, *Diplomatičeskij Slovar'*, vol. 3, edn of 1964, p. 102; edn of 1973, pp. 97ff.
112. *Ibid.*, vol. 2, Moscow 1986, p. 495.
113. *Ibid.*, vol. 3, 1964, p. 293; 1973, pp. 386ff; 1986, pp. 367ff.

was granted not a single word; the entry stated only that the communiqué included an agreement to continue talks about a peace treaty.[114]

This handling of facts, manipulation of documents and other measures were evidently backed by the politically rooted intention of reaffirming the historical foundation of the Soviet claim to all the islands at issue north of Hokkaido, and of destroying all prospects of revising the actual property aspect. During the early years of Gorbachev's rule, the formulation that a territorial problem in Japanese-Soviet relations did not exist, an expression which did not become current until the 1960s, was still traced back to the Joint Declaration of 1956.[115] This all made the possibility of Soviet concessions on the territorial question seem very remote.

Discussions on this issue in Japan were followed attentively by Moscow, although since the Japanese claim was rejected in principle, no official Soviet position concerning the details of the return was announced until towards the end of the Gorbachev era. The Japanese government, the LDP and organisations sympathising with the LDP held the view that all four islands – that is, the Habomai group, Shikotan, Kunashiri and Etorofu – would have to be returned to Japan *en bloc* (*yontô-ikkatsu* – 'four islands as a whole') before Japan would sign a peace treaty with the Soviet Union. However, occasional ideas or proposals diverging from this package solution and feeding speculations about Japan's willingness to compromise over the territorial question appeared in the Japanese press as early as the 1970s.

In 1975 Kazuhige Hirazawa, an eminent commentator on foreign affairs and confidant of the Prime Minister, proposed in the journal *Foreign Affairs* that Japan should sign a peace treaty with the Soviet Union under which, in accordance with the Joint Declaration of 1956, it would receive Habomai and Shikotan. He maintained, however, that the question of the return of Kunashiri and Etorofu should be left alone, unsettled, until the end of the century, but added that in his opinion Japanese fishing fleets should be given access to the waters around

---

114. *Ibid.*, vol. 3, 1986, p. 371.
115. See *Izvestiya*, 20 March 1987.

both islands. Hirazawa believed that the question of their return should only be re-examined after sufficient mutual trust had been built up between Japan and the Soviet Union through cooperation in other areas.[116]

The motive behind the publication of Hirazawa's proposal has never been fully explained. The usual claim in such affairs that the views published 'represent purely the private opinion of the author' is not credible in the face of such explosive material and the status of the author. It would not be too far-fetched to suspect that this proposal was planted by circles close to the government to sound out reactions at home and abroad.[117] Whatever its purpose, the government and people of Japan unanimously rejected the proposal. Prime Minister Miki expressly distanced himself from it in a Cabinet meeting and in Parliament, and emphasised that the previous policy of demanding a package solution to the territorial question had not changed.[118] Expressions of disapproval in the Japanese press concentrated on two questions: the precise meaning of 'freezing' the claim to Kunashiri and Etorofu, and whether there was any guarantee that in the next century the Soviet Union would take a seat at the negotiating table to discuss the territorial question.

One opinion held that if 'freezing' the claim meant recognition of the existing situation of Soviet occupancy until the end of the twentieth century, that was nothing more than a renunciation of both islands; such a unilateral concession would not be tolerated by the Japanese people under any circumstances. And as far as the second point was concerned, if Moscow was prepared to be persuaded by a spirit of mutual concession, then it would already have recognised Japan's dormant sovereignty over both islands, as the United States had done in the case of Okinawa; in this case, there would be a chance of negotiations later. As it was, however, the Soviet Union adhered immovably to its view that the territorial question had already been resolved.[119]

The Foreign Ministry also launched a sharp attack on Hira-

116. See *Foreign Affairs*, vol. 54, no. 1 (Oct. 1975), p. 165.
117. See *Sankei*, 21 Sept. 1975, in *DSJP*, 24–25 Sept. 1975, p. 1.
118. See *Nihon Keizai* (evening edn.), 19 Sept. 1975, in *DSJP*, 24–25 Sept. 1975, p. 23.
119. See *Yomiuri*, 21 Sept. 1975, in *DSJP*, 24–25 Sept. 1975, pp. 3ff.

zawa's proposal, taking the view that the concept would merely postpone the problems. The sole result would be the conclusion of a treaty of friendship and good neighbourliness instead of a peace treaty, which was exactly what the Soviet Union had been suggesting for some time.[120]

More than a decade after this 'episode', discussions on possible solutions to the territorial problem were once more widespread in Japan, following the resumption of Soviet-Japanese talks at Foreign Minister level. Renowned Japanese political scientists and publicists expounded their ideas on a solution to the territorial question.

The discussion was marked by some extreme emotions and polemics. Accusations of pro-Soviet sympathies were hurled at anyone who cast doubt on Japan's claims to all four islands by employing arguments from international law and who recommended a solution along the lines of the Joint Declaration of 1956 – that is, the return of the Habomais and the island of Shikotan. An internationally famous Japanese Sinologist expressed similar views to those of Hirazawa, calling for an acceptance of the return of two islands and for negotiations with the Soviet Union over the joint use and development of the other two, Kunashiri and Etorofu, while retaining all claims to them.[121] He argued in favour of improving relations with the USSR, posing the question of 'whether it can be right to cling to the return of the four islands in the north and to shake clenched fists', quoting Japan's growing economic attractiveness to Moscow and pointing out the possibility that the Soviet Union and China would develop 'towards the free world' in the twenty-first century. If this happened, it would become necessary for both Tokyo and Moscow to make compromises in order to bring about an improvement in their relations.[122]

During in the second half of the 1980s, other experts also publicly discussed a possible approach to settling the question by concentrating on winning back Habomai and Shikotan. While not actually speaking explicitly in favour of relinquishing

120. See *Asahi*, 19 Sept. 1975, in *DSJP*, 30 Sept. 1975, p. 8.
121. See Mineo Nakajima, 'Hoppô-ryôdo "nitô-henkanron" wa tabû ka?' (Is the Discussion of 'the Return of Two Islands' of the Northern Territories Taboo?), in *Shokun*, March 1987, p. 43.
122. *Ibid.*, p. 45.

territory, they attempted to loosen the deadlock over the islands, believing an improvement in relations between Japan and the Soviet Union to be necessary.[123]

Public debate about possible solutions, which did not even rule out the sale of Kunashiri and Etorofu,[124] was countered by the unchanged stance of the government which retained the idea of a package solution until the end of the 1980s. The simultaneous return of all four islands was demanded. This demand was reiterated by Prime Minister Nakasone in Parliament in view of speculation that Japan would be satisfied with the return of Habomai and Shikotan.[125]

But the *Gaimusho* itself appears to have fuelled such speculations. After the issue of a press report at the beginning of February 1986, an unnamed high-ranking official had posed the question of whether the population of Japan would not be happy if a visit by Prime Minister Nakasone to Moscow succeeded in returning the debate to the stance taken in the Joint Declaration of 1956. However, he went on, a return to that point would depend on future negotiations.[126] It is apparent from this that even the Foreign Ministry had occasionally considered a partial solution to the problem, and that at that time a return to the position of 1956 was seen as progress when compared with the current position.

Discussions on how to reach a solution received further impetus in autumn 1989, when the Soviets announced that Gorbachev would visit Japan in 1991. At the end of April 1990 Shin Kanemaru, then an influential LDP veteran and chairman of the strongest inner-party faction, declared that if the Soviet Union had no desire to return all four islands, then it should at least start by giving two back. He added the throwaway remark,

---

123. See Haruki Wada, 'Hoppô-ryôdo mondai-ni tsuite no kôsatsu' (Observations on the Question of the Northern Territories) in *Seika*, Dec. 1986, pp. 150–61; Gregory Clark, 'Hoppô-ryôdo-wa tabû shisuru na' (Do Not Place the Northern Territories under a Taboo), in *Voice*, Dec. 1986, pp. 96–105.
124. See Nakajima, 'Hoppô-ryôdo nitô-henkanron', p. 33.
125. See *Japan Times*, 11 Feb. 1986, Kenichi Itô, 'Strategy for Return of Northern Territory', in *SSJM*, March 1986, pp. 18–28. Itô rejects Gregory Clark's views, partly in a polemical tone.
126. See *Asahi*, 4 Feb. 1986, in *DSJP*, 15–18 Feb. 1986, p. 15.

'I think we can buy them too'.[127] Kanemaru maintained that he had already expressed these thoughts to Primakov, then director of the Institute for World Economy and International Relations (IMEMO) and Gorbachev's adviser.

There were varied reactions to this remark from party and government. While the government immediately reaffirmed the so-called package solution as the unchanged basis of its policies on the northern territories, although without explicitly criticising Kanemaru, high-ranking functionaries of the LDP hovered between surprise ('perhaps a way of sounding things out?'), affirmation (from the Abe faction) and misgivings, which were chiefly directed at the remark about buying the two islands and the silence about proceedings regarding the other two. This reaction, however, was essentially quite different from the energy with which Hirazawa's proposal of compromise had been rejected in 1975.

The fact that Kanemaru did not dissociate himself from his statements must be regarded as a further proof of the change in attitude. He explained before his faction that the four islands were Japanese territory; the demand for their return would change nothing. His proposal that two islands should be returned first referred, he said, to the Soviet offer in the Joint Declaration of 1956, and it had been in this sense that he had expressed the 'view of a gradual return' (*dankaiteki-henkan-ron*). As far as the proposal of buying the islands was concerned, he had intended to express the fact that Japan would have to cooperate actively with the Soviet Union in economic matters, in view of the Soviets' striving for economic cooperation.[128] It was remarkable that Kanemaru did not use the official expression for a package solution (*yontô-ikkatsu*).

The Soviets also fuelled speculation of this type during the second half of the 1980s. It is said that during a visit to Japan at the end of 1985, Primakov, in conversation with an official of the Japanese Foreign Ministry on the subject of the territorial question, made the sybilline remark that Japan should take note of the content of the Joint Declaration of 1956. He then made an unmistakable reference to the Soviets' intention of resolving

127. *Asahi*, 24 April 1990.
128. *Ibid.*, 27 April 1990.

the territorial question by returning the Habomai group and Shikotan.[129] Falin, the president of the news agency *Novosti*, also awoke Japanese hopes of more flexibility by remarking that the Soviet Union would not exclude any problem from the negotiations, even if it was only raised by the other side. Many observers in Tokyo perceived this as progress in comparison with previous stubborn denials of the existence of any territorial problem.[130]

It should be remembered that Primakov and Falin were not among the decision-makers; theirs were advisory capacities at best. However, it could very well have been their task to provoke reactions through such statements, thus enabling a more precise analysis of Japanese opinion to be conducted. Soviet political leaders showed no interest in compromising even after Gorbachev's ascent to power, as was evident during Foreign Minister Abe's visit to Moscow at the end of May 1986. After Abe had introduced the question of the islands, Gorbachev declared, 'You have brought up a problem which you have no right to bring up. The national boundaries are unchangeable. As a result of the Second World War, the borders of today have already gained legitimacy.'[131]

Signs of the 'New Thinking'

Since the Twenty-Seventh Party Conference of the Communist Party of the Soviet Union in February/March 1986, at which Gorbachev had promulgated 'New Thinking' as the basis of his foreign policy, there had been speculation as to when the USSR's relationship with Japan would be affected by this change. Foreign Minister Shevardnadze's visit to Tokyo at the end of December 1988, together with the outcome of the talks held by his Japanese opposite number, Sosuke Uno, in Moscow at the beginning of May 1989, made this question particularly pertinent for two reasons. First, in two key speeches made in Vladivostok in 1986 and in Krasnoyarsk in 1988, Gorbachev had announced a policy aimed at broadening attitudes towards the Asia Pacific area and at cooperation in economic and defence issues. Secondly, the

---

129. See *Nihon Keizai*, 27 Dec. 1985, in *DSJP*, 8 Jan. 1986, pp. 3–5.
130. See *Asahi* (evening edn.), 20 Nov. 1986.
131. *Japan Times*, 31 May 1986.

Soviet Union was attempting to strengthen both its trade and its relations with market economies involving capital and technology, seeing in this reorganisation a vital impetus to the restructuring of its own economic system. In keeping with this new political and economic orientation, it would have been logical for the Soviet Union to have aimed at improving relations with Japan, which Gorbachev had described as 'a power of first-ranking significance'.[132] Despite this positive attitude and the general dynamism of Soviet policies on Asia, Gorbachev's first three years in office left the impression that there had been few changes in Moscow's relations with the greatest economic power in the region.

Foreign Minister Shevardnadze's visit to Tokyo in January 1986 – the first visit to Japan by a Soviet head of the Foreign Ministry for ten years – chiefly signalled a change in atmosphere. While no discussion of the territorial problem actually took place, the Soviet guest was willing to listen to the arguments of his host, which marked a radical departure from Gromyko's time. In addition, hopes that discussions on a peace treaty would begin were nourished by the fact that a Soviet Foreign Minister had visited Japan after such a long gap, and that former agreements to hold annual consultations between the two countries' Foreign Ministers had been revived.

These hopes, however, proved false. During the Foreign Ministers' talks, there was no sign of even the slightest Soviet acquiescence. At a press conference in Tokyo, Shevardnadze declared that it had not been possible to reach a consensus on this problem; as far as the historical, legal and contractual background to the problem was concerned, the Soviet position remained unaltered. Shevardnadze added that there were additional unresolved problems;[133] an important remark, since it reiterated the distinction made by the Soviet Union between the territorial problem, which Moscow regarded as having been settled, and 'other problems', which were open to negotiation. What could it mean when Japanese sources optimistically reported in 1986 that Foreign Minister Abe had 'discussed' the

132. See Gorbachev's speech in Vladivostok on 28 July 1986, *Pravda*, 29 July 1986, English translation in *FEA*, no. 1 (1987), pp. 3–21.
133. See *SWB/FE/*8161/A2/5, 20 Jan. 1986.

territorial question with his guest? It is reliably documented that the talking was done by the Japanese, while the Soviets limited themselves to the remark that their standpoint had not changed. The Japanese, however, described this as 'negotiating'. The beginning of the Gorbachev era could be said at best to have introduced a change of style, but not of content. This was demonstrated by the reference by Shevardnadze himself to the territorial question before the Tokyo press, for example, and by his willingness to listen to Japan's claims. The Soviet Foreign Minister was quoted as saying, 'Although the Soviets and the Japanese differ in their interpretation of this problem, we on the Soviet side do not have the right to stop Japan talking about the problem.'[134] However, in official texts such as communiqués the Soviet Union permitted no direct reference to any 'discussion' of the territorial question.

A comparison of the Joint Communiqué of 1973 with the communiqués of Foreign Ministers Shevardnadze (in Tokyo at the beginning of 1986) and Abe (in Moscow in mid-1986) shows that the more recent texts contain weaker formulations. The statement in the communiqué of January 1986 that negotiations on a peace treaty had 'included the questions which could form its content' is no more than a commonplace. What else would there be to negotiate, if the conclusion of a peace treaty were the long-term goal? There is only an indirect reference to 'unsolved questions' in this document, in that the 1973 joint communiqué is mentioned but not quoted.[135] The communiqué issued on the visit of Foreign Minister Abe to Moscow at the end of May 1986 contains an even weaker formulation; again it refers to the communiqué of 1973, mentions the negotiations of January 1986 and cites the agreement to continue talks on the signing of a peace treaty during the next Foreign Ministers' Conference in Tokyo in 1987.[136] This meeting, however, was not to take place until December 1988.

The hopes of progress linked with the 1986 visit of Foreign Minister Abe to Moscow were soon subdued. Despite Gorbachev's denial of a settlement, delivered in the familiar style of

---

134. *Pravda*, 2 June 1986.
135. *Ibid.*, 11 Oct. 1985 and 20 Jan. 1986.
136. *Ibid.*, 2 June 1986.

old and quoted above, the new General Secretary tried to win promises of good neighbourliness and support for his policies from Abe. For his part, Prime Minister Nakasone attempted to persuade the Soviet party leader to visit Japan by repeatedly extending invitations. However, he was chiefly set on strengthening his own standing within his party, with the aim of securing another term in office. Moscow's reaction was reserved; a visit from the new man in the Kremlin would be the first visit to Japan by a Soviet party leader and head of state since the end of the war. Not until late autumn 1989 did the Soviet Union announce that Gorbachev would visit Japan in 1991.

The period after this sobering beginning was crowded with incidents which rendered any improvement in Japanese-Soviet relations impossible. After revelations in May 1987 about unauthorised deliveries of computer-operated milling machines to the Soviet Union by the Toshiba Machine Company, there followed the unmasking of three Soviet agents of the KGB and the military Secret Service. The United States believed the milling machines enabled the manufacture of submarine propellors which were so low in noise that locating the submarines' position became more difficult. The spying affair, uncovered at almost the same time as the Toshiba Affair, placed a further strain on relations. Soviet agents had allegedly obtained military documents concerning AWACS technology from a Japanese spy-ring. Japan protested to the Soviet Union and expelled a member of staff of the Soviet Embassy in Tokyo.[137] Moscow reacted by deporting the Japanese Naval Attaché and an employee of the Mitsubishi Company.[138] A further stage in mutual hostilities was marked by the almost simultaneous dismissal, in the autumn of 1987, of thirteen Soviet employees out of a total of forty-five at the Japanese Embassy in Moscow. This action, for which allegedly inadequate working conditions were used as justification, was linked by the Japanese with the insults to which the Soviet Embassy staff in Tokyo felt exposed when ultra-nationalist groups broadcast their slogans in the immediate vicinity of the embassy.[139]

137. See *Japan Times*, 23 May 1987; *SWB/FE*/8591/i, 11 June 1987.
138. See *Japan Times*, 21 Aug. 1987.
139. See *Asahi Evening News*, 6 Oct. 1987; *Japan Times*, 10 Oct. 1987.

The USSR's reactions to activities within Japanese foreign affairs also contained tones which had nothing in common with the much-vaunted 'New Thinking'. Japan's reiterated demand for a solution to the territorial problem was described by Moscow in the style of old as 'an artificially kindled campaign' aimed at 'revising events of the Second World War with regard to the border'. The criticism was accompanied by a stereotyped accusation concerning the acceleration of militarisation in Japan and its increasing integration into US military strategy.[140] This obdurate position was reinforced in May 1988 by Foreign Minister Shevardnadze's remark to the chairman of the Foreign Affairs Committee in the Lower House, Eitaro Itoyama, that on the basis of history and international law, the question had already been settled. 'The Soviet Union has extensive territory, but we have no superfluous land.'[141]

Meanwhile, another phenomenon made an occasional appearance in Soviet policy on Japan; the island state was either ostentatiously ignored, or its political significance played down. Gorbachev's speech in Vladivostok on Asian policies had targeted China and the United States; both were highlighted as important political powers, without which security in the region would be impossible to maintain. However, Gorbachev omitted any evaluation of Japan in similarly specific terms. On the first anniversary of Gorbachev's speech, the party newspaper printed reflections on the Asia Pacific region with regard to international security; the Soviet Union, China and the United States were the main focus of attention, while Japan was not even mentioned.[142] On the same occasion, another commentary dismissed Japan with the laconic remarks that in matters of regional security the country was oriented towards the US administration and that it attempted to justify its negative approach by quoting the existence of the so-called territorial question.[143] While the Soviet leaders regarded China as an independent agent in foreign affairs in the Asia Pacific region, they tended to view Japan's role as limited to a part of the strategy of the United States.

140. See M. Kapitsa, 'Paths to Peace and Security in the Asia Pacific Region', in *International Affairs*, Moscow, no. 8 (1987), p. 31.
141. TASS, 7 May 1988, quoted in *MD Asien*, 9 May 1988.
142. See *Pravda*, 29 July 1987.
143. See *Izvestiya*, 28 July 1987.

Even in matters of economic relations, the Soviet Union made it clear that it was not dependent on Japan's willingness to cooperate – for example, in the exploitation of natural resources in Siberia. This stance appeared from the very moment in autumn 1988 that economic cooperation between the Soviet Union and South Korea began to develop promisingly.[144] It is doubtful whether such a strategy, if it continues, will succeed in increasing Japan's willingness to compromise over political questions; however, the Tokyo government and Japanese industry must prepare for competition from Asia in the development of East Siberia. This in itself weakens Japan's position with regard to Russia. The 'New Thinking' had no effect on the structure of political relations with Japan until well into the second half of 1988. Only from the beginning of 1989 were there signs of a more flexible stance from Moscow in its dealings with Tokyo, leading to a cautious change of style.

As far as published sources allow conclusions to be drawn about the decisive processes, the meeting of ex-Prime Minister Nakasone and Gorbachev in Moscow at the end of July 1988 seems to have inspired changes in the Kremlin's approach to the central political problem of mutual relations. In almost three hours of talks, the Japanese politician had the opportunity of unfolding the historical details and legal basis of the territorial problem to the General Secretary. One of Nakasone's strongest impressions was the Soviet leader's ignorance of Japan.[145] In the discussion, Gorbachev repeated the view that the territorial problem had ceased to exist as a consequence of the Japanese-American security treaty of 1960, thus rejecting the Japanese claims.[146] However, he also demanded that the events of the war, rather than the resumption of diplomatic relations in 1956, should be taken as the starting-point for discussions of mutual

---

144. The vice-president of the National Committee for Economic Co-operation in Asia and the Pacific, W.I. Ilichev, declared at an international conference in Vladivostok in October 1988 that there were hopes of a marked improvement in economic and trade conditions between 'the Soviet Far East and the Western states of the USA, Australia, the ASEAN countries and the NICs' (W.I. Ilichev, unpublished manuscript of speech, p. 14). Japan was missing from this list.
145. Interview with Y. Nakasone, in *Sankei*, 3 Aug. 1988.
146. See *Asahi Evening News*, 23 July 1988.

relations.[147] Unlike his predecessor, Gorbachev did not simply dismiss the problem, but rather insisted that it should be discussed in full, going back to the time it first arose. In his speech in Krasnoyarsk, he stated that in the 'open talks' with Japan's ex-Prime Minister he had even found confirmation of his conviction that 'both sides aspired to more dynamic relations based on a balance of bilateral and regional interests'.[148] The willingness to participate in discussions that this statement demonstrated had a lasting influence on further developments. Even before the Soviet Foreign Minister's visit to Tokyo, prospects of a new approach to bilateral relations were strengthened by a staff decision in the international department of the CPSU Central Committee. On 30 September 1988, the deputy departmental head, Ivan Kovalenko, who had been in charge of Japanese affairs since the end of the 1970s, was relieved of his duties.[149] Since Kovalenko had gained little sympathy in Tokyo, being an uncompromising advocate of hard-line Soviet policies towards Japan, the Japanese leaders greeted this decision with hopes that the tension in relations between the two countries would be defused.

In November 1988 the Soviets publicly departed from their former stereotypes and, omitting one-sided accusations of blame, expressed criticism of the previous practice of simply rejecting Japan's demands without according them any consideration.[150] This new tone was soon to be heard in official sources. In the consultations between the two countries' Foreign Ministers in December 1988, Shevardnadze did not simply listen in silence to the arguments of the Japanese; a genuine discussion arose, during which the Soviet side also presented its stance on the controversial territorial issue. Shevardnadze later reported to the press that not only were questions concerning documents of the 1950s and 1960s discussed, but the participants also 'immersed themselves seriously in the history of the issue'.[151] He quoted 1855, 1875 and 1905 as examples – years of particular significance because this was when key treaties between Japan and

147. See *Pravda*, 23 July 1988.
148. *Ibid.*, 18 Sept. 1988.
149. See *Yomiuri*, 18 Oct. 1988.
150. See *Neue Zeit*, no. 45 (1988), pp. 14ff.
151. *Pravda*, 22 Dec. 1988.

Russia had been signed.[152] This occasion marked the first time both sides had discussed the territorial issue within its historical context since Prime Minister Tanaka's Moscow visit of 1973.

The Soviets' unwillingness explicitly to acknowledge the existence of a territorial problem between the two countries contrasted with the increased openness adopted towards the central issue. The communiqué skirted the problem, disregarding the frankness of the talks, and yet again completely avoided the term 'territorial question'.[153]

However, both sides agreed not to let the matter rest there. A permanent study group of Deputy Foreign Ministers was founded to prepare talks on the peace treaty. Since the Japanese view was that a peace treaty was impossible without first settling the territorial problem, the study group's discussions demonstrated the extent to which the 'New Thinking' was taking effect here. However, at first Gorbachev and his political advisers had great difficulties accepting substantial changes of position.

By the beginning of 1989 the new-style approach to Japan could no longer be overlooked; the government newspaper *Izvestiya* published an interview with Masamori Sase, an eminent political scientist and a professor at the Academy of Defence in Tokyo, in which he outlined the territorial claims of his country in detail and foresaw the development of mutually beneficial stable relations, should a settlement of the problem in the Japanese sense be agreed.[154] This was the first time that the Japanese standpoint had been presented in detail to the Soviet public, free from editing or misrepresentation. *Izvestiya*'s choice of interviewee was also noteworthy, since Sase was officially on the staff of the Ministry of Defence.

A month later, Prime Minister Takeshita was able to expound his political views to *Izvestiya* readers in a full-page interview. He stressed his dissatisfaction with the condition of bilateral relations, declared the willingness of his country to engage in talks and build up cooperation with the Soviet Union, and enumerated the reasons for the unsatisfactory situation in mutual relations: the Soviet Union's breach of the neutrality pact at the

---

152. See Maps 3 and 4 (pp. 34, 35).

153. *Ibid.*; German text in *BPA Ostinformationen*, 23 Dec. 1988, p. 1 (USSR–Japan).

154. *Izvestiya*, 2 Jan. 1989.

end of the war, its occupation of the four islands, its rescinding of the 1956 agreement to return two of the islands to Japan on the conclusion of a peace treaty, and Moscow's later denial that Brezhnev had verbally acknowledged the existence of the problem to Prime Minister Tanaka. Takeshita maintained that all these facts had 'aroused feelings of mistrust of the Soviet Union in the Japanese people', but evaluated the Soviets' recent change of position as a positive development, while regretting that their approach to the problem did not show any changes in the true sense of the word.[155]

A semi-official answer to these reflections could be found in a detailed statement by Deputy Foreign Minister Rogachov, who was responsible for the Asia Pacific area. Its very title revealed the Soviet stance: 'Groundless Claims.'[156] Its arguments, however, were more informed than those contained in previous statements, and were almost completely free from polemicising. The very fact that a member of the Soviet government had taken the trouble to refute the Japanese claims point by point was in itself something new. A certain willingness to compromise was evident in Rogachov's demand that solutions acceptable to both sides should be sought. Given the gulf between the two sides, it would not be easy to achieve a peace treaty, but it would nonetheless be possible. The inclusion of the 'geographical aspect' in such a treaty, Rogachov explained, would be a 'confirmation of the post-war border between the Soviet Union and Japan'.[157] This circumscription reduced the Japanese claim to a mere technicality involving borders, and thus implicitly rejected Japan's territorial claims.

Nevertheless, Rogachov's exposition mapped out the framework within which the Foreign Ministers' talks would be conducted in Moscow at the beginning of May 1989. Although no immediately discernible progress was made on the territorial question, both sides demonstrated the beginnings of a more flexible approach to the other's views:

– For the first time, a Soviet Foreign Minister declared in public that the conclusion of a peace treaty with Japan would be

155. *Ibid.*, 1 March 1989, p. 5.
156. *Ibid.*, 24 April 1989, p. 7.
157. *Ibid.*

possible without a consideration of the Japanese-American security treaty. Since in 1960 the Soviets had used the revision of the security pact as an argument for rescinding the 1956 agreement to return two of the four islands, Shevardnadze's statement could possibly have meant that the Soviet government was preparing to return to its 1956 position. It is certainly true to say that the Soviets were evaluating the situation in North-East Asia more realistically.
– Tokyo viewed as positive the Soviet Union's willingness to return to the state of affairs in existence until 1970 and to reinstate access for Japanese citizens to the island of Kunashiri (as well as Habomai and Shikotan) to visit graves.
– Finally, it is remarkable that in connection with the Foreign Ministers' conference the Soviet television company broadcast several reports about the difficulties in the two states' mutual relations. It also showed an interview with the head of the Japanese Foreign Ministry, in which he described the settlement of the territorial problem as a prerequisite of a peace treaty.[158]

It may be that the Soviet leaders wanted to prepare their own people for changes in this previously immutable issue by the impressive frankness of the discussions over the territorial question presented in the media. For the moment, however, a remark made by a Soviet commentator, that *glasnost* in the territorial question did not necessarily mean any change to the policies at its core, remained valid.[159] Foreign Minister Uno had precisely this experience when he was received by Gorbachev on 5 May 1989; the latter accused Japan of being guilty of double standards, for unlike its attitude to the Soviet Union, it had stopped pursuing problems with Korea and China over territorial claims (the islands Tok Do and Senkaku respectively), and maintained close relations with both countries. The Japanese Foreign Minister rejected all attempts to postpone the settlement of the territorial problem, saying that the claims mentioned were quite dissimilar.[160] In 1990/1, during the preparations for Gorbachev's

---

158. On these points, see Kimura Hiroshi in *Sankei*, 10 May 1989.
159. See *Neue Zeit*, no. 15 (1989), p. 14.
160. *Pravda*, 6 May 1989; *Asahi Evening News*, 8 May 1989.

visit to Japan, the territorial question was discussed with unprecedented openness in the Soviet press.

The Territorial Problem and Public Opinion

The significance of the territorial problem and the constantly shifting evaluations of the prospects of its settlement are evident in the findings of decades of Japanese opinion polls. They provide an additional analytical tool, whose significance should not be overestimated here; however, it is true to say that neither the Japanese nor the Soviet/Russian government could or can afford to ignore public opinion completely when formulating policies. On the other hand, opinions that are widespread among the populace can originate, in a way that is extremely difficult to evaluate, in the views published by official and unofficial media sources.

In Japan, the Soviet Union had a consistently negative image for decades. Only after Gorbachev took office could a shift in attitude be noted. The percentage of those surveyed who had a 'definitely positive' view of the Soviet Union was 4% during the 1960s, sank to under 3% after 1978 and fell in the following years to 1.2% (1984).[161] After this time there was a slow rise in positive attitudes, to 3.1% (at the end of 1988).[162] The proportion of those with a 'definitely negative' opinion of the Soviet Union was correspondingly high, reaching over 50% in 1981 and sinking, with minor fluctuations, to a level of 26.9% by the end of 1990.[163]

Growing optimism was also reflected in people's views on Japanese-Soviet relations. While in 1984 only 7.8% of those questioned evaluated relations between the two countries as positive, this figure had risen to 38.7% by the end of 1990.[164] This change is a direct expression of the improvement in climate between the two states.

161. As a comparison, the popularity figure for the United States stood at 45% in the mid-1980s, while since the re-establishment of diplomatic relations with China in the mid-1970s that country's popularity has been around 25%.
162. For these figures see Sôrifu Kôhôshitsu (Information Department of the Prime Minister's Office) (ed.), *Yoron-chôsa, gekkan* (Opinion Surveys, Monthly), no. 5 (May 1989), p. 24.
163. *Ibid.*, and *Yoron-chôsa*, no. 3 (March 1991), p. 47.
164. *Yoron-chôsa*, no. 3, p. 48.

In a national survey conducted in 1985, 52.3% stated that the principal reason for the especially bad image of the Soviet Union in past years was its refusal to settle the territorial problem. The proportion of people citing this reason fell steadily; in 1979 as many as 68.1% of those questioned had said this was the key factor, but in 1981 the figure was 56.2%. Further reasons given in 1985 were the Communist system (31.7%), unfriendly behaviour towards Japan (27.9%), foreign policies based on military power (23.6%) and deep mistrust of the Soviet Union (23.5%).[165]

In Hokkaido, where the population was more affected by the Soviet occupation of the Kuriles than people in other parts of the country, opinion polls produced some remarkable results. Here, in 1985, the unresolved territorial problem was also cited as the main reason for poor relations with the Soviet Union, but at 35.6% the proportion was far lower than the national average.[166] The results of the surveys in Hokkaido are interesting for their revelation of swings of opinion during the course of the 1980s, but they are chiefly remarkable for showing feelings on the extent of the territorial claims and the possibility of settling the issue.

In 1981 and 1985, 59% and 55.9%, respectively, of those surveyed in Hokkaido demanded the return of all the Kuriles, percentages which are remarkably high. The return of only four islands, which was the government's demand, was supported by 11.9% in 1981 and by 14.7% in 1985. Estimations of the chances of the territory being returned were somewhat different. In 1985, 27.5% of those questioned believed that the Soviet Union would respond to the territorial demands; 66.2% were doubtful. By 1988 these figures had clearly shifted: 37.4% believed the USSR would accept Japan's demands, while 53.4% doubted it. The changes introduced after Gorbachev's rise to power, including those in foreign policy, had evidently nourished hopes of a solution to the territorial question.[167]

Another interesting phenomenon is that the decade-long ban

---

165. See Tsuyoshi Hasegawa, 'Japanese Perceptions of the Soviet Union 1960–1980', in Hasegawa (ed.), *The Soviet Union Faces Asia: Perceptions and Policies*, Sapporo 1987, p. 53; *Yoron-chôsa*, no. 10 (Oct. 1985), p. 59.
166. Hasegawa, 'Japanese Perceptions', p. 54.
167. See Haruki Wada, *Hoppô ryôdo-mondai wo kangaeru* (The Problem of the Northern Territories), Tokyo 1990, pp. 313ff.

on fishing in the vicinity of the islands led some of the people of Hokkaido to shift their focus away from the territorial question in favour of fishing rights. In the first half of the 1980s a growing number would have been prepared to renounce the territorial claims in exchange for fishing rights: 10.95% in 1981 and 13.1% by 1985.[168]

Opinions do not diverge quite so widely in the survey conducted at the end of 1989. At that time 68.6% supported the return of four islands, and 46.5% the return of two (Habomai and Shikotan) as a first step towards a solution. And 10.1% of those questioned would have been satisfied with the return of only two islands.[169] On the other hand, 46.5%, almost half of the survey sample, were in agreement with aiming for the return of Habomai and Shikotan first of all and then trying for the return of the other two islands.[170] The clear decrease in demands for the return of all the Kuriles, and an evidently growing willingness to accept a lesser solution (the return of Habomai and Shikotan) appeared to signal a continuing trend that was especially clear among those inhabitants of Hokkaido employed in the fishing industry, whose chief desire was the return of two islands. According to a survey conducted by *Nemuro Shimbun*, 52% of those questioned approved of such a solution.[171] Despite some regional variations, the fact remained that the demand for the return of the Soviet-occupied islands found widespread support among the population.

A most informative picture is produced by dividing answers according to the ages of those surveyed. In 1981, the question of whether the individuals surveyed were interested in the problem of the northern territories was answered in the affirmative by 50% of those aged over sixty, 45% of those over fifty, 37% of those over forty, 21% of the over-thirties and only 10% of those over the age of twenty.[172] Even in Hokkaido, where interest in the territorial question was strongest, interest in the

---

168. *Ibid.*
169. *Ibid.*, p. 321; *Tokyo Shimbun*, 12 Nov. 1989, in *DSJP*, 18–20 Nov. 1989, p. 5.
170. *Ibid.* The survey is reproduced in Appendix D.
171. See Wada, *Hoppô-ryôdo mondai-ni tsuite* (Observations on the Issue of the Northern Territories), p. 308.
172. See Hasegawa, *Japanese Perceptions*, p. 56.

problem was recorded as decreasing with the age of those surveyed. Despite national support for the demands for the islands' return, interest in the question slowly declined. The Soviet leaders would certainly have been aware of this tendency, and during the pre-Gorbachev era may have taken it as a further reason to prepare for a gradual process of erosion and simply wait for this trend to become more pronounced over the generations, until no more substantial concessions would be needed.

This realisation was probably behind various activities initiated by the government in Tokyo to keep the territorial problem alive in the people's consciousness, including the decision to declare 7 February 'Northern Territories Day', an occasion observed for the first time in 1981. It was on this date in 1855 that Japan and Russia had concluded the Treaty of Shimoda and had first decided on a common border, to run between the islands of Etorofu and Uruppu.

The Prime Minister and members of the Cabinet, as well as members of the opposition parties, always attend events on Northern Territories Day. The introduction of a commemoration day presented Prime Minister Suzuki in 1981 with the opportunity of being the first government leader in office to undertake a tour of inspection through the northern territories, starting with the northern coast of Hokkaido.[173] The prefectures too have now begun to celebrate Northern Territories Day with various events.[174] In this way, within six years the organised movement of support for the demand for the islands' return spread from just thirteen prefectures at first, to all forty-seven prefectures. The function held in 1986 was the largest to date, with 1,200 participants.

Supporters of the nationwide movement were filled with optimism by the general improvement in the climate of Soviet-Japanese relations and by Gorbachev's agreement to visit Japan in 1991; on the other hand, the gulf between the government's propagated formulation of 'four islands at once' and the pragmatic position in northern Japan became more obvious. On Northern Territories Day in 1990, the director of *Nemuro Shim-*

---

173. See *Nihon Keizai* (evening edn.), 7 Feb. 1986, in *DSJP*, 21 Feb. 1986, pp. 13ff.
174. See *Nihon Keizai*, 7 Sept. 1981, in *DSJP*, 9 Sept. 1981, p. 3.

bun, Masaichi Takamoto, spoke in favour of the initial return of only two of the islands; in his opinion, this solution would double the size of the fishing grounds available to Japanese fishermen. His criticism of Tokyo and of the Foreign Ministry's policies was unmistakable; he dubbed the government funds which flowed into *Nemuro* to support the movement demanding the islands' return 'hush-money', seeing them as simply a means of preventing the spread of support for any solution deviating from the official one.[175]

Another campaign aimed at keeping the territorial problem alive in the minds of the populace is a petition calling for the return of the northern territories, first circulated in 1965. The signatures collected have been passed on to the Prime Minister and Parliament since 1972; by 7 February 1990, their number was estimated at 50 million.[176] However, this should not be allowed to obscure the fact that the driving force behind the movement is not gaining momentum. The number of people who actually come from the islands now under Russian occupation is shrinking year by year from natural causes; in 1946 there were 17,000 inhabitants, in the mid-1980s only 11,000.[177]

Gradually, then, the memory of these territories will fade. Even if the majority of the population demands the return of the islands, only a few Japanese are prepared to participate actively in the movement to win back the territories – a figure of 2–3% according to survey results.[178] Half the population said they definitely would not engage in active participation.

In the face of the decades of unsuccessful Japanese policies concerning the territorial question, it is understandable that the chances of winning back the islands are being judged with increasing pessimism. An opinion poll conducted at the beginning of the 1980s showed that nearly 70% of those questioned saw no possibility of a solution, against a mere 20% who were optimistic. The changes occurring in the Soviet Union under Gorbachev caused a swing in the population's mood; in 1988,

175. See *Asahi*, 7 Feb. 1990.
176. *Ibid*.
177. See *Mainichi*, 20 March 1984, in *DSJP*, 27 March 1984, p. 5.
178. Results of an unpublished survey of the Prime Minister's Office conducted between 1983 and 1986; quoted in Hasegawa, *Japanese Perceptions*, p. 57.

37.4% were optimistic about the return of the islands, whereas 53.4% remained pessimistic.[179] The new atmosphere was accompanied by increased interest from northern Japan in setting up economic and tourism exchanges with the islands' Soviet inhabitants. 73.7% of those surveyed in 1989 desired such a development.[180]

It is not possible to determine whether the younger generation's decline in interest in the territorial question, so clearly evident at the beginning of the 1980s, will gradually increase again in the light of changes in Moscow's policies on Japan, particularly in the aftermath of the dissolution of the USSR. Quite apart from this, strong nationalist feelings nourished by Japan's economic and technological prowess may be expected to arise, and these in turn will tend to diminish Japanese willingness to renounce a claim that is legitimate both historically and – as far as Habomai and Shikotan are concerned – under international law. The possibility of compromise, however, should not be excluded, although first Soviet, now Russian, behaviour remains the unknown factor in such speculations. A return to the Joint Declaration of 1956 by offering the return of the Habomai group and Shikotan to Japan would create a new situation and confront the government in Tokyo with a difficult decision. To judge from the signs of evidence since mid-1990, this could happen. Before Gorbachev's visit to Japan, Soviet statements – not only from publicists, but also from sources within the circle of Gorbachev's advisers – had created the impression that a compromise of this nature was not to be ruled out.[181]

The difficulty of evaluating the complex opinions of the Japanese with even partial accuracy is evident from the political parties' behaviour over the territorial question. Doubtless their views are formulated with an eye to their electorate; however, at the end of 1985 there were moves by parliamentary representatives to found an independent association to work on the territorial problem. This proposal is said to have come from the Democratic Socialists (DSP) and was taken up by the LDP,

---

179. See Wada, *Hoppô-ryôdo mondai-ni tsuite*, p. 319.
180. See *Hokkaido Shimbun*, 12 Nov. 1989.
181. See Part III below.

although even the Communist Party of Japan (CPJ) appeared not to oppose it in principle.[182] This initiative apart, it is remarkable that all parties across the political spectrum, from left to right, condemn the Russian occupation of the islands and demand the return of the northern territories, offering varying solutions to the problem and different time-scales for them to be effected.

In this matter the Japanese Communists gave their Moscow comrades little cause for rejoicing after 1969. Around the end of the 1960s deep-seated differences arose between the CPJ and the CPSU. The largest non-ruling Communist Party in Asia not only condemned the Soviet invasion of Czechoslovakia in the strongest possible terms, it also began to criticise the Soviet Union's policies on the territorial question, demanding the implementation of the 1956 agreement to return the Habomais and Shikotan. This was in March 1969. Until then the CPJ had, at least outwardly, supported the Soviet takeover of the Kuriles on the basis of the Yalta Agreement.[183]

In 1971 the General Secretary of the CPJ, Kenji Miyamoto, reported that he had been assured by leading functionaries of the CPSU that the Soviet Union would submit the demand for Kunashiri and Etorofu(!) to serious examination if Japan gave up its military links with the United States.[184] In 1974 the party newspaper *Akahata* published a secret arrangement with the CPSU dating from 1959, in which the Soviet Union had agreed to the possibility of adopting a 'new stance' on the question of the southern Kuriles. The conditions, however, would be Japan's withdrawal from all imperialist military blocs, its cancellation of all military agreements with the United States, the withdrawal of US troops from Japan and the closure of their bases on Japanese territory.[185]

In its talks with Brezhnev in 1979, the CPJ then reintroduced the territorial question and demanded the return of the Habomai

---

182. See *Nihon Keizai* (evening edn.), 10 Dec. 1985, in *DSJP*, 17 Dec. 1985, pp. 6ff.
183. See John Stephan, 'The Kuril Islands: Japan versus Russia', in *Pacific Community*, vol. 7, no. 3 (April 1976), p. 324.
184. *Ibid.*
185. See *Sankei*, 15 Sept. 1974, in *DSJP*, 18 Sept. 1974, pp. 16ff.

group and Shikotan to Japan at the earliest possible opportunity, independent of any peace treaty. The party argued that these islands belonged to Hokkaido and were not part of the Kuriles, to which the Japanese government had renounced its claim in San Francisco. In addition, the CPJ proposed its own idea that Japan should sign an interim agreement excluding the Habomais and Shikotan from the area to which the Japanese-American security pact applied and stipulating that they would not be used for military purposes.

The CPJ further demanded that the Tokyo government rescind the relinquishment of the Kuriles laid down in the San Francisco peace treaty, in order to pave the way for new negotiations on the problem and for a peace treaty with the Soviet Union. The Japanese no longer accepted the Soviets' arguments based on the Treaty of Yalta. The CPJ also accused the Soviet Union of having infringed the principle of non-expansion of territory with its unilateral claims to these islands in February 1946 and their integration into Soviet territory in 1947.[186] Incidentally, the CPJ continues to lay claim to the entire Kurile chain in accordance with its demands to the CPSU in 1979; this was reiterated at the Seventeenth Party Conference in 1985 in the declaration, 'This party endeavours to attain the return of the Habomais and Shikotan in addition to the entire Kurile chain [*zen-Chishima*] by the use of peaceful and diplomatic means.'[187]

Of the other three opposition parties, the DSP and the Komeito Party agree with the package solution but make additional claims to the remaining Kuriles. The left-wing Socialists (SPJ) propose a three-phase solution: return of the Habomais and Shikotan on the conclusion of a peace treaty with Russia; cancellation of the security treaty with the United States; implementation of the concept of unarmed neutrality and – on the basis of trust gained by the last action – reopening of

---

186. See *Akahata*, 21 Jan. 1986, in *DSJP*, 31 Jan. 1986, pp. 7ff; *ibid.*, 4 Sept. 1990, in Central Committee of the Japanese Communist Party (ed.), *Bulletin, Information for Abroad*, no. 676 (Sept. 1990).

187. See Heinz Timmermann, 'Japans Kommunisten nach ihrem 17. Parteitag vom November 1985' (Japan's Communists after their 17th Party Conference of November 1985), Cologne, 22 Jan. 1986 (Bundesinstitut für Internationale und Ostwissenschaftliche Studien, *Aktuelle Analysen*, 1986, no. 2), p. 6.

negotiations over the entire Kurile chain.[188] All the opposition parties thus demand a further-reaching 'revision of frontiers' than the ruling conservatives do. The broad range of territorial demands has increased Russia's reservations over accommodating the Japanese claims, since its fear is that any sign of concession would spawn a whole string of further claims from the Japanese.

Under Gorbachev, it became possible to express opinions deviating from the CPSU party line, and thus the Soviet Union came to show a far more widely differentiated range of opinions assessing Japan and commenting on the long-taboo territorial question than had been expected after the years of anti-Japanese propaganda. The first publication in this new strain was based on a survey planned by the news agencies TASS and *Kyodo* and conducted in both countries in February 1988, covering the cities of Moscow, Leningrad, Kiev, Khabarovsk and Vladivostok as well as the regions of Kanto, Tohoku, Kyushu, Shikoku and Hokkaido. Citizens of voting age were questioned, a total of 635 in the Soviet Union and 1,090 in Japan. The party newspaper *Pravda* published the findings in March 1988. From these the Soviets could learn that their country was not held in high esteem by the majority of Japanese, while Japan had almost without exception an excellent image in the Soviet Union. For example, 47.4% of Japanese questioned said that they felt no particular affinity with the Soviet Union and the Soviet people; only 17.6% responded positively. However, a mere 2.4% of the Soviet citizens questioned gave such a negative answer, while 88% were sympathetic to Japan. The question of whether the other country could be considered democratic was answered affirmatively by just 12.1% of the Japanese subjects, whereas nearly 75% denied that this quality could be attributed to the Soviet Union. On the other hand, 26.3% of Soviet responses agreed with the description as applied to Japan, 35.1% gave a negative answer and the majority (38.6%) had no firm opinion – an astonishing result after years of negative reports on Japan. The desire for improved relations between the two countries was affirmed by an overwhelming majority in both countries: 98.9% in the Soviet Union, 84.2% in Japan. Finally, far more Soviets than Japanese

---

188. See Mayer, *Der japanisch-sowjetische Territorialstreit*, pp. 30ff.

believed that an expansion in bilateral trade would bring benefits: 96.5% and 61.8%, respectively.[189]

The first Soviet publication of a survey concerning Japan still dodged the tricky territorial question. Two years later, this taboo too had been conquered. An opinion poll organised by the newspapers *Hokkaido Shimbun* and *Sovyetskaya Rossiya* and the news agency *Novosti* was carried out by the Institute for Sociology of the Academy of Sciences in Moscow. The area surveyed included Moscow and thirty-seven other areas in the RSFSR; that is, the Russian part of the Soviet Union, stretching from Moscow up to Sakhalin and the southern Kuriles. As the Soviet commentary on the survey explained, this factor was important because the history of relations with Japan had affected the inhabitants of the Russian regions differently from non-Russian segments of the population. A total of 1,194 subjects of both sexes, selected to reflect the population structure, were questioned in both rural and urban areas. In Japan the same questions were put to 1,000 people in 100 residential areas of Hokkaido, the most northerly prefecture – without doubt a more limited basis for a survey than that offered by the RSFSR areas.

The somewhat biased formulation of the question of whether Japanese territorial demands were of an anti-Soviet nature was answered in the affirmative by both sides (56% of Russians, 56.1% of Japanese), although significantly more Japanese than Russians denied the premise (40.4% as against 18.9%). In addition, 48.3% of Russians did not see acceptance of Japanese territorial claims as a necessary prerequisite for the development of neighbourly relations (as against 4.3% of the Japanese), while the solution of this problem was regarded by 79.5% of the Japanese as a necessary condition, demonstrating the fundamental difference between both sides in the question of territorial demands.[190]

From the publication of the survey's findings the Soviet readers learned that Japan's territorial claims were not supported solely by a small minority of revanchists, as had been maintained

189. *Pravda*, 11 March 1988.
190. See 'Sovetskij Soyuz, Japonija: kak my smotrim drug na druga' (The Soviet Union and Japan: How We See Each Other), in *Mirovaja Ekonomika i Meždunarodnie Otnošenija*, no. 3 (1990), pp. 134–41. For the complete text of the survey see Appendix D.

for decades; they also discovered that almost a fifth of the Russian citizens questioned did not regard Japan's territorial demands as anti-Soviet, a completely new factor in Soviet information policies. This objectivity and openness prepared Russian public opinion for calmer discussions of the territorial question, which, considering Gorbachev's visit to Japan and the anticipation of a compromise solution, seemed inevitable.

The diversity of opinions on relations with Japan was also demonstrated by the mid-1989 formation of a group in Vladivostok under the heading 'I love Japan' (*Ja ljublju Japoniju*), which planned demonstrations supporting the Japanese stance on the territorial question during the preparations for Gorbachev's visit to Japan. The group comprised around 100 members and was led by a thirty-five-year-old Soviet citizen called Kasantsev. Over 1,000 people were to be mobilised for the demonstration. Kasantsev openly supported the return of the four islands under dispute and believed the Japanese claim was historically justified.[191] However, this opinion can hardly be seen as representative of the Soviet population. At a conference held in Manila at the beginning of 1990, the spokesman for the Soviet government, G. Gerasimov, mentioned a survey according to which 85% of Soviet citizens questioned had rejected the idea of the four islands being returned to Japan. According to Gerasimov, the rejection was based on the argument that the return of territory represented a 'dangerous precedent'. He gave no further details of this claim, and no information concerning the survey's organisation or technical details.[192]

It is clear that in Russia's increasingly free climate, the openness of discussions of the Japanese territorial claims since 1989/90 has influenced a process that may achieve a solution to this central problem of relations between the two countries, although in all probability without simplifying the route to the solution.

---

191. See *Sankei*, 23 May 1990.
192. See *Asahi Evening News*, 20 Feb. 1990. See also Part III below (p. 213).

6
BEGINNINGS OF ECONOMIC COOPERATION

The proximity of Japan – a highly industrialised land but without raw materials and energy sources of its own – to the Soviet Far East – an area under-developed yet rich in resources – has constantly engaged the imagination of observers at home and abroad, who have perceived in the regions' disparity ideal conditions for close economic cooperation. However, there have always been political obstacles to achieving this. Successive Japanese governments held the opinion: 'First solve the territorial problem, then improve the atmosphere and work on economic cooperation.' Moscow, on the other hand, urged a reversion of this order. Since Gorbachev's visit to Japan in April 1991, and especially after the dissolution of the Soviet Union, relations between the two countries have apparently been moving closer towards Moscow's ideas. Tokyo, while holding to the principle that politics and economics are inseparable, is not implementing this principle as uncompromisingly as in previous years. While formerly the fundamental difference in position did not exclude limited cooperation, no Japanese government was prepared to agree to a long-term binding settlement or to large-scale low-interest state-backed loans. We need to examine the situation in the 1970s and 1980s before we can understand the position today.

Projects in the Soviet Far East and Siberia

The intransigence over the territorial question and the negotiations over fishing rights, which for the most part were lengthy and tedious, and which for years enabled the Soviet Union to flex its muscles and force Japan into submission, was accompanied by a complex of bilateral relations in which Moscow found itself, if not actually in the role of demander, then in that of a partner with especially strong interests. This complex comprised barter and economic cooperation. While up to the present day neither of these areas of economic activity has been as vibrant as Moscow hoped, because of the territorial/fishing issues, even so there have been periods when trade and economic cooperation reached relatively high levels. A perceptible revival was noticeable as early as the end of the 1960s, coinciding with an upturn in trade, when both sides cooperated to produce an umbrella agreement on supply conditions for specific projects.

At the beginning of the 1970s, Soviet writers painted a rosy picture of the trade situation and its prospects, describing 'broad perspectives for growth and the consolidation of Soviet-Japanese economic relations'.[1] Elsewhere there was talk of a range and level of Soviet-Japanese relations unprecedented in the history of relations between the two countries.[2] At the time of Prime Minister Tanaka's visit to Moscow in the autumn of 1973, overall trends in economic relations gave rise to expectations of further growth. The volume of trade had expanded from the equivalent of US$822 million in 1970 to US$1,560 million by 1973, and to US$2,500 million in 1974 (see survey in Appendix C). Several joint projects concerning the exploitation of natural resources in Siberia had already been agreed, and further steps were in the process of negotiation.

Japan's interest in supplying part of the growing demand for raw materials and energy from its immediate vicinity was welcomed by the Soviet government at the time of the worldwide fears of shortages at the beginning of the 1970s. This interest rose sharply with the development of the oil crisis of 1973, dubbed the 'oil shock' by Tokyo. Japan's politicians and economists were confronted with the realisation, clearer than ever before, that their country's survival and performance depended on stable supplies of energy and raw materials.[3]

Naturally the Soviets also had a specific interest in the ex-

---

1. H.P. Širjaev, 'Ekonomičeskie otnošenija SSSR i Japonii' (Economic Relations between the USSR and Japan), in *Problemy Dal'nego Vostoka*, no. 1 (1972), p. 97.
2. See N. Nikolayev, 'USSR–Japan: Fifty Years of Diplomatic Relations', in *FEA*, no. 4 (1975), p. 18.
3. See Dagmar Ahrens-Thiele, *Japans Rohstoffpolitik im Kräftefeld Moskau-Peking* (Japan's Raw Materials Policies within the Force-field of Moscow–Peking), Hamburg 1977, pp. 24ff.

ploitation and utilisation of Siberia's rich reserves of raw materials.[4] Energy sources in the region are chiefly in the form of fossil fuels. Over half of the Soviet Union's oil drilling took place in Siberia, principally in the area around Tyumen in the north-west; 90% of the Soviet coal seams lay within Siberia, in particular in the Kuznetsk Basin, in the area around Kansk-Atchinsk and southern Yakutiya. In addition, the reserves of precious metals and diamonds were and are said to be considerable. However, at first the exploitation of Siberian resources concentrated, as did cooperation with Japan, on energy and timber.[5]

At the beginning of the 1950s the Soviet Union had applied itself to the development of the gigantic region to the east of the Urals. Over the time-span of several Five-Year Plans (1951–75), between 15.6% and 16.3% of the total investment budget was allocated to this region.[6] In August 1962, the Soviet government presented Japan with proposals for a range of joint development projects in Siberia, to exploit the region's energy reserves and timber resources.

The creation of a Joint Japanese-Soviet Economic Committee (JJSEC) was agreed on 1 July 1965 as a practical vehicle for negotiations. At its first meeting in March 1966, the following projects were discussed: the tapping of natural gas in northern Sakhalin and of oil and natural gas in western Siberia; the construction of an oil pipeline between Irkutsk and Nakhodka; the working of copper deposits in Udokan; a harbour expansion in the Soviet Far East; and the exploitation of timber reserves in the Amur area.

The JJSEC was composed of leading Japanese business people,

4. The term 'Siberia' is used here to refer to the three regions of west and east Siberia and the Soviet Far East. West Siberia extends from Tyumenskaya Oblast' to Tomskaya Oblast', east Siberia from Krasnoyarskii Krai to Chitinskaya Oblast', and the Soviet Far East covers the entire area east of these, including the Yakutskaya Avtonomnaya Oblast'.

5. On this individually, see Hermann Clement, 'Sibirien: Reserve oder Bürde?' (Siberia: Reserve or Burden?), in Bundesinstitut für Internationale und Ostwissenschaftliche Studien (ed.), *Soviet Union 1984/85. Ereignisse, Probleme, Perspektiven*, Cologne 1985, pp. 190–201.

6. See Robert W. Campbell, 'Prospects for Siberian Economic Development', in Zagoria, Donald S. (ed.), *Soviet Policy in East Asia*, New Haven, Conn./London 1982, p. 231.

most of whom were members of *Keidanren*, the umbrella organisation of Japanese businesses. No government representatives took part, although they were consulted in important matters. The Joint Soviet-Japanese Economic Committee (JSJEC), the Soviet equivalent, was led by the First Deputy Foreign Minister for Trade, Ivan F. Semichastnov. The other members were high-ranking officials of the ministries involved with Siberian development.[7]

Over the succeeding years, the two sides conducted negotiations alternately in Tokyo and Moscow, within this institutional framework. Nine projects emerged from the first proposals under discussion:

1. The KS-I Agreement, so named for the initials of each side's leader of negotiations, Kawai and Sedov. In return for capital goods for highway construction and forestry and consumer goods from Japan, the Soviet Union agreed to supply a certain quantity of industrial and construction timber between 1969 and 1973.

2. Cooperation in the construction of a new harbour in Wrangel Bay opposite the port of Nakhodka. The planned completion date was the end of 1975, although the official opening took place at the beginning of 1974. The harbour was named Vostochny – 'the eastern one'.[8]

3. Import of mechanical wood pulp (wood chips) and industrial pulp from the Soviet Union. Japan was to deliver the necessary capital goods and building materials, together with consumer goods, between 1972 and 1974.

4. Supply of raw coal from southern Yakutiya. Japan was to supply capital goods and building materials for the exploitation

---

7. See Kiichi Saeki, 'Towards Japanese Cooperation in Siberian Development', in *Problems of Communism*, vol. 21, no. 3 (May/June 1972), p. 5.

8. The expansion of the harbour, with Japanese help, was based on a second agreement and took place over several years. In 1976 a turnover volume of 1.4 million tonnes in imports, exports and transit goods, including 124,000 containers, was reached, consisting chiefly of Japanese goods destined for Europe. See V.B. Spandaryan, 'Major Landmark in Soviet-Japanese Trade', in *FEA*, no. 2 (1978), p. 96. These data are significantly higher than the Japanese figures, according to which around 110,000 containers were transported in both directions. Around 25% of the total trade between Japan and Europe is conducted via the Siberia land bridge (SLB). Freight costs via this route are 15%–20% lower than sea transport. See *Nihon Keizai*, 7 March 1980; *DSJP*, 25 March 1980, p. 9; *Asahi Evening News*, 17 Oct. 1981.

of coalfields in southern Yakutiya (Neriyungura) and for the construction of a railway between Bam and Berkakit, and was to receive in return a total of 104.4 million tonnes of raw coal between 1983 and 1988. From 1985 the maximum quantity supplied was to be an annual 5.5 million tonnes of coal from Neriyungura and an annual 1 million tonnes of raw coal from Kuznetsk.

5. The KS-II Agreement. In exchange for supplying the capital goods necessary for forest exploitation, together with construction materials and timber transport ships, Japan was to receive a certain quantity of timber from the Soviet Union between 1975 and 1979.

6. Supply of crude oil from Tyumen. In return for the construction of vital infrastructure elements necessary for the exploitation, drilling and transport of crude oil from the fields in Tyumen in western Siberia, Japan was to receive an annually increasing quantity of crude oil from 1981 onwards, with an annual figure of 25 million tonnes envisaged from 1985 to the year 2000.

7. Supply of natural gas from Yakutiya. In return for constructing the necessary infrastructure and supplying consumer goods, Japan and possibly the United States were each to receive an annual quantity of 10,000 million cubic metres of natural gas over twenty-five years, starting from 1982.

8. Natural gas and oil exploration on the Sakhalin mainland. Japan was to provide the financial and technological wherewithal for the exploitation of oil and natural gas on the Sakhalin mainland. If this was successful, Japan was to receive over 50% of the oil extracted during the period of interest repayment on the loans granted and for ten years after the end of that period. As in Project 7 above, US participation in this project was also considered.

9. Establishment of a paper and pulp industry. In exchange for supplying the equipment required and constructing industrial complexes at Khabarovsk and Amurskin, Japan was to receive a certain quantity of products over the long term.[9]

The Soviets asked Japan for loans on favourable terms for all

---

9. See technical details of these projects in Appendix C below; for the story of negotiations, see Ahrens-Thiele, 'Japans Rohstoffpolitik'.

these projects, in order to finance the necessary investment. According to fairly conservative estimates, the loans required totalled around US$6,700 million. In fact the Soviet Union received only around US$1,500 million, as not all the projects planned were realised.[10] If industrial plant business crediting from 1975 is included, the total of official (that is, state-backed) loans from Japan for the economic development of the Soviet Union had reached almost US$4,000 million by 1979.[11]

The start of actual negotiations or the conclusion of treaties in connection with the projects planned took place in the relatively brief period of mid-1968 to the end of 1974, and attained its greatest intensity in the years from 1971 to 1973, the first years of the Soviet Union's ninth Five-Year Plan. Projects 1 to 5 had been wholly or partly completed by the second half of the 1980s. The chief concern was thus the development and exploitation of timber and coal reserves and the expansion of Vostochny harbour, which was equipped for container traffic between Japan and Europe and for the loading and sea transport of raw materials. All projects to do with the exploitation and transport of natural gas and oil proved to be fraught with problems.

The mining of copper deposits in Udokan, mentioned at the JJSEC's first meeting in March 1968, had not matured into a negotiable project by the end of 1991. Here the Soviet Union vainly sought a Western partner. According to expert opinion, Udokan is 'a project for the 1990s, if not indeed the next century'.[12] Another analysis attributes the non-materialisation of the Udokan project to faults on both sides, namely the lack of systematic Soviet studies and the lack of Japanese interest. Development costs are estimated at between US$1,000 million and US$2,000 million. World copper prices had fallen at the end of the 1970s and Japan had ready access to an adequate supply of sources; thus Tokyo saw no reason to take on the costly, technically complex process.[13] This judgement is supported by the

10. Author's calculations; see survey in Appendix C below.
11. See Allen S. Whiting, *Siberian Development and East Asia, Threat or Promise?*, Stanford, Calif. 1981, p. 137 (the figures quoted here are based on information obtained from a Japanese interviewee).
12. See Clement, 'Sibirien: Reserve oder Bürde?', p. 193.
13. See Whiting, *Siberian Development*, p. 155.

fact that at the end of 1980 the Soviet Union imported 1,500 tonnes of refined copper from Japan; while this says nothing about the standard of Soviet copper mining, it certainly reveals the technological level of ore processing.[14]

Difficulties with Tyumen

A range of factors, such as changes in world markets and insufficient exploration, were responsible for projects being postponed or abandoned altogether. Other reason for this include Soviet political stratagems or tactical finagling, aptly demonstrated by the example of the Tyumen oil-drilling project. The offer to supply crude oil from the Tyumen fields was an object lesson in the Soviet Union's strategy of awakening Japan's interest in a particular project and then altering conditions to suit its own interests.[15] When the Soviets first proposed participation in the Tyumen project to Japan at the first meeting of the JJSEC in 1966, they requested a long-term loan of US$1,000–1,500 million for the project (Japanese sources vary on this point). The loan was to be used chiefly to finance 7,500 kilometres of Japanese-manufactured pipeline from western Siberia to Nakhodka on the coast of the Soviet Far East. In return, Japan was offered the prospect of an annual 10 to 12 million tonnes of crude oil.

At first, other cooperative plans for the exploitation of natural gas in Yakutiya and northern Sakhalin took precedence over the oil project. In the spring of 1971, the Soviet Union returned to the Tyumen project in the context of its ninth Five-Year Plan (from 1971 to 1975); at the fifth meeting of the Joint Economic Committee in February 1972 it was one of the main points to be discussed. Japan's loan was now allocated to uses including the expansion of oil prospecting by means of supplying the necessary equipment, pipeline construction, primarily over the 4,200 km. from Irkutsk to Nakhodka, and the construction of all facilities necessary for sea transport. In return, between 25 and 40 million tonnes of crude oil would be delivered annually over a period of twenty years.

14. See *Asahi Evening News*, 30 Dec. 1980.
15. See Project 6 in Appendix C below.

In 1973 the Soviets again changed their offer concerning the Tyumen project. In August of that year, the president of Japan's Exim Bank was informed that the extent of the loan was no longer US$1,000 million, but US$1,380 million. Almost simultaneously the Deputy Minister of Foreign Trade, Semichastnov, reduced the quantity of oil to be delivered, stating that the Soviet Union would be able to deliver a maximum of 25 million tonnes of crude oil to Japan.[16]

One year later, in 1974, Semichastnov intimated in an interview that the crude oil drilled in Tyumen would be able to be transported not by pipeline but on the Baikal-Amur-Magistrale (BAM), the second Trans-Siberian Railway, which at that time was under construction. In addition, he changed the quantity of crude oil offered to an initial 5 million tonnes, to be followed by an annual increase of 5 million tonnes up to 25 million tonnes by 1985. This quantity would then be maintained until the year 2000.[17] Surprisingly, the Soviet Ministry of Transport then deviated from this promise by announcing in mid-1974 that the oil would be transported by pipeline over a stretch of over 1,000 km., but that over the remaining route a new type of eight-axle giant tanker wagons with a capacity of 150 tonnes would transport the oil via the second Trans-Siberian Railway, completion of which was planned for 1982. He specified that there were no plans to construct a pipeline exclusively for the transport of Tyumen oil.[18]

A report on this subject in the Soviet specialist railway periodical *Gudok* gave credence to the Japanese impression that plans to transport oil from Tyumen were unrealistic because of Siberia's lack of infrastructure; the writer calculated that at a load capacity of 1,300 tonnes per train, thirty-nine trains per day would be necessary to transport the planned annual supply of 25 million tonnes of crude oil to Japan. Since this would be too great a burden, *Gudok* pictured trains with a capacity of 8,000 tonnes, so that five trains per day would suffice to deliver the same quantity. One Japanese commentator's laconic comment was that the locomotive capable of drawing this weight had not

---

16. See Kazuo Ogawa, *Shiberia-kaihatsu to Nihon* (The Exploitation of Siberia and Japan), Tokyo 1974, pp. 219ff.
17. See *Asahi* (evening edn.), 20 July 1974, p. 2.
18. See *Sankei*, 3 Aug. 1974, p. 2.

yet been invented, so this could only refer to a development in the distant future.[19]

In Japan, doubt was cast on the feasibility of such plans, and with it on the reliability of Soviet promises to deliver. By now Soviet demands for Japanese loans had increased to US$3,200 million. A new source of uncertainty followed. According to reports in the Japanese press, Valentin Shashin, Soviet Minister for the Oil Industry, had claimed that no promises to deliver oil had been made to Japan.[20] A correction of this report on the following day at least made clear that the growth of the Soviets' (and Eastern Europeans') own needs left little surplus for large-scale deliveries to Japan.

The distrust of the Japanese, stemming from these uncertainties and from the Soviets' unwillingness to allow on-the-spot inspections, not only had an adverse effect on the Tyumen negotiations but also affected Tokyo's attitude to all Soviet offers of cooperation. Japan's captains of industry wondered whether there was really any point in investing over US$3,000 million in order to be able to import unspecified quantities of Soviet crude oil after twenty years.[21]

Occasionally, the Soviet Union even tried to link the development of the Tyumen oilfields with the construction of the new Trans-Siberian Railway, also attempting to engage Japan's support (in the form of construction machinery and loans) for this undertaking. Moreover, in an interview with the daily newspaper *Mainichi*, Semichastnov made Japanese assistance in constructing the BAM a prerequisite for Soviet oil deliveries to Japan:

> However, we said that if Japan desires to buy 25 million tonnes of oil annually over a long period of time, it must take part in this construction [of the BAM], by granting credit for the Soviet Union's purchasing of materials and facilities.[22]

Prime Minister Tanaka was informed of the Soviet intentions after Uemura and Nagano, the respective presidents of the

19. See Kenichi Kitahara, 'Shiberia-kaihatsu no tenbô' (Survey of Exploitation in Siberia), in *Seiji-keizai*, no. 3 (1975), pp. 25–38.
20. See *Asahi Evening News*, 28 May 1974.
21. *Ibid.*, 21 May 1974.
22. *Mainichi* (evening edn.), 4 April 1974, in *DSJP*, 16 April 1974, p. 7.

Keidanren and the Chamber of Industry and Commerce, had visited Moscow, and warned that restraint should be practised. He held the view that Japan's participation in the construction of the railway would have strategic implications; such a decision would not only displease China, it would also have a profound influence on Japanese-American relations.[23] Tanaka's caveat strengthened industry's increasing unwillingness to make any commitment to the Tyumen project.

Another retarding factor proved to be the standpoint of the United States. American participation in the Tyumen project, which came under periodic consideration and which was desired by the Japanese as a way of spreading the financial and technological risks, never materialised. In September 1974 both Houses of the US Congress voted for an amendment to the Exim banking regulation, imposing severe restrictions on the financing of Soviet projects to exploit energy resources. The amendment stated that the financing of such Soviet projects by the export bank could not exceed US$25 million and that the overall credit line over the next four years was to stay below a limit of US$300 million.[24]

There was one other political factor that reduced the willingness of Japanese industry to participate in the Tyumen project in any form whatsoever: criticism from Peking. In March 1973 Liao Chengzhi, a member of the Central Committee, remarked in an allusion to Japan's role in the development of Siberia that 'bitter feelings' were evoked in China by Japan's participation in Soviet projects concerned with oil drilling and transport, and that China could be moved to 'counter-measures'.[25] Later, Peking repeatedly made clear that it would prefer Japanese-American participation in Siberian projects to participation by Japan alone.

Apart from this, the Japanese business world saw the Soviets' fluctuating oil offers as increasingly dubious, and moreover unnecessary as more oil deals with China were confirmed. After the normalisation of diplomatic relations, China had offered to

23. See *Nihon Keizai* and *Tokyo Shimbun*, 4 April 1974, in *DSJP*, 10 April 1974, pp. 17–19.
24. See *Nihon Keizai*, 29 Sept. 1974, in *DSJP*, 2 Oct. 1974, p. 1; Kitahara, 'Shiberia-kaihatsu no tenbô', p. 29.
25. See *Yomiuri*, 12 March 1973, p. 3.

supply Japan with oil at an initial quantity of 1 million tonnes in 1973; the following year oil exports to Japan totalled 4 million tonnes, and in 1975 they reached 8.1 million tonnes.[26] In mid-1974 China announced that as a sign of friendship it was prepared to export 10% of its entire petroleum output to Japan, which according to Japanese estimations could mean 40 million tonnes by 1980.[27]

However, this never came to pass. Even the official targets of a total of 10 million tonnes of Chinese oil imports for 1977 and 15 million tonnes for 1981 were never fulfilled.[28] In 1985 imports of Chinese oil covered 6.5% of total Japanese demand, or 12.74 million tonnes. In 1988 delivery quantities had risen to 15.7 million tonnes, or 7.9% of total demand.[29] By 1989 imports had sunk to 12.37 million tonnes.[30]

But in the mid-1970s, when Peking made its offer, it achieved its effect against the backdrop of Soviet equivocation. As an expression of Sino-Soviet rivalry over Japan, the essential motivation was political. China declared itself willing to supply Japan with exactly the quantity of oil which the Soviet Union had promised from the Tyumen fields: 40 million tonnes. Japan was interested in Chinese oil, despite its relatively high price, because it was not beset with conditions of technological participation and financial risks and was immediately available – unlike the Soviets' offer, which only promised delivery after 1981. The only disadvantage was the relatively high wax content of some Chinese crude oil, necessitating the use of specially designed refineries.

After the Chinese intervention, Japan's virtual rejection of participation in the Tyumen project in October 1974 came as no surprise. Since Tyumen was the largest Soviet project, this was a major success for China's oil diplomacy, concerned about its position of competition with the Soviet Union. The project's abandonment dampened hopes of spectacular developments in

26. See 'Chûgoku-ni okeru saikin-no sekiyû-jijô' (China's Oil Situation in Recent Times), in *Chôsa Geppô*, vol. 21, no. 5 (1976), p. 4.
27. *Mainichi*, 7 July 1974, p. 1.
28. See *China Trade Report*, vol. 14 (Feb. 1976).
29. See Keizai Koho Center – Japan Institute for Social and Economic Affairs (ed.), *Japan 1990: An International Comparison*, Tokyo 1989, p. 66.
30. *China Trade Report*, vol. 28 (Sept. 1990).

Japanese-Soviet economic relations, although other large-scale projects of far lower strategic importance continued to operate unaffected.

In hindsight, the timely withdrawal from the Tyumen project can only have been a relief to Japanese industrialists. Not only is the BAM still far from being an efficiently functioning railway line, but oil drilling in Tyumen is also beset with enormous technical difficulties and manpower problems, with no prospect of solution in the mid-term.[31]

Economic Relations within Narrow Limits

It is surprising, given the Soviet offers of cooperation over the exploitation of Siberian resources and Japan's frequent laments over its dependence on other countries for raw materials and fuels, that the two neighbours on the Pacific coast never managed to agree on close long-term cooperation. Moscow focused its arguments on a range of reasons emphasising the advantages of such a development, which a Soviet political scientist has summarised in two main points:

- the Soviet Union's need to accelerate the development of productivity in its eastern territories, and in particular to create more rapid growth in economic potential in its Far Eastern regions;
- Japan's need, stemming from its economy's enormous dependence on foreign trade, to locate more profitable, more stable markets and sources for the raw materials and energy sources essential for survival.[32]

The second point implies that Japan desperately needed Siberian

---

31. See on this point Allan Kroncher, *Siberian Oil becomes a Problem*, Munich, 10 April 1984 (Radio Liberty Research, RL 147/84); Bernd Knabe, 'Her mit dem BAM-Programm' (Make Way for the BAM Programme), Cologne, 16 Oct. 1985 (Bundesinstitut für Internationale und Ostwissenschaftliche Studien, *Aktuelle Analysen*, 1985, no. 31). On the difficulties involved with the BAM, see *Pravda*, 11 June 1987; 'Endlose Sorgen mit der Baikal-Amur-Bahn' (Endless Problems with the Baikal-Amur Railway), in *Neue Zürcher Zeitung*, 18 June 1987.

32. See V.B. Spandaryan, 'Perspektivy sovetsko-japonskich otnošenji' (Perspectives of Soviet-Japanese Economic Relations), in *Problemy Dal'nego Vostoka*, no. 2 (1972), p. 32.

raw materials – an assumption which it has confounded in the two decades or so since the first oil crisis. Expert Soviet publicists were fond of pointing out that the Soviet Union 'could – and would – exploit the rich deposits in Siberia and the Soviet Far East itself', but that there also existed 'objective conditions and interest on the part of both countries in driving economic cooperation forward on a long-term and large-scale basis'.[33] Japanese participation in the exploitation of Siberian reserves of raw materials and energy was portrayed as desirable, but in general the Soviet side avoided giving any impression that it was dependent on outside help. Party leader Brezhnev himself emphasised this point with reference to Japan and stated in an interview with the newspaper *Asahi*:

> I should not like the readers of your paper to gain the impression that the Soviet Union could not exploit the enormous reserves in Siberia and the Soviet Far East using its own resources. It is completely clear, and has been proved throughout our country's history, that we have all the possibilities at our disposal to fulfil this task. Cooperation with other nations merely enables us to fulfil our plans for the development of these regions more quickly.[34]

Closer to the truth, however, is a statement by the editor of *Pravda*, V. Afanasyev, who declared freely in a podium discussion in Tokyo, 'Frankly, the Soviet Union does not possess enough materials or funds for the investment. The Soviet Union needs the cooperation of foreign countries, and Japan is the most ideal partner. Japan is a neighbouring nation, and the distance for transport is short.'[35] Afanasyev continued putting the case for cooperation with Japan by stating that oil supplies from the Near East were 'highly unreliable', while the Soviet Union was a reliable partner for Japan:

> By cooperating in Siberian development, Japan has nothing to lose but will have many things to gain. It is a worldwide phenomenon that demand for resources and energy will continue to grow, while supplies are running short. Therefore,

33. Spandaryan, 'Major Landmark', p. 98.
34. *Pravda*, 7 June 1977.
35. *Yomiuri*, 26 May 1979, in *DSJP*, 7 June 1979, p. 13.

cooperation in Siberian development will be more important to Japan than to the Soviet Union.[36]

In the fifteen years and more since this statement, developments have not borne out Afanasyev's concluding assessment. Indeed, Gorbachev's speech in Vladivostok on 28 July 1986 rather produced the impression that the Soviet Union was desperately dependent on foreign assistance for the development of its Far Eastern regions. He began his heavy criticism of the Soviet Far East's economic backwardness by stating that the economy of this region was beginning to develop more slowly than the economy of the country as a whole; he called for a definite increase in the region's contribution to the country's economic potential. His criticism was specifically directed at the chronically under-developed fuel and energy complex in the Far East and the decades of delay in utilising the natural gas and petroleum reserves in Sakhalin and on its continental shelf. His own words were, 'Meanwhile, hundreds of trainloads of oil go to the Far East from western Siberia! We are compelled today to transport millions of tons of oil to the Far East from other parts of the country.' Gorbachev used this image as a basis for his demand that in future the Soviet Far East should not only be supplying neighbouring regions with fuel and energy; it should become 'their large exporter'. He repeatedly demanded that the region should begin to orient itself towards exports, and bemoaned its extremely low contribution to Soviet exports as a whole. In this context Gorbachev underlined the necessity of fundamental alterations and new methods of revitalising trade on the coast and at the border, calling for 'progressive forms of economic ties with foreign countries, including cooperation in production and joint enterprises' as well as the creation of a specialised export base. The Soviet Far East was 'no longer to be regarded only as a raw materials base'. Cooperation with neighbouring countries was also to play a role in resolving problems in agriculture. In his unsparing criticism of the supply position among the population, he quoted the horrifying fact that 'nearly half of all food products required' came from outside the region itself, and that in the previous two decades the *per capita* production of milk, potatoes and vegetables in the Far East had fallen. Even animal

36. *Ibid.*

feed had to be brought in from outside in enormous quantities. The Soviet party leader also envisaged the creation of a sophisticated economic complex for the fishing industry, oriented towards utilising the full resources of the ocean.[37]

This summary of a region's backwardness lists a wide range of tasks involving closer economic cooperation with Japan, and anyone believing Gorbachev capable of subtlety would have taken his comment on Vostochny harbour, built by Japan under commission from the Soviet Union, as a veiled compliment to Japanese achievement: 'This is an excellent modern port. It can serve as an example for many.'[38]

In attempting to win Japan over to a greater degree of participation, the Soviets occasionally referred to potential competitors in Western Europe and existing government agreements on economic cooperation with France, the Federal Republic of Germany, Italy, Finland and other countries, which had been agreed for periods of between ten and twenty years.[39] These references were intended to motivate Japan to conclude a long-term, official economic agreement, for a period of ten to fifteen years, by quoting examples of competing Western partners.

Such an agreement would have made it easier for the Soviet Union to gain access to state-backed low-interest loans from the Japanese Export-Import Bank. The government in Tokyo, however, categorically rejected an official agreement over long-term economic cooperation with the Soviet Union, with a reference to the inseparability of politics and economics, a view reiterated by Prime Minister Nakasone in talks with the Polish head of the Council of State, Jaruzelski, during a visit to Eastern Europe at the beginning of 1987. He commented that he was prepared to expand cooperation with the Soviet Union in economic and technological areas, provided that progress was made on the territorial question.[40]

The link between willingness to engage in economic coopera-

37. *Pravda*, 29 July 1986; *FEA*, no. 1 (1987), pp. 8–9.
38. *Ibid.*, p. 9.
39. See I. Kazakov, 'Soviet-Japanese Economic Relations', in *FEA*, no. 2 (1976), p. 89; Spandaryan, 'Major Landmark', p. 100; ditto, 'Soviet-Japanese Trade Relations', in *FEA*, no. 4 (1980), pp. 91ff.
40. *Nihon Keizai* (evening edn.), 17 Jan. 1987, in *DSJP*, 28 Jan. 1987, p. 2.

tion and demands for the favour to be returned in a political form was maintained until the dissolution of the Soviet Union. The talks on the conclusion of a new tariffs and trade agreement at the end of November 1989 provide an example of this; while the Soviet Deputy Minister for Foreign Trade, V. Korolev, urged a rapid expansion of trade and economic relations without 'politicising' the situation, the Japanese pointed out that it would be rash to enter into long-term economic commitments without considering the political aspects of bilateral relations. These talks resulted in both sides agreeing to conclude a new tariffs and trade agreement for the period 1991–5 before the agreement then in effect expired at the end of 1990. The long-term agreement on general principles of economic and industrial cooperation which the Soviets repeatedly proposed was rejected by the leader of the Japanese delegation, Deputy Foreign Minister Koji Watanabe, in the same way as a treaty on mutual investment protection or the setting up of branches of the Soviet Chamber of Industry and Commerce and the Soviet Bank for Foreign Trade in Japan were also rejected.[41] The present situation indicates that Moscow's demands for a long-term basis and broader scope for economic relations with Japan will remain on the agenda of Russian-Japanese talks.

A further Soviet argument in favour of close economic relations concerned the alleged reduction of Japanese unemployment brought about by Soviet commissions, for which one economics expert quoted plant construction as an example. In the period between 1964 and 1979 the Soviet Union was said to have bought fifty complete industrial plants and nineteen petrochemical refineries from Japan, at a total cost of US$3,000 million.[42] This argument was weakened by Soviet participation in Japanese foreign trade, including the plant construction industry; in 1982, when Japan's exports to the USSR had reached a peak of US$3,890 million, they still totalled only 2.8% of all Japanese exports, and by 1985 this figure had dropped to 1.5%. Even less impressive was the ratio of the volume of Japanese-Soviet trade to Japan's total foreign trade; in 1982 it reached 2%, by 1985 it stood at only 1.36%. A Soviet survey was also forced to concede

41. See *SWB/FE/0628/A2/1*, 1 Dec. 1989.
42. See Spandaryan, 'Soviet-Japanese Trade Relations', p. 89.

that the USSR occupied 'overall a fairly modest place' in Japanese exports.[43]

Individual areas naturally yield more differentiation. Thus the Japanese iron industry supplied 8% of its total exports to the Soviet Union, chiefly in the form of pipes. But in 1982 the Soviet Union headed the list of customers for Japanese large-bore pipes, with a 21.3% share. Machine construction showed a similar picture. In terms of this industry's total exports, the Soviet Union occupied sixteenth place, with a 1.7% share; in terms of textile machinery, however, it was in fifth place in 1982, accounting for 5.5% of exports, while it also took 13.1% of exports of loading and unloading equipment, putting it in second place.[44] Japan's trade with the USSR was thus concentrated in a few areas and products, so that fluctuations in economic relations between the countries hit individual companies hard.[45]

As we have seen, the Soviet Union continually referred Japan, a country so dependent on outside supplies of raw materials and energy, to the richness of natural resources in Siberia, emphasising the complementary nature of the two countries' economic structures. At a general level this was correct, but the idea seemed to encourage the Soviet Union to overestimate the strength of its own negotiating position and to underestimate Japan's capacity for diversification in policies involving raw materials and energy. In the two decades or so since the first oil crisis, Japan has admirably demonstrated that its economy is by no means dependent on supplies of raw materials and energy from the Soviet Union. While Japan's economic leaders have always

43. See on Japan's trade with the Soviet Union Appendix C below; and Avtorskij kollektiv (Authors' Collective), *SSSR-Japonija: Problemy torgovo-ekonomičeskich otnošenij* (The USSR and Japan: Problems of Trade and Economic Relations), Moscow 1984, p. 192.

44. *Ibid.*, p. 193.

45. In the mid-1970s 90% of all Japanese-Soviet trade was conducted by fourteen companies: Mitsui Bussan, Mitsubishi Corp., Sumitomo Shôji, Marubeni Corp., Itôchû Shôji, Nichimen Jitsugyô, Chôri, Nisshô Iwai, Kanematsu Gôshô, Ataka Sangyô, Kyôhô Tsûshô, Tôyô Menka, Tôkyô Bôeki and Iskra Sangyô. Hundreds of small firms worked with these companies. In the second half of the 1970s, the companies actively trading with the Soviet Union had twenty-three permanent branches in the Soviet Union. See Kazakov, 'Soviet-Japanese Economic Relations', p. 84. Overall, however, trade with the Soviet Union/Russia was and is of minor importance for Japan.

reacted positively to enticing offers from the Soviet Union, Tokyo has in practice proved a cautious negotiating partner, avoiding risks and frequently put off either by the Soviets' constantly shifting business conditions or by the lack of flexibility.

Despite Japan's dependency on oil imports, its crude oil requirements, which had grown since the 1970s, were not filled by Soviet imports. In fact the figures show quite the contrary. In 1965, Japan had imported 3.34% of its oil requirements from the Soviet Union, or 2.9 million tonnes, but by 1970 this figure had fallen to 557,000 tonnes (0.28%) and by 1979 it constituted a negligible quantity (44,000 tonnes, or 0.02%). China, on the other hand, supplied around 3% of annual Japanese requirements between 1975 and 1979.[46]

Japan's crude oil requirements are met chiefly from the Middle East and Indonesia. In 1990 the three largest suppliers of crude oil were the United Arab Emirates (21.4% of total requirements), Saudi Arabia (19.5%) and Indonesia (12.6%).[47] The Soviet Union was not even among the three main suppliers of coal to Japan; in 1979 it was in fourth place with a mere 2.34 million tonnes (3.4%), behind Australia (42.6%), the USA (28.8%) and Canada (17.3%).[48] In 1990 too these three countries supplied almost 83% of Japan's coal imports.[49] The picture in timber imports is similar. Here the USA (31.2%), Malaysia (21.4%) and Indonesia (20.9%) were the three most important sources for imports in 1979. By 1990 Canada (15.0%) had replaced Indonesia.[50]

The significance of Japanese-Soviet economic relations is thus severely limited as far as Japan is concerned. In the period between 1978 and 1990 the proportion of Japan's total imports provided by the Soviet Union fluctuated between 1.8% (1978) and 1.4% (1990); in 1984 it even plummeted as low as 1%. The downward trend was even more apparent in Japan's exports to the Soviet Union over the same period: 2.6% (1978) and 0.89% (1990) of the country's total exports.[51]

46. See Keizai Koho Center, *Japan 1980*, p. 38.
47. *Ibid.*, *1992*, p. 65.
48. *Ibid.*, *1980*, p. 44.
49. *Ibid.*, *1992*, p. 66.
50. *Ibid.*, *1980*, p. 44 and *1992*, p. 66.
51. See OECD, *Monthly Statistics of Foreign Trade, Foreign Trade of OECD Members by Partner Countries*, Paris, various years; 'The Summary Report on

The situation looks quite different from the Soviet standpoint. The economic significance of trade with Japan and the Soviets' interest in extending economic cooperation were not only mentioned constantly in writings on the subject and by Soviet politicians, but were also reflected in Japan's position among the Soviet Union's Western economic partners. Between 1977 and 1986 the Soviets imported more from Japan than from any other Western industrial country apart from the Federal Republic of Germany, with Japan accounting for 4.8% (1977) and 3.5% (1986) of total imports. However, Japan's share of 2.6% (1977) and 1.1% (1986) of total Soviet exports over the same period clearly fell behind the proportion taken by the Federal Republic of Germany, Italy, France and Britain.[52]

These figures are tiny compared with the 26.8% of the foreign trade of the People's Republic of China that Japan took in 1975.[53] This sheds some light on the different levels of importance accorded to Japan by its two Communist-led neighbours; for China, Japan provides its most important outside support in the modernisation of the country, while for Russia Japan is a highly desirable partner, although cautious to commit itself, for reasons already described.

During the second half of the 1970s Japanese industry gradually lost all interest in participating in large-scale Soviet projects.[54] The first sign of this development was the withdrawal from the Tyumen project in 1974. The complex reasons for this change in attitude were chiefly political; at that time, Japan had begun to turn towards China in terms of politics and economic affairs, resulting in an expansion of trade in favour of Peking from 1977 onwards, after a period in which both Communist neighbours

---

Trade of Japan, December 1990', in Manfred Pohl (ed.), *Japan 1990/1991. Politik und Wirtschaft* (Politics and Economics), Hamburg 1991, pp. 337ff.

52. Ministersvo vnešnich ekonomičeskich svjazej SSSR (Ministry for Foreign Trade of the USSR) (ed.), *Vnešnaja torgovlja SSSR v 1987 g* (Foreign Trade of the USSR 1987), Moscow 1988 and other years; Avtorskij kollektiv, *SSSR-Japonija*, p. 222.

53. See *Far Eastern Economic Affairs, Asia 1977 Yearbook*, Hong Kong 1977, p. 159.

54. The rise in Japanese exports to the Soviet Union in 1981 and 1982 is attributed to big orders for large pipes, machines and transport equipment; see Avtorskij kollektiv, *SSSR-Japonija*, pp. 220ff.

had been favoured more or less equally in trade. By 1978, Japanese trade with China had already exceeded trade with the Soviet Union by US$2,270 million, a lead which increased to the impressive figure of US$13,400 million by 1988. In 1990, trade with the Soviet Union stagnated at US$6,000 million, whereas trade with China reached over US$18,000 million.[55] Japan was generous in granting China the state-backed loans which it awarded sparingly and hesitatingly, or not at all, to the Soviet Union. In addition, in 1978 the Japanese government concluded a long-term state economic agreement with China (covering thirteen years), a step for which the Soviet Union had been pressing for more than a decade in its desire to intensify economic cooperation.

Since the acceleration of Sino-Japanese *rapprochement* came at a time of bitter Sino-Soviet conflict, the overall climate of Japanese-Soviet relations deteriorated.[56] This general strain was compounded by individual events which further complicated bilateral relations, including their economic aspect: the complex, arduous negotiations over fishing rights in the first half of 1976, and the escape of a Soviet pilot in a MiG 25 to northern Japan in the autumn of the same year. Eventually, during 1977 Tokyo accelerated negotiations with the Chinese leaders over the conclusion of a Sino-Japanese peace and friendship treaty, which in turn provoked the Soviet Union into exerting massive diplomatic pressure, issuing heavy anti-Japanese propaganda and conducting a demonstration of military power in the waters and air space around the Japanese islands.

The Sino-Japanese treaty concluded in August 1978 marked a trough in bilateral relations which proved difficult to eliminate, for an event followed which again placed a lasting burden on economic and political relations: the invasion of Afghanistan by Soviet troops at the end of 1979. Japan endorsed the sanctions that the USA called for in retaliation. The atmosphere now prevailing in East–West relations was hardly favourable to any improvement in Japanese-Soviet economic relations, and this continued to be the case into the 1980s. The shooting down of a Korean Airlines passenger jet by a Soviet fighter plane in the

55. See Keizai Koho Center, *Japan 1992*, pp. 38ff.
56. See first section of chapter 7 below.

autumn of 1983 was a further obstacle to a return to more relaxed relations. These events all affected the activities of the Joint Economic Committee, which normally met every second year; a good five years elapsed between the eighth and ninth meetings of this important body.

After Gorbachev took office in March 1985, the meetings of the Joint Economic Committee were once more arranged as normal, but achieved no noteworthy results. Japan's caution became apparent at the twelfth meeting in August 1989, in negotiations over joint ventures; of the total of more than 800 joint ventures operating in the Soviet Union at that time, 19 were with Japan, but over 100 were with the Federal Republic of Germany.[57]

Oil and Natural Gas Exploitation off Sakhalin

The oil and natural gas exploitation project off the island of Sakhalin is one of the cooperative enterprises which continued through the years of stagnation. Its fluctuating progress is typical of the problems of economic cooperation which beset Japan and the Soviet Union. Discussions on this project, the largest Soviet/Russian-Japanese joint venture to date, show no sign of drawing to a conclusion.

At the fifth meeting of the Joint Economic Committee, in February 1972, both sides had agreed to begin exploiting the petroleum and natural gas deposits presumed to lie under the continental shelf off Sakhalin.[58] In January 1975 the Sakhalin Oil Development Cooperation (SODECO) and the Soviet Ministry for Foreign Trade concluded a treaty whereby Japan would grant the Soviet Union a loan to the value of US$100 million for equipment and machinery. In addition, each side would bear half the costs of the exploitation work. Work began in June 1976; in 1979 the joint prospecting project phase was extended by a further two years and the loan increased by another US$70 million.[59]

57. See *Asahi*, 26 Aug. 1989.
58. On the beginning and progress of the negotiations, see Ahrens-Thiele, *Japans Rohstoffpolitik*, pp. 103–12.
59. See *Japan Times* and *Pravda*, 7 June 1979. See also Map 5.

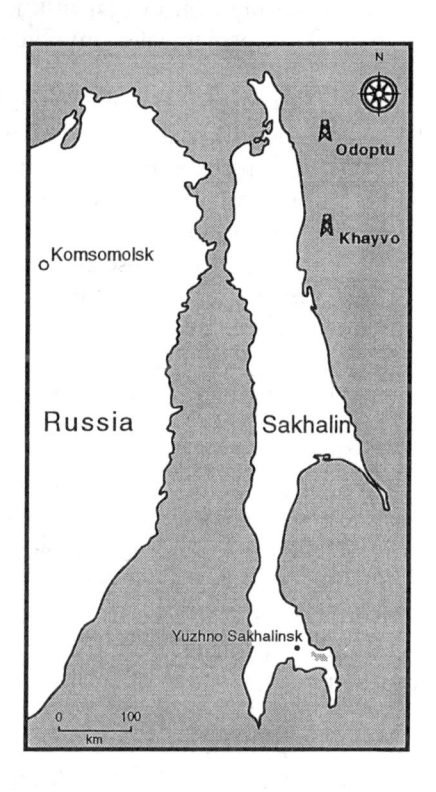

Map 5. OIL AND NATURAL GAS EXPLOITATION OFF SAKHALIN

Since the sea was frozen for long periods, work was only possible between June and October. Positive results were achieved, however, and in the autumn of 1980 the Soviet Union offered Japan an annual 5,000 million cubic metres (or 3 million tonnes) of natural gas over a period of twenty years. Hokkaido, separated from the southern tip of Sakhalin only by the La Perouse or Soya Straits, was to receive the gas by pipeline, but gave its requirements as only 2,500 million cubic metres annually and eventually reduced this quantity to 100 million cubic metres. On the strength of this reduction, it was decided to abandon the plan of building a costly pipeline from Sakhalin to Hokkaido and instead to transport the gas in liquid form in special tankers;

it would be available not only to north Japan but to other parts of the country too. This project also involved considerable costs.[60]

In mid-1981 both sides agreed to make extensive alterations to the original plan of exploiting natural gas and petroleum, and to focus the joint venture on the extraction and liquefaction of natural gas. In addition, the total costs of the project were fixed at 800,000 million yen (around US$4,000 million), one-quarter of which was to be used for the construction of liquefaction plants. During these negotiations the Soviet Union let it be known that it intended to give priority to the extraction of gas, for which there were more commercial takers than there were for oil. The Soviets had marked 1985 or 1986 for the start of deliveries. Japan considered this too early, because of its existing import obligations for natural gas, and pressed for 1988 as the earliest date for supplies to begin.[61]

These plans were soon overshadowed by the Soviet invasion of Afghanistan and the sanctions subsequently decided by Washington. At the beginning of April 1980 it was still said that the American government had agreed to except the oil and gas prospecting operations off Sakhalin from the sanctions, since the project was important as a guarantee of Japanese energy requirements.[62] However, in mid-February 1982 the US government informed Tokyo that it would be necessary to include this project in economic sanctions against the Soviet Union; it was to be treated in exactly the same way as the project involving the construction of gas pipelines from Yamburg in north-west Siberia, in which several Western European industrial states were involved.[63]

Japan found itself in an unpleasant situation. Failure to fulfil a treaty that had already been signed could possibly give the Soviets grounds for declaring the treaty void; loans already made to the value of US$180 million, as well as the oil and gas concessions, would be lost. Japan endeavoured to regain permission to use special American prospecting equipment by June 1982, when work would have been able to continue in the

60. See *Asahi*, 9 Nov. 1980.
61. See *Nihon Keizai*, 1 June 1981, in *DSJP*, 13–15 June 1981, pp. 12ff.
62. See *Nihon Keizai*, 3 April 1980, in *DSJP*, 11 April 1980, pp. 7ff.
63. See *Nihon Keizai*, 16 Feb. 1982, in *DSJP*, 18 Feb. 1982, pp. 9ff.

ice-free sea. The Japanese argued that, unlike the Yamburg project, there was no reason for concern that the Sakhalin project would make the Japanese dependent on Soviet energy supplies, since Japan's dependence on the Soviet Union for energy would increase by only around 3% when deliveries began.[64] Washington remained obdurate.

The Soviet Union exploited this situation to pressurise Japan and place Japanese-American relations under strain, declaring that it would continue the project alone if Japan were not in a position to carry out prospecting as agreed.[65] Additionally, at the beginning of July 1982, during Japanese-Soviet discussions of these problems in Moscow, the Soviets attempted to improve their loan interest conditions by demanding that they receive the same treatment as China, which Japan had granted loans at 4% interest over a twenty-year period. Tokyo, in turn, referred Moscow to the OECD regulations.[66]

At the end of July 1982, Japan and the Soviet Union resumed prospecting operations off Sakhalin, but were unable to utilise a special Japanese ship fitted with American electronic equipment to locate oil and gas deposits; only a Soviet drilling ship with American equipment was available, which led to delays in operations. The deadline for the start of gas deliveries (1988) could no longer be met – a not unwelcome prospect for the Japanese energy industry, which at the time was faced with a glut of gas.[67]

Sadao Kobayashi, the president of SODECO, declared that the American embargo had delayed the project by a year, adding that although the Soviets had been able to begin studies on commercial methods for the project after concluding prospecting operations in the area south of Chayvo (in August 1982), prospecting was also to have been completed in the northern exploration field of Odoptu by 1982. From a legal standpoint, the Soviet Union would have been within its rights to terminate the contract. To judge from Kobayashi's statements, American actions had, at least in those areas of Japanese industry which they had immediately affected, engendered reactions of bitterness

---

64. *Ibid.*
65. See *Asahi*, 29 May 1982, in *DSJP*, 3 June 1982, p. 16.
66. *Ibid.*, 4 July 1982, in *DSJP*, 14 July 1982, p. 13.
67. See *Nihon Keizai*, 30 July 1982, in *DSJP*, 7–9 Aug. 1982, pp. 14ff.

and strengthened the urge to eliminate technological dependence on the United States in any such future projects.

Kobayashi was cautious in his evaluation of the significance of the Sakhalin project for Japan's energy budget. According to his estimation, when the project came on stream Japan would receive only a small amount of oil, a condensate known as natural gasoline and an annual 3 million tonnes of natural gas over a period of twenty years. This would cover 7% of Japan's natural gas requirements and around 0.7% of the country's total energy consumption.[68]

As expected, when the chances of the Sakhalin project's swift resumption improved at the beginning of 1983 as the US embargo policies weakened, the problem of Japan's excess of gas received new prominence. It is unclear whether Moscow was adjusting to this market situation or whether it was realistically re-estimating the as yet unresolved production problems; in any case, at the end of 1983 the Soviet Union presented a revised timetable in which the export of liquid gas to Japan was planned for 1990 or 1991. Even this was considered 'one or two years too early' by members of the Japanese energy industry. Japan's natural gas consumption was secured by long-term contracts with other suppliers (the United States, Brunei, Indonesia) until the mid-1990s.[69]

Since for this reason Japan's energy industry showed little inclination to accept gas from Sakhalin, the Ministry for International Trade and Industry (MITI) threw the full weight of its authority behind the project: 'We want to realise it as a national project, by all means.' In practice, this was as much an attempt to win support for the acceptance of gas supplies from Sakhalin as it was a demand addressed to the Soviet Union for flexibility in the fixing of delivery conditions and price levels.[70]

Behind MITI's commitment stood the Japanese government's political aim of revitalising relations with the Soviet Union by re-forming the Joint Economic Committee in December 1984 after a break of over five years. While both sides agreed to continue the project,[71] there could be no question of overcoming

68. See *Asian Wall Street Journal*, 25 Nov. 1982.
69. See *Nihon Keizai*, 30 Dec. 1983, in *DSJP*, 7–9 Jan. 1984, p. 1.
70. See *Mainichi*, 16 Oct. 1984, in *DSJP*, 27–29 Oct. 1984, p. 13.
71. See *Japan Times*, 15 Dec. 1984.

the fact that economic relations were stagnating. A few months after this meeting, a further obstacle to progress in the project arose. The Soviet study of the operation's commercial feasibility, which the Japanese gas purchasers had intended quoting in support of their position, was no nearer completion. Japan's leading economic newspaper reported that the government in Moscow was suppressing the study, since its contents would allegedly place the Soviets at a disadvantage in price discussions with Japan.[72]

Whatever the reason for the delay, business with the Soviet Union presented a depressing contrast to the smoothly running negotiations between Japan and Canada over supplies of natural gas. These contracts, signed in September 1985, guaranteed Japan's requirements for natural gas until the end of 1995.[73] The fact that at the time Japan's energy industry was also signing contracts for natural gas supplies with other countries may be interpreted as an expression of the industry's extremely limited interest in the Sakhalin deal.

In order to break the stalemate in the Sakhalin project, for which the Soviet Union bore joint responsibility, the Soviets began to pile pressure onto Japan, declaring that no petrochemical plants would be purchased from Japanese manufacturers unless the Tokyo government guaranteed its purchase of the gas and appointed consumers for it; in addition, the Exim Bank was to specify conditions for further loans for the development of commercial applications. The linking of plant imports with the Sakhalin project brought great problems for the Japanese, since it represented orders to the value of around 650,000 million yen (around US$3,250 million) for those companies involved in plant manufacturing (principally Mitsui Bussan, Mitsui Zosen and Toyo Engineering). The Soviets estimated the development costs to be around 910,000 million yen, or US$4,550 million, 50% of which Japan was to supply in the form of Exim Bank loans. The cost of the natural gas to be delivered over a period of twenty years from 1991 would, according to the Soviets, be fixed at a level oriented towards international energy markets.[74]

72. See *Nihon Keizai*, 18 Oct. 1985, in *DSJP*, 30 Oct. 1985, p. 7.
73. *Ibid.*
74. See *Nihon Keizai*, 31 Oct. 1985, in *DSJP*, 13 Nov. and 19 Dec. 1985; *Asahi*, 14 Dec. 1985.

Despite Soviet ruthlessness, MITI was satisfied, since at last the results of the Soviet study of the project's commercial feasibility were available. The ministry also seemed extremely interested in gradually restarting Soviet-Japanese economic cooperation.

Expectations of a new, optimistic era in Japanese-Soviet relations were awakened by the resumption of Soviet-American dialogue after the summit talks between President Reagan and General Secretary Gorbachev in Geneva at the end of 1985, and the prospect of Soviet Foreign Minister Shevardnadze's visit to Tokyo in January 1986 - the first visit at this level for ten years. This would perhaps explain the letter from a high-level MITI member to a representative of the electricity works responsible for the matter, advising that in negotiations with the Soviets over the Sakhalin project the Federation side should 'avoid anything which may irritate the Soviet delegation, such as showing a quick refusal or acceptance' of their proposals.[75]

The project remained on the agenda; however, the lack of interest and motivation on both sides, though arising from different causes, was obvious. In Japan, energy companies could not be persuaded to purchase liquid gas from Sakhalin; on the other hand, the Soviet Union found the development costs of US$4,550 million too high, and at the beginning of 1986 suggested a re-examination of its own plans with the aim of achieving a reduction in costs and the price of supply.[76] In autumn 1986, the over-supply of natural gas forced the Japanese to propose further postponements of oil deliveries until 1994 and gas deliveries until 1995.[77]

At the twelfth meeting of the JSJEC in Moscow at the end of August 1989, the Sakhalin project reappeared on the agenda. The Soviet Union had previously presented SODECO with a comprehensive development plan, and both sides had agreed in principle to begin drilling operations. The decisive points of the agreement were as follows:

75. In November 1985 the Soviet Union had sent a seventeen-strong delegation to Tokyo under the leadership of the Deputy Minister for Foreign Trade, Sushkov, to discuss the Sakhalin project; see *Nihon Keizai* 29 Nov. 1985, in *DSJP*, 4 Dec. 1985, p. 7.
76. See *Sankei*, 21 Feb. 1986, in *DSJP*, 4 March 1986, p. 15.
77. See *Nihon Keizai* (evening edn.), 2 Sept. 1986, in *DSJP*, 9 Sept. 1986, pp. 8ff.

- Oil drilling would take priority, with production to begin in 1994.
- The Japanese would take the entire supply of crude oil produced (90,000 barrels per day).
- The total costs of drilling both oilfields would be around US$4,000 million, half of which was to be covered by Japan with the help of loans.[78]

Details were discussed at the JSJEC meeting; the joint communiqué on the Sakhalin project, however, gave no more information than the agreement to continue operations with greater intensity.[79] In April 1991 Gorbachev was still complaining to Japanese business people in Tokyo that operations were proceeding slowly.[80] Now, in the mid-1990s, the situation can be summarised thus: more than twenty years after the first negotiations took place, and almost twenty years after the signing of a treaty concerning the exploitation of oil and natural gas in the mainland off Sakhalin, Japan has invested around US$200 million but has as yet received not one tonne of oil or gas. Even if it is agreed that both sides have contributed to the problems, this project may still provide Japanese industrialists with a valuable lesson on the difficulties of economic cooperation with the Soviet Union and now with Russia.

Tentative Revival of Economic Relations

Other areas in Japanese-Soviet economic relations also proved to have their own specific difficulties; they were noticeably affected at the end of the 1970s by the overall shift in direction towards trading with China, and then from 1980 onwards by American sanctions. Japan supported the US government's measures in principle and imposed restrictions on trade with the Soviet Union, at first strictly, and then, following the European example, with increasing leniency. During 1980 sanctions were gradually relaxed, so that by the end of the year it was already possible to discuss the possibility of Japan's granting the Soviet

---

78. See *Nihon Keizai*, 13 July 1989, in *DSJP*, 18 July 1989, pp. 13ff.
79. See *Asahi Evening News*, 26 Aug. 1989.
80. See *Pravda*, 18 April 1991.

Union a loan of thousands of millions of yen at favourable conditions through the Export-Import Bank.

At the beginning of 1980, after sanctions had been imposed, Japan had also made loans available to the Soviet Union for projects decided before the invasion of Afghanistan. These included loans for supplies of large-bore pipes for that year, as well as for the third Five-Year Plan for the development of timber resources (KS-III) and coke-coal mining in southern Yakutiya. However, no new loans had been granted since then. During 1981 industrialists began to exert such pressure on the Japanese government that Prime Minister Suzuki informed the USA of the difficulty of withholding further loans.[81]

An initial trading arrangement was settled, involving the export of coal conveyor belts to the value of 2,000 million yen for the mining project in south Yakutiya. The Japanese government agreed to grant an additional loan worth US$40 million via the Exim Bank.[82] Trade in natural gas pipelines also looked somewhat rosier at the beginning of 1981. Here Japan kept a watchful eye on Europe's decisions; the Japanese steel industry waited for the results of negotiations with Western Europe, in particular with the Federal Republic of Germany, before beginning its own negotiations. The Soviet Union wanted to order 3.5 million tonnes of large-bore pipes from Japan to be delivered over a four-year period starting from 1981, an order which initially required a loan of around US$3,000 million.[83] In May 1981 the Japanese government decided to grant the Soviet Union a loan of around US$400 million via the Export-Import Bank as a first step towards financing the pipe deal.[84]

Japanese-Soviet negotiations on Japan's participation in the natural gas project at Yamburg in north-west Siberia went on until the autumn of 1981. There were particular difficulties over the delivery of components for the compression stations, an area in which Japanese willingness to supply clashed with American restrictions. Financing for the Japanese large-bore pipes, to be

81. See *Japan Economic Journal*, 2 June 1981, in *Japan Monitor*, June 1981, p. 9.
82. See *Asahi Evening News*, 24 Nov. 1980; *Mainichi*, 25 Jan. 1981, in *DSJP*, 3 Feb. 1981, pp. 11ff.
83. See *Nihon Keizai*, 28 March 1981, in *DSJP*, 4–6 April 1981, pp. 7ff.
84. See *Nihon Keizai*, 29 May 1981, in *DSJP*, 10 June 1981, pp. 6ff.

provided by the Exim Bank in cooperation with Japanese private banks, was secured at the end of 1981. The value of the loan was 89,300 million yen or around US$400 million, amounting to 85% of the costs of importing 700,000 tonnes of steel pipes from Japan. Surprisingly, at the beginning of 1982 the Soviet Union approached Japanese private banks directly for loans to cover the remaining 15%, a sum of around US$70 million.

However, the banks showed little interest in agreeing to Soviet requests. This was partly due to the Soviets' request for a low interest rate, 0.3% to 0.5% below the norm; in addition, the United States had already approached various Western industrial states with the request for a moratorium on private loans to the USSR in view of possible Soviet intervention in Poland.[85]

The Japanese government had scarcely begun to consider further reductions in sanctions against the Soviet Union – considerations in which the example of Western European industrialised nations played a decisive role - when further political pressure was placed on Japanese-Soviet relations by the imposition of martial law in Poland on 13 December 1981. Tokyo was obliged to commit itself at least verbally to supporting the continuation and tightening of sanctions policies. On 23 February 1982 the Tokyo government added four relatively mild measures to the existing sanctions against the Soviet Union:

- indefinite postponement of the official annual Soviet-Japanese trade talks;
- postponement of the regular meetings organised as part of the agreement on scientific and technological cooperation, and thus reduction of the scientific exchange programme;
- rejection of the Soviet request to open commercial agencies in other Japanese cities as well as Tokyo;
- advance warning that Soviet businesspeople would no longer be able to obtain preferential visas.[86]

Despite the inclement political climate, however, a certain vitality could be seen in economic relations. A gradual expansion in exports to the Soviet Union was accompanied by the resumption of high-level talks. In February 1983 a private business and trade

85. See *Nihon Keizai*, 4 Feb. 1982, in *DSJP*, 9 Feb. 1982, p. 9.
86. See *Japan Times*, 24 Feb. 1982.

delegation of over 250 members travelled to Moscow under the leadership of Shigeo Nagano, president of the Japanese Chamber of Industry and Commerce, and was received by dignitaries including the Soviet Prime Minister Tichonov. The Japanese industrialists felt encouraged to undertake this visit by the example of American industrialists who had organised the visit of a similarly sized delegation to the Soviet Union in November 1982.[87]

Before setting off, Nagano is said to have waved aside the *Gaimusho*'s request not to separate economic questions from the political problems with the Soviet Union, describing the request as an inappropriate admonition.[88] Prime Minister Nakasone did not take advantage of Nagano's offer to convey a letter on his behalf to the general secretary of the CPSU Central Committee, Y.V. Andropov. There was evidence of a certain discrepancy between the views of government and industry as to the necessity of such a lavishly planned visit; the Foreign Ministry informed Nagano that in the event of involvement in Siberian projects, Japanese industrial concerns would not necessarily be able to count on state-backed loans.[89]

While the delegation's two-day talks in Moscow did not achieve concrete results, the leaders of the delegation, Nagano, and his Soviet counterpart, Sushkov, the Soviet Deputy Minister of Foreign Trade, described the talks as extremely significant for the future expansion of Japanese-Soviet trade.[90] Nagano took the view that an increase in trade could be achieved even without a prior solution to the territorial question, and although not in full agreement with the concept of the unity of politics and economics propagated by the Japanese government, is said to have mentioned the territorial question to Prime Minister Tichonov and emphasised that this was a matter of national interest.[91]

The Soviets proposed resuming meetings of the Joint Economic Committee (suspended since 1979) from 1984, to include discussions on the continuation of development projects in

87. See *Asahi Evening News*, 28 Jan. 1983.
88. *Ibid.*, 1 March 1983.
89. *Ibid.*, 17 Feb. 1983.
90. *Pravda*, 25 Feb. 1983; *Izvestiya*, 28 Feb. 1983; text of the Joint Declaration in *Asahi*, 26 Feb. 1983, in *DSJP*, 8 March 1983, p. 11.
91. See *Asahi Evening News*, 1 March 1983.

Siberia, and seemed extremely interested in including cooperation with Japan over the working of Siberian resources in their twelfth Five-Year Plan (1986–90). Finally both sides agreed to discuss general questions of trade and economics, rather than the Siberian projects, at the next meeting of the JSJEC in Tokyo. The Soviet Union's interest in signing a long-term cooperation agreement with Japan along the same lines as those with Western states remained undiminished. The meeting ended with the passing of a Joint Agreement, which was fundamentally insubstantial, its sole concrete agreement concerning the continuation of talks in Tokyo in April 1984.[92]

The general improvement in climate was reinforced by the visit of Foreign Minister Shevardnadze to Tokyo and the reciprocal visit of his opposite number Shintaro Abe to Moscow, in January and May 1986 respectively. Under the aegis of 'New Thinking', optimistic expectations were formed and found expression on both sides in the activities of institutions and individuals concerned with economic relations; in January 1986, for instance, Japan and the Soviet Union had agreed on a commodities and payment agreement for the period 1986–90. In April 1986 the JJSEC met for its tenth conference, with a Japanese delegation of 230 members. Both sides expressed willingness to investigate new forms of cooperation, which chiefly meant joint ventures, whose organisation and legal aspects are specified in a Soviet law of 1 January 1987. At the meeting of the JJSEC the Soviet Union proposed joint ventures in foodstuffs and timber processing.[93]

In addition, both sides agreed to carry out a fourth five-year project to exploit forestry resources (KS-IV), which was to be ready for signing by the end of 1986. Japan also agreed to purchase coal from south Yakutiya and to participate in a harbour expansion project (presumably Vostochny).[94] The hopes awakened by this positive beginning were, however, quickly dampened by the setbacks in political relations described above. Moscow's Japanese policies betrayed no more evidence of 'New Thinking'.

92. See *Japan Times*, 26 Feb. 1983.
93. See *Japan Times*, 18 April 1986.
94. *Ibid.*

Those Japanese industries which had focused on trade with the Soviet Union now expressed their concern at current events and their fear at the effects of these events on economic relations.[95] These fears, although they could not be directly linked to the deterioration in climate, proved to be justified; pleading other commitments, the Soviets requested a postponement of the eleventh meeting of the JJSEC, which was finally held in Tokyo at the beginning of 1988. The Japanese press spread speculations of a drop of 20–30% in trade volume as a result of stricter export controls, but the strong yen and the Soviets' shortage of hard currency also curbed the growth of Japanese exports to the Soviet Union.[96] At the beginning of 1988, Moscow confirmed a fall of 20% in trade volume for 1987.[97] While in 1987 imports from the Soviet Union had risen by 18.9% over the previous year to US$2,350 million, exports to the Soviet Union had, for the reasons already mentioned, fallen by 18.6% to US$2,560 million.[98]

At the eleventh meeting of the JJSEC, which took place from 27 January to 2 February 1988, the Soviet Union, represented by an eighty-strong delegation, tried to promote a revitalisation of trade. The leader of the delegation, V.L. Malkevich, invited the Japanese to participate actively in joint venture companies. Since the Joint Venture Law had been passed, he said, twenty-three such joint ventures had been founded, one with a Japanese firm, and a further 250 were under discussion, of which only forty were with Japanese firms.[99] Malkevich also called for Japanese industrialists to participate in larger-scale Siberian projects. Within this sector of cooperation, a contract to supply a polyester plant on a compensatory basis was signed; moreover, both sides agreed in principle to the fourth step of the Siberian timber working project, and reached an agreement that the bilateral trade structure was to be rearranged by increasing Japan's imports of Soviet finished goods. To this end, proposed the Soviets, Japan should send a delegation to the Soviet Union to

95. See *Japan Times*, 26 Aug. 1987.
96. *Ibid.*
97. See *SWB/FE/0061/A2/1*, 29 Jan. 1988.
98. See *Japan Times*, 27 Jan. 1988; Pohl, *Japan 1990/91*, pp. 337ff.
99. *Ibid.*, 28 Jan. 1988. The result remained modest until the dissolution of the Soviet Union at the end of 1991.

study potential areas of cooperation in the modernisation of manufacturing plants.[100]

The Japanese reacted coolly to these ideas; the Toshiba Affair still cast a palpable shadow, and political relations, especially the question of the northern territories, showed no signs of fundamental improvement. Although Japanese-Soviet trade and economic relations had been reviving since 1988/9, Tokyo still adhered firmly to the principle of refusing to discuss wide-ranging contracts of long-term economic cooperation while no fundamental change was visible in political relations. Even though Prime Minister Takeshita spoke of 'immense potential for cooperation' in an *Izvestiya* interview at the beginning of 1989 and claimed a 'record level' of US$5,900 million for foreign trade between the two countries in 1988,[101] it should not be forgotten that this figure was equivalent to only one-third of the volume of Sino-Japanese trade.

Japanese politics at the time aimed at stabilising the level of trade and economic relations or possibly at achieving slight improvements, depending on circumstances, and this was also the inter-governmental aim behind the decision to sign a new agreement for the period 1991–5 before the expiry of the then current tariffs and trade agreement at the end of 1990. The Soviets, represented by the Deputy Minister for Foreign Trade, V. Korolev, pressed for a treaty protecting mutual investments and for increased representation of Soviet trade organisations in Tokyo; for example, the opening of a Soviet Chamber of Industry and Commerce and a branch of the Bank of Foreign Trade. These initiatives, however, were rejected by the Japanese, whose Secretary of State of the Foreign Ministry, Koji Watanabe, explained that Moscow would itself first have to improve the unsatisfactory investment conditions, and that it would be rash to implement changes with possible long-term implications at a time of such rapid change within the Soviet Union.[102]

The twelfth meeting of the JJSEC, held in Moscow in August 1989, brought positive results to join the other small steps towards an improvement in economic relations that were chiefly

100. *Ibid.*, 3 Feb. 1988.
101. See *Izvestiya*, 1 March 1989.
102. See Kyodo, 29 Nov. 1989, quoted in *SWB/FE/0628/A2/1*, 1 Dec. 1989.

being initiated by the private sector. At this meeting the Soviets gave the Japanese delegation, under Ryoichi Kawai (president of Komatsu Ltd.), a list of military technology which was to be offered for sale to other countries after its conversion to civilian applications. According to Malkevich, leader of the delegation and president of the Soviet Chamber of Industry and Commerce, this list included the technology used in the Soviet space shuttle.[103]

The most important results of the meeting were:

- discussion of various new forms of cooperation (joint ventures, consortia, projects involving joint research and production, regional exchanges, special economic zones), to achieve structural improvements in bilateral trade;
- reiteration of the necessity of bilateral visits to companies and industries by experts;
- agreement in principle to stimulate the progress of the Sakhalin project on the basis of the existing treaties;
- the establishment that negotiations of some large-scale projects were in their concluding stages, and the conclusion of feasibility studies for joint ventures in western Siberia;
- discussion of questions on the reorganisation of an industrial complex and on environmental improvements at the Amur Pulp and Cardboard Factory, within the sub-committee of the paper and pulp industry.[104]

To the surprise of the Japanese participants, the Soviets informed their guests that Vladivostok would not be opened to foreign business representatives before 1992 — a direct contradiction to earlier announcements. Tokyo presumed that military commanders had refused to approve a speedy release of the naval base.[105]

Trade also seemed to be reviving in more limited regional areas. In October 1989, in the fourth conference of its kind since 1984, around 440 leading representatives from governmental and commercial circles met to discuss the possibility of commodity barter between Hokkaido and the Soviet Far East and signed

---

103. See *Asahi Evening News*, 26 Aug. 1989.
104. *Ibid.*
105. See *Radio Japan*, 24 Aug. 1989, in *MD Asien*, 25 Aug. 1989, p. 6.

supply contracts worth a total of 4,200 million yen. Both sides also agreed to initiate specific negotiations on ten or so joint ventures. Discussions on an expansion of trade and tourism were delegated to sub-committees, with proposals to be presented at the next conference in 1991.[106]

It was noticed with surprise in Tokyo that the two rival companies Mitsubishi and Mitsui were already participating in a joint venture involving the manufacture of plastic base products in the Soviet Union, with a contribution of US$2 million per company. A complex consisting of three factories was planned in Tobolsk, with contributions of US$800 million to come from companies in the USA and Finland. The products of this chemical complex were intended to be desirable exports – this is said to have been a not inconsiderable factor in the two Japanese giants' decision to participate.[107]

A further Japanese joint-venture participation was also set up at the end of 1989. Fanuc Ltd., world-famous manufacturer of numerically controlled machine tools, together with the Mitsui Bussan trading company, concluded an agreement with the Soviet Union to start up a joint venture in April 1990 under the name of Stanko-Fanuc Service, for the servicing and sale of modern machine tools. The initial capital input totalled 100 million yen (US$699,000); 50% of the company was to be owned by Stanko Service, and 25% each by Fanuc and Mitsui Bussan. The company was to take over the servicing of machines delivered to the Soviet Union by Fanuc Ltd.[108] The amount of capital involved indicates that this is a relatively small-scale project.

Remarkably, at the beginning of 1990 a loan of 15,000 million yen (US$99.3 million) was granted to the Soviet Union by a consortium of six Japanese banks under the leadership of the partly state-controlled Export-Import Bank. The Exim Bank was to raise half the loan, with five private Japanese banks providing the remainder. The loan was to be used as payment for supplies from the companies of Sanyo Electric Co., Nissho Iwai Corp. and Tokyo Engineering Corp., participants in the construction of a manufacturing plant for cooling plant compressors in

106. *Asahi Evening News*, 11 Oct. 1989.
107. *Ibid.*, 23 Dec. 1989.
108. *Ibid.*, 28 Dec. 1989; *Pravda*, 29 Dec. 1989.

Lithuania. Production start-up was planned for the end of 1992; the production target is 1 million compressors per year. The last loan from the Exim Bank was granted to the Soviet Union in March 1988.[109]

In general it can be said that the Japanese business community has the will to increase bilateral trade and expand economic cooperation, but is not willing to set broad limits to facilitate this process. There are several reasons for this:

- No improvement is expected in the foreseeable future in the present unsatisfactory hard currency situation in Russia.
- Japan is not interested in delivering plants to be paid for later out of running production; the increasingly stiff competition this kind of compensation deal presents to the Japanese economy holds no attraction. Only raw materials and energy remain as potential areas of cooperation; but owing to contractual obligations with other suppliers Japan's purchasing potential in these sectors is limited, until the mid-1990s at the earliest and to some extent until the end of the century.
- The first attempts to improve Japanese-Soviet economic relations came at a time when trade in the East was generally suffering a decline. Investment capital was at a premium over the entire Comecon area, and urgently required investments for modernisation ceased.[110] The difficulties of the economic situation, particularly the overall fall in productivity in the Soviet economy, were compounded from mid-1989 by the political disintegration of the Soviet power bloc. No long-term improvements in the competitiveness of Russian manufactured goods can thus be expected; however, in view of the stagnation in oil prices, this would be the only area which could bring about a dramatic increase in Russian exports.
- Finally, the permanent intransigence of both sides on the territorial question led to continual tension in the political climate, and during Gorbachev's visit to Japan in April 1991 it even obstructed the realisation of a long-term government agreement on economic cooperation.

109. *Asahi Evening News*, 10 March 1990.
110. See *DIW Wochenbericht* (Berlin), no. 14/87, 2 April 1987.

Any attempt to summarise Soviet-Japanese economic relations since the beginning of the 1970s cannot avoid focusing on three main features: the changeability of Soviet intentions; the reorientation of Japan's economic interests, and the subjection of economic relations between the two countries to political fluctuations and to the intransigence of both sides on the territorial question. These factors preclude any definite predictions of further developments. If, however, Russia should one day launch a planned, concentrated operation to exploit natural resources in Siberia, including the Russian Far East, Japan would have the chance of becoming its most important foreign cooperative partner — thus of necessity improving its negotiating position. Whether this situation could be exploited politically is another question.

For Tokyo, considerations of this kind do play a part. According to one Japanese observer in mid-1986, there was no reason why the exploitation of Siberia was essential for Japan. He came to the conclusion that the Japanese government today still fundamentally holds, though now with regard to Russia:

> But for the Soviet Union the necessity of exploiting Siberia is growing more and more urgent. For geographical and economic reasons, the Soviet Union's degree of dependence on Japan with regard to the exploitation of Siberia will inexorably grow; and precisely because of this there will be a chance of regaining the northern territories. For this reason, where the Soviet Union is concerned the inseparability of politics and economics is emphasised.[111]

Such a development can no longer be rejected out of hand. The catastrophic state of Russia's economy only increases the urgency of cooperating with its highly developed, financially powerful neighbour. If both sides make progress in discussing the territorial question within the foreseeable future, then Japan's reservations could disappear, and an intensification of Japanese-Russian economic relations can be expected.

---

111. Hidetake Sawa, 'Fue fukedo odorezu - kane-kui mushi-no shiberia-kaihatsu' (The Piper's Paid, but There's No Tune — The Development of Siberia is Devouring Money), in *Sekai Shûhô*, 27 May 1986, p. 15.

7

JAPAN'S ENTANGLEMENT IN THE SINO-SOVIET CONFLICT

Japan was the only industrialised democracy in the world to have both the Communist-ruled great powers, China and the Soviet Union, as its immediate neighbours. Up to the dissolution of the USSR, this posed delicate problems of equilibrium for Tokyo's foreign policy. Japan's relationship with these two countries was determined on the one hand by the changeable relations it had experienced throughout its long history with the continent of Aisa, and on the other hand by the relationship of the two Communist states with each other.

Japan and China have a special relationship, founded on the common aspects of their cultural history and the expansionist adventures of Japanese imperialism. On the Japanese side this relationship is characterised by a curious emotionalism, countered on the Chiniese side by a composure stemming from that country's feeling of cultural superiority and from the resolution to do everything necessary to prevent any new threat from Japan from its very outset.

Tokyo's relationship with Russia, and formerly with the Soviet Union is, however, relatively uncomplicated. The two nations are culturally alien to each other, and their contact has no deep historical roots. Japan's view of the Soviet Union was primarily of a Communist superpower which, immediately before the end of the war, breached a neutrality pact in order to swell its own coffers from the spoils of war, and which achieved this by the occupation of several islands at the southern end of the Kurile chain. This action has remained fresh in Japan's memory, even if reference to it is coloured by a good measure of self-righteousness.

The Soviet Union's relationship to Japan, on the other hand, seems to have been marked by awe and fear: awe of the latter's impressive industrial performance and the high technological level of its industry, fear of a threat from the Japanese-American alliance or even from too close a *rapprochement* of Japan and China. With the normalisation of Sino-Japanese relations in September 1972, the former aspect receded somewhat into the background. Japan subsequently became an object of rivalry in the conflict between China and the Soviet Union until the beginning of the 1980s, with both countries attempting to move their economically powerful neighbour to commit itself one way or the other by means of treaties of peace and friendship. China emerged the winner.

Not until the phase of détente between Peking and Moscow began in the autumn of 1982 with the commencement of consultations did rivalry over Japan cool. At this stage China was able to feel satisfied with the results of its policies on Japan; a basis for close economic cooperation had been created and the long-desired treaty of peace and friendship had been concluded in 1978, largely in accordance with the conditions set by the Chinese. The Soviet Union had been ousted as competition for Japan's economic and political favours, or more precisely had out-manoeuvred itself by its inflexibility on the territorial question and by its direct threats to Japan.

Japan's position in the field of tension between China and the Soviet Union was of supreme significance, not only for the balance of power in the Asia Pacific region but also within a global context. The ruling politicians in Tokyo have always been mindful of this consideration and have endeavoured – not always successfully – to avoid involvement in the Sino-Soviet conflict.

During the 1970s China's conflict with the Soviet Union became the core of the former's foreign policies, and as a result its leaders exploited every opportunity of making anti-Soviet statements and supported military alliances directed against Soviet threats (NATO, the American-Japanese security alliance) and regional organisations aimed at countering Soviet influences (the EC, ASEAN). Western politicians known for their right-wing conservative, anti-Soviet views were received in Peking with open arms and treated to Chinese corroborations of the dangerous expansionism of the Soviets; less critical guests were nonetheless treated to this interpretation. Every declaration of principle of Chinese foreign policy from these years included a call to establish a global united front 'against the hegemonism of both superpowers' – at times directed against the Soviet

Union alone. The core of this extremely biased interpretation of the dangers threatening the peoples of the world was supplied by a 'Theory of the Differentiation of the Three Worlds', the basics of which were presented to the public in 1974 by Deng Xiaoping and a reworked version of which was later published in the party organ as the spiritual legacy of Mao Zedong.[1] In this, Mao used a simple formula to express the defensive nature of the USA – in the Chinese view – and the threat from the Soviet Union: 'The United States wants to protect its interests in the world, and the Soviet Union wants to expand; this can in no way be changed.'[2]

Given that this formulation was a constant element in Chinese foreign policy at the time, it was unsurprising that Peking also introduced Soviet policies on Japan into its own polemics. From the time relations were normalised in 1972 the Chinese leaders, regardless of their propagandist activities, attempted to prevent any improvement in Japanese-Soviet relations and to strengthen China's own relations with Japan by means of concrete proposals. Their activities in this field revolved around the Japanese claims to the Soviet-occupied islands at the southern end of the Kuriles; the conclusion of a peace and friendship pact, including an anti-hegemony clause; the strengthening of Japanese defence capabilities; and Japan's participation in the exploitation of Siberian natural resources.[3]

China and the Japanese-Soviet Territorial Question

China's policy on Japan had two aims. In the first place, it focused on exploiting the latter's industrial, technological and financial potential for its own expansion; the second intention was to gain a certain influence in Japanese politics, so that Japan would never again become a threat to China. From the end of 1974 onwards, these long-term goals were accompanied by a sudden interest in concluding a peace and friendship treaty with Japan as soon as possible.

1. Chairman Mao's Theory of the Differentiation of the Three Worlds is a major contribution to Marxism-Leninism; Chinese text in *Renmin Ribao*, 1 Nov. 1977; English translation in *Peking Review*, no. 45 (4 Nov. 1977).
2. *Ibid.*, p. 22.
3. See above, pp. 102ff.

The achievement of the first aim could have been at least obstructed by any all too intensive participation on the part of Japan in the development of Siberia, while any substantial improvement in relations and the creation of close political contacts between Tokyo and Moscow could have jeopardised the second aim. In China's view, the goal of concluding a treaty with Japan could best be achieved by the continual presentation of examples of the Soviet Union's hegemonism and by provoking the Soviet Union itself into hegemonistic actions. Peking was therefore necessarily interested in the continuation of the territorial problem, since this was the primary obstacle to Japanese-Soviet *rapprochement*. In the climate of Sino-Soviet confrontation, the existence of this question could best be maintained by China's unceasing support of Japanese claims.

Until the assumption of diplomatic relations between China and Japan which followed Prime Minister Tanaka's visit to Peking in September 1972, Chinese commentaries had always included the Tokyo government in its attacks on the Soviet Union. For instance, the Chinese had considered Gromyko's visit to Tokyo in January 1972 a 'step taken by Soviet revisionist social-imperialism to step up collusion with the Japanese reactionaries'.[4]

Mao Zedong had already been aware from a much earlier stage that the territorial problem was a thorn in Moscow's side. On 10 July 1964 he declared to a delegation of the Socialist Party of Japan, in response to a question from its leader, Kozo Sasaki: 'As far as the Kurile Islands are concerned, there is no doubt in our view; they must be returned.'[5] When Prime Minister Zhou Enlai himself received parliamentary SPJ representatives at the beginning of 1972 and announced that he would support Japan's demands for the return of the islands under discussion, Gromyko was about to set off for a visit to Japan. During his talks with government members in Tokyo, the Soviet Foreign Minister is said to have repeatedly declared, in reference to Zhou's statement, that intervention in Japanese-Soviet relations by an outside country was inadmissible.[6]

The Soviets' susceptibility actually seemed to goad the

4. See *Peking Review*, no. 6 (11 Feb. 1972), pp. 19ff.
5. *Asahi Shimbun*, 14 July 1964.
6. *Tokyo Shimbun*, 29 Jan. 1972, in *DSJP*, 1 Feb. 1972, p. 10.

Chinese into supporting Japan's claims; the Chinese press reported with evident sympathy on events and demonstrations during which it was demanded that the Soviet Union should give back the northern territories. In the second half of 1972, the *Peking Review*, re-edited with an eye to foreign favour, published four detailed reports on the subject, three of which appeared during the period directly after the establishment of diplomatic relations with Tokyo.

The Chinese leaders had doubtless calculated that the Japanese public would react with satisfaction to this demonstration of support. In talks held before Tanaka's visit to Peking, Prime Minister Zhou Enlai had informed Takeiri, chairman of the Komei Party and influential in Japan's policies on China, that China would support Japan's position as soon as diplomatic relations between the two countries were established.[7] At the beginning of 1973 Takeo Kimura, former Housing and Construction Minister, reported after returning from Peking that Zhou had not only reaffirmed the Chinese position, but had also confirmed Japan's rights to the four islands and to the entire Kurile chain.[8]

With this, a leading Chinese politician had made a statement on the territorial question for the first time after the establishment of diplomatic relations to Japan. The support reported in the Japanese press for a Japanese claim to the *entire* Kurile chain, a claim maintained by Japan's Communist Party but not made by the LDP, is especially remarkable. Zhou called on Mao's statement of 1964 as corroboration; later, however, no further Chinese statement could be located which went beyond the demands of the Japanese government.

In December 1973 even the Chinese Ambassador to Japan, Chen Chu, visited Cape Nosappu in northern Hokkaido, the point closest to the Soviet-occupied islands; he inspected the area, criticised the Soviets' position on the territorial question and encouraged the movement calling for the return of the islands which the population had supported.[9] The Chinese gave unstinting support to the Japanese territorial claim; even at the United Nations General Assembly in 1973 Chiao Guanhua,

7. See *Nihon Keizai*, 9 Aug. 1972, in *DSJP*, 11 Aug. 1972, p. 9.
8. *Tokyo Shimbun*, 27 Jan. 1973, in *DSJP*, 2 Feb. 1973, p. 27.
9. See *Yomiuri*, 7 Dec. 1973, in *DSJP*, 7 Dec. 1973, p. 30.

leader of the Chinese delegation, demanded that the Soviet Union 'return the four islands to Japan'.[10] Chiao spoke on 3 October. Four days later Prime Minister Tanaka was expected in Moscow; he had linked this visit to hopes of progress in the repeatedly postponed negotiations on a peace treaty between Japan and the Soviet Union.

The timing of the support expressed by leading Chinese politicians for Japan's territorial claims was based on tactical calculation. Zhou Enlai had made his statement at the beginning of 1972, immediately before Gromyko's visit to Tokyo; Chiao's support was expressed a few days before Tanaka's arrival in Moscow. Chinese support came at times when it was least welcome to the Japanese.

The Japanese Foreign Ministry admitted that it had noted China's unsolicited support in the United Nations with mixed feelings. The *Gaimusho* feared − correctly − the opposite effect to that intended, as a result of involving the Japanese-Soviet territorial problem in the conflict between China and the Soviet Union. In agreement with Moscow, Japan desired negotiations on the problem with the Soviet Union on a purely bilateral basis, independent of third parties.[11] Peking's intentions were obvious; it could not have the slightest interest in improvements in Japanese-Soviet relations, let alone in a solution of the territorial problem as a prerequisite for such improvements. Japanese politicians were constantly aware of the duplicity of China's support over the territorial question and never expressed any doubt in private talks that its neighbour was pursuing its own national interests. It seems that at that time, out of consideration for newly normalised relations with Peking, Tokyo had made the decision to suffer Chinese actions in silence.

Against this backdrop, the statement of Japanese Foreign Minister Miyazawa on 9 July 1976 created a sensation. He declared before the Foreign Affairs Committee of the Upper House that it would be undesirable for China to become involved in the question of the northern territories, since this problem concerned Japan and the Soviet Union alone. He continued, '[The involvement] will not be of service for an

10. *Peking Review*, vol. 16, no. 40 (5 Oct. 1973), p. 13.
11. *Tokyo Shimbun*, 4 Oct. 1973, in *DSJP*, 4 Oct. 1973, p. 34.

amicable settlement of the problem.'[12] Since Chinese delegations made frequent visits to Hokkaido and voiced anti-Soviet views on the territorial question, Miyazawa had already given instructions to all staff receiving Chinese groups to proceed with caution, but had not criticised such incidents as the delegations were not composed of official diplomatic visitors; now, however, he believed it appropriate to speak out over Chinese interference.

China's initial reaction was one of indirect criticism; its press quoted Japanese sources with pro-Chinese views who 'condemned the anti-Chinese statement of Japan's Foreign Minister'. After a few days, however, the Chinese news media launched a direct attack, accusing Miyazawa of treading in Brezhnev's footsteps – this accusation was especially severe in view of China's occasional comparisons of the Soviet party leader with Hitler – and describing his behaviour as perverse and a betrayal of Japan's national interests. The Japanese Foreign Minister, wrote a Xinhua correspondent, had not dared to defend his country's national interests in a head-on battle over the hegemonistic Soviet occupation of the Japanese northern territories. China announced that it would, as before, 'resolutely support the Japanese people's just struggle for the recovery of the northern territories'.[13] In Peking, the Japanese Ambassador was summoned to the Foreign Ministry and an official complaint was lodged about Miyazawa's statement.

China had been openly criticised by a member of the Japanese government for the first time since relations were normalised in September 1972, and this resulted in a perceptible cooling in relations which was greeted with satisfaction in Moscow. *Pravda* reported 'new rifts in Sino-Japanese relations' with gratification. The party organ, while not explicitly informing its Soviet readers that the subject was the territorial problem with Japan, occupied itself with 'the attempts of the People's Republic of China to hinder the progress of Japanese-Soviet relations and draw Japan into an anti-Soviet alliance', complacently quoting Miyazawa's reaction to these attempts.[14]

However, to assume Miyazawa's statement – which he in-

12. *Sankei*, 10 July 1976, in *DSJP*, 14 July 1976, p. 28.
13. Xinhua News Agency, *Daily Bulletin*, no. 6688 (19 July 1976); *Peking Review*, vol. 19, no. 30 (23 July 1976), pp. 15ff.
14. *Pravda*, 25 July 1976.

cidentally toned down as soon as he learned of China's reaction – implied even a temporary *rapprochement* between Japan and the Soviet Union would not be accurate. In addition to the Foreign Minister's probable aims of self-publicity within the LDP, it is also reasonable to assume that he was using the Chinese leaders' loss of authority, as a result of being weakened by their power struggles, to indicate increased freedom of movement in his country's foreign policy. With remarkable firmness the *Gaimusho* rejected Peking's claim that Japan was softening towards the Soviet Union, stating that, as was generally known in Japan, it was impossible that Japan and China should agree in their attitude towards the Soviet Union, and confidently continuing, 'Accordingly, if the Chinese side resolves to conclude a Japan–China peace and friendship treaty, even if no agreement with the Soviet Union has been reached on the understanding, the treaty can be concluded.'[15]

These resolute words were followed by a demonstration of Japan's independence from Moscow; on 10 and 11 September 1976, Foreign Minister Miyazawa visited Hokkaido to inspect the Soviet-occupied islands by telescope. Pictures of this, the first visit ever of a Japanese Foreign Minister to northern Japan, appeared in the Japanese press.[16] Miyazawa declared on the occasion:

> The Soviet Union should also know I have come here. The demand for the return of the northern territories is the demand of all the Japanese people. The Soviets are wrong when they claim that this is a desire for strength. I believe that through this tour of inspection I can give emphasis to our demand, and this is necessary.[17]

Japan's sensitivity on the territorial question, however, seemed to make little impression on China. When a leading representative of the Hokkaido Society for the Support of the Return of the Northern Territories visited Peking at the end of 1976 as part of a cultural delegation, Tan Chenlin, vice-president of the People's Congress Standing Committee, used the opportunity

15. *Sankei*, 20 July 1976, in *DSJP*, 22 July 1976, p. 18.
16. See *SWB/FE*/5306, 8 Sept. 1976.
17. *Sankei*, 14 Sept. 1976.

to launch a caustic attack on the Soviet Union, including the territorial problem in a long line of Soviet acts of aggression and intimidation, from Stalin's policies on China to the Soviet invasion of Czechoslovakia and intervention in Angola. He appealed to his Japanese guests, 'Unless you fight, the Soviet Union will not be satisfied with obtaining the four islands as its territory, and it will lay its hands on Hokkaido, too. It will advance into all fields, including the cultural, economic and military fields.'[18]

In the years that followed, the territorial question was to reappear constantly in Chinese commentaries on Soviet-Japanese relations; however, its appearances became more infrequent and more objective in proportion to the increase in détente between Peking and Moscow.[19] At first, all Chinese statements on the problem stressed the Japanese viewpoint by using the expression 'islands under Soviet occupation since the end of the Second World War'; however, no further mention was made of hegemonistic Soviet occupation. Polemics had vanished since China's commitment to the return of the northern territories to Japan had lost its former importance in the Sino-Soviet conflict. As President Gorbachev's visit to Japan drew nearer and speculations about a solution to the problem were rife on all sides, China became even more wary of making statements in Japan's favour. On 21 March 1991 the Chinese government issued a statement of deliberate neutrality: 'The northern territories represent a problem between Japan and the Soviet Union. We hope that this matter will be settled by negotiations between the two states.'[20] What China understood by 'settlement' was not explained. When Foreign Minister Nakayama was discussing Japanese-Soviet relations in Peking a few weeks before Gorbachev's visit to Japan, he received from both Prime Minister Li Peng and Foreign Minister Qian Qichen only the laconic comment that China's stance over Japanese-Soviet relations had not changed.[21] There was not the slightest hint of China's support

18. *Mainichi*, 16 Dec. 1976, in *DSJP*, 21 Dec. 1976, p. 5.
19. See articles on this problem in *Beijing Review*, no. 44, 29 Oct. 1984, pp. 12ff; *ibid.*, no. 4, 27 Jan. 1986, pp. 10ff and *ibid.*, no. 45, 10 Nov. 1986, p. 11; *China Daily*, 8 Feb. 1990 and 27 July 1990.
20. *Sankei*, 22 March 1991.
21. *Ibid.*, 6 and 7 April 1991. The same response came from Foreign Minister Qian at a press conference on 27 March and party leader Jiang Zemin

for the Japanese position. Once again, Peking's actions were hardly beneficial to Japan.

China's strategy was aimed at the achievement of three goals: first, provocation of the Soviet Union, with correspondingly negative effects on Soviet-Japanese relations; secondly, improvement of the chances for a Sino-Japanese treaty of peace and friendship, including an anti-hegemony clause; finally, the exclusion of any settlement of the territorial problem in the foreseeable future. All three aims had been achieved.

Offers of Competing Treaties

Japan owed its involvement in the conflict between the two Communist superpowers not only to the territorial problem, but also, perhaps even more importantly, to the issue of concluding friendship pacts. The race between China and the Soviet Union to agree such a treaty with Japan had accelerated from the moment in the autumn of 1974 when China had announced its interest in the swift realisation of a treaty of peace and friendship, which was seen as the ultimate goal of normalising relations. China's artful manoeuvring of the discussions over the treaty's objectives considerably exacerbated existing Soviet-Japanese tensions. In January 1975 the Chinese made it clear that they wanted the text of the treaty to include a clause by which both sides would not only renounce any attempts at hegemony, but would also commit themselves to combating hegemonist activities by any other states or groups of states. The Soviets reacted to this with extreme sensitivity, interpreting the clause – not without reason – as a move by Peking to win Japan's alliance against the Soviet Union.

As early as November 1974, the Soviet Embassy in Tokyo had formed an impression that the Japanese viewpoint on peace treaties with China and the Soviet Union was inconsistent; the embassy pointed out that although Japan was willing to exclude a still-unsettled territorial question from negotiations with China, in this case the claim to the tiny, uninhabited Senkaku Islands (in Chinese, Diaoyütai) between Okinawa and Taiwan, in its

---

in an interview on 29 March 1991 in *Beijing Review*, no. 14, 8–14 April 1991, p. 11 and no. 15, 15–21 April 1991, p. 10.

dealings with the Soviet Union Tokyo insisted that the territorial problem must be resolved before a treaty could be concluded.[22] The *Gaimusho* countered that a Sino-Japanese treaty of peace and friendship was not aimed at settling the situation between both countries after the end of the Second World War, and so would not include territorial issues; however, any peace treaty with the Soviet Union would be intended precisely to settle the post-war situation, and thus the resolution of the territorial problem was an imperative prerequisite for the conclusion of a Japanese–Soviet peace treaty.[23] Even the sinologist Tadao Ishikawa, known at that time for his critical attitude towards Peking, opposed the Soviets' attitude that the two territorial questions should be accorded equal status.[24]

After preliminary Sino-Japanese talks had got under way, the Soviet approach became more overt. On 3 February 1975 Oleg Troyanovski, the Soviet Ambassador to Japan, appeared before Shiina, the deputy chairman of the LDP who had considerable influence within the party, and declared bluntly that the conclusion of a Sino-Japanese treaty of peace and friendship would have an unfavourable effect on the Soviet Union.[25] Ten days later he handed Prime Minister Miki a letter from the General Secretary of the CPSU, Brezhnev, containing the familiar proposal that a treaty of good neighbourliness and cooperation should be concluded while negotiations for a Soviet-Japanese peace treaty were still under way. The Soviet Union's intentions in this appeared to be twofold: to limit the unfavourable effects of Sino-Japanese negotiations; and to postpone the territorial question, with its adverse effect on relations, *ad calendas Graecas*, with the possibility that Japanese-Soviet relations would gradually improve in the mean time.[26] Neither this nor the Soviets' second attempt could deflect the Japanese government from its aim. Miki reacted to the Soviet Ambassador's *démarche* with unaccustomed directness, pointing out that the conclusion of a treaty of peace and friendship with China was not only specified

22. See *Asahi*, 6 Nov. 1974, p. 2.
23. See *Yomiuri*, 6 Nov. 1974, in *DSJP*, 8 Nov. 1974, p. 7.
24. 'Hoppô Senkaku wo kondô suru na' (No Mixing of the Northern Territories with Senkaku), in *Sankei*, 19 Nov. 1974, p. 7 (Seiron).
25. See *Sekai-Shûhô*, Tokyo, 11 March 1975, p. 7.
26. *Ibid.*

Offers of Competing Treaties

in both states' Joint Declaration of September 1972, but also had the support of all in the Japanese government.[27]

In a letter to Soviet party leader Brezhnev, Miki again rejected the former's proposal, rejected in Moscow four weeks earlier by Foreign Minister Miyazawa, and simultaneously emphasised the necessity of concluding a peace treaty.[28] Despite the firm rejection of the Soviet proposals, it must be stressed that the Moscow's reaction to the anti-hegemony clause caused the Japanese to hesitate further over capitulating all too swiftly to Chinese insistence. Tokyo did not yet dare accept a sustained deterioration in relations with Moscow as the price for unilaterally good relations with Peking.

There was another reason for Japan's hesitation. At that time Tokyo was unclear about the political intentions which China was attaching to the establishment of the anti-hegemony clause. Speculation arose as to whether perhaps one day the clause could be interpreted against the United States just as readily as against Japan and its economic influence in South-East Asia. In the Chinese use of the word, 'hegemony' was synonymous with 'the policies of the Soviet Union'. Since, however, the Chinese Communists referred to the striving of both superpowers for hegemony, Japan's doubts were fully justified.

The Soviets could have let the interpretation rest, but committed the error of assuming that the anti-hegemony clause referred to them, although it was not specifically directed at any country. Their outraged reaction and their crude attempts at intervention over the inclusion of the clause in the Sino-Japanese treaty only seemed to bear out China's accusation.

At the end of 1977 the Soviet Ambassador to Japan, Polyanski, attempted to whip up an atmosphere of criticism of the treaty with China among members of the ruling LDP. With this intention he met around twenty LDP representatives, chiefly of a pro-Soviet tendency, for individual talks. He also gave lectures in provincial areas. His primary aim was to strengthen the gradually dwindling group of politicians calling for the exercise of caution over the treaty.[29] At the same time Radio Moscow warned, 'If Japan accepts an anti-hegemonism clause proposed

27. See *International Herald Tribune*, 12 Feb. 1975.
28. See *SWB/FE/4890*, 29 April 1975.
29. See *Japan Times*, 15 Dec. 1977.

by China, like it or not, Japan will be turned into an enemy of a third nation against which the clause is directed.'[30] The Soviet press had a predilection for quoting Japanese comments warning against involvement in China's anti-Soviet policies;[31] countless Soviet publications expressed the view that the Sino-Japanese treaty would run counter to both Japan's national interests and to peace and detente in the Far East.[32] China practised less and less self-restraint in its distorted interpretation of the anti-hegemony clause; as early as mid-1975, Deputy Prime Minister Deng Xiaoping had declared to Japanese journalists that the clause directed against attempts at hegemony by outside states which was to be included in a future treaty of peace and friendship was primarily aimed at the Soviet Union.[33] The Japanese government was gradually pressurised into making the difficult decision either to sign a treaty with an anti-Soviet bias or to risk the deterioration of relations with China.

For China, a treaty was only acceptable if it included the anti-hegemony clause in the form agreed in 1972; all Japan's attempts to conclude the treaty without this clause, or at least to tone it down, foundered against Chinese intransigence. However, the area to which the rejection of hegemonistic aims was applied was no longer confined to the Asia Pacific area, but was extended to include any region. Peking eliminated Japanese doubts over another issue, namely the treaty of friendship and alliance signed by China and the Soviet Union in 1950, which was to run for thirty years. The treaty, which was massively biased against Japan, had long since reverted to a meaningless scrap of paper in the face of the Sino-Soviet rift, but was nonetheless still legally valid. Tokyo demanded that China distance itself from the treaty. The Chinese agreed they would under no circumstances revive the treaty with Moscow;[34] in fact, the Chinese leaders had already informed their Soviet counterparts a year before the treaty expired that they did not wish to extend it.

30. Radio Moscow, 24 Nov. 1977, quoted in *Japan Times*, 15 Dec. 1977.
31. See *Pravda*, 15 Dec. 1977; 7 Jan., 19 Jan., 25 Feb. and 20 March 1978.
32. *Ibid.*, 6 April 1978.
33. See *SWB/FE/4962*, 23 July 1975.
34. See *Yomiuri* (evening edn.), 17 Nov. 1977, in *DSJP*, 23–25 Nov. 1977, p. 9.

Offers of Competing Treaties

In the late summer of 1978, the climate which had developed between Japan, China and the Soviet Union combined with some incidents of hair-raising diplomatic clumsiness on the part of the Japanese to create a situation in which the Tokyo government had no choice but to sign the treaty. Soviet attempts to hinder or devalue the signing of the treaty failed owing to Moscow's complete lack of flexibility on the territorial question, even to the extent of issuing threats; at the end of November 1977 a commentary stated, 'In the event that a Japan-China treaty is concluded, the Soviet Union will take retaliatory measures against Japan.'[35] A more specific statement followed a few days later: 'In the event that the treaty is signed in a form including the hegemony clause, the Soviet Union will ban Japanese fishing boats' operations within the 200-nautical-mile exclusive fishing zones of the Soviet Union.'[36] This was the first threat of concrete reprisals.

In the Cabinet reshuffle of December 1977 Prime Minister Fukuda appointed Sunao Sonoda, a firm supporter of the treaty with China, to the post of Foreign Minister. Moscow invited the new head of the Foreign Ministry to take part in the long-overdue Soviet-Japanese ministerial consultations. Sonoda's predecessor, Iichiro Hatoyama, a colourless politician, had never received an invitation to Moscow despite all his attempts to restart the consultations.[37] The Soviet interest in re-establishing contact at Foreign Minister level can probably be attributed to the fact that the Sino-Japanese treaty negotiations were entering their final phase.

For Soviet-Japanese relations, then, 1978 began with the fifth consultational meeting of the two Foreign Ministers, which was to shape the political climate between the two countries for a considerable time to come. As far as concrete results were concerned, Sonoda's visit to Moscow was not a success. Japan's Foreign Minister had made it his aim to persuade the Soviet participants to reaffirm the formulation agreed with Prime Min-

35. *Pravda*, 26 Nov. 1977; *Asahi*, 27 Nov. 1977, in *DSJP*, 1 Dec. 1977, p. 3.
36. *Tokyo Shimbun* (evening edn.), 1 Dec. 1977, in *DSJP*, 8 Dec. 1977, p. 7.
37. The Soviet side explained this as resulting from difficulties in Gromyko's appointment planning; see *Japan Times*, 15 Dec. 1977.

ister Tanaka in 1973, that before the conclusion of a peace treaty 'certain questions open since the end of the Second World War' should be settled. This was understood by Japan to refer chiefly to the territorial question.[38]

Sonoda did not achieve his aim. Foreign Minister Gromyko, who described the overall state of relations between the two countries as stable, stressed the regularity of their political contact – although two years had passed since the last Foreign Ministers' meeting – and praised the development of mutual trade and economic relations. He also appealed, with hints at the territorial question, for existing problems to be evaluated from the standpoint of political realism which would take both sets of interests into consideration. For the Soviet Foreign Minister, political realists were those who could recognise common elements in the viewpoints of both sides and who did not permit 'considerations of a temporary nature' – probably a reference to Japan's *rapprochement* to China – to distract from the decisive trend of Soviet-Japanese relations.[39] A 'realistic' viewpoint meant finally dropping the claim to the northern islands and acceding to Soviet demands.

Gromyko attempted to entice Japan into cooperation over policies of détente by hinting at the treaties of friendship his country had concluded with India and other Asian nations. The circle of Asian governments maintaining 'friendly and lasting' relations with the Soviet Union was to be expanded; this, he said, was one of the essential (*neot'emlemyi*) elements of security and cooperation on the continent of Asia.[40] In other words, Japan was to contribute towards the realisation of Soviet plans for collective security in the region. The Soviets presented Foreign Minister Sonoda with the draft of a treaty of good neighbourliness and cooperation, with which they hoped to achieve two aims: first, the indefinite deferral of Japan's claim to the islands under discussion, and secondly, the preemption of a possible Sino-Japanese treaty of peace and friendship by producing an equivalent document, thus neutralising the former.

The Soviet Union did not come close to achieving either

38. *Pravda*, 11 Oct. 1973.
39. *Ibid.*, 10 Jan. 1978.
40. *Ibid.*

Offers of Competing Treaties

aim. After some resistance Sonoda took the Soviet treaty draft, but refused to study it, insisting that a peace treaty between Japan and the Soviet Union – which Japan also desired – had to be preceded by the settlement of the territorial problem, and that this condition could not be circumvented by an interim solution as envisaged in the draft he had been given.[41] The Japanese stance, which had remained unchanged for years, was rejected by the Soviet Union with equal inflexibility; in that country's view Tokyo's territorial demands were groundless and unacceptable, for there was no unsettled territorial problem with Japan.[42] The irreconcilability of the two viewpoints meant that Sonoda's visit ended without a joint communiqué; he even returned to Tokyo a day earlier than planned. The only concrete result of the consultations was the extension of the bilateral cultural agreement, which ran for a period of two years. The Japanese Foreign Minister had incidentally left no doubt that the treaty would shortly be concluded with Peking.

Since Moscow's leaders were not prepared, even by the merest hint of willingness to negotiate, to show flexibility on the territorial question to which Japan attached such importance, the Tokyo government decided after the Foreign Minister's return to resume talks with China over the planned treaty.[43] This decision encapsulated the political significance of Sonoda's Moscow talks for Japan's foreign policies: Prime Minister Fukuda had recognised that the time was ripe for the continuation of treaty discussions with China. Moscow's intransigence had smoothed a path in national politics for his decision.

Disregarding this, the Soviet Union continued its attempts to win Japan's acquiescence to an improvement in political relations according to the Soviet understanding of the idea. On 22 February 1978 Ambassador Polyanski presented Prime Minister Fukuda with a letter from Brezhnev proposing once again the conclusion of a treaty of good neighbourliness and cooperation and inviting Fukuda to visit Moscow.

Fukuda answered that since Prime Minister Tanaka had visited

---

41. See *Asahi Evening News*, 10 Jan. 1978.
42. *New Times*, no. 4 (Jan. 1978) and no. 8 (Feb. 1978), p. 8.
43. *Asahi Evening News*, 12 Jan. 1978; *Mainichi* (evening edn.), 10 Aug. 1978, in *DSJP*, 17 Aug. 1978, p. 11.

Moscow in 1973, it was the Soviet leader's turn to visit Tokyo. He emphasised again that friendly relations between both countries were dependent on the territorial question and that Japan would not conclude a treaty of neighbourliness and cooperation with the Soviet Union before this problem was solved.[44] Two days after the letter from Brezhnev had been handed over, the Soviet government took an unaccustomed step by publishing, without consulting the other side, the draft of the treaty it had proposed.[45]

The draft consisted of a Preamble and 14 Articles.[46] The intentions of the Soviet Union's policies on Japan may chiefly be gleaned from Articles 3, 5, 12 and 13. In Article 3, Japan is forbidden to allow its territory to be used for activities which could prejudice the security of the Soviet Union. Acceptance of such a prohibition would mean the end of the American-Japanese security alliance, under the terms of which the United States is permitted to maintain military bases on Japanese territory. Article 5 contains an obligation to participate in consultations in the event of a threat to world peace and security; with this article Japan would basically accept the Soviet proposal to found a system of collective security in Asia. Article 12 is the Soviet version of the anti-hegemony clause taken over from the Chinese; it reads: 'The Union of Soviet Socialist Republics and Japan do not claim and do not recognise anyone's claims to any special rights or advantages in world affairs, including claims to domination [*dominirovanie*] in Asia and in the area of the Far East.' According to Article 13, the treaty is not directed against any third country.[47]

If Moscow had intended by its unusual action to use public opinion to pressurise the Tokyo government to evaluate the treaty more positively, it had reckoned wrongly. The majority of Japanese supported their government's policy in this respect; in surveys of public opinion examining the reasons for the poor state of Japanese-Soviet relations, 54% of those questioned in

44. See *Mainichi Daily News*, 23 Feb. 1978.
45. See *Izvestiya*, 24 Feb. 1978, English version in *Japan Times*, 25 Feb. 1978.
46. See Appendix B.
47. See *Izvestiya*, 24 Feb. 1978.

1978, and 68% in 1979, gave as the primary reason the Soviet Union's refusal to settle the territorial problem.[48] The obvious aim of slowing down Sino-Japanese negotiations by publishing the draft also failed. The reaction of the Japanese public to the Soviets' action clearly showed that the Kremlin's action had achieved the opposite of what it had presumably intended.

The Soviet press either completely ignored or made only oblique allusions to the Japanese government's refusal even to discuss the draft and to the unanimously negative reaction of the Japanese media, excluding left-wing socialist and Communist-influenced organs. The official Soviet government organ accused 'influential circles' in Japan of twisting the Soviet Union's honourable intentions and falsifying the contents of the draft by insinuating that the Soviet Union wanted to take away Japan's independence, cut Japan off from the United States and China and turn it into a Soviet satellite.[49]

Despite an incident on Senkaku or Diaoyütai, islands claimed equally by both Japan and China, the Japanese government resumed treaty negotiations with China at the end of May 1978 after a temporary break.[50] Upon this the Soviet government sent word via their Ambassador in Tokyo that the Soviet Union 'cannot remain a spectator in a question which could involve its own interests'.[51] Should the anti-hegemony clause be included in the treaty, the Soviet Union threatened 'to draw the necessary conclusions and to make any alterations necessary in its own politics with reference to relations with Japan'.[52] The Japanese government replied that the treaty with China was not directed against any third party, that Japan alone decided its foreign policy

48. See *Yoron chôsa*, no. 12 (Dec. 1979), p. 13.
49. See *Izvestiya*, 7 March 1978.
50. On 12 April 1978 Chinese fishing vessels had gathered near the group of islands to call attention to China's claim. Their banners proclaimed: 'Diaoyütai is a part of Chinese territorial waters!' The government in Tokyo and the Japanese public were displeased; the Soviet press spoke of a Sino-Japanese conflict and claimed the incident was proof of a Maoist foreign policy allegedly characterised by border provocations and territorial claims; see *Pravda*, 17 and 20 April 1978.
51. Kyodo, 19 June 1978, German text quoted in *MD Asien*, 20 June 1978, p. 7.
52. *Ibid.*

and that concluding the treaty would not lead to any coordination of the signatories' foreign policy.[53]

The Soviet Union believed Fukuda's decision to resume negotiations was made under pressure from both China and the United States.[54] In fact, Washington was interested in further *rapprochement* between China and Japan, and emphatically supported the conclusion of a treaty.[55] Private sources yielded the information that the US President's Security Adviser, Brzezinski, who visited Tokyo at the end of May on his way home from Peking, had discussed the question of the treaty with Japan's leading politicians and reaffirmed the US government's positive attitude to the plan. A Japanese government would hardly have overruled the will of the United States to initiate negotiations, let alone to sign the treaty.

The Soviet Union continued its campaign against the proposed treaty throughout the entire negotiating period, focusing its warnings on China's allegedly hegemonistic intentions and its tireless efforts to involve Japan in its 'peace-endangering plans'. The Soviet Prime Minister also joined in with advice to Japan to exercise 'extreme caution' in negotiations with China. In talks with a delegation from the Association of Japanese Newspaper Publishers, Kosygin claimed that the approval some Japanese newspapers expressed for a treaty with China was support for a policy of war against the Soviet Union, since China, convinced that war with the Soviet Union was unavoidable, was preparing for war.[56]

These warnings, together with the threats of deterioration in Soviet-Japanese relations and the announcement of specific retaliations, eventually made it easier for the political leaders in Tokyo to conclude the treaty including the anti-hegemony clause; for it was not the case that a significant majority of the population unreservedly supported the treaty with China. Foreign Minister Sonoda spoke of 'only 20 to 30%', and claimed

53. *Mainichi Daily News*, 22 June 1978.
54. See *Pravda*, 26 May 1978.
55. The conclusion of the treaty was, according to information from Foreign Minister Sonoda, also the subject of a conversation between Prime Minister Fukuda and President Carter in May 1978; see *Mainichi* (evening edn.), 10 Aug. 1978, in *DSJP*, 17 Aug. 1978, p. 11.
56. Kyodo, German text quoted in *MD Asien*, 2 June 1978, p. 3.

that the great majority were in favour of 'a cautious approach'.[57] Moscow's actions, however, wounded Japanese pride, a reaction typified by a Japanese commentary on the actions announced by the Soviet Union, the last sentence of which ran: 'However, even if such measures are taken, it will be impossible for Japan to bow its head from its side [and give in].'[58]

The effects of a second phenomenon, of a psychological nature which, typically, had been hinted at by two of Japan's leading politicians, should not be discounted; this was Japan's differing perceptions of its two Communist neighbours. The Japanese people naturally felt close links with China, said Foreign Minister Miyazawa, but they were not able to experience such feelings for the other country (in other words, the Soviet Union).[59] Some years later, Foreign Minister Sonoda made a similar comment: 'When China and the Soviet Union are compared, the Japanese people somehow feel an attachment and nostalgia for China.'[60]

The treaty was signed in Peking on 12 August; however, no immediate announcement of political counter-measures came from the Soviet Union. A 'wait and see' attitude took over from the previous intermittent threats. 'The future will show whether Japan will succeed in following an independent course in foreign policy', was the comment appearing in identical articles in the official government and party newspapers the day after the treaty had been signed.[61] Japan's politicians, it was said, would prove, not by their words but by their concrete actions, whether Tokyo had the foresight to avoid involvement in Peking's dangerous policies.[62] These views demonstrated that the Soviet leaders did not overestimate the treaty's political significance and that they had not overlooked the disquiet with which Japan's political leaders and general public had received the treaty.

For some time Soviet commentaries continued to express negative attitudes towards the treaty, criticisms of the anti-Soviet aims China had allegedly pursued in the treaty, and doubts over

57. *Mainichi* (evening edn.), 10 Aug. 1978, in *DSJP*, 17 Aug. 1978, p. 11.
58. *Asahi*, 27 Nov. 1977, in *DSJP*, 1 Dec. 1977, p. 3.
59. See *Asahi*, 18 Sept. 1975, in *DSJP*, 20–2 Sept. 1975, p. 13.
60. *Mainichi* (evening edn.), 10 Aug. 1978, in *DSJP*, 17 Aug. 1978, p. 11.
61. *Izvestiya* and *Pravda*, 13 Aug. 1978.
62. See *New Times*, no. 45 (Nov. 1978), p. 3.

Japan's ability to resist Chinese pressure and attempts to win support. Moscow dealt at length with the criticisms from Japan's Communist Party, whose general secretary, Kenji Miyamoto, had described the treaty as proof of the aim of hegemony and had stated that Sino-Japanese *rapprochement* was a *rapprochement* based on the Japanese-American military alliance,[63] views which echoed the Soviets' opinion. However, the CPJ had not gone so far as to reject the treaty upon its ratification in Parliament, simply modifying its assent by adding riders directed against the 'hegemonial and great power policies of Peking's leaders' and their attempts 'to draw Japan into an anti-Soviet alliance'.[64]

Later Soviet analyses of the treaty and the history of its development took a different approach. Criticism of China's role was proportionally reduced as Sino-Soviet relations improved.

In 1980 the Soviet Union still faced the power grouping of the United States-China-Japan. Relations within this grouping were said to be based on anti-Soviet efforts to counteract any further surge of development in favour of socialism within the international balance of power.[65] Of the trio, China's attitude was alleged to be one of cunningly calculated hostility towards socialism; Peking was said to have plunged into the military venture planned in Vietnam only after reinforcing its position by means of the treaty of friendship with Japan and the establishment of diplomatic relations with the United States. During *rapprochement* with Japan and the Americans, it was said, Peking had increased its attacks on the treaty of friendship and support with the Soviet Union, finally dissolving the treaty on 3 April 1979.[66] The Maoists had attempted to bring about a deterioration in Soviet-Japanese relations, but the leaders of the United States and Japan had not been prepared to allow themselves to be drawn into conflicts directed against their own interests and intentions.[67]

At this point, then, China was still allotted the role of the

63. See *Pravda*, 18 Sept. 1978.
64. *Ibid.*, 20 Oct. 1978.
65. See V.M. Mazurov, *SSA–Kitaj–Japonija:* perestrojka mežgosudarstvennych otnošenij, 1969–1979 (The USA–China–Japan: Restructuring International Relations), Moscow 1980, p. 183.
66. *Ibid.*, p. 184.
67. *Ibid.*, p. 190.

influential trouble-maker. Just two years later a different picture could be seen: the role played by Japan and the United States in the development of the treaty was alleged to have been far more active, while China's role was treated with surprising lenience and objectivity. This shift led to an analysis of the situation[68] which if anything over-valued Japan's degree of independence in this process and ignored the sophisticated manoeuvrings of China's anti-Soviet movement. Statements made by Deng[69] can prove the claim that China had replaced the firm demand for a united front against hegemonism by propositions compatible with Japan's position and that this flexibility had paved the way for the signing of the treaty of peace and friendship; however, this is only half the truth, for the same period saw an equal number of appeals to form just such a united front. Chinese politicians declared one thing one day and another the next, depending on whom they were talking to and on their own interests, but always referring to their 'principles'; the truth of the matter is more likely to be that dealings with Tokyo demonstrated flexibility without there being any alteration in China's actual attitude to the treaty.

Kunadze, the diplomat and expert on Japan, saw American pressure on Japan as an important factor in the treaty's development and believed that for the USA the treaty had become part of a strategy in the conflict with the Soviet Union.[70] As proof of this he cited 'the decisive role of the USA in Sino-Japanese *rapprochement*, the meetings of Prime Minister Fukuda and President Carter in May 1978, the assurance by the latter that the anti-hegemony clause engendered no US doubts in the concerning Japan, and Brzezinski's visit to Tokyo on his return from Peking the same month.[71]

It is correct to say that an early conclusion of the treaty was in accordance with American interests, and it can be assumed that Washington informed its Japanese allies of this. However, there is no reference as to whether Washington went so far as to exert pressure in this matter.

68. See G.F. Kunadze, *Japono-kitajskie otnošenija na sovremennom etape, 1972–1982* (Japanese-Chinese Relations of the Present Day), Moscow 1983.
69. *Ibid.*, p. 81.
70. *Ibid.*, pp. 81 and 167.
71. *Ibid.*, p. 87.

Kunadze's analysis of the treaty itself is enlightening as an example of the modified Soviet viewpoint on the role of China. On the one hand, the alteration to the anti-hegemony clause desired by Japan, in which the field of application was extended beyond the Asia Pacific region, was interpreted as a certain concession to conditions stipulated by Foreign Minister Miyazawa in September 1975. On the other hand, according to Kunadze, this extension exactly corresponded to the US government's plans, the intention of which had been to suggest China's inclusion not only in US anti-Soviet policies concerning the Far East, but also those applying far outside the region.[72]

As a result, the United States – or indeed, as other conclusions drawn by the Soviet observer show, Japan – had taken over from China as the source of anti-Soviet policies. Kunadze concluded from Foreign Minister Sonoda's statement that the Soviet Union occasionally committed hegemonistic acts, that Japan reserved the right to accuse it of hegemonism when appropriate. He evolved tortuous arguments in attempts to prove that Article 2 (the anti-hegemony clause) and Article 4 (dealing with the signatories' relations to third states) were no more than an 'instrument of Japanese pressure on the Soviet Union'.[73] Kunadze no longer employed the justified Soviet accusation, produced frequently both before and immediately after the signing of the treaty, that China was attempting to draw Japan into its anti-Soviet policies by means of the treaty of peace and friendship; instead he described the United States, and in its wake Japan, as protagonists who were using China as an instrument in their anti-Soviet policies – a complete inversion of the picture given by Mazurov in 1980.

This reinterpretation was caused by changes in Sino-Soviet relations. After 1982 Soviet efforts at creating détente with their Chinese neighbours once more met with a positive reaction; both sides subsequently called a halt to all unnecessary criticism of their counterparts. Mazurov's analysis was released for publication in April 1980 – that is, before this Sino-Soviet détente – while Kunadze's was retained until August 1983, after the resumption of Sino-Soviet consultations at Foreign Ministry

72. *Ibid.*, p. 90.
73. *Ibid.*, p. 92.

level. Considerate treatment of the Soviet Union's Chinese negotiating partner was the order of the day. It has already been shown that Chinese publicists' treatment of Japan and its problems with the Soviet Union underwent a similar development. Soviet accounts published from the late 1980s onwards either cite the negative effects of the Sino-Japanese treaty on relations between Tokyo and Moscow, or simply ignore the whole episode.[74]

Japan's Armed Forces and the Sino-Soviet Conflict

A third factor drawing Japan into the conflict between China and the Soviet Union can be added to the territorial question and the Sino-Soviet jockeying over treaties. This was China's clear attempt to build closer contacts with the Japanese armed forces, including Peking's interest in Japanese military technology and its encouragement of Tokyo to make greater defence efforts.

This was another tactical move on China's part, aimed at further increasing the already high degree of tension in relations between Japan and the Soviet Union, an aim confirmed by subsequent actions. From the end of 1982, as soon as Peking and Moscow began to reach agreements on improving their relations, China's provocatively ostentatious interest in military cooperation with Japan soon dwindled. In the same way, the Soviet Union's criticisms, occasionally bordering on the hysterical, of China's alleged collaboration with 'Japanese militarism' were shifted to accusations that Japan was using the issue of military cooperation in attempts to mobilise China against the Soviet Union. Thus, from the middle of the 1970s to the beginning of the 1980s Japan was basically no more than a pawn in the Sino-Soviet conflict. What was going on?

At first the Soviets' suspicions were directed at the invitations issued by China to Japanese military officials. Hisao Iwashima, director of the First Research Department for Military History of the National Defence College in Tokyo, visited the People's

74. Avtorskij kollektiv (Authors' Collective), *SSSR i Japonija* (The USSR and Japan), Moscow 1987, p. 366; L.N. Kutakov, *Moskva-Tokio, Očerki diplomatičeskich otnošenij 1956–1986* (Moscow–Tokyo, Summary of Diplomatic Relations), Moscow 1988.

Republic of China on 15–18 April 1977. This was the first visit to China by a member of this institute, which was under the jurisdiction of the Defence Agency. Unlike all previous Japanese visitors, Iwashima was permitted to inspect a Chinese military unit, the 124th Infantery Division in Guangzhou, and to film them during exercises. At that time, visitors whom China considered important were taken to inspect this unit. Iwashima was received by Chen Xiliang, the deputy chairman of the State Council and commander of the Peking military district, and he met the chairman of the Association for Sino-Japanese Friendship, Liao Chengzhi, and its secretary-general, Sun Pinghua, for talks.

Iwashima had been informed before his departure of the topics his Chinese hosts were interested in discussing. Themes concerning the Soviet Union included the following:

- the most urgent problems of Soviet society;
- conflicts within the Soviet leadership;
- problems of national minorities;
- Soviet military strategy and doctrine; and
- strategies concerning Asia.

On international topics, the Chinese wanted to find out whether there had been any recent developments in the rivalry between the United States and the Soviet Union, how high the likelihood was of a Third World War and how the international situation would develop in the 1980s. With regard to Japan, Iwashima was to give information about the actual strength of its national defence forces, the present and future export possibilities for Japanese weapons and Japan's reaction to the MiG-25 incident, involving the escape of a Soviet pilot to Hokkaido in September 1976.

The Chinese explained to their guest that it was only natural that Japan should maintain military forces for purposes of self-defence (SDF), and that China would not protest as long as their build-up did not assume an aggressive character. While China rejected US imperialism, they continued, in view of the current international situation Peking had complete understanding for the view that the Japanese-American security treaty was the basis of relations with the United States; in Asia the United States was the chief opponent of the Soviet Union, followed by Japan and

China. They concluded that even given one's own desire for peace, one could never be sure of one's opponent, and that warnings about the Soviet Union were not to be taken lightly.[75]

The Soviet Union allowed itself to be goaded into reacting to such provocations. Iwashima's visit to China was accorded such a degree of significance that the editors of the yearbook *Japonija* devoted not only an article to the event, but also an entry in the chronicle of the year's events in Japanese foreign relations.[76]

Iwashima's visit to China was not the only one of its kind. China issued invitations to a whole string of retired Japanese army officers, who were always given a high-profile reception. Until the autumn of 1978 – that is in the eighteen months after the first visit – the Soviet government newspaper reported on the visits of twelve Japanese military delegations, whose members included Osamu Kaihara, the former secretary-general of the Defence Agency, H. Miyoshi, the former Chief of Staff of the Territorial Army, and Nagai, the former Vice-Admiral of the Navy.

The Soviet Union reacted to China's diplomacy of invitations with scathing commentaries, seeing in it the beginnings of a military cooperation between Japan and China which had anti-Soviet aims. Chinese statements along these lines also strengthened this impression; thus Deng Xiaoping informed a former divisional commander of the Japanese Army, K. Matsuoka, that China would be buying new weapons and technology abroad, including from Japan, to modernise its army.[77] Soviet commentators noted critically that the military potential of the Soviet Union was among the themes discussed by Chinese and Japanese military.[78]

The Japanese periodical *Toyokeizai* was among those that published reports, difficult to verify here, that China was obtaining spare parts for arms as well as military technology. This information gave the Soviet press the idea that Peking was attempting to gain access to the newest Japanese military tech-

75. Interview with Prof. Hisao Iwashima conducted by the author.
76. See Akademija Nauk SSSR, *Japonija 1978, Ežegodnik*, pp. 88 and 317.
77. Ibid., p. 88.
78. Ibid.

nology.[79] In corroboration of this premise, Soviet commentaries referred to the brisk business contacts of Japanese companies in China. The agreement between Deng Xiaoping and Konosuke Matsushita, head of National, Japan's largest electronics firm, over the foundation of a joint venture in Peking was interpreted by a Soviet commentator as preferential treatment for 'Peking's military expansion'.[80]

Japan's Prime Minister Ohira had refused to supply armaments to China; however, it was noted that there was a growing exchange of military information and cooperation in areas of technology where civil and military applications could no longer be separated. The Soviet Union diligently registered all Sino-Japanese activities in this field, evaluating and documenting their apparent significance. Thus it was noted critically that the first Chinese visitor to Japan after the signing of the treaty of peace and friendship had been the Deputy General Chief of Staff of the People's Liberation Army, Zhang Caitian, allegedly invited on the recommendation of the Foreign Ministry in Tokyo.[81]

Chinese statements evaluating the Japanese-American alliance in a positive light and encouraging Tokyo's politicians to make significant increases to Japan's defence efforts[82] were soon followed by more concrete desires. For example, in 1980 Prime Minister Hua Guofeng proposed to Nakasone that the Japanese Air Force should be expanded to protect shipping routes, while Deputy General Chief of Staff Wu Xiuquan recommended raising the proportion of GNP allotted to defence from the traditional 1% to 2%.[83]

79. See *Izvestiya*, 25 Oct. 1978; *Pravda*, 6 Dec. 1979.
80. See *Izvestiya*, 2 Sept. 1979.
81. *Ibid.*, 25 Oct. 1978.
82. In 1973 the chairman of the Sino-Japanese Friendship Society was still saying that China could not support the Japanese-American security treaty, and he continued, 'We shall not, however, regard this system with enmity, because it has already been nullified in practice as a system directed against China' (*Tokyo Shimbun* [evening edn.], 2 Aug. 1973, in *DSJP*, 3 Aug. 1973, p. 24). Some years later, Deng Xiaoping expressed rather different views: 'I support the strengthening of Japan's defence power. I also support the improvement of relations with the US. [For Japan] Japan–US relations are important above all' (*Mainichi*, 15 Sept. 1977, in *DSJP*, 22–26 Sept. 1977, p. 17).
83. See *Mainichi*, 1 May 1980, in *DSJP*, 3–6 May 1980, p. 16. When

For years Moscow over-dramatised cautious increases in Japanese military potential, issuing exaggerated commentaries on the subject. However, it was none other than the Soviet Union which, by expanding its Pacific fleet and demonstrating its military presence off Japan's coasts and in Japanese air space, had significantly contributed to the lowering of national political opposition to the expansion of Japanese defence capacity. Chinese encouragement was not necessary to fuel this feeling, but it fitted the Soviets' image of the resurrection of Japanese militarism to dwell on it.

Soviet commentaries on the visit of Prime Minister Hua Guofeng to Japan at the end of May 1980 also expressed suspicions that there was increased Sino-Japanese cooperation on military and technological matters. At the start of the visit, the Soviet party organ published an article under the headline 'Japanese militarism raises its ugly head', in which the increase in Japanese military potential desired by the Americans was discussed and linked with the claim that Hua's visit to Japan served not least to 'encourage the country's mood of militarism' and to give support to a doubling of the defence budget which would transform the country into a military power – another commentary even spoke of a 'military superpower'.[84]

The government newspaper propagated the view that the actual aim of Hua's visit was to persuade Japan's leaders to agree to 'broadly based military cooperation with China', to obtain from Japan 'the maximum solidarity with China's implementation of its own aggressive anti-Soviet policies' and to convince Japan and the United States to initiate 'more active trilateral military and political cooperation' through the exertion of diplomatic pressure.[85]

In the years that followed, Sino-Japanese contacts at military level were intensified at China's instigation, while Moscow concentrated its criticism on Japan in the interests of the con-

---

Japan did actually raise the 1% limit slightly, Deng Xiaoping reacted with unmistakable concern. The Chinese party newspaper followed with a critical commentary warning of a Japan which was a military power (*Renmin-ribao*, 11 Feb. 1987). See also on this problem *Asahi* (evening edn.), 13 Jan. 1987, in *DSJP*, 22 Jan. 1987. p. 8.

84. *Pravda*, 28 May 1980; *Izvestiya*, 31 May 1980.
85. *Izvestiya*, 27 May 1980.

tinuing détente between the Soviet Union and China. At the end of 1984 Minister of Defence Zhang Aiping visited Japan. The return visit of Defence Minister Kurihara took place from 29 May to 4 June 1987 and, according to Japanese reports, appears to have been successful, although at that time the Chinese had begun to express concern over a revival of Japanese militarism, and other problems were also overshadowing relations between the two countries. Kurihara, who was the first head of defence to visit China, explained at a Peking press conference that while his Chinese counterpart had made no reference to the defence budget increase over the limit of 1% of GNP, he had spoken positively of the security treaty with the United States.[86]

The Soviet Union saw the Japanese Defence Minister's visit to China in a rather less favourable light; Kurihara had been 'heavily criticised' by the Chinese for exceeding the 1% limit and had spent much of his time in Peking apologising for this.[87] In one and the same report Japan is portrayed as dangerous and negative, yet no blame is even obliquely attached to China for inviting such a sinister guest; this exactly fits the pattern of Soviet attitudes to Sino-Japanese defence contacts which applied from the beginning of the 1980s, while since that time open criticism of China's policies on Japan has vanished. 'Japan's rulers evidently hoped that by organising so many visits [of the Japanese military] they would sound out the prevalent political views of the People's Liberation Army', wrote a Soviet observer in 1982.[88]

During the visit of the Chinese Minister of Defence, the Soviet party newspaper had confined itself to giving brief information formulated to create the impression that Japan was attempting to form closer defence contacts. After Zhang Aiping's visit to Tokyo while returning from an initial visit to the United States, it also emphasised the Pentagon's interest in a 'consolidation of military and political links between the USA, Japan and China'.[89]

Although the Chinese leaders issued statements criticising the Soviets, criticism of the People's Republic was kept to a mini-

86. See *Nihon Keizai*, 30 May 1987, in *DSJP*, 4 June 1987, p. 12; *Asahi*, 31 May 1987, p. 13.
87. *New Times*, no. 24, 22 June 1987, p. 7.
88. Kunadze, *Japono-kitajskie otnošenija*, p. 74.
89. See *Pravda*, 10 July 1984.

mum in Soviet reactions to Prime Minister Nakasone's visit to China in March 1984. Japan was again the target of Soviet attack, accused of wanting to draw China into its military and strategic alliance with the USA, of laying the foundations for China's gradual integration into Western economic structures and of obstructing the normalisation of Sino-Soviet relations.[90] In fact, Japan sought to avoid any provocation of the Soviets, behaving with demonstrative caution over the expansion of its military contacts with China.

What were the motives behind the Soviets' actions? Moscow had been concerned about developments in Eastern and North-Eastern Asia since the beginning of the 1970s. As détente and cooperation grew between China on the one hand and the United States and Japan on the other, America, China and Japan found themselves on the same side for the first time in modern East Asian history. The smallest point they had in common amidst their otherwise differing interests was the restriction of Soviet influence in the Asia Pacific region. This national grouping had drastically reduced the Soviet Union's chances of extending its influence in East Asia; and the core of its Asian policies – the initiative of founding a system of collective security – stood not the slightest chance of winning Moscow that influence.

Instead, the Soviet Union, confronted by accusations of hegemony, feared that the combined support of the United States, Japan and the Western European industrialised nations for China's modernisation policies could considerably strengthen Peking's economic and military potential over the coming decades. The Soviet Union's prime intention was to influence this development in its own favour.

Under Brezhnev, the Soviet leaders had realised that any improvement in the USSR's position in Eastern Asia would not be achieved through confrontation with China, but by normalising relations with this influential neighbour. This was an insight that Gorbachev, despite being forced into making considerable concessions, was later to translate into practical politics.

Japan only played a role in these considerations as long as the Soviet leaders were interested in preventing not only the development of close cooperation, including military cooperation,

---

90. *Ibid.*, 29 March 1984.

between Tokyo and Peking, but also any qualitative and quantitative expansion of Japanese military forces that was backed by both the United States and China.

As already described, under Brezhnev's rule the Soviet Union had used propaganda, diplomatic influence, thinly veiled threats and offers of a competing treaty of friendship in its attempts to disrupt Japan's *rapprochement* with China. The KGB's activities had the same goal. The Soviet Secret Service's operations in Japan were known from statements of the former KGB Major Stanislav A. Levchenko, made in July 1982 before a Congress Committee in Washington (the House Permanent Select Committee on Intelligence).[91] Levchenko claimed to have spent four years after 1975 in Japan as correspondent of the Soviet weekly *Novoe Vremya* (New Times), until in October 1979 he applied for political asylum at the US Embassy in Tokyo, whereupon he was taken to the United States the same day. Levchenko's occupation as a journalist served solely to conceal his real tasks: espionage and disinformation. He held the rank of Major in the Active Operations Division of the KGB. According to his statements, the KGB in Japan consisted of two groups, one concerned with counter-espionage and the other larger group with the collection of classified information on science and technology. Approximately fifty or sixty members of Soviet intelligence, many disguised as journalists, some in industry, worked in the Tokyo region. Around half the staff of the Aeroflot office in Tokyo, for example, had been KGB members working chiefly in the areas of science and technology.[92] At the time of Levchenko's operations in Japan the KGB had maintained a network of 200 recruited agents. In his own words:

> Among the most efficient agents were a former member of the Japanese government, several leading functionaries of the Socialist Party of Japan, one of the most eminent Sinologists

---

91. The Japanese government was not informed of Levchenko's statement until the end of 1982. The unconvincing reason given at the time for the delay was that Washington had wanted to counteract an impending improvement in relations between Japan and the Soviet Union by revealing the KGB's activities in Japan. See *Asahi Evening News*, 11 Feb. 1982.

92. See *Mainichi*, 2 Dec. 1982, in *DSJP*, 10 Dec. 1982, p. 9, and 10 Dec. 1982, p. 11; *Asahi*, 11 Dec. 1982.

with close contacts with government officers, and several members of the Japanese Parliament.[93]

The former member of the Cabinet was identified as the former Minister for Employment, Hirohide Ishida. As a piquant twist, Ishida was also the chairman of the Parliamentary League for Japanese-Soviet Friendship, which was said to have received financial support from the Soviet Union through his offices.[94] One of Levchenko's tasks was to disrupt Sino-Japanese *rapprochement*. According to his confession, the text published in 1976 in *Sankei Shimbun* and other organs of the press under the heading 'Last Will and Testament of Zhou Enlai' was nothing more than a forgery carried out by the KGB with the aim of arousing Japan's mistrust of China. This 'document' chiefly dealt with the internal conflicts, unreliability and instability of the Chinese leadership; its aim was thus to retard the process of *rapprochement* with China.[95] Levchenko had been directly involved in distributing the forged text.[96]

This episode underlines the urgency of the Soviet Union's interest in obstructing close Sino-Japanese relations. If in the mid-1990s Russian commentators have been objective and scrupulous in their treatment of relations between Japan and China, this is at least an indication of a shift in their perception of the relationship between the two countries. On the one hand, despite differing theoretical evaluations and practical realisations of 'socialism', Sino-Russian relations have nonetheless grown easier. Their normalisation has been most successful at state level. On the other hand, even observers in Moscow have noticed that the relationship between Japan and China is extremely complicated and by no means tension-free.[97] A Sino-Japanese alliance lies outside the scope of *realpolitik*; nevertheless, Japan's future role in the modernisation of China will continue to be an important one. It will, however, continue to suit Russia's

93. *Asahi Evening News*, 11 Dec. 1982.
94. See *Tokyo Shimbun*, 28 May 1983, in *DSJP*, 3 June 1983, p. 9.
95. See *Mainichi*, 2 Dec. 1982, in *DSJP*, 10 Dec. 1982, pp. 9–11.
96. On the details of this agent's fate see Stanislav Levchenko, *On the Wrong Side. My Life in the KGB*, Washington 1988.
97. See on this the analysis of Sino-Japanese relations in E.P. Bažanov, *Kitaj i vnešnij mir* (China and the Outside World), Moscow 1990, pp. 233–47.

and China's interests for Japan not to assume a dominant political role in the Asia Pacific region and, where possible, not to develop an independent military power, in order to maintain the *status quo*.

8

ASPECTS OF SECURITY POLICY

The Japanese-American security treaty of 1951 formalised the transformation of the United States' erstwhile wartime enemy into its military and political protegé and ally. From the treaty's inception it and the subsequent organisation of independent defence forces were branded by the Soviet Union as a revival of Japanese militarism. The Soviets slated the development as an infringement of Article 9 of the Constitution the United States had drawn up in 1947, according to which Japan renounced the right to wage war and to acquire and maintain the necessary weaponry for so doing. However, it would be erroneous to conclude from the Soviet Union's ceaseless attacks on the existence, training and weapons of Japanese troops that Moscow saw Japan as a threat; this massively armed nuclear power, whose troops at times numbered 5 million, confronted a conventionally armed island state whose sole fighting force was a volunteer army of 243,000 regular soldiers, and whose deployment possibilities were moreover severely limited by its legislature. It was not Japan's modest military power that shook the Soviet Union, but Tokyo's alliance with Washington represented the foundation of the country's security and formed the target of Soviet criticism; well into the era of Gorbachev, Soviet policy on Japan retained the aim of shattering this foundation.

Historical Background

Soon after the end of the Second World War, Japan became a base for the US military presence in East Asia following growing conflicts in interest between the Soviet Union and America, a development which was seen by the Soviet Union as a potential threat to its Far Eastern regions. The treaty of friendship and alliance signed by Moscow and Peking in February 1950 contained a mutual assistance clause in the case of an attack by Japan or one of its allies; it is uncertain whether Stalin intended this precaution against clashes on the Korean peninsula, which began only four months later with the Soviet-aided invasion of Communist forces from the north of Korea, in which China later intervened. Stalin was certainly convinced that Japan and Germany would regroup their forces and based his policy on this eventuality, explaining in one of his last speeches that one would have to believe in miracles to assume that Germany and Japan would not attempt to 'get back on their feet', to break the 'régime' of the United States and strike out towards independent development. Stalin continued, 'What guarantees exist, I wonder, that Germany and Japan will not get back on their feet again, that they will not attempt to break out of their servitude to America and lead an independent life? I believe there are no such guarantees.'[1]

Stalin's theory of 'getting back on their feet' was confirmed. Only the break with 'servitude' proved unsuccessful, since this servitude proved both for Japan and for (West) Germany to be an indispensable guarantee of security. The Korean war gave vital momentum to American Far Eastern policies, which even before the outbreak of this conflict had been moving towards the retention of a US military presence in Japan. The accomplishment of the island state's rearmament forced Moscow and Peking to realise Japan's renewed potential as a threat, especially since the change in principle in the US policy of occupation had the specific purpose of limiting the influence of Communism in Asia. The 'loss' of China following Mao Zedong's victory in 1949 and the subsequent formation of a Sino-Soviet alliance were further factors indirectly influencing Washington's Far Eastern policies.

Japan gained a more equal footing in the alliance with the 1960 revision of the security treaty with the United States, still in force today. At that time its defence forces, formed from a national police force reserve, had grown from around 146,000 men to 206,000, and US forces based in Japan had been reduced over the same period from 210,000 to 58,000.[2]

1. Speech at the Nineteenth Party Congress of the CPSU on 14 Oct. 1952, German text in J.W. Stalin, *Über den Kampf um den Frieden*, Berlin 1954, pp. 334–6.
2. They decreased further before reaching their lowest level of 26,500 in 1971. In the middle of 1993, US troops in Japan numbered 43,100, and active Japanese defence forces 237,700. Individual defence departments of the United

In reply to criticism directed at the build-up of national forces, the Japanese government refers to the Charter of the United Nations, which concedes every sovereign state the right to self-defence, and maintains that this was all Japan ever intended – an argument ignored by Soviet critics until the beginning of 1990. China's attitude in this question was more realistic. For more than two decades Peking had united with the Soviet Union in denouncing the alleged aggression of the Japanese-American security treaty; however, as early as 1953, (that is, before the official creation of the self-defence forces) China's Prime Minister Zhou Enlai had declared to Ikuo Oyama, 'We are of the opinion that an independent, democratic, peaceful and free Japan must have the right to possess arms for its own defence.'[3]

While over the years the USSR modified its criticisms of Japan out of political opportunism, it was not until the era of 'New Thinking' that Moscow cautiously began to abandon its decades of obsession, exaggerated to the point of absurdity, with a revival of Japanese militarism. Over three-quarters of all published Soviet statements on Japan dealt with the threat to peace in the region posed by the alleged revival of Japanese militarism and revanchism and by the USA's encouragement of this.[4]

The perceptible increase in Japan's self-confidence from the mid-1960s onwards – the glittering Olympic Games in 1964,

---

States stationed in Japan now total 1,900 (army), 7,300 (navy), 15,600 (air force) and over 22,000 marines. See International Institute for Strategic Studies (IISS), *The Military Balance 1993–1994*, London 1993, pp. 28 and 158–9.

3. Talks between Zhou Enlai and the president of the Japanese Committee for the Defence of Peace on 28 Sept. 1953; see *Xinhua*, 9 Oct. 1953, quoted in Kenichirô Maiya (ed.), *Shû Onrai Nihon-wo kataru* (Zhou Enlai on Japan), Tokyo 1972, p. 23.

4. Many Soviet monographs appeared on this topic, e.g. I. Sergienko, *Vozroždenie militarizma v Japonii* (Revival of Militarism in Japan), Moscow 1968; A.P. Markov, *Japonija: Kurs na vooružrenie* (Japan: On Course to Rearmament), Moscow 1970; Akademija Nauk SSSR. Institut Voennoj Istorii Ministerstva Oborony SSSR (Academy of Sciences of the USSR, Institute for Military History of the Ministry of Defence of the USSR, ed.), *Japonskij militarizm* (Japan's Militarism), Moscow 1972; S.T. Mazorov, *Voenno-ekonomiceskij potencial sovremennoj Japonii* (Japan's Military and Economic Potential), Moscow 1979; M.I. Ivanov, *Rost militarizma v Japonii* (The Growth of Militarism in Japan), Moscow 1982; V.G. Leske, *Japono-amerikanskij sojuz – itogi trech desjatiletij* (The Japanese-American Alliance – Results of Three Decades), Moscow 1983.

the no less prestigious World's Fair Expo '70 and the country's economic prosperity – also influenced the country's defence policies. The growing self-confidence was expressed in freer discussions of the question of Japan's own security and defence, which up to then had been regarded as a taboo subject; this development was probably connected with the fact that Japan did not publish a Defence White Paper until this time (1970).[5] The White Paper was edited under the leadership of Yasuhiro Nakasone, Director-General of the Defence Department, then aged fifty-two and professing nationalist views; he became Prime Minister twelve years later and occupied that office until October 1987 as one of its most distinctive representatives.

The White Paper contained no statements that had not previously been issued and supported by Japanese politicians. However, it presented a summary of these views, ordered into a unified defence concept, for the first time in Japan's post-war history. A sensation was caused by the document's renunciation of nuclear weapons, although this was posited as purely conditional and hedged about with qualifying clauses:

> Even though it would be possible to say that in legal and theoretical sense possession of small nuclear weapon, falling within the minimum requirement for capacity necessary for self-defense and not posing a threat of aggression to other countries, would be permissible, the government, as its policy, adopts the principle of not attempting at nuclear armament which might be possible under the Constitution.[6]

This development explains the view of Soviet observers that in the 1960s and the beginning of the 1970s, Japan's military theory and practice began to demonstrate Tokyo's striving for partial autonomy and independence of the USA in questions of defence.[7] The so-called revival of militarism in Japan was, however, shifted by Soviet commentators to the second half of the 1970s

---

5. See Bôeichô (Defence Agency) (ed.), *Nihon-no bôei* (Defence of Japan), Tokyo 1970. Not until six years later did a second Defence White Paper follow, opening a series published annually up to the present day. References following are to the English version whenever available.

6. *Ibid.*, p. 40. (English as in original.)

7. See B.G. Šapožnikov, 'Problemy "nacional'noj oborony"' Japonii' (Problems of Japan's 'National Defence'), in Akademija Nauk SSSR, *Japonija 1972, Ežegodnik*, p. 103.

and the beginning of the 1980s, a time when they alleged this process was taking on 'particularly turbulent' features.[8]

Primary Targets of Soviet Criticism

All Soviet statements of the time on this subject focused on the accusation of growing military cooperation between Japan and the United States. The framework formulated in 1976 for Japan's national defence engendered Soviet criticism of the military and political alliance with the United States, 'the most powerful country in the capitalist world'. The alliance, it was said, was in the main anti-Soviet and anti-Communist and was intended to unite the ruling circles of Japan and the United States in consolidating their positions in Asia. Over the following years, the maintenance and development of the US alliance would remain one of the most important tendencies in the military policies of Japan's leaders. This process was opposed by the development of socialist forces, euphemistically described as 'consolidation of the positions of peace and socialism in Asia', which was probably a metaphor for the Communists' victory in Indochina.[9]

Claims that in the 1970s Japan was developing into an 'independent military centre' pose something of a contradiction to this viewpoint. The chief example given to support the claim was Prime Minister Sato, with his statements on 'the necessity of military independence' for his country.[10] Soviet commentators also supported their theory by quoting the automatic extension of the security pact by one year, agreed by Japan and the United States in 1970. Japan's ruling circles, they maintained, could abandon the military alliance with the USA, should they conclude that its continuation was no longer advantageous; on the other hand, Tokyo now had leverage over Washington, which given its own weakening position in Asia had shown especial interest in continuing the alliance with Japan.[11]

8. See V. Bunin, 'Usilinie militaritskich tendencij' (Increase in Militaristic Tendencies), in Akademija Nauk SSSR, *Japonija 1984, Ežegodnik*, Moscow 1985, p. 91.
9. See A.A. Panov and L.P. Pinaev, 'Voenno-političeskie koncepcii pravjaščich krugov Japonii' (Concepts of Military Policy of Japan's Ruling Circles), in Akademija Nauk SSSR, *Japonija 1978, Ežegodnik*, Moscow 1979, pp. 107ff.
10. *Ibid.*, p. 98ff.
11. *Ibid.*, p. 97ff.

The contradiction between Japan's alleged striving for greater independence in defence policies on the one hand, and the view that ever-increasing cooperation could be detected in the Japanese-American military alliance on the other, was countered by Soviet commentators with claims that Japan was being pressurised by the United States into stepping up its activities within the American system of military strategy.[12] The Soviet attacks repeatedly focused on US strategy, with Japan apparently Washington's pawn. The following developments evidently presented a particular challenge to Soviet critics:

- the formulation of guidelines on Japanese-American cooperation over defence issues ('Guidelines for Japan–US Defense Cooperation') in November 1978; in this context specific mention was made of plans to block the three straits of La Perouse or Soya (between Hokkaido and Sakhalin), Tsugaru (between Japan's main island of Honshu and Hokkaido) and Tsushima or the Korea Strait, which would obstruct the route to the open sea for Soviet ships;[13]
- the expanding contacts between Japan's self-defence forces and NATO, with discussions on the possibilities of an exchange of state-of-the-art technology for arms production, with the aim of standardisation;[14]
- the extension of Japan's military contacts with South Korea and the inclusion of Tokyo's contacts with ASEAN in Japan's concepts of military strategy – a development which Tokyo attempted to justify with the expression 'comprehensive security';[15]
- the growing number of joint Japanese-American military exercises and manoeuvres; between 1970 and 1982 alone approximately fifty large-scale naval manoeuvres of up to fourteen days' duration were held.[16]

12. *Ibid.*, p. 94.
13. See V.N. Bunin, 'Koncepcija "kompleksnogo obespečenija nacional'noj bezopasnosti"' (The Concept of 'Comprehensive National Security'), in Akademija Nauk SSSR, *Japonija 1982, Ežegodnik*, Moscow 1983, p. 71.
14. *Ibid.*, p. 78.
15. *Ibid.*, pp. 78ff.
16. See V. Bunin, 'Tokyo – A Course toward Militarization', in *FEA*, no. 2 (1983), pp. 68ff.

Other points at issue were:

- the collection and exchange of information by the military leaders of Japan and the United States concerning the activities of the Soviet forces;[17]
- the installation of the American Loran-C system on Japanese ships, including submarines, to pinpoint the coordinates of Soviet sea vessels whose positions had been locked on; proof of the degree to which the SDF had been integrated into the US forces;
- the exchange of military technology, in which Japan, in accordance with an agreement of November 1983, provided the United States with relevant military technology, including parts used in the guiding systems of intercontinental missiles;
- the setting up of coordination centres to function as joint command centres in case of conflict;
- the extension of the naval SDF's radius of operation to 1,000 nautical miles off the Japanese coast, in accordance with a decision of May 1981; this was claimed to ease the burden on the US Seventh Fleet and to open up the possibility of operations in other areas, for example the Indian Ocean;[18]
- the agreement reached in the autumn of 1982 concerning the stationing of forty-eight American F-16 bombers on the Japanese air base of Misawa;[19]
- the inclusion of Japan in American nuclear strategy. Here Japan was accused of avoiding the legislative establishment of the three principles of the renunciation of nuclear weapons – no production, no possession and no deployment of nuclear weapons. It was claimed that the use of Japanese ports by ships of the US Navy repeatedly infringed the third principle. The Soviets had a convenient source of evidence for this in the statements made in 1981 by Edwin O. Reischauer, former US Ambassador to Tokyo, in which he declared that in accordance with a secret agreement dating from the 1960s the Japanese government would not oppose warships carrying nuclear weapons docking in Japanese ports. Moreover, Japan

17. *Ibid.*, p. 69.
18. See V. Bunin, 'The Defeat of Japanese Militarism: Lessons for Our Time', in *FEA*, no. 3 (1985), pp. 33ff.
19. See V. Bunin, 'Tokyo – A Course toward Militarization', p. 69.

was providing American atomic submarines with the navigational and intelligence information they required, was planning to document the movements of Soviet ships and submarines using various methods and to deliver the data to the United States, and had agreed to accompany American warships including those carrying nuclear arms. These activities occasioned a Soviet commentator to conclude that Japan was gradually becoming an important US nuclear base.[20] Reference has already been made to the years of Soviet accusations stating that China's leaders were attempting to involve Japan in their anti-Soviet, anti-socialist strategy and in the US-Chinese-Japanese triple alliance which they claimed was China's goal.[21]

Departure from Traditional Positions

The changes in Soviet leadership after Brezhnev's death, in particular Gorbachev's rise to power, created the conditions necessary for changes to occur in the Soviet Union's evaluation of the Asia Pacific region, and with it Japan, in terms of security policy. This process of change was irregular, however, and the fact that it was still not complete by 1991 implied the radical nature of the re-evaluation.

Two important speeches by Gorbachev, then General Secretary, in Vladivostok (July 1986) and Krasnoyarsk (September 1988) outlined the main points of the Soviet Union's new policy on Asia.[22] It was remarkable from the standpoint of domestic policy that Gorbachev, unlike his predecessors, visited the Asian region of the Soviet Union very soon after taking power. While Brezhnev did not visit Siberia and the Soviet Far East until 1978, after having been head of the party for fourteen years, Gorbachev

20. See D. Petrov, 'Japan in the Nuclear Strategy of the United States', in *FEA*, no. 3 (1984), pp. 55–8.
21. See last section of Chapter 7 above.
22. They had been preceded by Gorbachev's proposal (in 1985) to found a pan-Asian forum modelled on the Conference of Helsinki, by particular emphasis on the 'Asia Pacific direction' in Soviet foreign policy at the Twenty-Seventh Party Congress of the CPSU (February 1986) and by a statement of the Soviet government on issues of security in Asia and in the region of the Pacific Ocean (April 1986).

Departure from Traditional Positions

travelled to this strategically vital area in his second year of power.[23]

Unlike his predecessors, Gorbachev was the first Soviet leader since 1945 to devote a number of his speeches exclusively to the problems of the Asian region of the Soviet Union and to matters of Soviet policy on Asia. The creation of a National Committee for Economic Cooperation with Asian and Pacific countries in the spring of 1988, the Soviet efforts to be included in the Pacific Economic Cooperation Conference (PECC) and the Asia Pacific Economic Cooperation (APEC) were all further indications of a newly awakened interest in the 'Asia Pacific region', which soon became firmly integrated into Russian speech as a set phrase abbreviated to 'ATR'.[24]

The causes of this interest are principally to be found in the catastrophic economic situation of the Soviet Union as a whole and the Far Eastern regions in particular, to which Gorbachev referred in both his speeches on Asian policy. He stated that 'the economy of the Far East is now developing at a slower rate than the national economy as a whole', criticised the 'chronic lagging behind of the fuel and energy complex' and described food distribution as 'the most pressing of current problems'.[25] The economic situation in the Soviet Union's Far Eastern regions was particularly striking in comparison with the flourishing economies of neighbouring Asian countries such as Japan and South Korea. Even China, despite serious problems of domestic policy, was better able overall to provide for its population than was the Soviet Union.

The contrast between the inefficiency of the Soviet economy on the one hand and Asia's dynamic market economies and the pronounced successes of Chinese economic reforms on the other was perceived by the leaders in Moscow as a serious challenge to the Soviet Union's credibility as a world power. It caused them to initiate efforts to participate in economic cooperation in the Pacific region, an operation promising the maximum advantage for the development of eastern Siberia, which though

---

23. Brezhnev's visit to Vladivostok in 1972 only concerned his meeting with President Ford.
24. ATR = Aziatsko-Tichookeanskij Region.
25. Speech by Gorbachev in Vladivostok on 28 July 1986, English text in *FEA*, no. 1 (1987), pp. 3–21.

backward is rich in raw materials. The region's ability to contribute structurally and technologically to such cooperation is another story. Apart from the basic prerequisites of infrastructure and organisation, which will not be detailed here, economic cooperation in the development of Siberia and the Russian Far East is only possible given the necessary political climate; however, for over two decades the Soviet leaders reacted to political developments in the Asian Pacific region with demonstrations of increasing military strength.

Gorbachev was the first to attempt to reduce the political and military costs of Soviet policy on Asia, and thereby to correct his country's negative image in that area. He began to create a basis for trust. His first and most important step was the improvement of relations with China; Gorbachev wooed his vast neighbour, devoting many of the passages of his Vladivostok speech concerning foreign policy to China. The Soviets' new leader had grasped that the Soviet Union could never hope for success in its policies on Asia without China's assent, let alone against China's will. In 1969, Brezhnev had tried to hedge China in with his proposal of a system of collective security in Asia. He failed; his proposal received not a single positive reaction from all Asia, with the exception of the Mongolian People's Republic, the Kremlin's closest satellite. None of China's neighbours wished to support an initiative directed against China, which, moreover, had modelled itself on the CSCE and taken as its aim the fixing of existing borders; given the number of unresolved territorial issues, such regulations would be premature.

After making a number of concessions Gorbachev finally succeeded in normalising political relations with China, after decades of frost. His visit to Peking in May 1989 and the return visits to Moscow of Prime Minister Li Peng in April 1990 and the party head Jiang Zemin in May 1991 signalled the external course of the procedure; however, this should not obscure the fact that the two sides were divided by deep differences of opinion over ideological matters – although, in contrast to past eras, these divergences no longer seemed to affect relations. Trade and economic cooperation had increased since the mid-1980s, and contacts at military level also began to re-form in 1990, occasioned at first by negotiations over reductions in troop numbers stationed each side of the common border. During the visit of Soviet Minister for Defence Yasov to Peking in May 1991, however, other issues played a part; for example, Soviet arms supplies and the problems of conversion.

The success of Gorbachev's new Asian policies depended on the United States as well as China. He acknowledged the presence of the United States in the region and referred to the nation in his Vladivostok speech as a 'great Pacific power' with 'important economic and political interests in the region'. Without US participation, continued Gorbachev, 'it is impossible to resolve the problem of security and cooperation in the Pacific Ocean in a way that would satisfy all'.[26]

The explicit acknowledgement of American interests in the Pacific region was new, and signified that China and the United States were regarded as decisive partners in Soviet policies on Asia. This trilateral responsibility is reflected in the speech Gorbachev made in Krasnoyarsk, where he even proposed that the Soviet Union, China and the United States should, in their capacity as permanent members of the UN Security Council, discuss the creation of a negotiating mechanism for reviewing individual proposals in Asian policies.[27]

It is striking that Japan's involvement was not cited as an essential element in resolving the security problems in the Asia Pacific region; Japan was not even mentioned in this context. Other Soviet statements gave the impression that Japan, unlike China, was not seen as an independent protagonist in international relations within East Asia until well into 1990. Even in comments on economic matters – Japan's chief strength – the Soviet Union was reserved in its acknowledgement of Japan as an economic superpower and was quick to emphasise that it was in no way beholden to the latter's economic strength. Tokyo, which unlike Moscow insisted on the inseparability of politics and economics, was not to be encouraged to over-confidence through an awareness that it possessed a way of applying political pressure.[28]

26. *Ibid.*, p. 17.
27. See extracts from the Krasnoyarsk speech in *FEA*, no. 1 (1989), p. 3; complete text of the speech given in *Pravda*, 18 Sept. 1988.
28. See also on this the last section of Chapter 6 above.

This aim was freely admitted by the Soviets. It was hoped that, with the help of South Korea, the link supported by Tokyo, between Soviet concessions on the territorial issue and Japanese participation in the development of Siberian raw materials, could be avoided. When Gorbachev met the President of South Korea, Roh Tae Woo, in San Francisco in 1990, Soviet commentators pointed out this link: 'Now that Seoul is ready to provide capital, technology and equipment for this (the development of Siberia), there is no longer any point in Tokyo's "hard line".'[29] The rivalry between South Korea and Japan, once discerned, was duly exploited. Another analysis stated that it was now possible to get everything the Soviet economy would theoretically want to buy from Japan more easily and under more favourable conditions from Korea, which had not yet attained Japan's level of technological sophistication.[30]

Gorbachev's comments about Japan oscillated between admiration of the country's economic and industrial prowess ('a power of front-rank importance') and criticism of Tokyo's defence policies. In 1986 he launched the accusation that Japan 'has lately . . . circumvented ever more openly' the three non-nuclear principles and the constitutional regulations limiting armaments.[31] His Krasnoyarsk speech of 1988 was even more direct, describing the growth of Japanese military potential within the framework of burden-sharing with the United States as disquieting; the 1% proportion of GNP used for military purposes sounded modest, but in view of the country's economic power still gave serious grounds for concern. Gorbachev saw developments in Japan as proof that a country could attain the status of a great power without basing itself on militarism, and linked this with the question as to why Japan wanted to discredit its unique 'experience from which all humanity could learn' and burden the exceptional dynamism of its global economic presence with historical associations from the pre- and post-war periods.[32]

The idea of a strategically dependent Japan bound to the

29. *Pravda*, 1 July 1990.
30. *New Times*, no. 27 (July 1990).
31. Gorbachev's speech in Vladivostok, English text in *FEA*, no. 1 (1987), pp. 13–14.
32. See *Pravda*, 18 Sept. 1988.

United States permeated Soviet analyses of the late 1980s. One commentator concluded that NATO leaders were making efforts to turn the Asia Pacific region into a kind of NATO wing, in which Japan, South Korea and other allies would form 'an "Eastern front" of nuclear confrontation with the Soviet Union'.[33] However, not all Soviet observers agreed with this extremely conservative interpretation. The former Deputy Foreign Minister, M. Kapitsa, believed that 'from the Soviet point of view' it was important for Japan to find its own image 'within its relations as an ally with the USA',[34] a remarkable statement from Soviet lips, since it revealed that the subject had been rethought and that as a result the Japanese-American alliance had apparently been accepted.

As a result of increasingly open discussions, Soviet specialist publications began to present more diversified, more realistic estimations of Japanese policies, gradually abandoning their former stereotyped accusations. The LDP, it was now acknowledged, had had its hands tied in issues of foreign policy, not so much by its country's allegiance to a military and political bloc with the United States, but rather by its efforts at strengthening Japan's role within a community of free-market economies. Objective accounts were presented of the debate between the conservative supporters of a Japan in possession of military strength and the defenders of a Japan of civil power whose potential was based on economic and technological capability; the outcome of this conflict was declared to be open.[35]

Japan's economic power replaced the once-decried revival of Japanese militarism as an aspect of interest. In a discussion among Soviet experts it was pointed out that Japan's global influence was out of proportion to its 'relatively modest armed forces', a discrepancy said to be convincing proof that the concept of the balance of power was dwindling in importance as a general foundation for international politics, and for defence issues in particular. The constant emphasis placed by Japanese foreign pol-

33. V. Bunin, 'Japan and Washington's Asian Pacific Strategy', in *FEA*, no. 3 (1987), p. 42.
34. *Ibid.*, no. 6 (1987), p. 8.
35. See B. Pospelov, 'The Japanese Approach', in *FEA*, no. 6 (1988), p. 30.

icy on the importance of non-military methods in international politics was even described as characteristic of its ideology.[36]

Probably the most radical move away from conservative and ideological images of Japan and its allied relations with the United States was made at the same time that Moscow expressed acceptance of the inclusion of a reunited Germany in NATO as vital for the Soviet Union's own security. A foreign affairs correspondent of the Moscow *New Times* wrote that 'thanks to her military alliance with the USA', Japan had 'not developed into a military power', and that the US forces stationed on Japanese territory had saved Japan from maintaining its own army.[37] It may be concluded from this statement that the Soviets were gradually coming to recognise the United States as a power whose military presence was actually a contribution to stability in the Asia Pacific region rather than a threat to the Soviet Union. Sergei Solodovnik, a member of staff at the Institute for International Relations of the Soviet Foreign Ministry, drew attention to this shift in perception:

> It was not until recently that, to judge by some indirect signs, the Soviet leadership began to realize that the US capability in the APR [Asia Pacific region] serves primarily regional stability, and that its very deployment makes it practically impossible to attack our territory in order to achieve a classic strategic goal by seizing land mass as well as economic and manpower resources.[38]

In the second half of 1988, the perception of the Japanese-American alliance as a stabilising factor was still dismissed as 'patently absurd'.[39] In this context the reaction to NATO Secretary-General Manfred Wörner's visit to Tokyo in mid-September 1991 was remarkable. While the Western media collectively ignored the event, although it was the first time a leader of that defence organisation had ever visited Japan, *Izvestiya* published a detailed commentary on the visit in which the consequences

36. See *FEA*, no. 1 (1990), pp. 24 and 28.
37. I. Mlechin, in *New Times*, no. 27 (July 1990), p. 19.
38. Sergei Solodovnik, 'Is there Room for US in the APR?' in *International Affairs*, Moscow, no. 3 (1991), pp. 62ff.
39. See B. Zanegin, 'US Strategy in the Asian Pacific Region', in *FEA*, no. 6 (1988), p. 19.

of the NATO–Japan dialogue were evaluated as 'significant for the future of the world order'.[40] The crux of Japan's interests was the European 'model' for stabilising international relations, which despite regional differences suggested 'the necessity of regional dialogue also for the Asia Pacific region' – a necessity pointed out by Gorbachev time and time again in his statements on Asian policy. The correspondent found 'nothing wrong' in the agreement between Tokyo and NATO to expand their relations. There could hardly be clearer proof that the 'New Thinking' was permeating even Soviet policies on Asia. This unmistakable alteration in attitudes is a vital prerequisite for meaningful Russo-American dialogue over regional arms control and disarmament, and for the development of a system of international security in the Asia Pacific region.

The Soviet Union as a Threat to Japan

The biased Soviet attitude to Japan's defence and security policies which persisted until the end of the 1980s must be balanced out with Tokyo's views. While Japan began only relatively late to speak of a threat from the Soviet Union, it still clung unremittingly to this image after it had been outstripped by the changes in Moscow. At the end of the 1960s Tokyo first registered an increase in Soviet military presence in the Far East, which continued into the early 1970s; this military potential in the region rose again at the end of the 1970s after a phase of relative stability. While the first period of military concentration was clearly linked to the deterioration in Sino-Soviet relations and affected Japan only indirectly, the marshalling of Soviet armed forces from the end of the 1970s onwards was no longer directed exclusively at China, but by its very nature at Japan too.[41] Several motives seemed to be involved, including the USA, Japan and China's formation of a coalition of interests against Soviet influence within the region, reflected in the establishment of the antihegemony clause in Sino-American and Sino-Japanese agreements and not least in the Treaty of Peace and Friendship of 1978.

40. *Izvestiya*, 19 Sept. 1991.
41. See Hisahiko Okazaki, *A Grand Strategy for Japanese Defense*, Lanham/New York/London 1986, pp. 104ff.

The White Papers on Japanese defence issues published annually from 1976 onwards expressed the potential threat from the Soviet Union more clearly from year to year. At the same time, Tokyo noted with concern that US military strength in the Asia Pacific region was undergoing reductions. In May 1977 President Carter made the decision to withdraw the last division of land forces stationed in South Korea, thus completing US withdrawal from the Asian continent. This, together with increased American interest in the so-called 'swing concept', a plan to deploy naval forces from the Pacific for NATO operations, and the reductions announced to President Ford's fleet construction programme, aroused the disquieting impression in Japan that the United States was gradually abandoning Asia. The expression *Ajia-banare* – turning away from Asia – was in frequent use. The Defence White Paper of 1977 stated, 'Over the last decade a remarkable expansion of Soviet forces has taken place, contrasting with a fall in the numbers of US military forces from their once-impressive superiority.'[42] Two years later, the Japanese standpoint was expressed in terms of still harsher criticism:

> Regarding the capability of the US Seventh Fleet to maintain control of sea lanes, while the Seventh Fleet has substantial capabilities for anti-submarine warfare for its own defense, judging from force quantity it does not have sufficient capabilities to protect merchant shipping in the Indian Ocean and western Pacific, and therefore will have difficulty in completely preventing the Soviet Union from interdicting sea lanes.[43]

Such statements provided a clear expression of the threat emanating from the Soviet Union as it was perceived by Japanese defence experts, who based their impressions on the following incidents and developments:

– the increase in strength of the Soviet Pacific fleet;
– the stationing of Soviet troops in the disputed islands at the southern end of the Kurile chain;

---

42. Bôeichô, *Nihon-no bôei 1977*, p. 7.
43. Defence Agency (ed.), *Defence of Japan 1979*, Tokyo 1979, p. 48.

- the demonstration of Soviet military power off Japan's coasts and in Japanese air space;
- the increase in the number of medium-range missiles and bomber aircraft in the Soviet Union's Asian regions.

Incidents also occurred which over a short period gave the Japanese public ample proof of the efficiency with which the Soviet military machinery could react and the ease with which a Soviet aircraft could penetrate Japan's inadequately monitored air space. The first such incident occurred in the autumn of 1976, when the pilot of a MiG-25 landed in northern Japan, having decided on his own initiative to leave the Soviet Union and ultimately seek asylum in the USA; the second, on 1 September 1983, concerned the shooting down of a Korean passenger aircraft with 269 passengers on board. We will examine the MiG incident in detail, since it occurred during the first stages of the public perception and discussion of a Soviet threat, and occasioned investigations into improvements in Japanese air surveillance.

Once the Soviet Union had been informed that Lieutenant Belenko had landed a MiG-25 at Hakodate in northern Japan, Moscow demanded the immediate return of the aircraft and its pilot. Japan, however, permitted Belenko to leave for the United States, initially retaining the aircraft for a thorough inspection by American experts. On 15 November 1976 the dismantled machine was transported out of Japan on a Soviet freighter. The inspection had had considerable military value for the West, since this type of Soviet bomber, the most modern of its time, had been imagined to be far faster, lighter and more powerful.

Moscow protested at the way Japan had handled the incident, with specific criticism of the involvement of outsiders – in this case representatives of the United States. The Soviets threatened consequences for current and future Soviet-Japanese relations, questioning the report that the pilot was seeking asylum and claiming that he had been forced into his action by the US Secret Service.[44] Analysis of the data stored by the flight recorder disproved the Soviet claims; Belenko's flight movements proved

---

44. See *Pravda*, 29 Sept. 1976; *Yomiuri*, 23 Sept. 1976, in *DSJP*, 28 Sept. 1976, p. 9.

that he had attempted to evade the Soviet radar network and avoid pursuit by other planes.[45]

Soviet demands for compensation of 7.7 million roubles (around 3,000 million yen) were met by a Japanese counter-demand and by Japanese criticisms that the Soviets' actions represented an infringement of international regulations since the Soviet Union had not even found it necessary to apologise for the act of trespassing on Japanese air space.[46]

Moscow demonstrated its anger in several concrete ways of no great import. The Soviets refused to exchange messages with Tokyo upon the twentieth anniversary of the end of war between the Soviet Union and Japan. At the October meeting of the Central Committee, party chief Brezhnev referred to the subject, concluding that 'a complex struggle' lay ahead before truly good relations could be established. The incident with the aircraft, he noted, had seriously troubled the general atmosphere of relations between the two countries and had left doubts as to the sincerity of Japanese declarations of improvements in their relationship.[47] Finally, the Soviet Union informed the Japanese on 28 October that the meeting of the Joint Japanese-Soviet Economic Committee planned for 25 November would have to be postponed, since such a meeting required neighbourly relations and a correspondingly positive atmosphere. No direct reference to the aircraft incident was made. The Soviet Ambassador, Polyanski, is said to have intimated to Deputy Foreign Minister Sato that his country did not wish any change in its relations to Japan.[48]

The consequences of the MiG incident for Tokyo concerned defence policies and the expansion of radar surveillance in particular.[49] The incident also occasioned questions of principle, outlined by a former top official of the Defence Ministry in the words:

> If the faults [of Japan's defence] are really to be eliminated, we must have the courage to challenge the irrational dogma

45. See *Nihon Keizai*, 16 Nov. 1976, in *DSJP*, 19 Nov. 1976, p. 2.
46. See *Mainichi*, 19 April 1977, in *DSJP*, 21 April 1977, pp. 3ff.
47. See *Pravda*, 26 Oct. 1976.
48. See *Asahi Evening News*, 29 Oct. 1976.
49. Details of this in the Japanese Defence White Paper of 1977.

The Soviet Union as a Threat to Japan 185

which limits defence spending to less than 1% of GNP. The MiG affair was a prime example of the need for Japan fundamentally to rethink its defence.'[50]

The expansion of the Soviet fleet in the Pacific provided continuous fuel for Japanese discussions of the Soviet threat, although it is hard to estimate the extent to which this information motivated independent decisions on defence policy. According to Japanese data, in 1976 the Soviet Pacific fleet numbered around 750 vessels with a total tonnage of 1.2 million tonnes, constituting over a quarter of the entire Soviet war fleet;[51] by the eve of the 1980s this proportion had risen to just under a third. In April 1970 the first worldwide Soviet sea exercises, code-named 'Okean', took place, in which thirty cruisers and numerous aircraft from the Pacific fleet also participated. The operations extended from the fleet base in Vladivostok to the vicinity of Guam. After small-scale Soviet manoeuvres in the summers of 1971 and 1973, 'Okean 75' followed in April 1975 – a further worldwide sea manoeuvre monitored by satellite from Moscow and the largest military exercise ever conducted by a navy in peacetime. Around fifty vessels and numerous aircraft stationed in the waters around Japan carried out mock convoy attacks, attacks on aircraft carriers, submarine battles and amphibian exercises.[52]

The expansion of the Pacific fleet accelerated in the first half

---

50. Osamu Kaihara, 'Migu 25 to Nihon-no bôei' (The MiG-25 and Japan's Defence), in *Sekai Shûhô*, 28 Sept. 1976, p. 5. Public opinion in Japan immediately reflected the contempt for the crudeness the Soviets had revealed in the MiG incident. In a survey of 1,200 people at the beginning of November 1976 concerning the most and least popular countries, the Soviet Union was top of the list of unpopular countries for 50% of those surveyed. In April of the same year, before the incident, 34% of those asked the same question had considered the Soviet Union to be unpopular. See *Sankei*, 5 Nov. 1976.

51. See Masamori Sase, 'Die militärische Dimension der sowjetischen Asienpolitik' (The Military Dimension of Soviet Policy on Asia), in Joachim Glaubitz and Dieter Heinzig (eds), *Die Sowjetunion und Asien in den 80er Jahren* (The Soviet Union and Asia in the 1980s), Baden-Baden 1988, p. 37 and table on p. 311.

52. See Defence Agency, *Defence of Japan 1976*, pp. 17ff with detailed outlines of the procedure and scope of the manoeuvres 'Okean 70', the exercises held in the summer of 1973 and 1975 and 'Okean 75', as well as the location and extent of the exercise area.

of the 1980s. According to the London International Institute for Strategic Studies, by 1991 it consisted of 63 main warships, including 2 aircraft carriers, 14 cruisers, 7 destroyers and 40 frigates, in addition to 98 submarines, 24 of which were intended for strategic use, 70 for tactical tasks and 4 for other tasks.[53]

Both aircraft carriers of the Kiev class, the *Minsk* (40,000 tonnes) and the *Novorossijsk* (42,000 tonnes) were transferred to the fleet in 1979 and 1984 respectively; in other words, two out of a total of three to four aircraft carriers belong to the Pacific fleet. However, both were smaller than the largest American aircraft carriers, and the deployment of the helicopters and vertical takeoff jets they carried was limited to potential submarine attacks. At the beginning of 1984 the potential for amphibious attacks was increased when the fleet was allocated a vessel of the Ivan Rogov class (*Aleksandr Nikolaev*). The Soviets' state-of-the-art LASH (lighter aboard ship) vessel, which although actually part of the Soviet trading fleet could also be used for military purposes, was also stationed in the Far East in the mid-1980s.[54]

There is a piquant twist in the fact that one of the largest Japanese shipbuilders, Ishikawajima-Harima Heavy Industries, was commissioned by the Soviets to construct a floating dock with a capacity of 80,000 tonnes, which was delivered, with the authorisation of the Japanese government, to Vladivostok, the main base of the Pacific fleet, in November 1978. Among other advantages, this dock enabled the Soviet Union to carry out on-the-spot repair work on the aircraft carrier *Minsk*, which docked in Vladivostok only a few months later, and thus contributed significantly to the operational powers of the largest vessels of the fleet. Given the significance of such a strategic decision, internal Japanese cooperation was shown in a dubious

53. See IISS, *The Military Balance, 1991–1992*, p. 45. Japanese figures of the same time for the Soviet Pacific fleet were considerably higher: the Defence White Paper spoke of 'about 100 major surface combatants and about 140 submarines' (Defence Agency, *Defence of Japan 1989*, p. 40); the unofficial Research Institute for Peace and Security (RIPS) quoted in its yearbook eighty-four main fighting vessels, see Research Institute for Peace and Security (ed.), *Asian Security 1989–1990*, Tokyo 1990, p. 48.

54. See Defence Agency, *Defence of Japan 1985*, p. 29. A detailed survey of increases in the individual types of submarine and surface ships during the period 1974–84 can be found in RIPS, *Asian Security 1985*, p. 54.

light when it was reported in January 1978 that the Ministry of Defence had 'recently learned of this'.[55]

Japanese views on the Pacific fleet emphasised its threatening aspect. With regard to total Soviet military power in the region, the Ministry of Defence had concluded as early as 1985 that the expansion of this power had not only increased the level of tension in the region's international military situation, it also contained 'a growing latent threat' for Japan[56] – a statement which grew in significance when viewed against Japan's then relatively cautious evaluation of the US deterrent. Statements evidently intended to calm the concern arising from the situation were made to the effect that the United States would try to step up its own military strength in the area to increase the credibility of its deterrence, in reaction to the Soviets' remarkable expansion of military power in the region around Japan.[57]

It is worthy of note at this point that even within the ranks of the Socialist Party of Japan a voice was raised describing the Soviet Pacific fleet as a threat to Japan. Since the end of the war the SPJ has clung to the illusion that there will be no hostile powers in the vicinity of Japan as long as Japan itself refrains from endangering its own security; the party also demands that its country adopt a state of unarmed neutrality. The surprise was thus all the greater when Hiroyuki Maruyama, member of the Secretariat of the SPJ Central Executive Committee, expressed his views on the threat posed by the Pacific fleet. Maruyama based his ideas on the newest data available from American sources at the time, concluding that the Soviet Union intended to exert heavy political and military pressure finally to 'neutralise' Japan and to secure 'unhindered use' of the three international straits around Japan – the straits of Tsushima, Tsugara and Soya.[58]

As a parallel process to the reinforcements of the Pacific fleet, air forces stationed in the Far East were modernised. According to Japanese sources, approximately 22,000 aircraft, in other words a quarter of the total Soviet contingent, were accessible in this region in the mid-1980s. Older models were replaced at remark-

55. *Asahi Evening News*, 12 Jan. 1978; *International Herald Tribune*, 10 Jan. 1978.
56. See Defence Agency, *Defence of Japan 1985*, p. 23.
57. *Ibid.*
58. See *Shokun*, Nov. 1985, in *SSJM*, Nov. 1985, pp. 41–50.

able speed by newer, higher-performance craft, so that by 1985 some 80% of all fighter craft stationed in the Far East were third-generation types such as the MiG-23, MiG-27 and SU-24.[59] In addition, there was the formidable weapon power of 85 TU-22 Backfire and 135 SS-20 medium-range missiles, all sited within range of Japan in central Siberia and to the east of Lake Baikal.[60]

Japanese authorities first reported an increase in the stationing of Soviet SS-20 medium-range missiles at the end of the 1970s; in the autumn of 1979 the Japanese press, citing an American source, reported that SS-20s had been stationed near Chita along the River Schilka.[61] Two-and-a-half years later, approximately one-quarter of the total of 250 SS-20 systems in existence at the time had been stationed in Asia, and a similar proportion of a total of 150 Soviet Backfire bombers in the Far East.[62]

The subject took on new urgency when the Soviet leaders openly began to consider deploying medium-range missiles in Asia which up till then had been aimed at Western Europe. The Japanese government vainly attempted to convince the Soviet Union to remove the rockets by means of official protests and direct talks with Soviet government representatives, for example during Kapitsa's visit to Tokyo at the beginning of April 1983. It was known at the beginning of 1983 that 108 SS-20 systems were stationed in twelve launching bases across Siberia, a number confirmed by the Soviets; in 1984 numbers increased to 117 SS-20 systems east of the Urals, and over the two subsequent years to 135 and then 162.[63] These missiles would have enabled the Soviets to strike Japan, South Korea, China and most of South-East Asia.

Interestingly, the Socialist Party of Japan joined the LDP's protest against the stationing of SS-20 missiles in the Asian region

59. See Defence Agency, *Defence of Japan 1985*, p. 28.
60. *Ibid.*, p. 27.
61. See *Tokyo Shimbun* (evening edn.), 24 Oct. 1979, in *DSJP*, 1 Nov. 1979, p. 16; RIPS, *Asian Security 1985*, p. 57.
62. See *Asahi Evening News*, 10 Feb. 1982; Dieter Heinzig, 'SS-20 in Asien' (I) and (II), Cologne, 5–6 Feb. 1983; Bundesinstitut für Internationale und Ostwissenschaftliche Studien, *Aktuelle Analysen*, 1984, nos 6/7.
63. See RIPS, *Asian Security 1985*, p. 56; Sase, *Die militärische Dimension*, p. 39.

of the Soviet Union and informed the CPSU by letter that the missiles of this type already stationed were 'the cause of great concern to the Japanese people and to those in other regions of Asia'.[64]

International support for the Japanese government over the issue of missile stations came chiefly from the USA. The Americans declared that any Far Eastern deployment of the Soviet medium-range missiles previously aimed at Europe would be unacceptable. Foreign Minister Shultz assured the Japanese government in Tokyo in February 1983 that Washington would never agree to reductions in the INF medium-range missile system at the expense of Japan's security or the security of other non-European countries.[65] China also supported Japan's protests against the Soviets' missile stationing policy, although with somewhat less intensity. Prime Minister Zhao Ziyang assured Prime Minister Nakasone of his agreement to an exchange of information over increases in Soviet military strength, including the positioning of SS-20s.[66]

The Japanese demand for the withdrawal of missiles already in position was countered by the Soviets with the stereotype answer that the missiles were not aimed at Japan; this answer was also given by the Soviet Foreign Minister when receiving the new Japanese Ambassador in Moscow for the first time, eight months after the latter's appointment.[67] G. Arbatov, member of the Central Committee and director of the Institute for the USA and Canada, gave a similar reply in an interview for the *Asahi Shimbun*, in which he expressed the opinion that China should be included in all negotiations over reductions of medium-range missiles in Asia and the Far East, continuing that the Soviet Union was as interested in reducing arms in this region as it was in concluding security agreements with the West. Tokyo understood this statement to be an expression of Soviet concern over China's growing missile potential.

Arbatov countered denials that Soviet missiles represented a threat to Japan with the veiled threat that Japan would have to

64. See *Frankfurter Allgemeine Zeitung*, 11 March 1983.
65. See *Japan Times*, 8 Feb. 1983.
66. See *Asahi*, 3 Jan. 1984, in *DSJP*, 31 March–2 April 1984, p. 5.
67. See *Asahi Evening News*, 24 Feb. 1983.

remain a nuclear-free zone if it wanted to avoid being the target of a Soviet attack. Moreover, he continued, Japan should neither permit the installation of nuclear weapons on its territory nor allow an attack to be launched on the Soviet Union from Japanese territory.[68] A few days later, Foreign Minister Gromyko followed this with the remark that Okinawa was a huge nuclear base[69] – a statement which Tokyo repudiated with protests. The claim that American nuclear weapons were stationed on Japanese territory was quoted by the Soviet leaders as justification for the stationing of their own medium-range missiles. The chief aim behind this was naturally to cause turmoil in Japan, to whip up pacifist feelings and to sow the seeds of mistrust in the Japanese-American alliance.

The subject was soon reopened and used as a massive threat; a report in *Sotsialistitscheskaya Industriya*, repeated by TASS, threatened Japan with massive reprisals if an attack were launched against the Soviet Union from Japanese territory using American nuclear weapons. American-Japanese cooperation over the stationing of nuclear weapons on Japanese territory could cost Tokyo dear. In the case of an attack from Japanese territory, the report warned, reprisals would follow which could mean the end for Japan. Moreover, Washington was sadly mistaken to rely on the idea that in the event of an attack from Japan or Europe reprisals would only be directed against those areas, for reprisals would inevitably affect the United States as well.[70]

This stick had been preceded by a carrot; at the beginning of the year the Central Committee of the CPSU had sent a letter to Japan's two socialist opposition parties, the SPJ and the Democratic Socialist Party (DSP), offering to guarantee Japan's security in exchange for its adherence to the three principles of renunciation of nuclear weapons. However, the letter contained no precise details about the nature of the guarantee. It was dated 19 January 1983, the second day of Prime Minister Nakasone's visit to Washington, and was clearly intended to cause unrest among the Japanese people over the Japanese-American alliance.[71] Secretary General Brezhnev had made a similar proposal

68. See *Asahi Evening News*, 14 March 1983.
69. *Pravda*, 3 April 1983.
70. *Neue Zürcher Zeitung*, 22 April 1983.
71. See *Asahi Evening News*, 4 Feb. 1983.

the previous year to Japanese writers, offering Japan negotiations over nuclear non-aggression on condition that Japan refrained from the production, purchase and importing of nuclear weapons.[72] These were principles to which Japan already felt committed, with the exception of the right of passage through Japanese waters granted to American ships carrying nuclear weapons.

The lures and threats missed their target, and even seemed to have the opposite effect to that intended; at the summit conference of the seven leading Western industrial nations in Williamsburg in May 1983, Prime Minister Nakasone was among the signatories of the Declaration of Disarmament and Arms Control, thus accepting the statement that the security of the Western industrial nations and Japan were inseparable and were to be seen within a global context.[73] The counter-productive nature of Soviet policy had made Japan move closer to Western political standpoints, including those on defence issues; however, Nakasone's move was not solely a reaction to Moscow's threats, but was also aimed at preventing the consensus of Europe, America and the Soviet Union on the INF issue, which would be to Japan's disadvantage.

A further demonstration of Soviet military force was necessary, however, before the threat to Japan became the subject of public discussion. Soviet forces were stationed on some of the islands of contention to the north of Hokkaido. In mid-1978 the Japanese press printed reports that Soviet troops had landed on Etorofu, the most northerly of the Soviet-occupied islands claimed by Japan; apparently, ten Antonov-12 transporters each carrying ninety men had landed on Etorofu, and three or four ships of the Soviet Navy had approached the island to carry out amphibian exercises. This, the reports continued, was the first time that the 4,500 Soviet marines of the Pacific fleet had practised landing manoeuvres on one of the islands at issue.[74]

The Japanese government protested to Moscow about the manoeuvre, which had been announced as target practice, because the area involved extended 12 miles into the Japanese

---

72. See *Kommunist*, no. 4 (March 1982), pp. 20ff.
73. See *Europa-Archiv*, vol. 38, no. 12 (June 1983), pp. D333ff.
74. See *Asahi Evening News*, 7 June 1978.

territorial waters of Etorofu, leaving Japanese fishing vessels operating within the danger-zone;[75] however, Tokyo was unclear as to what interpretation to place on the manoeuvre. Opinions in the Ministry of Defence were apparently so fundamentally divided that General Kurisu, the chairman of the Committee of Chiefs of Staff, was relieved of his post, allegedly because his dramatisation of the threat which the Soviet Union presented to Japan was irreconcilable with the standpoint of his civilian superior, the Director-General of the Defence Agency.[76]

The Soviet Union's intentions did not become clear to Tokyo until the beginning of 1979, when it became known that the Soviet Union had built new military facilities – barracks, protection devices and radar stations – on the islands of Etorofu and Kunashiri, and had stationed troops at brigade-level strength: 2,300 soldiers with tanks and artillery. This raised the total number of troops on the islands to around 30,000 or 40,000 men.

Only a few months later, the Japanese government was informed of further Soviet actions in the military conversion of the northern territories. An American source reported on 24 September 1979 that over the past months the Soviet Union had founded an additional base on the island of Shikotan, closely resembling the existing bases on Etorofu and Kunashiri.[77] This news caused uproar in Japan, for unlike the other two islands, Shikotan is geologically part of Hokkaido. Since the Soviet Union had proposed in 1956 that upon conclusion of a peace treaty Shikotan and the Habomais should be 'transferred' to Japan, the Japanese took the news of the erection of a military base on the island far more seriously than the news concerning Etorofu and Kunashiri. This action had yet again underlined the Soviet Union's claim to the islands and still further reduced the chances of a solution to the territorial dispute, even under the terms of the Joint Declaration of 1956.

Another remarkable aspect of the incident was the intervention by the United States with its military reconnaissance findings

75. *Ibid.*, 8 June 1978.
76. *Ibid.*, 9 June 1978.
77. See *Mainichi*, 26 Sept. 1979, in *DSJP*, 3 Oct. 1979, p. 12. Shikotan is approximately 255 square kilometres in area and in 1940 had one village of 1,177 inhabitants.

and its evident feeling that its interests of security had been impinged upon, resulting in the abandonment of Washington's previous view that the territorial problem was primarily a Japanese-Soviet one. On 15 October 1979, a hearing took place in a closed session of the Military Forces Committee of the House of Representatives, in which the stationing and reinforcement of Soviet troops on the islands at issue was discussed. The session determined total Soviet troop strength on Etorofu, Kunashiri and Shikotan at some fewer than 6,000; the Japanese Ministry of Defence had estimated 10,000, and Prime Minister Ohira had spoken of 10,000–12,000 at a press conference.[78] Once again the Japanese figures considerably exceeded the American statistics, a tendency probably rooted in domestic policy which is also in evidence in the Defence White Papers.

The Soviet decision to convert the three largest of the islands at issue into military bases was interpreted by the Americans as a reaction to the Sino-Japanese treaty of peace and friendship. Washington believed the decision was probably intended as a warning against any further *rapprochement* of the United States, China and Japan, and as a means of intimidating Tokyo in its claims to the islands.[79] The Soviet Union reacted to Japanese reports of the stationing of troops on Shikotan with the claim that this anti-Soviet campaign was serving to justify the continuation of Japanese armament, the consolidation of the Japanese-American military alliance and the creation of a three-cornered alliance between Washington, Tokyo and Peking.[80]

On 2 October 1979 the Tokyo government issued a strong protest against the recent expansions of Soviet military presence on the islands at issue and criticised the Soviet Union for ignoring Japan's protest of 5 February.[81] Ambassador Polyanski rejected

---

78. See *Asahi* (evening edn.), 17 Oct. 1979, in DSJP, 25 Oct. 1979, p. 7; *Asahi Evening News*, 28 Sept. 1979. In the summer of 1991, the commanding officer of the Soviet Far East military district, General Victor Novozhilov, stated to the newspaper *Yomiuri* that an infantry division of 7,000 soldiers and forty tanks, an air force unit and a small radar reconnaissance unit were stationed on the islands; see *International Herald Tribune*, 1–2 June 1991.

79. See *Sankei*, 23 Oct. 1979, in *DSJP*, 30 Oct. 1979, pp. 12ff; RIPS, *Asian Security 1980*, p. 17.

80. See *Pravda*, 28 Sept. 1979.

81. See *Asahi Evening News*, 5 Feb. 1979.

Japan's 'unfounded territorial claims', describing the protest as interference in his country's domestic affairs and demanding the Japanese government cease 'encouraging anti-Soviet campaigns' in Japan.[82]

The protests against the stationing of troops in Shikotan revealed the Japanese government's insecurity over its Soviet policies. While the head of the Defence Agency, Ganri Yamashita, declared that the USA and Japan shared the view that Soviet military activity represented a threat to the Far East, the Foreign Ministry hastened to play down the incident by requesting more restraint in the use of the term 'threat'.[83]

At the time the Defence White Paper was published in the summer of 1979, divergencies had already emerged between the Foreign Ministry and the Defence Department in their evaluation of Soviet armament in the Far East. The Foreign Ministry's verdict on the White Paper was condensed into the cry: 'The Russians are coming!' The formulation of the text was said to have caused heated discussions, in which officials of the *Gaimusho* had also participated, with particular emphasis on the assessment of the international military situation. The Foreign Ministry, according to one of its officials, did not deny the strength of the Soviet military forces in the Far East; however, this development was not sudden, but could be seen as a natural consequence of the USSR's global strategy.[84] In reference to the Defence Department's attitude, Foreign Minister Sonoda declared that it would be premature to view the Soviets' actions – by which he meant the stationing of troops in Shikotan – as a threat. Japan was to remain calm; if the incident blew up into an affair, this would only be doing the Soviets a favour.[85]

Over the next few years, the Soviet Union continued to expand its military presence in the islands at issue, chiefly in qualitative terms. Even Suisho, an island belonging to the Ha-

---

82. See *Japan Times*, 3 Oct. 1979.

83. A conservative Japanese newspaper wrote: 'The Japanese public, however, regards the stationing of Soviet forces in northern Japan as a "threat", and we call upon the government to acknowledge this fact and to implement counter-measures without delay. The government's prime task is to improve the quality of our defence capabilities' (*Sankei*, in *Japan Times*, 5 Oct. 1979).

84. See *Mainichi Daily News*, 30 July 1979.

85. See *Asahi Evening News*, 10 Sept. 1979.

bomai group, was involved. In the autumn of 1980 the Japanese Defence Department confirmed the existence of a heliport, communications equipment and living quarters and perhaps a tunnel on the small island, and expressed the view that the quarters had been constructed during the last year or two for the border troops stationed there, a total of just under 100 soldiers.[86] At the end of 1982 it was reported that the Soviet Union had replaced two dozen of the older MiG-27s, since withdrawn, by around ten MiG-21 fighter jets.[87] Almost a year later, further information from the Defence Department contained the report that more than ten MiG-23s, at the time the most modern fighter aircraft in existence, had been stationed in Etorofu, possibly as replacements for the MiG-21s.[88]

At the end of the 1980s approximately forty MiG-23s and a number of MI-24 fighter helicopters were stationed in Etorofu, while ten MiG-31s were seen in Sakhalin, in other words directly in the vicinity of Hokkaido.[89] The Japanese press published the news, although without official confirmation, that the Soviet Union had stationed SSC-1 cruise missiles (NATO code Seapal) in Etorofu from October 1985.[90]

A large-scale landing manoeuvre which took place in Etorofu in the autumn of 1985 also caught the attention of the Japanese press. It differed from a similar manoeuvre in 1978 in that this time a large number of aircraft, including Backfire bombers and MiG-23 and MiG-27 fighter aircraft, were involved from their bases on the Siberian coast and Sakhalin. Three shiploads of troops were transported from Sakhalin to participate in the exercise.[91] Military commentaries on the manoeuvre took the

86. See Kyodo, 4 Oct. 1980, in *SWB/FE/6541/A2/1*, 6 Oct. 1980.
87. See *International Herald Tribune*, 17 Dec. 1982.
88. See Radio Japan IS (English broadcast) 31 Aug. 1983, in *MD, Allgem. Teil*, 1 Sept. 1983.
89. See Bôeichô, *Nihon-no bôei 1986*, p. 35; RIPS, *Asian Security 1985*, p. 56.
90. See *Sankei*, 5 Feb. 1986; *DSJP*, 19 Feb. 1986, p. 12. The SSC-1 is described as a cruise missile from the first half of the 1960s, relatively large, adaptable for nuclear or conventional warheads and with a range of 450 km. According to the source quoted above the most advanced version, SSC-3, was stationed on the Kurile island of Simushir, a mere 300 km. north of Etorofu.
91. See *Sankei*, 7 Sept. 1985, in *DSJP*, 18 Sept. 1985, p. 8.

view that the Soviet Union wanted to seize sole control over access to the Sea of Okhotsk, a maritime region which appeared to have considerable strategic importance in the operations of Soviet nuclear-powered SS-N-8 and SS-N-18 submarines, missiles from which would be able to reach the American continent.[92] In the years following Gorbachev's rise to power, official Japanese statements on the threat from the Soviet Union tended to increase their criticism of that country. The Defence White Papers for 1987 and 1988 concurred in registering a 'growing potential threat to this country'.[93] In 1989 it was even stated that Soviet military operations in the Far East not only represented a potential threat to Japan, but also caused military tension. Moreover, Gorbachev's initiatives and proposals for a reduction of Soviet troops in the Far East were described as 'imprecise in many respects and generally vague'. The chances of a let-up in the military pressure exerted by the Soviet Union were assessed sceptically.[94] An initial report on the 1990 Defence White Paper stated that in the Japanese view, a potential threat to Japan from the Soviet Union still existed, and that some quantitative reduction in Soviet troops in the Far East would bring about a qualitative improvement which would considerably exceed the Soviet Union's defence requirements.[95]

Although the Defence Agency insisted that it had not intended unduly to emphasise the Soviet threat, it was undeniable that Japanese assessments of the changes the Soviet Union was undergoing and of their effect on Moscow's military capabilities differed from assessments made by Western Europe and America. Japan's more conservative attitude towards events in the Soviet Union was based on two factors. First, changes in the Soviet Union's level of military presence in the Far East had been far smaller in recent years than those in Europe; troop reductions along the Sino-Soviet border and in Mongolia did not affect Japan, while in maritime armaments, seen by Japan as a major threat, nothing had yet changed between the two superpowers. The second factor was linked to the further expansion of Japan's

92. See Georges Tan Eng Bok, *The USSR in East Asia*, Paris 1986 (Atlantic Papers, no. 59/69), p. 62.
93. Defence Agency, *Defence of Japan*, 1987 and 1988 edns, pp. 29ff.
94. *Ibid.*, 1989, p. 40.
95. See *Sankei*, 27 June 1990.

own defence potential; for the Defence Agency, the threatening image of the Soviet Union had to be maintained in order to justify the annual budget increases.

More and more gaps began to appear in this line of argument. In the mid-1980s the Defence Agency had already been aware of the imbalance between the Soviet Pacific fleet's impressive size and relative inactivity. It had been observed that the aircraft carrier *Minsk* had been launched only three times within the previous five years, for a total of nine months, against the record of the US aircraft carrier *Midway* (51,000 tonnes), moored at Yokosuka near Tokyo, which had left port six times during 1983 to sail the Indian Ocean and the Pacific for a total of 191 days; an analysis even stated that this was rather less than normal owing to lay-up days necessitated by repair work.[96] Despite the major shortcomings of the Pacific fleet, of which Japan was well aware, the image of its menacing power continued to be propagated. Only in the middle of 1990 did some willingness to make cautious corrections appear. The head of the Defence Agency declared before a parliamentary committee that around half the Soviet warships in the Pacific were outdated, in other words more than twenty-five years old, and that this fact had caused the department to reduce its estimate of the fleet's combat strength.[97] A comparison of available data concerning the Soviet Union's military presence in the islands at issue to the north of Hokkaido showed that since Gorbachev's ascent to power Japanese sources had been unable to prove any increase in either the quantity or the quality of troops present.[98]

In the autumn of 1990, shortly before the publication of the Defence White Paper, the reference to the continued Soviet threat in the Far East, which had been included for years as a matter of course, was deleted on the recommendation of the Prime Minister. Kaifu demanded that the content should reflect

---

96. Reasons given by the Japanese for the limited mobility of the Soviet fleet were: restrictions on the grounds of budget savings and fuel conservation; frequent engine defects owing to inadequate inspection; bureaucratic delays over ship repairs; irregular availability of spare parts and low crew training standards – see *Asahi Evening News*, 17 May 1984.

97. See Radio Free Europe/Radio Liberty, *Daily Report*, no. 112, 13 June 1990.

98. See Defence Agency, *Defence of Japan 1987*, p. 38 and 1989 edn, p. 45.

the moves towards global détente that were taking place, and should agree with the statements published in the concluding documents of the summit conference which the seven leading industrial nations had attended in Houston.[99] The commander of the Soviet Far East military region, General Victor Novozhilov, announced in the interview with *Yomiuri* already cited that the forces stationed in the islands at issue would be reduced by one-third by the end of the year.[100] At what point the Japanese defence planners will draw the logical conclusions from these insights and facts remains to be seen. At the beginning of 1994 a Defence Ministry spokesman announced that a discussion would start soon to re-define roles for the armed forces and to overhaul Japan's military doctrine.

The Threat and its Effect on Public Opinion

As already described, the Soviet Union's continuous expansion of military power and the demonstration of its permanent presence in the Far East did not leave the Japanese people unaffected. Even a cursory survey of Japanese reactions makes one thing clear; unlike the effect Soviet power had on Western Europe, and on the Federal Republic of Germany in particular, in the case of Japan – and in East Asia generally – the Soviet Union did not succeed in making political capital out of showing off its military might.

The unity of the Japanese people in their perceptions of the development of Soviet power can be seen from long-term surveys of public opinion. The question 'Do you see a military threat coming from the Soviet Union?' was answered in the affirmative by 55.2% of those surveyed in 1981, 72.5% in 1983 and 80.2% in 1985; the proportion of those replying in the negative fell accordingly, from 36.4% in 1981 to 16.8% in 1983 and 16% in 1985. The percentage of 'don't knows' fell over the same period from 10.7% to 3.8%. It is remarkable that this perception of threat was shared by the majority of those surveyed, irrespective of political tendency. In a survey carried out by *Yomiuri* in 1981, over 70% of subjects with conservatively ori-

---

99. See *Pravda*, 20 Aug. 1990; *International Herald Tribune*, 19 Sept. 1990.
100. See *International Herald Tribune*, 1–2 June 1991.

ented views (supporters of the LDP, *Komeito*, DSP and the New Liberal Club) felt that the Soviet Union posed a military threat to Japan. The proportion of SPJ supporters who held this view was 65%, that of CPJ supporters 59%.[101]

Despite this feeling of being threatened, there was no noticeable demand for a dramatic change in Japanese defence policies or for an increase in defence spending. Opinion polls on this theme show a stable picture that gives no support to the accusation of Japan's remilitarisation, at least as far as the mood of the people was concerned.[102] The necessity of having Self-defence forces was affirmed in 1984 by 82.6% of those surveyed — a result that varied only slightly from the number agreeing in 1965 (81.9%). At that time 4.9% had denied the necessity of SDF, a figure which had risen to 7.5% by 1984.[103]

Surveys investigating opinions on the alliance with the United States, the basis of Japan's national security, showed a stable majority in favour of the security treaty, which at the end of 1978 was supported by 65.5% of Japanese questioned, at the end of 1984 by 71.4% and in 1988 by 67%. Those most in favour were those aged forty to forty-nine (77.6%); in other words, the post-war generation. Even in the twenty to twenty-nine year old age group, 72.4% in the mid-1980s declared their support for the defence alliance with the USA.[104] These figures had not changed significantly by the end of the 1980s.

The view that Japan should be defended through national means alone, that is by using purely Japanese military forces with

101. See Hasegawa, *Japanese Perceptions*, p. 64.
102. For years, a growing majority has spoken out in favour of retention of the present budget: in 1969 a total of 38.2% of those questioned; in 1984, 54.1%. An increase in defence spending was desired by 24.1% in 1969, but by only 14.2% in 1984; the percentage of those desiring a reduction in defence spending totalled 13.8% and 17.7% for those years respectively. See *Yoronchôsa*, no. 8 (Aug. 1985), p. 92. Here too the survey in 1988 revealed a drop in the numbers supporting an increase in the defence budget (11.2%); see *ibid.*, Aug. 1988, p. 11.
103. It is interesting to note age-related divergences in the results of 1984. Older subjects gave the most support to the necessity of self-defence forces: 86% of those aged sixty and over. Other age groups gave the following results: 50–59 years: 85.6%; 40–49 years: 83.2%; 30–39 years: 79.5%; 20–29 years: 76.2%. See *ibid.*, Aug. 1985, p. 85.
104. See *ibid.*, p. 94; and Defence Agency, *Defence of Japan 1989*, p. 200.

appropriate reinforcements and after the annulment of the security treaty with the United States, has had but few supporters over the course of the last two decades.[105] The proportion of those supporting Japan's defence within the US alliance in its present form and with the assistance of SDF rose over the same period from 40.9% in 1969 to 67% in 1988. Those few believing in the illusion that Japan's security can be maintained without autonomous military forces and without the treaty with the United States fell from 15.5% in 1972 to 5–6% in the 1980s.[106]

These figures are derived not from isolated random surveys taken after major events, but from national surveys using standardised methods which have been carried out for years with identically formulated questions. One is left with the overall impression, at least on an examination of the opinion polls, that Japan is a long way from striving to build up a military power in proportion to its economic strength, let alone from striving to revive militarism. There is also no perceptible movement towards dissolution of the security pact with the United States. Not only does Japan have no alternative to this alliance; the mood of the population is such that the government will have a rough ride should it decide to lead the country into such an insecure future in terms of defence. The survey results clearly show that while the Soviet Union increased Japan's perception of a threat by increasing its military strength in the Far East, at the same time its actions heightened people's support for a moderate self-defence capability and for the US alliance. The Soviet Union's exaggerated propaganda, demonstrations of military strength and campaigns of intimidation have achieved precisely what that country wanted to avoid, namely the consolidation of the alliance between Japan and the United States.

Under the influence of 'New Thinking', the Soviet Union openly conceded the negative effects of its earlier policies on Asia and undertook efforts to improve its image. Some encourag-

---

105. In 1969 the idea of an autonomous defence of Japan was supported by just under 13% of those questioned. After this time the number fell to 5% (1984), and has since then risen gradually to reach the figure of 7.3% in 1991. See *Yoron chôsa*, Aug. 1991, p. 16.

106. This form of defence was affirmed in 1969 by 12.9%; 1972 by 10.8%; 1975 by 8.6%; 1978 by 8.2%; 1981 by 6.1%, and by the end of the 1980s by between 5 and 6% – *Defence of Japan 1989*, p. 200.

ing features of this process are already visible, and have already been reflected in public opinion. In the Soviet-Japanese survey of early 1990 already quoted, 62.1% of those Japanese questioned still saw the military potential of the Soviet Union as a threat to their country, while 9% denied any such threat.[107] Astonishingly, only 18.1% of the Soviet citizens questioned felt threatened by Japan, and 25.6% denied any Japanese threat – although for decades the Soviet media had bombarded the population with images of a revanchist, militaristic Japan. Georgi Kunadze, an expert on Japan and Deputy Foreign Minister of the Russian Federation since 1991, remarked in reference to the phenomenon that even in 1990 a high percentage of Japanese felt threatened by the Soviet Union's military power:

> Of course it is easiest to explain such a result by saying that the Japanese are more efficient at propaganda than we are, just as they are in many other fields. However, I believe that would be a clear case of over-simplification. The Soviets' military potential in the Far East is indeed inconceivably great. There is absolutely no reasonable explanation for the high specific concentration of troops based in the Soviet Far East compared with other regions of the USSR, and for this reason the neighbouring countries regard them with concern.[108]

There is no doubt that the withdrawal of troops from the islands at issue which has already been announced, together with Russia's current concentration on economic problems and problems of civil recovery, will make all fears of Russia's military threat to Japan completely groundless. However, by 1994 the withdrawal had not been completed.

---

107. See *Mirovaja Ekonomika i Mez̆dunarodnye Otnos̆enija*, no. 3 (1990), p. 137.
108. *Ibid.*, p. 141.

Part III

RECENT DEVELOPMENTS AND PERSPECTIVES

9

EXPECTATIONS BEFORE GORBACHEV'S VISIT TO JAPAN

When the Foreign Ministers of Japan and the Soviet Union met on the periphery of the UN General Assembly in New York in September 1989, Shevardnadze informed his Japanese colleague that Gorbachev intended to visit Japan in 1991. It was unusual for a state visit to be announced such a long way in advance, and this fact alone gave rise to speculation in Tokyo over the Soviet Union's intentions in such an action and the kind of political proposals the head of the Kremlin would make.

The immediate consequence of the announcement was an increase in diplomatic activity in the preparations for the visit. At the beginning of 1990 the former Japanese Foreign Minister Shintaro Abe headed a delegation of LDP members on a visit to Moscow; in September, Shevardnadze met his colleague Nakayama in Tokyo, and immediately afterwards another LDP delegation headed by Obuchi, later to become General Secretary, visited Moscow. In January 1991 Foreign Minister Nakayama was received by Gorbachev in the Kremlin for talks, and only a few weeks before the Soviet President arrived in Tokyo, the General Secretary of the LDP, Ichiro Ozawa, also travelled to the Soviet capital. In addition to these more or less high-level political meetings, a vigorous exchange of ideas developed between parliamentarians, scholars, experts and publicists on both sides, and was in part reported in the press and in specialist publications. All thoughts and discussions revolved around the unsettled territorial question, the central obstacle to any improvement in relations.

The announcement of Gorbachev's visit took the Ministry of Foreign Affairs in Tokyo by surprise; the most that had been expected in the autumn of 1989 had been a suggested date for the next visit of the Soviet Foreign Minister. Political observers close to the Japanese government wondered what Soviet strategy could be hidden behind the announcement, and how Japan should react. The discussions which took place in Japan may be summarised thus:

- An announcement so far in advance, it was said, made it clear that Gorbachev would not visit Japan in 1990. The Soviets wanted to place this negative information in a more positive light by announcing the visit for 1991, and possibly also wanted to avoid leaving the impression that they did not consider Japan very significant.
- The postponement could also mean that the Soviet Union did not yet see its relations with Japan as mature enough for the 'New Thinking' to take adequate effect. When the former Prime Minister Nakasone had repeated his invitation to Gorbachev to visit Japan in July 1988, Gorbachev was said to have replied that while he was willing to visit Japan, he did not believe that, given the situation, a visit would necessarily contribute to an improvement in relations.
- In addition, in the autumn of 1989 Japanese observers suspected that the postponement of the visit was due to domestic policy in both countries: on the one side, the impending regional elections in the Soviet Union and the announced Twenty-Eighth Party Congress of the CPSU, with personnel changes in the leadership committees; and on the other a bribery scandal in Japan known as the Recruit Affair, in which a group of top Japanese politicians was involved in insider share dealings and which severely weakened their position.[1]

Before the visit, thought was naturally given to ways of overcoming the wearisome territorial problem. Kiichi Saeki, an expert with a thorough knowledge of the problems, saw the search for a solution as faced with increasing difficulties,[2] explaining this in the context of the ever more prevalent problems of the various nationalities in the Soviet Union, which presented growing difficulties for any alterations planned in territorial

1. For the Japanese discussions of the announcement of Gorbachev's visit, see Kiichi Saeki and Shigeki Hakamada, '91en Gorubachofu-shokichô hô-Nichi hyômei-no Soren-senryaku-wo dô miru ka' (How Should the Soviet Strategy behind Gorbachev's Declaration of a Visit to Japan in 1991 be Evaluated?) in *Ajia-jihô*, no. 12 (1989), pp. 30–49.
2. At the time of the statements given here, Prof. Saeki was vice-president of the renowned International Institute for Global Peace in Tokyo.

status. In a clear departure from Tokyo's official views, Saeki maintained that no decision could be made on the basis that the Soviet claims were wrong and the Japanese right, but that a reasonable compromise would have to be sought; however, he continued, discussions from a legal standpoint would contribute little to solving the problem, which would have to be founded on a political decision. He referred to the transfer of Okinawa in 1972, which had only been possible because of the good relations existing between Japan and the United States; the logical consequence, then, was to seek an improvement in the climate of Soviet-Japanese relations. Saeki's views thus opposed the (official) stance that the return of the islands was the prerequisite for such an improvement. He saw the possibilities of development within the direction he proposed as existing chiefly in joint discussions of economic problems, questions of arms control and measures designed to build up mutual trust, and pointed out that with regard to the stimulation of economic relations and the exploitation of Siberian resources, it would be necessary to present the Soviets with the prospect of positive decisions.

In general, the chances of Gorbachev's visit bringing about any substantial progress were viewed with scepticism. On the one hand, the view was expressed that both the Prime Minister and his Soviet guest would need enormous powers of leadership and assertion in the field of domestic politics in order to achieve a political decision; on the other, it was also understood that Gorbachev's scope for action in the territorial question was reduced by the nationalistic tendencies emerging in the Soviet Union. Saeki therefore came to the conclusion that a 'one-stop' solution to the problem could not be expected, and that first steps towards a solution should be accepted as positive progress. In Saeki's view, Gorbachev's power base in domestic politics was not firm enough for him even to be able to imply the transfer of four islands, although an offer of partial withdrawal of the troops stationed in the islands at issue would be feasible.[3] The visit itself proved this prediction to be accurate.

The numerous statements made by other Japanese experts led to a general impression of cautiously optimistic composure, justified chiefly with references to the enormous difference in

---

3. See *Ajia-jihô*, no. 12 (1989), pp. 42ff.

the two sides' economic power. Frequent references were made to the catastrophic economic situation forcing Moscow to seek Japan's help, and the premature conclusion was drawn that Japan was in a stronger bargaining position, making a breakthrough towards a settlement seem not improbable, since the Soviet Union would be desperate enough to be forced into making concessions. Even Hiroshi Kimura, one of Japan's most eminent Soviet experts, recommended playing a waiting game, since 'the facts of the situation will develop in Japan's favour'.[4]

Evaluations of Soviet difficulties proved to be accurate; however, the anticipation of a Soviet willingness to compromise extending to the return of territory proved false, an error in judgement founded both in Japan's self-righteousness and in its misunderstanding of the German-Soviet Agreement over the reunification of Germany and Germany's continued membership of NATO. The impression had arisen in Japan that Gorbachev had given Germany 'territory in exchange for money', fuelling hopes that money would also resolve the territorial question. The influential conservative politician Shin Kanemaru had already distinguished himself in April 1990 by the arrogant remark that in any case Japan could buy the islands. Kimura also justified the use of Japanese economic power to regain the islands at issue by referring to the policies of Helmut Kohl and George Bush, in the case of the latter with specific reference to the American 'most favoured nation' clause; he ignored the fact that in both cases issues were at stake which were quite different from the relinquishment of territory.[5] From these statements speculations arose that a simple Soviet-Japanese purchase transaction could take place. The historian Yuri Afanasyev brought up the idea of selling the islands to Japan for 30,000–40,000 million roubles.[6] The visit of the General Secretary of the LDP, Ozawa, in March 1991 was accompanied by rumours that Japan intended to make the Soviet Union an informal offer of US$28,000 million in economic aid if the latter returned the islands. There was also

4. See Hiroshi Kimura, 'Chikara-kankei ga Nihon-yûri na no da kara seikan-subeki de aru' (Japan Should Observe Events Calmly, since the Balance of Power is in its Favour), in *Sekai Shûhô*, 10 March 1991, pp. 108–13.
5. See 'USSR-Japan: Is There a Way out of the Territorial Deadlock? FEA Round Table', in *FEA*, no. 2 (1991), p. 116.
6. See *Horizont International*, no. 38, 17 Sept. 1990.

talk of financial aid totalling US$450 million, should Moscow express willingness to begin talks over the return of the islands.[7] Boris Yeltsin refuted these speculations, declaring in Strasbourg that it was unimaginable that the Kuriles could be sold as Alaska had once been, no matter what the price involved; the Russian people would never agree to it.[8]

There was remarkably little readiness on the part of the Foreign Ministry and its supporters to seek a solution in compromise. Kimura even went so far as to declare that any government, whether LDP or any other stripe, would be doomed to failure by accepting even the smallest concession in this question.[9] Events were to disprove this view.

The government had grasped that such an attitude is not conducive to politics; no less a figure than Ichiro Ozawa referred at the beginning of 1990 to the necessity of a compromise solution: 'We must both take a step forward from our previous positions.'[10] A few weeks later Ozawa declared in an interview with the Soviet party organ that nothing would change without 'concessions from both sides';[11] he said nothing about the form such compromises could take.

The Japanese public paid scant attention to the role of Korea in Gorbachev's policies on Japan. Moscow's strategy was clear: with the assistance of improved relations with South Korea, Japan's monopoly as financier and partner in the exploitation and development of Siberian resources was to be relativised, its negotiating position founded on economic considerations weakened. The possibility should not be ruled out that it was for this very reason that Gorbachev initiated ostentatious measures to improve Soviet relations with South Korea before visiting Tokyo. In June 1990 he had an impromptu meeting with the South Korean President, Roh Tae Woo, in San Francisco; that autumn, Moscow and Seoul confirmed full diplomatic relations, and towards the end of the year President Roh made a state visit to the Soviet Union. South Korea granted the Soviet Union a

---

7. See *Yomiuri*, 21 March 1991; *International Herald Tribune*, 22 March 1991.
8. See *Asahi Evening News*, 16 April 1991.
9. Kimura, 'Chikara-kankei', p. 110.
10. See *Asahi Evening News*, 14 March 1990.
11. See *Pravda*, 9 April 1990.

loan of US$3,000 million and agreed to cooperate in exploiting reserves in Siberia and Sakhalin.

Japan's unexpected willingness to take up official contacts with North Korea in the autumn of 1990 indicated that its leaders had been disturbed by this turn of events. While Tokyo betrayed no readiness to compromise with Moscow over the territorial question, the more flexible attitude to Moscow initiated at the beginning of 1990 by former Foreign Minister Abe with his talks in the Kremlin was retained. Abe's offer differed fundamentally from previous Japanese offers; he had presented an eight-point plan proposing the development of economic and cultural exchanges without basing these on the settlement of the territorial question. The core of his proposal was the offer to contribute to the success of *perestroika* in the form of training, support and consultancy programmes.[12] Abe's request to allow visiting rights to the 1,400 or so graves in the island of Etorofu was solely linked with Japanese interests, and was granted by the Soviet Union after only a few weeks.[13]

Back in Tokyo, Abe saw his talks with Gorbachev in an extremely positive light, expressing optimism over future developments in mutual relations and speaking of a 'great change' in the Soviet attitude towards Japan.[14] One remark allegedly made by Gorbachev had attracted particular attention; he had said Japan had 'a sovereign right' to lay claim to the islands — at least, this was the interpretation placed by the Japanese press on the following statement from the Soviet president: 'We can accept what you say in a positive light. We cannot force you into decisions we believe to be necessary. The question involves your sovereignty. You have an inherent right.'[15] In the light of concrete developments, this disputed report more probably originated in the common Japanese tendency towards over-interpretation than in any actual statement made by Gorbachev. A speaker in the *Gaimusho* immediately described the interpretation as 'very daring', adding that no evidence could be found

---

12. See *Pravda*, 17 Jan. 1990.
13. See *Asahi Evening News*, 7 Feb. 1990.
14. *Ibid.*, 18 Jan. 1990.
15. *Ibid.*, 16 Jan. 1990.

for the postulation that the Soviet Union acknowledged Japan's right to lay claim to the islands.[16]

Abe's talks in Moscow may have been important in improving the atmosphere between both sides, since they had signalled a cautious departure from the familiar Japanese position of 'territory first, good relations later'; however, prospects of a settlement of the territorial question were as open afterwards as they were to remain in all subsequent Japanese-Soviet contacts at diplomatic level.

It is worth mentioning that no detailed ideas from the government on a settlement of the territorial question were publicised for discussion. If they had existed, they would certainly have appeared in the press in one form or another; it is likely that there were no such ideas outside the Foreign Ministry's demands for 'the return of four islands at once' and Shin Kanemaru's remark concerning a phased solution.[17] In view of the decades of vehement demands for a political solution to the territorial question, this was a little meagre. Only in March 1991, less than four weeks before the Soviet President's arrival in Tokyo, did an agency report appear in which it was said the LDP leaders intended dropping demands for the return of all four islands 'at once'; they were aiming for the return of the Habomai Islands and Shikotan as a beginning and would then agree to a phased return of the other two islands if the Soviets accepted Japanese sovereignty over the islands from the outset. In exchange, the LDP had in mind that Sakhalin would receive economic aid from the Japanese and Tokyo would grant perpetual rights of residence to those Soviet citizens who wanted to remain on the islands. In addition, Japan would pledge to refrain from founding military bases on the islands. These proposals, prepared with the agreement of General Secretary Ozawa, were to be presented to the Soviets during the visit of an LDP delegation to Sakhalin on 19 March.[18] While the Soviet reaction was not made public, it can be assumed to have been one of rejection.

Soviet public opinion, too, discussed the timing of Gor-

16. Kyodo News Agency, in *SWB/FE/0666/A2/1*, 19 Jan. 1990.
17. See section in Chapter 5, 'Fundamental Positions under Fire, 1973–1985', above.
18. See Kyodo News Agency, in *SWB/FE/1026/A2/1*, 21 March 1991.

bachev's visit to Japan. In general it can be said that the greater the political responsibility of the personality expressing his views, the more reserved his comments concerning concrete possibilities for the settlement of the territorial question.

Boris Yeltsin was the first example of this. During his visit to Japan as a parliamentary representative at the beginning of 1990, he unveiled a five-phase plan. In Phase 1 of his 'personal proposal' the Soviet Union was to issue a public acknowledgement of the existence of a territorial question, either in 1990 or during Gorbachev's visit to Japan in 1991. Phase 2 would see the islands being reorganised into a free enterprise zone, in which Japan would receive most favoured nation status; the duration of this phase was given as three to four years. In Phase 3, calculated to take five to seven years from 1990, the islands would be demilitarised; Yeltsin commented that they were in fact ruled by the Soviet military and not the Soviet government. In the fourth phase, in around fifteen or twenty years, Tokyo was to conclude a bilateral peace treaty, to include certain concessions, which would officially end the state of war between the two countries and create favourable conditions for the settlement of the problem. In the fifth and last phase there would be 'a new generation of people' on both sides, who, free from case-hardened preconceptions, would tackle the question with new ideas under different conditions.[19] Foreign Minister Nakayama rejected the proposals but agreed with Yeltsin that the door should be opened to a solution to the problem.[20]

Later statements show that Yeltsin still disregarded the idea of returning the islands to Japan. During a visit to Kunashiri, one of the four islands at issue, in August 1990, he rejected ideas of returning the islands; in February 1991 he stated in Kaliningrad (Königsberg), now speaking as President of the Federation of Russian States, that the Russian Republic had no intention of either giving up Kaliningrad or returning the four islands claimed by Japan. Yeltsin had already declared the Russian Republic responsible for resolving the territorial problem with Japan.[21] His decisive rejection of Japanese claims was in accordance with

19. See *Asahi Evening News*, 17 Jan. 1990.
20. Kyodo News Agency, in *SWB/FE/0672/A2/2*, 26 Jan. 1990.
21. See *Asahi Evening News*, 9 Feb. 1991.

public opinion, which was and is firmly against the return of the islands. In a referendum conducted in the Kurile Islands in March 1991, in which almost 90% of the population took part, between 70.2% (in Kunashiri and the Habomais) and 81.3% (in Etorofu) of respondents voted against a transfer of the islands to Japan.[22]

Gorbachev also said nothing to awaken hopes of a swift and united solution to the territorial question. He stated briefly in a speech before workers in Sverdlovsk in April 1990 that the Soviet Union had 'no superfluous territory'; it would retain the view of the inviolability of post-war borders stated in the Declaration of Helsinki.[23] In July 1990 he made a similar pronouncement before Yoshio Sakurauchi, head of the Japanese Lower House: 'Today, too, I can only repeat that for us there is no territorial question.'[24] In an interview with the president of *Asahi Shimbun*, one of Japan's largest daily newspapers, at the end of 1990, Gorbachev described the role of the territorial question in bilateral relations as exaggerated and as an end in itself (*samodovleyushchi kharakter*). This, he said, had done harm to both sides. He avoided making any prediction on the chances of finding a solution.[25]

On the other hand, statements were made within Soviet leadership circles which appeared not to rule out the possibility of concessions; for example, the spokesman of the Soviet government, G. Gerasimov, declared in Manila at the beginning of 1990 that arrangements for territorial concessions to Japan were under debate in the Supreme Soviet.[26] In a television interview in Tokyo in the autumn of 1990, the Politburo member responsible for international affairs, G. Yanayev, expressed the view that the Joint Declaration of 1956 should serve as a basis for negotiations over a Soviet-Japanese peace treaty.[27] This was evidently an allusion to the return of two of the four islands proposed by the Soviets at that time, which was to take effect after the signing of a peace treaty. Yanayev repeated his proposal

22. See Kyodo News Agency, in *SWB/FE*/1025/A2/1, 20 March 1991.
23. See *Asahi Evening News*, 28 April 1990.
24. TASS, quoted in *MD Asien*, 26 July 1990.
25. See *Pravda*, 30 Dec. 1990.
26. See Kyodo News Agency, in *SWB/FE*/0697/A2/2, 24 Feb. 1990.
27. See NHK Television, in *SWB/FE*/0895/A2/1, 15 Oct. 1990.

before the Congress of People's Deputies in Moscow at the end of December 1990.[28]

Speculations about these arrangements for the return of the islands were fuelled anew by reports in the Japanese press of a Soviet seven-point plan; Gorbachev, it was said, would offer the return of two of the four islands, namely Habomai and Shikotan, during his visit. This plan was said to have been presented verbally to the General Secretary of the Abe faction and former Foreign Minister, Hiroshi Mitsuzuka, in Moscow at the end of September, and sent to Shintaro Abe in Tokyo at the beginning of October.[29] The Foreign Ministry in Moscow immediately denied the existence of such a plan, an embarrassing disavowal for Abe, since, as already mentioned, he had believed he could perceive a change in the Soviets' attitude. The *Gaimusho* complained that Abe had not immediately passed on information concerning the alleged plan.[30]

Foreign Minister Shevardnadze was also reported as stating that the Kuriles and the island of Sakhalin should be transformed into a Soviet-Japanese zone for joint projects on environmental conservation. He left the question of sovereignty open.[31] A similar proposal came from the *Pravda* commentator Ovchinnikov, who thought the problem could be resolved by entrusting the islands at issue to the United Nations and thus making them into a special economic zone under joint administration.[32]

Soviet leaders continued their comments on the territorial question until Gorbachev's departure for Japan was imminent. At the end of February 1991 his adviser Marshal Sergei Akhromeyev informed the news agency Kyodo that Japan and the Soviet Union should open talks on the return of the Habomais and Shikotan on the basis of the Joint Declaration of 1956; if negotiations were to be conducted over this question, he said, then careful consideration should be given not only to the military advantages, but also to political, economic and other factors.[33]

28. See *Sankei Shimbun* (evening edn.), 28 Dec. 1990.
29. See *Asahi Evening News*, 8 Oct. 1990.
30. See *International Herald Tribune*, 9 Oct. 1990; *Neue Zürcher Zeitung*, 11 Oct. 1990.
31. See *Izvestiya*, 13 April 1990.
32. See *Pravda*, 1 July 1990.
33. See Kyodo News Agency, in *SWB/FE*/1010/i, 2 March 1991.

None of these considerations met with the official approval of the Japanese. The Foreign Ministry spokesman, Taizo Watanabe, declared without further ado that all proposals not envisaging the return of two islands or joint use of the islands were unacceptable; the return of four islands, he proclaimed, was a fundamental condition.[34]

Naturally the Foreign Ministers of both sides and the joint working groups played an important role in preparing for the Japanese-Soviet summit meeting. However, the visit of Foreign Minister Shevardnadze to Tokyo on 4–7 September 1990 was especially significant, since for the first time both sides reached an agreement over a joint communiqué concerning 'an acute problem of international dimensions'. The issue at hand was the situation in the Gulf, where developments were regarded with great concern by both Tokyo and Moscow. They sharply criticised Baghdad's invasion of Kuwait and pledged their full support for UN measures against Iraq.[35] In addition, Japan showed interest in a serious discussion with the Soviets on the military situation in the Asia Pacific region and on problems of security and stability in the region.[36] On the question of drawing up a peace treaty, and the territorial problems linked to it, Shevardnadze intimated that his government would be prepared to participate in an open discussion, although he noted that 'a long time' would be necessary before both states could reach a solution. He explained the difficulties by pleading that the Russian Federal Republic could afford to ignore public opinion as little as could the central government of the Soviet Union, and that this concern certainly applied to the Japanese government as well.[37]

A *rapprochement* between the two standpoints on the territorial question, or, as the Soviets called it, on the 'geographical aspect' of the peace treaty, was reached neither at the sixth meeting of the joint working parties on 15 November 1990 nor during the reciprocal visits of both sides' Foreign Ministers to Moscow in January and to Tokyo at the end of March 1991. It is remarkable, however, that at the beginning of 1991 Shevardnadze's successor,

34. See Kyodo News Agency, in *SWB/FE/0897/i*, 17 Oct. 1990.
35. Text of the communiqué in *SWB/FE/0862/C1/2*, 6 Sept. 1990.
36. See *SWB/FE/0863/C1/4*, 7 Sept. 1990.
37. See *SWB/FE/0865/C1/4*, 10 Sept. 1990.

Foreign Minister Bessmertnykh, dampened hopes which had arisen in connection with Gorbachev's visit with the comment that the territorial question could not be resolved at the first bilateral summit conference.[38] As had been the case with Shevardnadze, underlying this remark was the realistic acceptance that problems with nationalities within the USSR would further complicate the territorial question with Japan as well. This was demonstrated by the fact that Bessmertnykh was accompanied on his visit by Andrei Kosyrev, the Foreign Minister of the Russian Federal Republic.

Gorbachev himself also referred, in a television interview immediately before his visit, to the long and arduous process of finding a solution, speaking of a gradual approach to the territorial question; border issues affected the fate of nations and the future of the people, and should be resolved step by step, not in a single decision.[39] When Gorbachev broke his journey to Japan in Khabarovsk, shouts were heard from the crowd, 'Don't give them any islands, Mikhail Sergeiyevitch!' His reply was, 'I will do what you ask me!'[40] And so he did – but not exclusively because that was the wish of the people.

38. See *MD Asien*, 24 Jan. 1991.
39. *International Herald Tribune*, 13/14 April 1991.
40. *Moskovskie Novosti*, no. 17 (28 April 1991).

10

PROGRESS, RESULTS, REACTIONS

The Soviet President's visit to Japan on 16–19 April 1991 ended neither with disappointing results nor in clear-cut failure. Expectations which the Japanese media had driven sky-high with every speculation imaginable were forced to give way to disillusionment. Seen realistically, Gorbachev and his host Prime Minister Kaifu reached the limits of what was possible; they made serious and successful efforts to prevent the meeting ending inconclusively and to introduce an improvement in relations.

Gorbachev, whose authority in his own country appeared to be crumbling more and more rapidly just before his visit to Japan, made no concrete offer of a solution to the territorial question. The Japanese head of state was conscious of his guest's extremely limited scope for decisions; for this reason and because of the highly critical condition of the Soviet economy, clearly in a state of absolute chaos, he was not in a position to make any significant offers of help, which in any case his party would not have approved. Moreover, Japanese policies on the Soviet Union had been focused on the fundamentally trivial territorial question for decades, a constriction which left no room for concessions. In view of these factors, the actual political achievements of the meeting were realistic and should be assessed against the potential for development in relations, and also against the stagnation which had ruled in the past.

Immediately after their arrival, the Soviet President and Raisa Gorbachev were received by Emperor Akihito and the Empress in the guest-house in the heart of Tokyo used for state visits, and welcomed with the ceremony prescribed for such occasions. Gorbachev was accompanied by a group including not only Foreign Minister Bessmertnykh but also the Ministers of Culture (Gubenko) and Foreign Trade Relations (Katushev), the Secretary of the Central Committee and Chairman of the International Department of the CPSU Central Committee, Falin, the President's adviser Yakovlev, and – as an illustration of how the Soviet Union was changing – three high-ranking representatives of the Russian Federal Republic; the Foreign Minister already mentioned, Kosyrev, was accompanied by the Chairman of the Committee for International Affairs of the Supreme Soviet of the RSFSR, Lukin, and the Chairman for the Yakutiya-Sakhalin Region in the Supreme Soviet, Nikolayev. On the day of his guests' arrival, Prime Minister Kaifu met his counterpart for the first of three rounds of talks that were planned; at this stage nothing indicated that the two politicians would have to meet on a total of six occasions in order to reach accord on difficult points of the communiqué. At the first meeting, the Japanese leader outlined and justified Japan's territorial demands; both sides agreed not to release any particulars of the discussion over the territorial conflict. Gorbachev's spokesman described the first meeting as a good start.[1]

Two points on the visitors' programme are worthy of note: Gorbachev's speech before the Members of Parliament, and his meeting with top Japanese business people. In his speech to Parliament, he presented details of the disarmament process in the Asian regions of the Soviet Union. The perspectives he unveiled hardly exceeded his presentations of Asian policies in 1986 (at Vladivostok) and 1988 (at Krasnoyarsk); by maintaining them he took up, though not explicitly, the European model of a CSCE, which had never found favour in Asia.

Gorbachev proposed a dialogue on military questions with Japan, completed this point with the suggestion of initiating trilateral Soviet/Japanese/American consultations, and, alluding to his country's existing good relations with China, India, the ASEAN states, South Korea, the USA and Canada, pleaded for international structures of security policy in the Asia Pacific region, to create the 'mechanisms of a multilateral cooperation'. He proposed a Five Powers Conference, to include the Soviet Union, the United States, China, India and Japan. A similar proposal had been made in his Krasnoyarsk speech of 1988, albeit without the inclusion of India, an omission which at the time had produced critical reactions in Delhi. Then as now, the proposal was greeted with extreme reserve. In his speech before the Tokyo Parliament, Gorbachev linked the idea to Foreign Minister Shevardnadze's suggestion for a conference of Foreign Ministers of Asia Pacific states in 1993.

1. See Kyodo News Agency, in *SWB/FE/1048/A2/1*, 17 April 1991.

The Soviet guest briefly touched upon the problems in Soviet-Japanese relations, and spoke of finally settling the 'problems in existence since the war, including the most difficult problem of all, the territorial limits'. He asked for confidence to be placed in the reshaping process the Soviet Union was undergoing, while making no attempt to hide the colossal problems and dangers of this process and commenting that there was a possibility that the country would fall into chaos out of which a dictatorship would arise.[2]

Reactions to the speech from the Japanese public were reserved; those passages dealing with Asian policies were felt to be lacking in new approaches. The familiar attempt, repeated by Gorbachev, to apply European models to Asia was not supported by Japan, and China's rejection of the idea was well known; however, without the support of these two countries the Soviet proposal was impossible. Gorbachev's suggestion that trilateral consultations with the United States and Japan should be initiated was rejected by Kaifu with a reference to the functioning, proven alliance with the United States that was already in existence.[3] The constant rejection of Soviet multilaterally based initiatives indicated that European models of organisation would fare no better with the region's other main powers; on the other hand, five years of Gorbachev's Asian policies demonstrated that a bilateral approach to the problems did bring noteworthy results. Perhaps this approach was more suited to the more complex situation in East Asia, where – with the exception of Korea – clear boundaries between systems are absent.

Gorbachev's warning of the possibility of chaos arising in his country was a vain attempt to win more active commitment to the Soviet Union from Japanese business; however, he sought precisely this kind of commitment from the leaders of Japan's seven largest conglomerates and representatives of over 500 companies. His most important offers to this influential audience included:

– extensive exploitation of Russian gas and oil deposits in the Tyumen region of western Siberia;

2. Text of the speech in *Izvestiya*, 17 April 1991.
3. See *International Herald Tribune*, 23 April 1991.

- the modernisation of twelve oil refineries in the Soviet Far East and Siberia;
- supply of Soviet uranium products and components for atomic power stations;
- the purchase of Japanese equipment and technology for manufacturing consumer goods;
- Japanese participation in expanding the under-developed infrastructure of the Far Eastern region, in particular expanding the ports of Vostochny and Vanino and the airports of Khabarovsk and Vladivostok and organising modern transport links between these cities and Japan;
- the creation of free economic zones, for example in the vicinity of Nakhodka;
- the creation of a Soviet-Japanese regional development bank, which would also be open to other states;
- cooperation in the fields of high technology and conversion; that is, the 'elimination of our economy's excessive militarism'.

In conclusion, Gorbachev referred to the possibilities, which he saw as extensive, of a cooperation offering benefits to both sides, while conceding that Japanese companies were greatly concerned by the debts incurred by the Soviet Foreign Trade Organisation. He continued: 'We are counting on an understanding of our difficulties in this matter and hope for cooperation as regards rescheduling the payments. There is no need to panic.'[4]

Japanese industrialists' reactions to Gorbachev's speech were reserved. Gaishi Hiraiwa, chairman of the umbrella organisation of Japan's industries, stated that he regarded Gorbachev's efforts at gaining cooperation for a range of projects as nothing more than an expression of his hopes for cooperation at such time as it would be needed. Despite the reforms, he continued, the system of decentralised control in the Soviet economy was hardly likely to collapse overnight.[5] This was a polite but unmistakable expression of the Japanese industrialists' lack of interest in any significant commitment to the Soviet Union.

Of the protocol ceremonies arranged for the Soviet guests,

4. Text of the speech in *Pravda*, 18 April 1991; *SWB/FE*/1050 A2/5, 19 April 1991; *Asahi*, 18 April 1991 in *DSJP*, 23 April 1991, p. 4.
5. See Kyodo News Agency, in *SWB/FE*/1050 A2/5, 19 April 1991.

the banquet in the Imperial Palace is noteworthy because Gorbachev touched on a sensitive spot in the relations of the two states: the death of Japanese prisoners-of-war in Soviet camps. The Soviet President expressed his condolences (*soboleznovanie*) for 'the families of the prisoners of war who died on foreign soil'.[6] The Japanese criticised his choice of words as 'rather too light', although the Soviet Embassy had (deliberately?) chosen the perhaps too weak expression 'sympathy' in the English version of the text.[7] The degree of Japanese self-righteousness apparent in these criticisms is quite remarkable; when Emperor Hirohito managed a feeble expression of 'regret' (*ikan*) to the President of South Korea, Chun Doo Hwan, for Japan's brutal colonization of Korea, Japanese politicians accepted this as a wholly appropriate gesture. Other neighbouring countries which had suffered at the hands of Japan's military rule in the past have complained constantly of Tokyo's unwillingness to acknowledge the crimes committed on behalf of the Tenno. The 600,000 Japanese prisoners-of-war in Siberia, 60,000 of whom died, undoubtedly suffered terribly; however, Japan of all countries has little enough reason to criticise others for insufficient feelings of guilt.

At the end of the visit the Joint Declaration was published, which as the Japanese press was aware had only been finalised after enormous effort on both sides; there had been disagreement over the phrasing of references to the territorial problem. Eventually the delegations managed to agree on a document which may be judged a solid basis for further improvements in relations.[8]

The following points from the Joint Declaration are politically worthy of note:

– The Soviet Union recognised the existence of an as yet unresolved territorial question defined by its geographical scope. For the first time since the end of the Second World War the Soviets declared themselves prepared to discuss the issue of the frontier between the two states, including the

6. *Pravda*, 17 April 1991.
7. *Asahi Evening News*, 18 April 1991.
8. Text of the Joint Declaration of 18 April 1991 in *Nihon Keizai Shimbun*, 19 April 1991; *Pravda*, 20 April 1991; *SWB/FE/*1051, 20 April 1991; for English text see Appendix A.

territorial problem, with a peace treaty in view. The four islands were listed by name in the Declaration.
- The Soviet Union implicity acknowledged a difference in status between the territory at issue and the remainder of the Soviet Union, by mentioning the prospect of visa-free visiting rights to the islands for Japanese citizens.
- The Soviet Union and Japan agreed to discuss the initiation of joint economic activities in the islands and the reduction of the Soviet troops stationed there. While these two ideas still included areas of uncertainty, both sides nonetheless began to examine the questions involved. It was explicitly agreed to speed up preparations for signing a peace treaty.
- The Joint Declaration of 1956, the fundamental basis for this Declaration, was not mentioned specifically; however, a reference to the date, combined with the intention announced by both sides to employ 'all positive elements' from past negotiations, logically includes that document. It is still unclear as to whether this may be understood as an indirect reference to the offer made in 1956 to return two of the four islands after the signing of a peace treaty. In any case, the Japanese took the offer to be a 'positive element' towards a solution.
- A total of fifteen agreements, pacts and memoranda concerning cooperation in fields such as science/technology, fishing, ecology, transport technology and culture allow the possibility of creating closer relations than in the past. Whether this can be put into practice, and to what extent, will depend chiefly on internal developments in Russia after the dissolution of the Soviet Union.
- With regard to the Korean peninsula, both sides formulated an extensive agreement of their interests, with especial significance given to joint hopes of a safeguard agreement to be signed 'as fast as possible' by North Korea and the International Atomic Energy Agency (IAEA). There was open concern over the development of atomic weapons in North Korea; the dialogue unfolding between North and South Korea was welcomed. Japan also interpreted the assumption of diplomatic relations between Moscow and Seoul in a positive light; the Soviets for their part supported the beginning of talks between Japan and North Korea.

How may the results of the meeting be interpreted? Gorbachev's statements on the territorial question did not go beyond the ideas presented at the beginning of 1990 by Boris Yeltsin as the initial steps towards his own proposal for a solution. While the Joint Declaration contains no reference to the creation of a free-trade zone, future negotiations on economic cooperation in the islands could take this direction. The Soviet government is known to have considered the creation of free-trade zones in the Soviet Far East. Yeltsin, who had at first announced his intention to leave the solution of the territorial problem to 'successive generations', saw the process as ending not with the return of the islands, but with their administration by a 'joint protectorate'.[9]

The Soviets appeared to have enormous difficulty – other than had been widely assumed at first – in returning to the offer made in the Joint Declaration of 1956, that of returning two of the four islands at issue on the signing of a peace treaty. The Soviet Union had withdrawn the offer in 1960, referring to the renewal of the Japanese-American security treaty, and had made its reacceptance contingent on the withdrawal of all foreign troops from Japanese territory. Despite improvements in relations with the United States, by the end of 1991 Moscow had still shown no readiness to drop this biased stance, which actually represented an infringement of international law, since the Supreme Soviet had officially ratified the Joint Declaration of 1956. Soviet experts on Japan also described the annulment of even a single paragraph of this document as an illegal act.[10]

Back in Moscow once again, Gorbachev explained before the Supreme Soviet his reasons for refusing the request of Japan's head of government to mention the Declaration of 1956. In his view, it was only possible to rely on that part of the document which had become historical reality and had 'physical consequences and consequences of international law'; he continued, doubtless in allusion to the offer made at that time, that it was not possible simply to resurrect what had not happened in the subsequent period: 'The chance which existed at the time was

9. See *Asahi Evening News*, 17 Jan. 1990; *Moscow News*, quoted in RFE/RL *Daily Report*, no. 41 (27 Feb. 1990).
10. See *Ogonek*, no. 20 (May 1990), pp. 16–19; Georgi Kunadze in *Nezavisimaja Gazeta*, 24 Jan. 1991.

missed.'[11] Gorbachev believed that in the end decisions acceptable to both sides would be reached, but that for this to be achieved 'a different situation, a different character to mutual relations, the creation of their irreversibility, a high degree of mutual dependence and close reciprocal links' would be necessary.[12] The familiar Soviet view reappeared: the climate of relations would first have to change before any change could be made to the relations themselves. Or, along the lines of the Japanese principle of the inseparability of politics and economics, the two factors should function not consecutively, but as closely linked to one another.

The reference to the irreversibility (*neobratimost*) of relations is an interesting one. It probably masked the Soviets' concern that territorial concessions would result in only a temporary improvement in Japanese-Soviet relations, and that after a time there would perhaps be a strengthening of the same voices which today are calling for the return of the entire Kurile chain and Sakhalin; the result, the Soviets feared, would be a new confrontation. The 'irreversibility of relations' assumes a change in both peoples' understanding of one another – a lengthy process.

Russia, under whose administrative jurisdiction the islands fall, is now the sole negotiating partner after the dissolution of the Soviet Union, which explains the representation of the Russian Federation by its Foreign Minister in Gorbachev's delegation. As already explained, the majority of the islands' population had expressed their rejection of a return to Japanese rule, a fact which Gorbachev was also obliged to bear in mind in Tokyo. This aspect, together with Russia's growing nationalism, will play a role in future negotiations, and will certainly not simplify the process of finding a solution.

It is remarkable that the Soviets were willing to list the four islands by name in the Joint Declaration, without distinguishing between the islands always defined as geographically part of Hokkaido – the Habomai group and Shikotan – and the islands which belong to the Kuriles – namely, Kunashiri and Etorofu. The presence of such a distinction in the Soviet view may be

11. *Pravda*, 27 April 1991. The Soviet leaders had assumed in 1956 that Japan would take this chance and accept two islands, and had even begun to move the population of Shikotan to other Kurile islands in anticipation.
12. *Ibid.*

inferred from the offer of 1956 in which Habomai and Shikotan would be 'transferred' to Japan upon the signing of a peace treaty. As Japan renounced all claim to the Kuriles in the 1951 peace treaty of San Francisco, under international law it has lost all claim to Kunashiri and Etorofu; however, since 1955 the Japanese government has attempted to except Kunashiri and Etorofu from the renunciation by declaring them not to be part of the Kuriles, an untenable claim according to the traditional definition of the Kuriles. So it is an important factor for future negotiations that the Soviets/Russians agreed to the naming of all four islands without further distinction.

The Soviet military proved to be of little assistance in attempts to come to a solution. One week before Gorbachev arrived in Japan, Yasov, the Minister of Defence, emphasised the allegedly great significance of the islands for the security of the Soviet Union, declaring that they could not be exchanged for Japanese economic aid, and that this decision should not be left to Gorbachev alone.[13] The restricting influence of the military was also reflected in the Joint Declaration, which proposed not the withdrawal but only the reduction of troops in the islands.

A comparison of the results of the visit with both sides' opposing approaches to a solution gives the impression of a certain measure of concession on the part of the Japanese. Tokyo always held the view that 'first the territorial question should be solved, then the atmosphere improved and economic cooperation initiated'; Moscow urged the reverse procedure, or at least a linking of the two processes. In fact, the process actually seems to have started moving according to Soviet ideas; the principle of the inseparability of politics and economics is still upheld, but no longer practised as uncompromisingly as in earlier years. Between the end of 1990 and President Yeltsin's visit to Tokyo in October 1993, the total volume of Japanese loans to Russia was US$4,100 million, mostly offered by the Export-Import Bank. The largest part (US$2,900 million) were guarantees in the fields of trade and energy. In the same period Russia received US$500 million as non-refundable aid for food, medicine, education and cooperation in disposing of nuclear waste.[14] Before

13. See *Far Eastern Economic Review*, 2 May 1991, p. 12.
14. See *Nihon Keizai Shimbun*, 10 Oct. 1993.

the summit conference of the seven leading industrial nations, held in London in July 1991, Japan decided to grant the Soviet Union a limited amount of financial aid via the European Bank for Reconstruction and Development and to agree to a special status for the Soviet Union within the International Monetary Fund (IMF). In Moscow this 'change from a hard-line course' was greeted with approval.[15] On the other hand, there were no signs that Tokyo was prepared to grant Moscow a loan to repay Soviet debts to Japanese companies, which had by this time grown to US$450 million. The agreements and memoranda signed on the occasion of Gorbachev's visit seemed to encourage expectations of a certain degree of expansion in business relations; however, in view of Russia's catastrophic economic situation, Japanese industrialists would probably prefer to keep their distance. It was counted as a Soviet success that Japan intended to give its support to the Soviet Union's full membership of the Pacific Economic Cooperation Conference (PECC); until then Moscow had occupied only observer status, since its full membership had been obstructed by Japan for years.

All in all, the visit of the Soviet President to Japan may be evaluated as a vital first step on the doubtless long road to improved relations between the two states. Even after the dissolution of the Soviet Union, the result offers a sound basis for future high-level Russian-Japanese negotiations.

Immediately after Gorbachev's visit, both sides conducted studies chiefly to determine the results as assessed by informed, critical observers. The press on both sides saw the achievements as mainly positive. Japanese observers voiced the loudest disappointment, principally because of the Soviets' refusal explicitly to acknowledge the Joint Declaration of 1956.[16] The General Secretary of the LDP, Keizo Obuchi, viewed Gorbachev's acknowledgement of the need to accelerate negotiations on the territorial problem as a step forward, and affirmed that the concluding document could indeed be taken as a confirmation of the 1956 Declaration. Other respected members of the ruling party also took a positive view, intimating that this was the best

15. See *Pravda*, 2 July 1991.
16. See the discussion between Masamori Sase and Hiroshi Kimura in *Sankei Shimbun*, 20 April 1991.

result to be expected under the circumstances. Similar opinions were expressed by the General Secretary of the SPJ, Tsuruo Yamaguchi. The head of the International Office of the Buddhism-based Komei Party, Kazuyoshi Endo, warned that the Kremlin should understand that a swift solution to the territorial problem was necessary to place Japanese-Soviet relations on a firm and solid base. The head of the Japanese Communist Party International Committee stated that in his party's view the progress made on the territorial question was slight, adding, 'We do not accept the restriction of the problem to only four islands.'[17] His Party was known to demand the return of the entire Kurile chain. The Soviets' overall view of the results was positive, and they noted with satisfaction that the inseparability of politics and economics in Japan's relationship with the Soviet Union was undergoing a 'significant process of revision'.[18]

In a survey organised jointly by the dailies *Izvestiya* and *Yomiuri Shimbun*, both sides attempted to gain a picture of popular opinion in their own countries from answers given to identical sets of questions. Future developments in Soviet-Japanese relations were evaluated by 5% of Russians and 1% of Japanese as 'very good', by 19% and 29% respectively as 'good', by 44% and 21% respectively as 'medium' and 13% and 41% respectively as 'bad'. Interest in Gorbachev's visit to Japan was described by 17% of Soviet and 46% of Japanese citizens as 'high', by 24% and 14% respectively as 'limited'; 16% and 4% respectively had 'no interest'. Answers also differed sharply when the respondents were asked if they were satisfied with the acknowledgement of the territorial problem by the explicit naming of the four islands and the agreement to sign a peace treaty as soon as possible; 16% of the Russians and 5% of the Japanese surveyed stated they were 'completely satisfied', 19% and 40% respectively were 'somewhat dissatisfied'. Questioned on the prospect of more rapid future developments in Soviet-Japanese relations, respondents' answers showed a greater degree of convergence; 37% of Soviet and 44% of Japanese subjects expected swifter developments, while 32% and 38% respectively did not expect any change.[19] These opin-

17. *Asahi Evening News*, 19 April 1991.
18. *Izvestiya*, 23 April 1991.
19. *Izvestiya*, 27 April 1991. In the Soviet Union the survey was conducted on 22 April in fourteen Russian cities between Leningrad and Krasnoyarsk,

ions show that while the Japanese showed more interest in Gorbachev's visit to their country, they judged its results, and the state of bilateral relations, more sceptically than their Soviet counterparts did.

Gorbachev broke his return journey on the South Korean island of Cheju not only with the purpose of deepening contacts, but also to emphasise the difference in quality between the relations of his country with South Korea and those with Japan. The gradual improvement in relations with South Korea since 1988 was in part an element of Soviet policy on Japan, intended to signal to Japan's political leaders and industrialists that the Soviet Union was not solely dependent on the goodwill of the island state. This was a tactical blunder, and made a bad impression on the Japanese; the visit of the Soviet President to Tokyo was an exceptional event, and in certain ways also an historic one, but its combination with a mere stopover in South Korea relativised it. Soviet diplomacy had committed a blunder.

Gorbachev's talks in South Korea probably seemed a welcome break from the fierce struggles with Kaifu; his evaluations after the event clearly expressed a certain disappointment in Japan's reservedness in contrast to Korea's eagerness for economic cooperation. Back in Moscow, Gorbachev fulsomely praised 'those partners who have shown true solidarity with our country at this moment when our only need is support'.[20]

Acting on a Soviet initiative, Moscow and Seoul engaged in consultations over signing a treaty of good neighbourliness and cooperation, a delicate step since there was already a 'treaty of friendship, cooperation and mutual aid' with North Korea, dating from 1961. Furthermore, Gorbachev supported double representation for Korea in the United Nations; the initial resistance from Pyongyang which this support caused was dropped a few weeks later, probably under influence from Peking. These actions, together with the expression of straightforward commitment to international controls to be exercised over North Korea's development of nuclear technology, showed that the

---

with a total number of 1,072 subjects reflecting more or less the spread of the adult population. In Japan 1,500 persons over the age of twenty were questioned on 24–25 April.
20. *Pravda*, 27 April 1991.

Soviet leaders were interested in lowering the tensions in the Korean peninsula. Soviet policies were clearly focused on the era after reunification of the divided country and were preparing for a time when profitable relations would flourish. But Moscow was also certainly interested in securing the possibility of gaining influence within the unification process itself, the course of which can as yet hardly be considered peaceful. History has shown that Russian-Japanese relationships have always been influenced by events in the Korean peninsula; Tokyo was able to regard with detachment the Soviet Union's attempts to exploit the problem-filled relationship of Korea and Japan for its own Japanese policies. Korea has yet to undergo a similar experience to that of Japan in the 1970s over the Siberian development projects.

China's attitude towards Gorbachev's visit to Japan was illuminating for Tokyo; as long as China's policies towards the Soviet Union were openly critical, the leaders in Peking had, as shown, always supported Japan's claims to the return of the four islands, and had pursued this course to such an extent in the 1970s that Foreign Minister Miyazawa had been compelled to point out that Chinese support over the territorial question was completely unsolicited. For this he was sharply criticised in Peking. Naturally, Tokyo realised that exaggerated support from China hardly simplified the search for a solution, but then this was precisely Peking's aim.[21] The backing for Japan's territorial claim grew less vociferous in proportion to the improvements in Sino-Soviet/Russian relations, and latterly has been reduced to an objective remark that a territorial problem between the two sides exists. When Foreign Minister Nakayama travelled to Peking a few weeks before Gorbachev's visit to Japan and brought up the subject of Japanese-Soviet relations, he received a laconic answer from Prime Minister Li Peng and from Foreign Minister Qian: China's views on the question of Japanese-Soviet relations had not altered. There was not the slightest detectable allusion from the Chinese in favour of the Japanese position.[22] China's tactics were hardly helpful to Japan.

Another series of issues also made it clear that China's leaders

21. See first section of Chapter 7 above.
22. See *Sankei Shimbun*, 6 and 7 April 1991.

no longer believed it opportune to express public views which contradicted Soviet interests. It is also possible that the still unfinished negotiations over the joint Sino-Soviet border caused Peking to avoid every possible disruption. Whether in the course of time a Sino-Russian coalition of interests will form in opposition to Japan's dominant political role in the Asia Pacific region depends principally on whether and to what extent Japan will strive for a leading role in that region; at present there is little cause for alarm.

11

CONTINUATION OF THE DIALOGUE: PROSPECTS FOR THE FUTURE

The second half of 1991 was remarkable for two events which will positively influence Japanese-Russian relations over the long term: the failed putsch of 19 August in Moscow, and the end of the Soviet Union. The first of these strengthened the chances of developments in the direction of democracy and a market economy; at the same time, the meteoric rise of Boris Yeltsin clearly took place at the expense of President Gorbachev. The second event put a formal end to a state, to its inhumane apparatus of power and to the ideology with which its existence had been justified; instead conditions came into existence which will facilitate future dialogues between Japan and Russia. It is, however, unlikely that this will mean a speedier conclusion of a peace treaty including a solution of the territorial problem. A short examination of the development of relations after the failed putsch follows.

After 19 August 1991 hopes understandably developed in Tokyo that the Russians might prove more flexible, now that economic restructuring was freed from ideological restrictions, than they had been at the time of Gorbachev's visit. The openly admitted acute need for economic aid served to strengthen Japan's hopes in this direction. The granting of independence to the three Baltic states was seen by Tokyo as encouraging for its own cause, for this action reversed one consequence of Stalin's expansionism. Why, then, should it not be followed by a revision of the effects of this expansionism on the Russian-Japanese border? After all the drastic changes, the first impressions were that a decision from Moscow along the lines of Japan's territorial demands or an offer modelled on that of 1956 no longer appeared to be impossible.

Only a week after the failed putsch in Moscow in August 1991, Saito and Rogachov, the Deputy Foreign Ministers of Japan and the USSR, agreed to hold talks at working-group level aimed at reconciling the differences which prevented the signing of a peace treaty.[1] Unpredictable internal developments in the Soviet Union led to delays in these plans. Finally, Foreign Ministers Taro Nakayama and Boris Pankin met for talks on the periphery of the UN General Assembly. Again, both sides professed to desire a settlement to the undecided territorial question as soon as possible. The solution, according to Nakayama, would have to be preceded by 'a fundamental improvement' in relations, since it was such an important part of Japan's 'five principles' on Soviet policies. These principles, which strictly speaking are political intentions, were published at this time and covered the following:

– Increase in Japan's aid for Soviet reforms.
– Strengthening of cooperation with the Russian Federation.
– Support for the Soviet Union's efforts towards becoming accepted as a constructive partner in the Asia Pacific region.
– Support for the Soviet Union's efforts towards integration into the world economic order by means of special status in the IMF and the World Bank.
– Striving towards an early solution to the territorial question, with the aim of signing a peace treaty.[2]

In New York, Nakayama explained to his Soviet counterpart that all Japanese support for the Soviet Union in its processes of democratisation and conversion to a market economy would be in the form of humanitarian and technological aid and expertise in macroeconomic and fiscal issues.[3] Long-term state-backed loans, however, were still impermissible because their agreement was bound up with the territorial question.

Only a few weeks after this meeting, the Japanese Foreign Minister travelled to Moscow and St Petersburg for a working visit, meeting the Presidents of the Soviet Union and the RSFSR, Gorbachev and Yeltsin, and their Foreign Ministers, Pankin and Kosyrev, for talks on 12–17 October. The visit's timing was especially felicitous since just before Nakayama's arrival in Moscow the Tokyo government had decided to grant

---

1. See Kyodo News Agency, Tokyo, in *SWB/FE*/1163/A2/2, 29 Aug. 1991.
2. See Kyodo News Agency, Tokyo, 24 Sept. 1991, in *SWB/FE*/1186/A2/1, 25 Sept. 1991.
3. *Ibid.*

the Soviet Union loan aid for foodstuffs and medicines totalling US$2,500 million.[4] However, the reason for this rapid agreement to grant loans was not so much the Foreign Minister's visit to Moscow, but the G7 meeting planned for 11 October in Bangkok. The Japanese government feared it would be placing itself under pressure from the United States and the European Community by maintaining its reservations towards support for the Soviet Union.

Nakayama's talks in the Soviet Union brought positive results on three issues: the question of how negotiations on a peace treaty were to proceed, the matter of visiting rights and talks on security policy. With regard to the individual issues, it was agreed to reorganise the peace treaty working group which had been in existence since 1988. At the Soviets' suggestion, two sub-committees were set up, one of which was to concern itself solely with the treaty paragraph on the territorial question, while the other was to discuss all other questions arising from the peace treaty. The Soviets nominated the Deputy Foreign Minister of the RSFSR, Georgi Kunadze, as chairman of the first sub-committee,[5] thus entrusting this important position to an experienced diplomat and renowned expert in Japanese affairs, who saw the territorial question in an objective light and understood the Japanese viewpoint.

The agreement over visiting rights concerned procedures for visa-exempted tour groups from Japan to the four islands at issue and for Soviet island-dwellers to Japan. Furthermore, it was agreed to raise the number of journalists active in each country from thirty to fifty.[6]

With regard to the Asia Pacific region, both ministers expressed strong interest in the development and intensification of

4. See NHK Television, Tokyo, 8 Oct. 1991, in *SWB/FE/1201/A2/1*, 12 Oct. 1991. The aid comprised: US$500 million in the form of loans from the Export-Import Bank at low interest rates for the purchase of food and clothing; US$1,800 million in the form of trade assurances from Japanese companies contributing to the Soviet economic reform in the form of trade and investment; US$200 million as loans for exports from Japanese companies to the Soviet Union.

5. See 'Vestnik Ministerstva inostrannych del SSSR' (Messenger of the Ministry for Foreign Affairs of the USSR), 15 Nov. 1991, pp. 5ff; TASS, 16 Oct. 1991.

6. See 'Vestnik', p. 6.

talks on aspects of the region's security policies, agreeing in principle to involve military experts from both sides to contribute to this exchange of ideas. The possibility of a Soviet-Japanese agreement on the prevention of naval incidents was considered.[7] Finally, Foreign Minister Pankin informed his Japanese colleagues that in accordance with Gorbachev's proposal in Tokyo, 30% of the Soviet troops stationed in the south Kuriles at that time would be withdrawn.[8]

To sum up, both sides made serious efforts at government level to exploit the impetus towards an improvement in atmosphere which had arisen out of Gorbachev's visit to Japan and the events of that August, in order to achieve concrete results, if only in peripheral areas. This was certainly in accordance with the Soviet idea expressed in the past, of creating a basis for solving the core questions by means of an atmosphere of détente. When the Soviet Union dissolved into a Commonwealth of Independent States (CIS) at the end of 1991, not even the beginnings of negotiations on a peace treaty had been agreed, to say nothing of whether a solution to the territorial problem had been approached; for all that, the political climate between Japan and Russia seemed more favourable that at any time over the decades since the end of the Second World War. On 27 December 1991 Japan proclaimed official diplomatic recognition of the Russian Republic as the legal successor to the Soviet Union. Tokyo's negotiating partner was now the Russian President, Boris Yeltsin, whose five-phase plan for the solution of the territorial question has been described above.[9] According to statements of the acting chairman of the Supreme Soviet of the Russian Federation, Ruslan Khasbulatov, who had visited Japan on the LDP's invitation at the beginning of September 1991, Yeltsin was prepared to smooth over the territorial conflict with Japan. No details about how a solution would be achieved were discussed on this occasion; without establishing any connection with the territorial question, the guest placed the Russian leaders' desire for Japanese economic assistance at US$8,000–15,000 million.[10] He gave the Japanese Prime Minister a letter from

7. *Ibid.*
8. *Ibid.*
9. See Chapter 9 above.
10. See *International Herald Tribune*, 14/15 Sept. 1991.

Yeltsin in which the latter apparently begged Japan for economic and financial aid, and which apparently also contained the prospect of a possible solution to the territorial question within the next two years.[11] On his return to Moscow, Khasbulatov intimated that Yeltsin's intention was to review his original five-phase plan, which as it stood passed the final solution of the problem on to the coming generation;[12] the long-term perspective involving the next generation was to be deleted.[13] The Japanese government also believes it is important to avoid the impression that a solution to the territorial question is a commercial issue, particularly in consideration of Russian national feelings. It is not disputed that there is an internal political link between a peace treaty along the lines favoured by Japan and Tokyo's willingness to make comprehensive, state-backed contributions to the rebuilding of the Russian economy. It was hoped that by the time of President Yeltsin's planned visit to Tokyo in mid-September 1992, it would be clear whether his standing in domestic politics would be sufficient to allow him to revise his proposals, which in Japanese eyes are inadequate.[14]

Yeltsin's strength is an unknown quantity. In the autumn of 1991 expressions of mistrust were already appearing in the Soviet media, arising from the Japanese Foreign Minister's talks in Moscow, in which agreements had been made that could lead to a resolution to the territorial question in accordance with Japanese demands. One of the loudest voices in the protests was the Tokyo correspondent of *Pravda*, I. Latyshev, whose criticisms were directed at what he saw as the extremely sparse information on the talks with Nakayama supplied by the Foreign Ministries of the Soviet Union and the Russian Federation. He also attacked

11. *Ibid.*, 10 Sept. 1991.
12. See Radio Japan, German text in *MD Asien*, 20 Sept. 1991.
13. At the end of September Khasbulatov stated more cautiously, 'No politician in Russia and the Soviet Union can say that tomorrow he will be willing to renounce the islands. Public opinion will not accept such a stance' (TASS, on Radio Japan, in *MD Asien*, 24 Sept. 1991). Yeltsin himself had reaffirmed his five-phase proposal of a solution at the beginning of September, but had emphasised that the northern territories were not an object of trade, and aid for Russia from Japan could not be linked to them. See *Izvestiya*, 17 Oct. 1991; *Asahi*, 8 Sept. 1991.
14. The visit did not take place. For an account of subsequent events see the Epilogue below.

statements by the Russian and Soviet politicians Gorbachev, Yeltsin, Khasbulatov, Pankin, Kosyrev and Kunadze, with reference to reports in the Japanese press which had in his view awakened hopes among the Japanese that the islands would be returned, without taking the opinion of the islands' population into consideration. He reserved particular suspicion for the satisfaction of the Japanese press at the nomination of Georgi Kunadze as the leader of the territorial issue sub-committee; this man, said Latyshev, was the same diplomat who had recently attempted to persuade the Kuriles' inhabitants to submit to a takeover of Habomai and Shikotan by Japan, a move which had led to demonstrations of protest and outbreaks of violence.[15]

It was true that Kunadze had visited the Kuriles in September in the capacity of Russia's Deputy Foreign Minister. His statements after the visit had been particularly cautious, presumably because of the mood of the population.[16] Kunadze emphasised the efforts of the Russian government 'to solve the problem of the South Kuriles with the participation of the people'; he added that the government would not engage in any secret diplomatic moves. On the other hand, he stated that the government was also thinking of the 'criteria of legality, of justice and of adherence to the norms of international law', probably an allusion to the Joint Declaration of 1956, whose revision by the Soviets in 1960 constituted an infringement of international law.[17] Kunadze also made it clear that Japan's claim could be rejected: 'Should we conclude, on the basis of an independent and separate analysis, that the islands belong to us by right, no amount of Japanese capital will be able to persuade us to transfer the islands to Japan.' An impression of the people's mood was evident in his criticism

15. See *Pravda*, 23 Oct. 1991.
16. The mood of the islands' population was described on Soviet television as tense. The correspondent's words were, 'The people are living in tense anticipation of their fate. They are extremely outraged that their views are ignored and that somewhere up there decisions are made affecting their future without them being informed' (Soviet television, in Russian, 13 Oct. 1991). This mood has been politically exploited. The governor of Sakhalin, Valentin Fyodorov, called for a protest at a return of the islands to Japan. In his opinion, Kunadze's visit was intended to prepare the people for a transfer. See Radio Japan, German broadcast, 1 Oct. 1991; *ibid.*, 1 Oct. 1991, p. 3.
17. TASS, in Russian, 28 Sept. 1991, in German in BPA, *Fernseh/Hörfunkspiegel Ausland*, 30 Sept. 1991, p. 40.

that 'some leader or other of public opinion is throwing people's minds into turmoil by bandying about the possibility of some swift solution to the territorial question'. He explained soothingly that even if agreements were made with Japan, their realisation would 'take no little time, probably even decades'.[18] The disparity between this view and the desire voiced by Yeltsin to have the problem solved within two years indicates that attitudes within the Russian leadership are as yet unformed.

Around the end of 1991, the inhabitants of the southern Kuriles approached the United Nations with the request that the four islands at issue be included in the international trusteeship system. The letter concerning the request stated, 'The final solution is being worked out without consideration for the inhabitants of the southern Kuriles . . . We reserve the right to protect our interests and human rights with all the methods available to us and by all possible means.'[19]

In the atmosphere of tension that prevailed, Japanese press reports that Tokyo had allegedly already formulated policy on the treatment of the Russian inhabitants of the islands did not help matters. According to these reports, the Japanese government intended to grant the Russians living on the islands at the time of their transfer the right to stay, to award those wishing to move to the mainland financial compensation and to reimburse their moving costs. Furthermore, those intending to stay would be given either the opportunity of adopting Japanese nationality or the right of permanent residence. However, rights of ownership were to be transferred to the former Japanese inhabitants of the islands. The *Gaimusho* refused to comment on these reports, but explained that at the current stage of negotiations, and considering public opinion in the Soviet Union, any presentation of Japan's intentions could cause difficulties for the Soviets.[20]

At the end of January 1992 Japan's Foreign Minister Michio Watanabe travelled to Moscow. The talks planned with President Yeltsin for 27 January were cancelled at short notice by the

18. TASS, in Russian, 8 Oct. 1991, in German in BPA, 9 Oct. 1991, p. 23.
19. Soviet television, in Russian, 15 Dec. 1991.
20. See *Izvestiya*, 17 Oct. 1991.

Russians; the President was inexplicably unavailable for public comment for a few days. The most important result of Watanabe's meeting with his counterpart Kosyrev was the agreement to begin discussions on a peace treaty in February; Kosyrev's talks in Tokyo in March, however, brought no results. When Miyazawa and Yeltsin had held an hour-long meeting in New York on 31 January, arrangements had been made for the Russian president to visit Japan in mid-September 1992. Yeltsin had made no mention of his five-phase plan in New York, but repeated the formulation used in a letter to Prime Minister Kaifu in September 1991, of a solution to the question of a peace treaty including the territorial question based on 'law and justice'.[21]

This, then, was the position in Japanese-Soviet relations around the end of 1991 and beginning of 1992. On the one hand, there was a palpable improvement in atmosphere, and demonstrable willingness on the part of the Japanese to make slight modifications to their once inviolable linkage of politics and economics by guaranteeing 'humanitarian aid'; negotiations on peripheral matters had brought results with positive long-term effects; there were prospects of talks on the issues being initiated and of a visit to Japan by the Russian President before the end of the year. The other side of the coin was a split in Russian public opinion, with the conservatives, who were apparently in a majority in the islands, rejecting the return of the territory to Japan; and a Russian government in desperate need of Japanese financial aid but unable to ignore the opinion of its people for fear of the consequences.[22] The grim developments within Russia also influenced the situation.

Observers may ask how such a complex situation could have developed in the first place. Stalin's successors certainly com-

21. *Asahi*, 2 Feb. 1992.

22. A survey of 2,000 people, conducted in Russia at the end of 1991, gives a rough picture of public opinion. According to the results, 71% were against a return of the islands to Japan, 14% voted in favour and 15% had no opinion on the subject. In the results of individual groups, young (27%) and educated (22%) Russians were more positively inclined towards the return of the islands, while those with less education (80%) and older subjects (75%) were largely against the islands' return. Regional variations in opinion were also telling; in the Russian Far East 85%, in west Siberia 76% and in Moscow 49% of those surveyed rejected the return of the islands. See *New Times*, no. 3, Jan. 1992, p. 25.

mitted an error by failing to clear up the problem with a compromise. Even in the 1960s and 1970s, the Soviet Union could have gained political kudos by offering to return two islands. Facing this is the familiar Japanese intransigence and, it should not be forgotten, Washington's and Peking's discernible aversion to the achievement of any state of settlement between Tokyo and Moscow. The intransigence was understandable as long as the East–West conflict existed and the Japanese government saw the still-unresolved territorial question as a welcome argument in favour of its policies concerning Moscow. This situation is now a thing of the past. The United States in particular is interested in a settlement of the issue. The Tokyo government must face the question of whether it has lost all sense of proportion in this question. The eyes of the world gaze in horror at the consequences of the Soviet Union's disintegration and the rampant dissolution of its military apparatus; however, in Tokyo only one topic counts in relations with Russia: the return of four tiny islands. Russia's problems are affecting the entire world; Japan's territorial question is third-rate in comparison. For the Japanese government, this fundamentally trivial question determines whether and to what extent the Russia of today should receive aid. This has led to international pressure on Tokyo, in particular from the G7 countries, and to demands for Japan to increase the aid it grants to Russia. In Japan the expression 'internationalisation' (*kokusaika*) is frequently used to denote the spiritual and moral goal of the nation; if proof is necessary that Japan is still very far from attaining this goal, it is furnished by Tokyo's treatment of the problems forming the Soviet Union's heritage.

It was certainly correct that for decades demands for the return of the illegally occupied islands had been issued to the Soviet leaders, and that the expansionism of the Soviet empire had been pilloried; but was it also correct to cling to the principle of the linkage between politics and economics at a time when palpable changes were occurring within the Soviet Union? Would not generous state-backed aid for specific projects in the islands at issue have swung the islanders' opinions in Japan's favour?

Even if it is understandable that Japan wanted to keep its only trump card, its financial and economic power, for as long as possible, until its aim of the past decades had been wrested from

Russia, the question still remains of the relation between this aim and the problems of the present, the question of Japan's international responsibility. If Japan really took this responsibility seriously, should it then not commit itself to massive economic aid, at least in Eastern Europe? Japan has no unresolved political problems with the countries of Eastern Europe, and yet its commitment to and presence in that area remain limited. It is hard to avoid the impression that Japan is fundamentally incapable of directing its gaze at anything beyond limited national interests.

Beyond the boundaries of this problem arises the general question of prospects for the relationship between Japan and Russia. The foundations for further intensive negotiations have been laid, but complete normalisation of bilateral relations may take years, and the process is dependent to a great extent on developments within Russia itself. If President Yeltsin is increasingly forced to show consideration for his people's nationalistic tendencies – and there are indications that this may be so – then no return of the islands may be expected in the foreseeable future. The greatest concession which seems to be possible from Russia at present would be the solution of the return of two islands offered in 1956.[23] For Russia, the 'major solution' is linked to a limited extent with the danger that it could be used as a precedent for territorial revision at other points on the Russian border; this thinking lay behind the Supreme Soviet's decision to ratify in 1956. Japan's leaders would do well to prepare their population gradually for this solution; under international law, Japan's renunciation of all claims to the Kuriles in San Francisco

---

23. Indeed, Russia declared to Deputy Foreign Minister Kunihiko Saito in Moscow on 10 February 1992 that it accepted the Treaty of Shimoda (1855) as a fact. This means recognition of the Russian-Japanese frontier to the north of the island of Etorofu, and also implies the possibility of a return to the Joint Declaration of 1956, which in itself implies the revocation of the Soviets' note of January 1960 in which the acceptance of 1956 was withdrawn. See above, pp. 41–2, and *Nihon Keizai*, 11 Feb. 1992. At the end of April 1992 the *Gaimusho* unexpectedly switched to a phased solution; Foreign Minister Watanabe declared that Japan was prepared to accept Habomai and Shikotan if Russia would recognise Japan's sovereignty over all four islands and fix on a date for the return of the other two. See *Sankei* 21 April 1992 and above, pp. 74–5.

in 1951 leaves its demand for the return of all four islands open to challenge.

Should it come to such a 'minor solution', the relinquishment of two islands would mean a burden on mutual relations for Japan, and one whose importance would only become relative over the long term. Japan's relations with its Russian neighbours would remain difficult for a long time, because of a territorial problem seen either as unresolved, or – in the Japanese view – as inadequately solved. Even if all four islands are returned, Japan will be slow to overcome its distance from Russia under the heavy weight of psychological barriers and historical factors. Economic relations could prove a catalyst in their elimination. As long as the reorganisation of the Russian economy has laid no foundations for dynamic developments, as long as Russia's integration into global economic structures is unsuccessful, Japan will show no particular initiative in this field. The considerable technological and financial risks involved in the development of the Russian Far East would probably limit Japanese commitment, especially since Japan can meet its requirements for raw materials and energy from sources other than the CIS into the next century. This may change in the long term, especially if the energy requirements of South-East Asian countries rise sharply. Japan is not (yet) prepared to adopt a model role in the process of Russian modernisation in the same way that it is with China. Why is this so? The reason is that Japan's relations with China are emotionally coloured by historical and cultural links, but its relations with Russia have always been cool and distant. In Europe a parallel may be drawn with relations between Germany and Russia, which in certain respects are similar to those between Japan and China, especially when the period of the two world wars is included.

At the beginning of 1991 a thoughtful Russian observer remarked to Foreign Minister Nakayama that he knew of no other case in which two neighbours have lived 'with their backs to each other' for centuries. He continued by asking whether Nakayama believed that 'our politicians will be able to overcome this tradition of centuries', and received a non-committal answer. The questioner mentioned that there had been periods when there had been no territorial problems between Japan and Russia, and yet neighbourly relations had not existed, and asked pointedly, 'Do you really believe that it is sufficient to solve the problem of four islands to overcome this century-old tradition? Perhaps the problem is a deeper one.' Nakayama's answer once again avoided the nub of the problem with a banal statement that humanity was on the threshold of historic changes and all these questions must be solved in the spirit of the 'New Thinking'.[24]

This may have been a coincidence; however, the evasion may also be interpreted as confirmation that the problem has further dimensions and cannot be eliminated by an agreement over islands. A realistic assumption is that the relationship between Japan and Russia will remain complicated into the foreseeable future, even if their economic relations grow closer; these are only 'superficial', and have no immediate deep-seated effect. There, however, the roots of the problem in relations may be found. Involuntarily one recalls Fukuzawa's judgement of Russia from 1861 quoted at the start of this book. The mistrust accumulated by both sides in the past can only be reduced slowly and with great effort. For Russia to master this task a thorough restructuring of economic and social systems will be necessary; Japan will have to redetermine its role as a responsible partner and supporter of this internal Russian process, which affects all aspects of international relations.

24. Soviet television, 29 Jan. 1991.

EPILOGUE TO THE ENGLISH EDITION

In the two years since the completion of the German manuscript of this book in the spring of 1992, no fundamental changes have taken place in relations between Japan and Russia. However, events have reconfirmed the difficulties, both political and psychological, between the two countries.

The event with the most dramatic effect was the sudden cancellation of President Yeltsin's visit to Japan, planned for mid-September 1992. Yeltsin informed the Japanese Prime Minister by telephone a mere three days before the visit was due to take place that 'internal affairs' prevented him from visiting Japan. The Japanese reaction was one of disappointment and anger; while the disappointment could be traced to expectations of a certain progress on the eternal territorial question, the anger was caused by the method of cancellation. Yeltsin had first informed the South Korean President in a long telephone conversation that his visit would be postponed; he had intended to visit South Korea on his way back from Tokyo. Tokyo saw not only the order in which those involved were informed of the cancellation, but also its suddenness as both tactless and absolutely undiplomatic. However, the affair was blown up into a full-scale diplomatic insult when the President's press secretary had the audacity to blame Japan for the cancellation. According to Moscow, the Tokyo government and the LDP had attempted to exploit Yeltsin's visit for their own electioneering purposes; moreover, Japan's 'attitude of inflexibility, occasionally even to the point of delivering an ultimatum' had allegedly played an important role in the Russian leader's decision to postpone the visit.

The independent Russian press described this claim from Yeltsin's circle as 'uncivilised' and 'ill-mannered', taking the view that an excuse for the cancellation had been desperately sought for weeks. In the eyes of the press, the decision had finally been taken by the Security Council, a committee already known within the country as 'the new Politburo'; the President had ignored these people for too long, and now they had got their way. The cancellation of the visits to Japan and South Korea, concluded press observers, were proof of the insecurity of Yeltsin's position and the weakness of the democratic wing of the Russian leadership.[1]

This interpretation may correspond to Russian reality. Yeltsin was politically too weak to transform his visit to Japan into a success – 'success' meaning in this context large-scale financial aid from Japan and across-the-board support for restructuring the economy. In return for this, he would have had to move towards an acceptable solution of the territorial question, but he did not have the necessary scope for such a move; the conservative powers around him would brook no concessions.

Of course, there were and are limits to Japan's scope for action. For decades the Japanese leaders spoke in favour of a package solution to the territorial question (*yontô-ikkatsu*). In April 1992, however, Tokyo modified its demands; a return to the proposal of 1956 – that is, the return of Habomai and Shikotan – and simultaneously the recognition of Japanese sovereignty over Kunashiri and Etorofu. Under these circumstances Japan would be prepared to discuss the timing of the return of these two large islands.[2]

It was evidently known in Moscow that Tokyo was not prepared to concede anything in the question of sovereignty over all the islands. A look back at the first half of 1992 shows that during the preparatory talks between both sides and diplomatic contacts prior to Yeltsin's visit, no progress had been possible. At the end of July one of the President's advisers declared that owing to the increasing strength of patriotic trends in Russia, conditions for a solution to the territorial question had deteriorated for Yeltsin since the previous year. The situation was even more difficult than at the time of Gorbachev's visit in 1991. The longer normalisation of relations between the two countries was postponed, the greater the difficulties would be.[3] Russia's conservative constitutional commission is said to have demanded during a stormy debate that Yeltsin's visit to Japan

1. *Izvestiya*, 11 Sept. 1992.
2. *Sankei*, 29 April 1992.
3. *Ibid.*, 30 July 1992.

be postponed until a procedure for the solution to the territorial question was determined.[4]

The military also spoke out against any concessions. A document issued by the general staff even demanded a temporary halt in troop reductions in the islands and spoke against mentioning the possibility of returning the islands in further diplomatic communications. The military's central argument was that concessions over the issue of the Kuriles would endanger the country's strategic interests.[5]

In Tokyo the awareness of growing difficulties regarding Yeltsin's visit increased. The Foreign Ministry's estimation was that the issue was a power struggle within the Russian leadership, where 'people who have no understanding of the territorial problem unite with those who understand the problem in rejecting a solution'.[6] Despite this insight, Tokyo uncompromisingly maintained its demand for the recognition of Japanese sovereignty over Kunashiri and Etorofu. The question occurs to a foreign observer whether Tokyo had not misinterpreted Yeltsin's freedom of movement. Is it possible even now to count on a breakthrough along the lines of the Japanese demand?

Only a few weeks before Yeltsin's intended visit, this demand was categorically rejected. The chairman of the Highest Commission for International Questions and International Trade Relations, Arbatsumov, gave this advice to Yeltsin: 'In the present situation, recognition in any form whatsoever of Japan's sovereignty over any part of Russian territory whatsoever is extremely dangerous.'[7]

Apart from nationalist or patriotic trends, which will always oppose any transfer of territory, conservative circles also fear that a compromise with Japan will set a precedent for other as yet unresolved territorial questions between the CIS and China or other neighbouring countries. An important consideration in this context is Yeltsin's July 1992 agreement with Finnish President Koivisto, in which both parties agreed to drop territorial

4. *Nihon Keizai*, 28 July 1992.
5. *International Herald Tribune*, 30 July 1992.
6. *Nihon Keizai*, 31 July 1992.
7. *Ibid.*, 26 Aug. 1992.

claims regarding Karelia, which was partitioned from Finland at the end of the 1930s.[8]

In conclusion, it may be said that on the eve of the Russian President's visit to Japan prospects of any mutually satisfactory result arising from the Japanese-Russian summit talks were extremely slim. For different reasons, neither side was yet in a position to overcome the central problem. In view of this, a good case can be made that a postponement of the visit was more helpful to the cause than a fruitless meeting would have been.

After Tokyo's first anger at the cancellation had ebbed, both sides made efforts to contain the damage. However, a few examples of Russian tactlessness were to follow, including the proposal that during Yeltsin's visit to South Korea, planned for mid-November 1992, the Russian President could meet Prime Minister Miyazawa in Okinawa to discuss a rescheduling of his postponed visit.[9] This ludicrous feeler, put out in an interview with the Russian Vice-President, Poltoranin, demonstrated the uncoordinated and floundering methods of decision-making within the Russian leadership.

The most vital step towards calming the situation was the meeting of both Foreign Ministers on the fringes of the UN General Assembly in New York at the end of September 1992. Both politicians agreed that talks at vice-ministerial level and Foreign Ministerial visits would be resumed. It was agreed that first the Russian Foreign Minister would visit Tokyo and that vice-ministerial talks would be extended to include discussions which would not be limited to the territorial problem and the conclusion of a peace treaty, as in the past, but would also cover economic questions, security in the Asia Pacific region and the entire range of topics concerning bilateral relations as well as international problems. The peace treaty working group was to continue to concentrate on the territorial question.

After the meeting, Foreign Minister Watanabe spoke of a chasm between Japan and Russia which still had to be bridged, and it soon became apparent how deep this chasm still is. A few days after Yeltsin cancelled his visit to Japan it was announced

8. *Ibid.*, 12 July 1992.
9. *Sankei*, 15 Sept. 1992.

that Russia intended to lease land in Shikotan to foreign companies. An area of nearly 700 acres (278 hectares) for the construction of leisure facilities was to be handed over to foreign concerns on a fifty-year lease for the sum of 200 million roubles. The news of the planned deal was broadcast on Russian television on 13 September, the very day on which Yeltsin had previously intended to arrive in Tokyo. A Hong Kong firm, which proved to exist only on paper, was named as the agent; its representative had already signed the lease on 4 September. There is much to suggest that Valentin Fyodorov, the Governor of Sakhalin and an outspoken opponent of territorial concessions to Japan, intended this news to shake Yeltsin's credibility during his state visit to Tokyo. Fyodorov's deputy declared in a television discussion:

> What claims do the Japanese have? Up till now the entire Kurile chain has been under our jurisdiction, and we, the administrators of the area and the region, are free to dispose of this territory strictly according to Russian law; according to this law we are not forbidden to rent land to foreign partners. I would not connect this purely economic procedure with politics . . . The Kuriles need investment now, to develop the infrastructure and solve social problems. The Russian government will not give us any money, and the Japanese refuse to take part in joint economic activities on the islands; frankly, they take every opportunity of rubbing in our dependence on their favours. So we have shown that there are other countries which are extremely interested in working with us to the benefit of both sides.[10]

The *Gaimusho* issued an official protest at the lease, pointing out that according to the Joint Declaration of 1956 the question of the island of Shikotan belonging to Japan had already been settled; this meant that the Japanese would not tolerate any unauthorised actions connected with leasing and involving outside countries. Japan demanded an explanation of the affair and appropriate action from Moscow.[11] Immediately afterwards fur-

---

10. *Izvestiya*, 15 Sept. 1992.
11. *Ibid.*, 16 Sept. 1992.

ther plans to lease land in the island of Kunashiri were revealed. Again, Tokyo protested most strongly.[12]

These events, which seem obscure in themselves, show one thing clearly: Russia's leadership under Yeltsin is not able to exert effective control over unauthorised actions by the administrations of individual areas, or to prevent steps which may severely affect Russia's foreign interests. This applies even today. In its further treatment of the affair, however, the Russian leadership has trapped itself in a thicket of contradictions. At first it appeared as if Moscow were opposing the independent action of those responsible in Sakhalin. Then, however, the impression became clearer that even the Russian President tends to favour opening the Kuriles, including the islands at the heart of the controversy, to foreign investors. At the beginning of December 1992 the Russian weekly *Kommersant* reported that Yeltsin had signed an agreement under which the Kuriles would become a special economic zone within which regional administrations were allowed to lease land to foreign investors on ninety-nine-year leases.[13]

While the fate of the agreement is still undecided, the whole affair demonstrates how Yeltsin was forced step by step to yield to the pressure of the conservative elements. In this he felt he was supported by the prevailing mood of the Russian people. According to a joint Japanese-Russian survey at the beginning of November 1992, 72.2% of Russians questioned supported their President. Among the Japanese surveyed, 84% supported the claim to the islands.[14] Here, too, the wide chasm between both sides is visible.

In order to bridge the gulf, Tokyo and Moscow attempted to introduce a dialogue between the military bodies of both sides over questions of security. In mid-June 1992 the first Japanese-Russian talks on policy planning took place in the Foreign Ministry in Moscow. It was the first time that both countries had ever discussed the military position in East Asia with uniformed officers participating in the talks. The Japanese side included, among others, a General of the Joint Staff Council of the Self Defence Forces. At the beginning of September 1992

12. *Sankei*, 19 Sept. 1992.
13. *International Herald Tribune*, 3 Dec. 1992.
14. *Ibid.*, 30 Nov. 1992.

twenty-four officials, some former Japanese officers, undertook a seven-day inspection of Russian military facilities around Khabarovsk, Ussurisk and Vladivostok. Their experiences were positive, and were continued in January 1993 in a seminar in which Russian officers participated. These steps are important. The military in the Russian Far East belongs to the conservative sector of society, views all reforms critically, and rejects a solution to the territorial question along Japanese lines. For this reason it is all the more urgent that the Japanese should take the initiative to create an atmosphere of trust step by step. One member of the military was quoted at the joint seminar in Tokyo as saying 'unjust territorial claims will make Russia uneasy'.[15] A source close to the Russian Foreign Ministry conceded that after tactical considerations the general staff and the navy command had come to the conclusion that it would be completely senseless to hand the islands over to Japan.[16]

During the first half of 1993 a cautious change in Japan's policies on Russia was discernible. The usual demands for the return of the northern territories were dropped in favour of statements supporting President Yeltsin and his leadership. The Japanese Deputy Foreign Minister, Kunihiko Saito, announced, 'Japan's aim is to conclude a peace treaty, but economic aid will not be frozen if no progress is made on political questions.'[17] Foreign Minister Muto even announced the end of the 'linkage policy': 'Japan will no longer link extension of aid to Russia to parallel progress in resolving a bilateral territorial dispute.' This change was explained by the fact that the success of economic reforms and the formation of democracy in Russia were significant for Japan.[18] The development immediately preceded the summit of the G7 in Tokyo in April 1993. The Japanese government appeared to be concerned that its slowness in promising aid for Russia could call forth increasing criticism from the other members. At the meeting Japan promised financial aid of US$1,820 million, $320 million of which was to be regarded as a gift. This non-repayable aid is intended to be used in humanitarian projects ($100 million), for nuclear waste disposal measures

15. Kyodo, 24 Feb. 1993.
16. See *New Times*, no. 43 (1992), pp. 24–5.
17. *Nezavisimaya gazeta*, 9 April 1993.
18. Kyodo, 13 April 1993.

in Russia and CIS member countries ($100 million) and for technological aid and training and exchange programmes ($120 million). Of the loans, $1,100 million is intended as security for export risks (insurance cover and so on) and $400 million as export loans.[19] The Japanese government did not conduct any political talks with President Yeltsin, who had only guest status at the G7 summit in Tokyo. However, the Russian Foreign Minister made it clear to the Japanese premier that Yeltsin wanted to visit Japan in May. The Japanese side accepted and suggested 25–7 May for the visit.

The visit did not take place. Once again Yeltsin saw himself compelled to cancel owing to reasons of domestic politics. This time the Japanese made clear efforts not to over-dramatise the cancellation, since they did not want to add further burdens to the relations between the two countries, and a new date was soon fixed: September/October 1993.

Up to the eve of the Russian President's departure for Japan on 11 October, doubts were expressed as to whether this third attempt at a visit would fail too. Yeltsin had just managed, with the army's help, to quell an attempted putsch by his enemies in the Communist and nationalist camps, and had averted civil war at the last minute. By visiting Japan he wanted to demonstrate, both to his hosts in Tokyo and to the world at large, that he was once more master of the situation in his own country.

The demonstration worked. The visit can be regarded as a political and psychological triumph for the President and means a modest step forward for Japanese-Russian relations. Yeltsin began his stay in Tokyo by apologising for the unspeakable sufferings of over 600,000 Japanese prisoners-of-war, between 40,000 and 60,000 of whom died in Siberian camps. This gesture achieved its psychological aim and provided a sound basis for the political talks that were to follow. Yeltsin was also the first major Russian politician to confess openly that Japan had not initiated war with the Soviet Union.

The visit concluded with the publication of political and economic declarations as well as sixteen individual agreements on subjects such as 'Non-proliferation of Weapons of Mass Destruction' and 'The Nuclear Question on the Korean Penin-

19. *Neue Zürcher Zeitung*, 16 April 1993.

sula'. The central document is the Tokyo Declaration,[20] which specifies that all treaties concluded between Japan and the former Soviet Union and other international agreements are recognised as effective and will form the basis of negotiations on the conclusion of a peace treaty. While not explicitly referring to it, this includes the Joint Declaration of 1956, with its agreement to return the Habomai group and Shikotan on the conclusion of a peace treaty with Japan. While Yeltsin carefully avoided any direct reference to the Declaration of 1956, he may be assumed to be aware that in future negotiations the Japanese government will insist on this agreement as the first step towards a resolution of the territorial question. This is probably the most important political achievement of the Russian President's visit to Japan.

In April 1991 Gorbachev had refused to recognise the continued validity of the Joint Declaration of 1956. However, in other matters there are no major differences between the results of Gorbachev's and Yeltsin's visits to Tokyo. In some points, for example the naming of the islands under discussion and the declaration of intent to find a satisfactory solution to the problem, the two communiqués closely resemble one another.

With regard to economic relations, both sides declared their intention of extending trade under consideration of general conditions, a formulation which permits Japan to structure its economic commitment according to progress made in political questions.[21] This means that Japan can continue to maintain a certain link between politics and economics.

Yeltsin managed, unlike Gorbachev, to use psychological skill to bring about a better atmosphere in dealings with the other side. This important element in mutual relations was, however, soon to be threatened. Only a few days after Yeltsin's visit to Japan it was announced that ships of the Russian Navy had been discharging hundreds of tons of liquid nuclear waste into the Sea of Japan. After furious protests from the Japanese government this activity was suspended.

Since it had been known for some time that the Soviet Union had been dumping radioactive waste in the Sea of Japan since 1959, in April 1993 the Japanese government had presented

20. *Nihon Keizai*, 14 Oct. 1993. See Appendix A below.
21. Trade with Russia declined further in 1991 and 1992, to 0.99% and 0.61% respectively of Japan's total foreign trade.

Russia with a grant of $100 million to finance less hazardous methods of disposal, and founded a joint working group to discuss the issue. The problem was also raised with Yeltsin in Tokyo. Because of this, Russia's actions so soon after the President's visit were viewed as provocative. Either Yeltsin approved the undertaking, completely misinterpreting Japan's sensitivity on the issue, and nullified the positive achievements of his visit, or other interests are involved. It is not far-fetched to suppose that powers are in action which disapprove of Yeltsin's visit to Japan and want to demonstrate their strength to the President. Since the issue involves radioactive waste from submarines, it is probable that the military, highly critical of proposed solutions to the territorial question with Japan, is behind the actions. The event recalls the attempt of Sakhalin's administration in the autumn of 1992 to sabotage Yeltsin's planned visit by releasing information about land-leasing in Shikotan. Both affairs clearly show the high-handed methods of such groups, the limited scope of the Russian President and the continuing weakness of the foundations on which Japanese-Russian relations are based.

A great deal of patience will be required to overcome mutual distrust. In view of the situation in Russia it is unlikely that the problem will be resolved in the near future, and setbacks can be expected. Sudden reactions and unexpected decisions emanating from Moscow from time to time will continue to shock Japan. Finally, however, it should be possible to conclude an agreement that can be carried by a broad majority on both sides and does not contain the potential for new disputes. Since the time is not yet ripe for this development, the most sensible course is probably to leave the territorial question alone for some years. Meanwhile, Japan and Russia should set about improving mutual relations to pave the way for a future solution.

APPENDIXES

APPENDIXES

A

JOINT SOVIET-JAPANESE DECLARATIONS

Joint Declaration by Japan and the Soviet Union, 19 October 1956

From 13 to 19 October 1956, negotiations were held at Moscow between the delegations of Japan and the Union of Soviet Socialist Republics.

The following representatives of Japan took part in the negotiations:

Prime Minister, Ichiro Hatoyama,
Ichiro Kono, Minister of Agriculture and Forestry, and
Shunichi Matsumoto, Member of the House of Representatives.

The following representatives of the Union of Soviet Socialist Republics took part in the negotiations:

N.A. Bulganin, Chairman of the Council of Ministers of the USSR,
N.S. Khrushchev, Member of the Presidium of the Supreme Soviet of the USSR,
A.I. Mikoyan, First Vice-Chairman of the Council of Ministers of the USSR,
A.A. Gromyko, First Deputy Minister of Foreign Affairs of the USSR, and
N.T. Fedorenko, Deputy Minister of Foreign Affairs of the USSR.

In the course of the negotiations, which were held in an atmosphere of mutual understanding and co-operation, a full and frank exchange of views concerning relations between Japan and the Union of Soviet Socialist Republics took place. Japan and the Union of Soviet Socialist Republics were fully agreed that the restoration of diplomatic relations between them would contribute to the development of mutual understanding and co-operation between the two States in the interests of peace and security in the Far East.

As a result of these negotiations between the Delegations of Japan and the Union of Soviet Socialist Republics, agreement was reached on the following:

1. The state of war between Japan and the Union of Soviet Socialist Republics shall cease on the date on which this declaration enters into force and peace, friendship and good-neighbourly relations between them shall be restored.

2. Diplomatic and consular relations shall be restored between Japan and the Union of Soviet Socialist Republics. For this purpose it is intended that the two States shall proceed forthwith to exchange diplomatic representatives with the rank of Ambassador and that the question of the establishment of consulates in the territories of Japan and the Union of Soviet Socialist Republics respectively shall be settled through the diplomatic channels.

3. Japan and the Union of Soviet Socialist Republics affirm that in their relations with each other they will be guided by the principles of the United Nations Charter, in particular the following principles set forth in Article 2 of the said Charter:

 (a) To settle their international disputes by peaceful means in such a manner that international peace and security, and justice, are not endangered;

 (b) To refrain in their international relations from the threat or use of force against the territorial integrity or political independence of any State, or in any other manner inconsistent with the purposes of the United Nations.

Japan and the USSR affirm that, in accordance with Article 51 of the United Nations Charter, each of the two States has the inherent right of individual or collective self-defence.

Japan and the USSR reciprocally undertake not to intervene directly or indirectly in each other's domestic affairs for any economic, political or ideological reasons.

4. The Union of Soviet Socialist Republics will support Japan's application for membership in the United Nations.

5. On the entry into force of this Joint Declaration, all Japanese citizens convicted in the Union of Soviet Socialist Republics shall be released and repatriated to Japan.

With regard to those Japanese whose fate is unknown, the USSR, at the request of Japan, will continue its efforts to discover what has happened to them.

6. The Union of Soviet Socialist Republics renounces all reparations claims against Japan.

Japan and the USSR agree to renounce all claims by either State, its individuals or citizens, against the other State, its institutions or citizens, which have arisen as a result of the war since 9 August 1945.

7. Japan and the Union of Soviet Socialist Republics agree that they will enter into negotiations as soon as may be possible for the conclusion of treaties or agreements with a view to putting their trade, navigation and other commercial relations on a firm and friendly basis.

8. The Convention on deep-sea fishing in the north-western sector of the Pacific Ocean between Japan and the Union of Soviet Socialist

Republics on co-operation in the rescue of persons in distress at sea, both signed at Moscow on 14 May 1956, shall come into effect simultaneously with this Joint Declaration.

Having regard to the interest of both Japan and the USSR in the conservation and rational use of the natural fishery resources and other biological resources of the sea, Japan and the Union of Soviet Socialist Republics shall, in a spirit of co-operation, take measures to conserve and develop fishery resources, and to regulate and restrict deep-sea fishing.

9. Japan and the Union of Soviet Socialist Republics agree to continue, after the restoration of normal diplomatic relations between Japan and the Union of Soviet Socialist Republics, negotiations for the conclusion of a Peace Treaty.

In this connexion, the Union of Soviet Socialist Republics, desiring to meet the wishes of Japan and taking into consideration the interests of the Japanese State, agrees to transfer to Japan the Habomai Islands and the island of Shikotan, the actual transfer of these islands to Japan to take place after the conclusion of a Peace Treaty between Japan and the Union of Soviet Socialist Republics.

10. This Joint Declaration is subject to ratification. It shall enter into force on the date of the exchange of instruments of ratification. The exchange of the instruments of ratification shall take place at Tokyo as soon as may be possible.

Done in two copies, each in the Japanese and Russian languages, both texts being equally authentic.

Moscow, 19 October 1956

By authorization
of the Government
of Japan

I. HATOYAMA
I. KONO
S. MATSUMOTO

By authorization
of the Presidium of the Supreme
Soviet of the Union of Soviet
Socialist Republics

N. BULGANIN
D. SHEPILOV

Source: Northern Territories Issues Association (ed.), *A Border yet Unresolved – Japan's Northern Territories*, Tokyo 1981, pp. 102–5, following: 'Joint Communiqué of the Union of Soviet Socialist Republics', in *Neue Zeit*, vol. 14, no. 44 (Oct. 1956), pp. 35–6.

Joint Soviet-Japanese Communiqué of 18 April 1991

1. President M.S. Gorbachev of the USSR paid an official visit to Japan from 16th April through 19th April 1991, at the invitation of the government of Japan. President M.S. Gorbachev of the USSR was accompanied by Minister for Foreign Affairs A.A. Bessmertnykh of the USSR and other government officials.

2. President M.S. Gorbachev of the USSR and Mrs Gorbacheva had an audience with Their Imperial Highnesses the Emperor and the Empress of Japan on 16th April.

3. President M.S. Gorbachev of the USSR had frank and constructive discussions with Prime Minister Toshiki Kaifu of Japan on issues between Japan and the USSR, including the negotiations for the conclusion of a peace treaty, and on important international issues of mutual interest. President M.S. Gorbachev of the USSR invited Prime Minister Toshiki Kaifu of Japan to pay an official visit to the USSR, which invitation was gratefully accepted. The details of the visit are to be arranged through diplomatic channels.

4. Prime Minister Toshiki Kaifu of Japan and President M.S. Gorbachev of the USSR held an in-depth and thorough discussion of the total range of issues relating to the drafting and conclusion of a peace treaty between Japan and the USSR, including the issue of territorial demarcation, with consideration to the two sides' positions on the attribution of the Habomai islands, Shikotan, Kunashiri and Etorofu.

In the joint work thus far, and especially in the negotiations at the highest level, the series of conceptual approaches was confirmed, meaning that the peace treaty should be the document marking the final resolution of war-related issues, including the territorial issue, that it should open the way for long-term Japan–USSR relations on the basis of friendship, and that it should not infringe upon either side's security.

The Soviet side proposed that measures be taken in the near future to expand exchanges between residents of Japan and residents of the aforementioned islands, to establish a simplified visa-free framework for visits by Japanese to these islands, to initiate joint mutually beneficial economic activities in that region, and to reduce the Soviet military forces stationed on the islands. The Japanese side indicated that it wanted to discuss these issues further.

As well as emphasizing the primary importance of accelerating work to conclude the preparations on the peace treaty, the Prime Minister and the president expressed their firm resolve to make constructive and vigorous efforts to this end taking advantage of all positive elements that have been built up in the bilateral negotiations in the years since Japan and the USSR jointly proclaimed an end to the state of war and the restoration of diplomatic relations in 1956.

At the same time, they recognized that the development of constructive cooperation between Japan and the USSR, including the adjacent Russian SFSR, in the trade and economic, scientific and technological, and political as well as in the social activity, cultural, educational, tourism and sports fields through free and wide-ranging exchanges between the peoples of the two countries in mutual relations in an atmosphere of good-neighbourliness, mutual benefit and trust is consistent with these ends.

5. Affirming that expanded political dialogue is a useful and effective means of enhancing Japan–USSR relations, the two sides announced their determination to work to continue, deepen and advance this political dialogue through regular exchanges of visits at the highest level.

6. Noting the importance of holding regular foreign ministerial consultations, as agreed in 1966, the two sides affirmed that such consultations should be held at least once a year, and more frequently if necessary.

7. The two sides affirmed that they guide their bilateral relations in accordance with the principles elucidated in Article 2 of the UN Charter, particularly the principles of:
   i. Settling their international disputes by peaceful means in such a manner that international peace and security, and justice, are not endangered.
   ii. Refraining in their international relations from the threat or use of force against the territorial integrity or political independence of any state, or in any other manner inconsistent with the purposes of the UN.

8. The two sides are in agreement that this summit meeting was extremely useful for both sides. Noting the importance of expanding, and making more active, cooperation in practical fields, the two sides have produced the following:
   – memorandum on consultations between the governments of Japan and the USSR
   – agreement between the government of Japan and the government of the USSR on cooperation in regard to technical support for the reforms now under way in the USSR to shift to a market economy

- agreement on trade and payments between Japan and the USSR during the period 1991 through 1995
- exchange of notes on trade in consumer and other goods with the Far East region of the USSR
- Japan–USSR joint communiqué on encouraging the mutual holding of exhibitions and trade fairs
- Japan–USSR joint communiqué on progress in cooperation in the field of fisheries
- exchange of notes concerning amendment of Appendix 1 of the Japan–USSR aviation agreement
- exchange of notes between the government of Japan and the government of the USSR on expanding air services on the Siberian route
- agreement on cooperation between the government of Japan and the government of the USSR in the field of environmental conservation
- agreement between the government of Japan and the government of the USSR on cooperation in the field of the peaceful uses of nuclear power
- memorandum on cooperation between Japan and the USSR to reduce the impact of the Chernobyl atomic power station accident on the health of residents of the area
- exchange of notes approving the plans proposed for implementing the agreement between the government of Japan and the government of the USSR on cultural exchanges during the period 1st April 1991 through 31st March 1993
- memorandum on exchanges and cooperation between Japan and the USSR in the field of conserving important cultural properties
- Japan–USSR joint communiqué on cooperation relating to the activities of the Centre for Modern Japanese Studies
- agreement between the government of Japan and the government of the USSR on persons interned in POW war camps

9. The two sides were in agreement on the need to further deepen and develop practical relations between the two countries in various fields, including the political, economic, trade, industrial, fisheries, science and technology, transport, environmental, cultural and humanitarian fields, in a balanced manner and to the extent feasible on the basis of friendship and mutual benefit so as to contribute to the improvement of living standards for the people of Japan and the USSR and further progress in the international community.

10. Expressing their high regard for the activities of the Japan–USSR governmental trade and economic consultations, Japan–USSR and

USSR—Japan committees on economic consultations and other forums, the two sides announced their readiness to promote further expansion of trade and economic relations between the two countries on the basis of mutual benefit. The two sides share the understanding that the continued promotion of perestroyka in the USSR is of significance not only for the USSR but for the entire world.

11. The two sides evaluated highly the cooperation between the two countries under the existing governmental agreements in the fisheries field and were agreed on the desirability of continuing constructive exchanges of views so as to further develop such cooperation on a long-term and mutually beneficial basis.

In this regard, the two sides expressed the desire to see extensive development of relations between enterprises and organizations in Japan and the Far Eastern region of the USSR based on market economy principles. The two sides recognized the necessity of maintaining and developing close cooperation in international deliberations for the conservation, management, reproduction and optimal utilization of the world's biomarine resources (also in such activities of the international organizations to which both governments are parties).

12. The two sides announced their satisfaction with the activities of the committee on science and technology cooperation and the steady progress being made on cooperation in the field of science and technology between the two countries on the basis of mutual benefit and were in agreement on working to further develop such cooperation and to expand cooperation in such other fields as might be deemed necessary by the two sides.

13. The two sides announced their satisfaction that cultural exchange between the two countries has recently been becoming increasingly active and that mutual understanding between the peoples of the two countries is being continuously enhanced. The two sides also expressed their satisfction with the steady progress being made in developing cultural exchanges between the two countries under the existing agreement and were in agreement on the importance of exchanges to further promote mutual understanding of the two countries' traditional and contemporary cultures and societies.

14. The two sides recognized that cooperation between the two countries in the humanitarian field contributes considerably to enhancing mutual trust between the two peoples and expressed their satisfaction that such cooperation is being increasingly active as regards visits to gravesites, the issue of persons interned in POW camps, and the issue of Japanese permanently living in the USSR.

15. The two sides agreed that the process of improvement in the international situation is of an irreversible nature on a global scale and regional scale and should be further promoted. The two sides stressed the need to continue efforts to maintain international peace and security and the importance of attaining, in a balanced manner, the lowest levels of military forces and arms possible. In this connection, the two sides welcomed the results attained in arms control and disarmament and recognized the importance of faithful implementation and supported the attainment of early agreement in the bilateral and multilateral negotiations now under way in this field.

16. In light of the harsh lessons of the crisis in the Gulf and from the perspective of maintaining international peace and security, the two sides have a shared recognition of the need for the international comminuty to strengthen its efforts for the nonproliferation of nuclear arms, chemical weapons and other weapons of mass destruction and missiles, for the enhancement of transparency and openness on conventional arms transfers, and for the strengthening of self-restraint on conventional arms transfers by each country.

17. The two sides were in agreement that, given the fact that the current international order is changing rapidly with the end of cold war structures and in light of the positions that the two sides hold and the responsibilities that they ought to fulfil in international politics and economy, it is important to achieve a complete normalization of Japan–USSR relations and to pave the way for dramatic development of these relations and that achieving this will not only be in the two countries' own interests but will also contribute to peace and prosperity in the Asia-Pacific region and worldwide.

18. The two sides have a high regard for the activities of the UN and other international organizations and for the important contribution that they have made to the resolution of regional conflicts, to the strengthening of mutual understanding, trust and stability worldwide, and to the expansion of constructive cooperation and concert within the framework of the present international community. The two sides were in agreement that the UN has an important role to play politically, economically, and in the resolution of other international issues, including environmental issues and the fight against illegal trafficking in drugs. The two sides were in agreement in recognizing the need for the two countries to further promote their cooperation and consultations for supporting the full flowering of the UN's potential for peace and enhancing the role of the UN on global issues.

The two sides recognized that 'the former enemy clauses' in the UN Charter have lost their meaning and, mindful of the need to strengthen the UN Charter and system, agreed that appropriate ways should be sought to resolve this issue.

19. The two sides had shared awareness that the solidarity and cooperation of the international community centring on the UN in dealing with the crisis in the Gulf made the liberation of Kuwait possible and were in agreement that peace and stability must be restored to the region through Iraq's prompt compliance with the series of UN Security Council resolutions.

Recognizing that the Middle East region is extremely important to international peace, the two sides had a shared awareness that it is important that the international community as a whole, respecting the intentions and activities of the countries in the region, work in concert and cooperate actively for post-war economic reconstruction in that region to ensure peace and prosperity not only in the Middle East but worldwide.

The two sides believe that it is extremely important that, together with efforts to work for post-crisis reconstruction in the Gulf region, the international community should support efforts for the early resolution of other conflicts in the Middle East, which has become an urgent task, stressing particularly the need for a workable Middle East peace and the initiation of a meaningful peace process to that end.

20. The two sides evaluate highly the efforts being made for peace and prosperity in the Asia-Pacific region. In this connection, the two sides supported efforts for just and reasonable resolution of conflicts in this region through peaceful means and shared an awareness of the importance of providing constructive cooperation for the self-reliant efforts of the states of the region and of always respecting those states' own initiatives and decisions.

21. The two sides announced their grave concern for the attainment of peace and stability on the Korean peninsula and, sharing an awareness of the importance of progress in North–South dialogue for their attainment, supported the continuation of the North–South prime ministerial talks. In this connection, the Japanese side welcomed the establishment of diplomatic relations between the ROK and the USSR and the Soviet side the start of discussions between Japan and the DPRK for the normalization of their relations, both as contributing to the relaxation of tensions on the Korean peninsula. The two sides expressed their hope that the DPRK will promptly conclude a safeguards agreement with the IAEA [International Atomic Energy Agency].

22. The two sides touched upon the importance of the draft agreements on a comprehensive political settlement of the Cambodia conflict drawn up by the five permanent members of the UN Security

Council and the co-chairman of the Paris conference on Cambodia. In this connection, Japan expressed its appreciation for the contribution made by the USSR as a permanent member of the UN Security Council and the Soviet Union welcomed the recent efforts by Japan to encourage the Cambodian parties to accept the draft agreements on a comprehensive political settlement. The two sides were in agreement on the need to continue to endeavour for the early attainment of comprehensive peace in Cambodia.

23. The two sides were in agreement on the need to further strengthen the international trend towards relaxation of tensions and the importance of expanding the dialogue and exchange between the two countries on a broad range of issues, including security aspects, from the perspective of promoting peace and prosperity in the Asia-Pacific region. The two sides expressed their high regard for the policy planning consultations held between the two countries' foreign ministries in December 1990 as a means to that end and gave their approval for further continuing these consultations.

24. The two sides had a high regard for the cooperation taking place among the countries of the Asia-Pacific region and in the appropriate economic organizations for regional prosperity in keeping with the principles of freedom and openness. In this connection, Japan welcomed the desire of the USSR, sharing these values, to be a member of the Conference on Pacific Economic Cooperation, and the USSR had a positive regard for Japanese contributions to the promotion of economic development in the region.

Tokyo, 18 April 1991

President of the Union of Soviet   *Prime Minister of Japan*
Socialist Republics

Source: TASS, 19 April 1991; English transl. Foreign Press Centre, FE/1051/A2/1, 20 April 1991.

Tokyo Declaration on Japan–Russia Relations, 13 October 1993

The prime minister of Japan and the president of the Russian Federation,

Based on the recognition that with the end of the Cold War, the world is moving away from the structure of confrontation towards cooperation, which will open new vistas for advances in international cooperation on both global and regional levels as well as in bilateral relations between different countries, and this is creating favourable conditions for the full normalization of the Japan-Russia bilateral relations,

Declaring that Japan and the Russian Federation share the universal values of freedom, democracy, the rule of law and the respect for fundamental human rights,

Recalling that the promotion of market economy and free trade contributes to the prosperity of the economies of both countries and to the sound development of the global economy,

Believing firmly that the success of the reforms underway in the Russian Federation is of decisive importance for building a new world political and economic order,

Affirming the importance of building the relations between the two countries in accordance with the objectives and principles of the UN Charter,

Determined that Japan and the Russian Federation should work together on the basis of the spirit of international cooperation, overcoming the legacy of totalitarianism, to build a new international order and to fully normalize their bilateral relations,

Declare the following:

1. The prime minister of Japan and the president of the Russian Federation share the recognition that the democratic and economic reforms underway in the Russian Federation are of tremendous significance not only for the people of Russia but also for the entire world. They are also of the view that the Russian Federation's successful transition to a true market economy and its smooth integration into the democratic international community are indispensable factors for increasing stability in the world and making the process of forming a new international order irreversible. In this regard, the prime minister of Japan conveyed to the president of the Russian Federation the following message from the leaders of the G7 countries and the representatives of the European Community:

'We regret that the armed clash in Moscow which was provoked by the supporters of the former parliament resulted in many victims. We nevertheless welcome the fact that the situation has ended and law and order is being restored including respect of human rights.

'We reconfirm that our support remains unchanged for democratic reform and economic reform pursued by President Yeltsin. We strongly hope that a truly democratic society which reflects the will of the people will be born through free and fair election of the new parliament with broad participation of the people and that reform will be further promoted.'

2. The prime minister of Japan and the president of the Russian Federation, sharing the recognition that the difficult legacies of the past in the relations between the two countries must be overcome, have undertaken serious negotiations on the issue of where Etorofu, Kunashiri, Shikotan and the Habomai Islands belong. They agree that negotiations towards an early conclusion of a peace treaty through the solution of this issue on the basis of historical and legal facts and based on the documents produced with the two countries' agreement as well as on the principles of law and justice should continue, and that the relations between the two countries should thus be fully normalized. In this regard, the government of Japan and the government of the Russian Federation confirm that the Russian Federation is the state retaining continuing identity with the Soviet Union and that all treaties and other international agreements between Japan and the Soviet Union continue to be applied between Japan and the Russian Federation.

The government of Japan and the government of the Russian Federation recall that constructive dialogue has taken place in the peace treaty working group between the two countries, and that one of the fruits thereof has been the joint publication in September 1992 of the joint compendium of documents of the history of territorial problems between Japan and Russia.

The government of Japan and the government of the Russian Federation agree to take a series of measures aimed at increased mutual understanding, including further facilitation of mutual visits between the current residents of the aforementioned islands and the residents of Japan that have been conducted within the framework agreed upon between the two countries.

3. The prime minister of Japan and the president of the Russian Federation, convinced that expanded political dialogue is a beneficial and effective means to promote Japan–Russia relations, agree to continue, deepen and develop political dialogue through regular mutual visits at the levels of the heads of state and government, the ministers and the vice ministers for foreign affairs.

4. The prime minister of Japan and the president of the Russian Federation welcome the progress thus far achieved in the area of arms

Joint Soviet-Japanese Declarations 267

control and disarmament, confirm the need for faithful implementation thereof and share the recognition that it is important to further promote such a process and to make it irreversible.

They share the recognition that the dismantling of nuclear weapons and the ensuing storage, control and disposal of fissile materials have an important bearing on the security of the entire world, and confirm their intention to cooperate in these areas. Furthermore, they confirm that the ocean dumping of radioactive wastes raises a grave concern on a global scale, particularly due to its effects on the environment of the neighbouring countries, and agree to consult closely through the Japan–Russia joint working group to consider this problem further.

They welcome the signing of the convention on the prohibition of chemical weapons in Paris in January 1993 and express their expectation for as many countries as possible joining the convention and thereby contributing to peace and stability of the world. They also agree to cooperate closely for effectively securing nonproliferation of weapons of mass destruction, their delivery systems, related materials and components, and technologies and knowledge, as well as for promoting increased transparency in transfers of conventional weapons.

5. The prime minister of Japan and the president of the Russian Federation, based on the common principles of freedom and openness, share the recognition of the potential for remarkable development which the Asia-Pacific region may demonstrate in the world in the 21st century. They confirm the significance of the Russian Federation's becoming an active and constructive partner in the region by implementing the principles of law and justice to further contribute to the development of political and economic relations among the countries in this region. They also share the recognition that the full normalization of the relations between Japan and the Russian Federation, both of which play important roles in the Asia-Pacific region, is of essential importance, in the context of making this region a region of peace and stability as well as a place for developing economic countries and regions, including the Russian Federation.

The prime minister of Japan and the president of the Russian Federation, based on their shared recognition of the need for promoting peace and stability in the Asia-Pacific region, confirm the importance of dialogue between the authorities of their two governments on a wide range of issues including security, and agree to further activate such issues.

6. The prime minister of Japan and the president of the Russian Federation note the ongoing deliberations at the United Nations on such issues as how the United Nations should function and be struc-

tured, so that it can play a central role in maintaining and creating a new world peace while adapting itself to the changing international circumstances, and agree to engage in common efforts to enhance the authority of the United Nations by further activating the contributions by both countries to the United Nations' efforts for solving global and regional problems.

In Tokyo, the thirteenth day of October nineteen hundred ninety-three:

MORIHIRO HOSOKAWA,   *Prime Minister of Japan*
BORIS NIKOLAYEVICH YELTSIN,   *President of the Russian Federation.*

Source: SWB/FE/1819 D/6-8, 14 Oct. 1993.

B

DRAFT OF A TREATY OF GOOD NEIGHBOURLINESS AND COOPERATION BETWEEN THE USSR AND JAPAN, 24 FEBRUARY 1978

The Union of Soviet Socialist Republics and Japan, seeking to promote the consolidation of peace and security in the Far East, in the Pacific basin and throughout the world:
Convinced that peaceful cooperation between both states on the basis of the aims and principles of the United Nations charter accord with the aspirations of the Soviet and Japanese peoples, the broad interests of international peace,
Guided by the desire fully to overcome the elements of estrangement and distrust in their mutual relations, engendered in the past,
Prompted by solicitude for creating an atmosphere of good neighbourhood and goodwill between both countries,
Reaffirming their intention to continue talks on the conclusion of a peace treaty,
Desiring to express in contractual form their resolve to create a firm and long-term foundation for the development of all-round cooperation between them, above all in the political sphere, and also in the sphere of the economy, science, technology and culture, have agreed as follows:

Article 1
The Union of Soviet Socialist Republics and Japan regard the maintenance of peace, extension and strengthening of relaxation of tension and strengthening of international security as one of the main aims of their policy.

They express a desire to exert efforts for the consolidation of universal peace on the Asian continent, in the Pacific basin and throughout the world.

Article 2
The Union of Soviet Socialist Republics and Japan shall settle their disputes exclusively by peaceful means and undertake in their mutual relations to refrain from the threat of force or its use.

The above contracting parties shall develop and strengthen relations of good neighbourhood and mutually advantageous cooperation on the basis of peaceful coexistence.

Article 3
The Union of Soviet Socialist Republics and Japan undertake not to allow the use of their territories for any actions which could prejudice the security of the other party.

Article 4
The above contracting parties undertake to refrain from any actions encouraging any third party to take aggressive actions against either of them.

Article 5
The Union of Soviet Socialist Republics and Japan shall maintain and widen regular contacts and consultations on important international issues concerning the interests of both states through meetings and exchanges of views between their leading statesmen and through diplomatic channels.

Should a situation arise which in the opinion of both sides is dangerous for maintaining peace, or if peace is violated, the sides shall immediately contact each other with the aim of exchanging views on the question of what can be done for improving the situation.

Article 6
The Union of Soviet Socialist Republics and Japan declare their determination to continue efforts for ending the arms race, of both nuclear and conventional weapons, and attaining general and complete disarmament under effective international control.

Article 7
Considering trade relations to be an important and necessary element of strengthening bilateral relations and attaching great significance to economic cooperation between the Union of Soviet Socialist Republics and Japan, the parties shall actively promote the growth of such relations, contribute to cooperation between the appropriate organizations and enterprises of both countries and to concluding appropriate agreements and contracts, including long-term ones.

Article 8
Attaching great significance to scientific and technical cooperation between the Union of Soviet Socialist Republics and Japan, the parties will promote in every way possible an expansion of mutually beneficial and all-round cooperation in these fields on the basis of the treaties and agreements which exist or which will be concluded between them.

Article 9

Being interested in the preservation and rational use of biological resources of the world ocean, the Union of Soviet Socialist Republics and Japan shall continue broadening cooperation in this field on the basis of the appropriate agreements and with due regard for the legislation of the parties.

Article 10

The above contracting parties shall encourage the development of relations between Government institutions and public organizations in the field of science, arts, education, television, radio and sports, contributing to a mutual enrichment of achievements in these fields, to strengthening the feeling of respect and friendliness of the peoples of those countries for each other.

Article 11

The Union of Soviet Socialist Republics and Japan shall strive that the relations and cooperations between them in all the above listed fields and any other fields of mutual interest be built on a durable and long-term basis. With this aim in view, the parties shall establish, where it is deemed advisable, joint commissions or other joint bodies.

Article 12

The Union of Soviet Socialist Republics and Japan do not claim and do not recognize anyone's claims to any special rights or advantages in world affairs, including claims to domination in Asia and in the area of the Far East.

Article 13

This treaty shall not affect the bilateral and multilateral treaties and agreements concluded earlier by the Union of Soviet Socialist Republics and Japan, and is not directed against any third country.

Article 14

This treaty shall be subject to ratification and enter into force on the day of the exchange of instruments of ratification to be done in the city of . . . done at . . . on . . . in two copies, each in the Russian and Japanese languages, both texts being equally authentic. For the Union of Soviet Socialist Republics . . . for Japan . . .

Source: *Izvestiya*, 24 Feb. 1978; *Japan Times*, 25 Feb. 1978.

C

JAPANESE-SOVIET ECONOMIC RELATIONS

LARGE-SCALE PROJECTS OF THE 1970s

The nine Japanese-Soviet projects described below were planned, discussed and partly embarked upon during the first half of the 1970s, the most promising phase of cooperation between the countries. Only Projects 1 to 3 and 5 achieved results which corresponded to the original plans. With regard to the remaining projects, either the results are not exactly known (Projects 4 and 9) or they never progressed beyond the planning stage (Projects 6 and 7). The oil and natural gas exploitation off the coast of Sakhalin (Project 8) has not even been started after twenty years of discussions.

1. KS-I Agreement

Japan shall supply the necessary capital goods for road construction and forestry in connection with the working of the timber resources in the Soviet Far East in the Sichote-Alin Mountains between 1969 and 1971 to the value of US$133 million; in addition it shall supply consumer goods (total value for 1969 and 1970 US$15 million annually).

The Soviet Union shall supply 7.6 million cubic metres of utilisable timber and 420,000 cubic metres of construction timber over a five-year period from 1969 to 1973.

Negotiating partners
Japan: Timber Committee (Chairman: Seiichi Kawai).
Soviet Union: Ministry for Foreign Trade (Director: L.I. Sedov).

Contracting partners
Japan: KS-Sangyo plc (Director: Seiichi Kawai).
Soviet Union: All-Soviet Timber Exporting Association (President: V.N. Akratov).

Implementation
July 1968: basic treaty is signed and comes into effect. Financing by Japanese loan of US$130 million, interest rate 5.8%.

Results (1969–1973)
Export of capital goods to the value of US$119 million (89.5% realised).

Export of consumer goods to the value of US$29.88 million (99.6% realised).
Import of utilisable timber: 7.555 million cubic metres (99.4% realised).
Import of construction timber: 64,000 cubic metres (owing to USSR's lack of supply capacity, only 15.2% realised).

2. Cooperation over construction of Wrangel port

In construction of a new port with modern equipment in Wrangel Bay opposite the port of Nakhodka, Japan shall undertake to supply:
- execution of construction blueprints for coal landing stage and in addition coal, timber and container facilities for the entire port;
- equipment, building materials and port facilities for coal, wood chips and containers over the period from 1971 to 1973 (total value US$80 million).

Negotiating partners
Japan: Sub-Committee for Cooperation over Construction of Wrangel Port of the Port Transport Committee (Chairman: Katsumi Yamagata).
Soviet Union: Ministry of Foreign Trade (Director: V.N. Sushkov).

Contracting partners
Japan: Waipui plc (Director: Katsumi Yamagata).
Soviet Union: All-Soviet Machinery Import Association (Vice-President: V.P. Panyushkin).

Implementation
December 1970: basic treaty is signed and comes into effect.
July 1974: agreement of both partners to an extension of delivery period for equipment and building materials to 1975.

Financing
Japanese loan of US$80 million, interest rate 6.5% and 6.8%, period seven years.

Results
Treaties signed concerning supply of machinery and other goods to the USSR totalled the equivalent of US$62.5 million.

Execution of construction
Timber port: completed December 1973 (annual capacity: 400,000 cubic metres).
Wood shavings port: completed end 1974 (annual capacity: 300,000 cubic metres).
Container port: completed mid-1975 (annual capacity: 140,000 units).

Coal landing stage: completed end 1975, start-up 1976 (annual capacity: 5 million tonnes).

Remarks
The completion of this project improved Japan's access to the Soviet transport system and facilitated container traffic between Japan and Europe.

3. *Project concerning imports of mechanical wood pulp (chips) and mash for industrial purposes*

Japan shall supply the necessary capital goods for the manufacture of mash and wood pulp and building materials between 1972 and 1974 to a total value of US$45 million; also to supply (cash payment) consumer goods to the value of approximately US$5 million.

The *Soviet Union* shall supply 4.7 million cubic metres of timber for mash and 8.5 million cubic metres industrial wood pulp (supply quantity was reduced to 8 million cubic metres in an individual contract).

Negotiating partners
Japan: Japan Chip Trading Company plc (Director: Fumio Tanaka).
Soviet Union: All-Soviet Timber Export Association (President: V.N. Akratov).

Implementation
December 1971: basic treaty is signed and comes into effect.

Financing
Japanese loan of US$50 million, interest rate 6%.
Repayment: 12% cash on delivery; the remainder within six years in kind.

Results
Exports (to September 1974): to the value of US$27.76 million (62% realised), including supply of two special transport ships for wood pulp to the value of US$18 million against cash.
Imports (to end September 1974):

		m^3	% realised
Pulp	1972	272,000	91
	1973	251,000	63
	1974	122,000	24
Wood chips	1972	34,000	68
	1973	89,000	44
	1974	192,000	48

4. Project concerning supplies of raw coal from southern Yakutiya

Japan shall grant a bank loan to the value of US$450 million in yen (including US$60 million 'local costs') and between 1975 and 1981 shall supply capital goods and building materials necessary for the working of coalfields in southern Yakutiya (Nerijungura ore deposit), including the construction of a railway between Bam, Tynda and Berkakit.

The *Soviet Union* shall supply coal from Nerijungura: 3.2 million tonnes in 1983; 4.2 million tonnes in 1984; 5.5 million tonnes annually in 1985–8. Total: 84.4 million tonnes. It shall also supply from Kuznetsk: 1 million tonnes annually in 1979–98 (total: 20 million tonnes) on the basis of a long-term contract.

Negotiating partners
Japan: Coal Committee (Chairman: Hisao Makita)
Soviet Union: All-Soviet Iron and Industrial Goods Export Association (President: B. Z. Nikolayenko).

Contracting partners
Japan: Association for Cooperation in Coal Mining in Southern Yakutiya plc.
Soviet Union: All-Soviet Iron and Industrial Goods Export Association (President: B. Z. Nikolayenko).

Execution
August 1970: inspection of coalfields in southern Yakutiya.
February 1972: proposals of USSR at fifth meeting of Joint Japan-Soviet Economic Committee (JJSEC).
April 1973: negotiations start in Tokyo.
June/July 1973: technical discussion in Moscow.
March 1974: second negotiations in Moscow.
April 1974: third negotiations in Tokyo.
April 1974: negotiations over loan to value of U$340 million in Tokyo (agreement on most important conditions: interest rate 6.375%, for 'local costs' 7.25%, repayment 1980–7, the portion for 'local costs' within five years).
June 1974: signing of basic contract in Moscow.
June 1974: signing of contract for loans in Tokyo, basic contract takes effect. Project is declared Energy Development Project no. 1.
December 1975: first business meeting in Tokyo over fulfilment of Japanese-Soviet cooperation agreements in southern Yakutiya coal project.

Results
No known individual results.

5. *KS-II Agreement*

Japan shall grant a bank loan to the value of US$550 million (including US$50 million "local costs") to be paid in yen, and supply all capital goods, building materials and timber transport vessels necessary for the development of timber resources to the Soviet Union over the period 1975–8. Interest rate 6.375%, 'local costs' interest 7.25%, repayment to take place 1979–5. The loan is included in the yen framework credit agreement of 23 April 1974.

The *Soviet Union* shall supply 17.5 million cubic metres of utilisable timber and 0.9 million cubic metres timber goods to Japan over five years, 1975–9.

Negotiating partners
Japan: Timber Committee (chairman: Yoshiichi Kawai).
Soviet Union: All-Soviet Timber Exporting Association (President: V.N. Akratov).

Contracting partners
Unknown.

Execution (to December 1974)
October 1972 to July 1973: preliminary negotiations in Moscow.
August 1973: initial negotiation meeting in Tokyo.
December 1973: meeting of Kawai and Vakhtov in Tokyo (agreement on primary conditions).
May 1974: meeting of Uchida and Vakhtov in Moscow.
June 1974: meeting of Kawai and Vakhtov in Moscow.
July 1974: basic contract is signed in Tokyo.
October 1974: contract concerning loans is signed in Moscow; basic contract comes into effect.

Results
Over the following years several new KS agreements were concluded and successfully realised.

6. *Petroleum project in Tyumen*

Japan shall grant a bank loan to the value of 240 million roubles (or US$1,300–1,700 million) to the Soviet Union and shall supply capital goods, machinery, ships, building materials and consumer goods necessary for the expansion of prospecting work in the Tyumen oilfields, for the completion of drilling plants, for oil transport to Japan and for the expansion of an overseas export port.

The *Soviet Union* shall supply crude oil to Japan on the basis of a long-term contract over a period of twenty years in the following instalments: 1981: 5 million tonnes, 1982: 10 million tonnes, 1983: 15 million tonnes, 1984: 20 million tonnes, 1985–2000 25 million tonnes annually.

Negotiating partners
Japan: Petroleum Committee (Chairman: Hiroki Imasato).
Soviet Union: Ministry for Foreign Trade/Secretary of State N.G. Osipov).
USA: Gulf Oil (planned).

Contracting partners
No contract concluded.

Execution until present
February 1972: repeated proposals from Soviets at fifth meeting of the Joint Japanese-Soviet Economic Committee (JJSEC).
June 1972: inspection of Tyumen oilfields.
August 1973: first joint board meeting of the JJSEC; Soviets present a 'protocol of intention'.
March 1974: second board meeting; Soviets present draft of contract (see above).
October/November 1974: sixth meeting of JJSEC; Japanese state they are not able to discuss the Soviet proposals.
June 1976: Hiroki Imasato states there are no intentions to resume negotiations.

Results
The project did not develop beyond the negotiating stage.

7. *Natural gas project in Yakutiya*

Japan and the USA shall grant bank loans to the value of US$3,400 million dollars (including US$400 million for consumer goods) and shall supply equipment, building materials and consumer goods necessary for the working of natural gas in Yakutiya, for pipeline construction, for liquefaction and overseas transport of gas. The first step shall take the form of a joint bank loan to the value of US$200 million for the prospecting of 1 billion cubic metres, furthermore equipment for additional exploration work and materials shall be supplied to the Soviet Union.

The Soviet Union shall supply an annual quantity of 10,000 million cubic metres of liquefied natural gas (LNG) to Japan and the USA on the basis of a long-term contract over a period of twenty-five years. Delivery to commence from 1982.

Negotiating partners
Japan: Natural Gas Kondankai (Chairman: Hiroshi Anzai).
USA: El Paso Natural Gas, Occidental Petroleum.
Soviet Union: Ministry for Foreign Trade (Secretary of State N.G. Osipov).

Contracting partners
Japan: Siberia Tennen Gas plc (Director: Hiroshi Anzai).
USA: American Siberian Natural Gas plc (Director: Harvard Boid) and Occidental LNG (Director: Armand Hammer).
Soviet Union: Ministry for Foreign Trade (Secretary of State N.G. Osipov).

Execution
October 1972: initial negotiations in Moscow.
July 1973: second negotiations in Tokyo.
August 1973: negotiations in Moscow on loan grant for prospecting.
December 1973: inspection of natural gas fields in Yakutiya.
January 1974: meeting of Anzai and Osipov in Moscow.
April/May 1974: Japanese-Soviet negotiations in Tokyo concerning ground exploration and loan grant for prospecting work (agreement on conditions of major importance). Talks between Anzai and the US government and the Board of the Export Bank. Conference between Japan, the USA and Soviet Union.
September 1974: Japanese-American consultations on G/A prospecting.
November 1974: trilateral conference in Paris; agreement between Japan, the USA and the Soviet Union on a basic contract for the implementation of prospecting work.
December 1974: signing of basic contract limited to technical matters; comes into effect as soon as the various agreements such as loan grants have come into effect.
July 1975: initialling of an agreement on loan extension to 29,400 million yen (approximately US$98 million) by Deputy Minister for Foreign Trade Alkhimov and the President of the Exim Bank, Satoshi Sumita, in Tokyo.
February 1976: Deputy Minister for Foreign Trade Alkhimov proposes reduction of original loan of US$100 million to US$25 million. This would reduce the total amount of loans including loans to be

granted by the USA to US$50 million instead of the originally planned US$200 million. Interest rate 8%.

Results
None known.

8. Oil and natural gas exploration on the Sakhalin continental shelf

Japan shall grant a loan to the value of US$100 million at 6% interest, with the option of an increase of a further US$100 million if necessary. Repayment only on achievement of results. Granting of an ordinary loan of US$30 million for 'local costs' and a loan of US$22.5 million for the construction of permanent exploration equipment. Hire or use of drilling equipment and materials necessary for oil and natural gas exploration on the Sakhalin shelf. In the case of successful exploration, capital goods and materials necessary for drilling and production to be supplied. Financing via bank loan, the value to be decided separately.

The *Soviet Union* shall carry out drilling in the event of successful prospecting and during the period of loan repayment, and for ten years after this period shall supply Japan with one half of the oil thus drilled. The Soviet Union shall also grant discount as agreed of 8.4% of the price for ten years after production start-up as compensation for Japan's assumption of the risk. Separate agreements regarding natural gas shall be made at a later date.

Negotiating partners
Japan: Committee for Exploration on the Sakhalin Continental Shelf (Chairman: Hiroshi Anzai; Chairman of Technical Affairs; Hiroki Imasato).
Soviet Union: Ministry for Foreign Trade (V.N. Sushkov).
USA: Gulf Oil.

Contracting Partners (probable)
Japan: Association for Oil Drilling in Sakhalin plc (Director: Hiroki Imasato).
Soviet Union: Ministry for Foreign Trade (V.N. Sushkov).

Execution
February 1972: proposals from the USSR at the fifth meeting of the JJSEC.
September 1972: inspection of Sakhalin.
November 1972: initial conference in Tokyo.
January/February 1974: second negotiations in Moscow.
April 1974: third negotiations in Tokyo.
July 1974: fourth negotiations in Moscow.

October/November 1974: fifth negotiations in Moscow.
November/December 1974: sixth negotiations in Moscow (provisional agreement on G/A contract text).
January 1975: agreement signed in Tokyo within basic contract on loan grant for US$100 million, over a period of five years, repayable in eighteen years in the event of succesful prospecting; interest rate 6%. No Soviet-American negotiations on the project. The Soviets would not object if Japan and the USA reached agreements on the project. Total extent of loans required estimated by Japanese experts as US$600–700 million dollars.
July 1975: agreement on Japanese loan of US$100 million dollars initialled (Association for Petroleum Development in Sakhalin and Deputy Chairman of the Soviet Bank for Foreign Trade, Nikitkin).
September 1975: on consideration of the basic contract, the Soviets demand a Soviet investigation ship instead of a Japanese ship to conduct geophysical investigations on the continental shelf.
November 1975: three agreements signed in Moscow by Nikitkin and Imasato concerning the awarding of loans already mentioned to the value of US$100 million, 2.5 million and 30 million assuming an exchange rate of 300 yen = 1 US$. Soviet concession to allow foreign, that is American, technicians into consultations if necessary.

Results
In October 1993 the project was again on the agenda of President Yeltsin's talks in Tokyo. No specific results are known.

9. *Paper and pulp project*

Japan shall supply the equipment necessary for the construction of a paper and pulp plant in Khabarovsk with annual production capacity of 7.05 million tonnes and for the construction of a pulp plant in Amurskin with annual production capacity of 250,000 tonnes by granting a loan of US$500 million.
    The *Soviet Union* shall supply Japan with a certain quantity from the production of both plants on the basis of a long-term contract (details not known).

Negotiating partners
Japan: Paper and Pulp Committee (Chairman: Fumio Tanaka).
Soviet Union: Ministry for Foreign Trade (V.N. Sushkov).

Contracting Partners
No contract as yet.

Execution:
October 1973: proposed by Soviet Union during visit of Prime Minister Tanaka to Moscow.
March 1974: proposal by Soviet Union at second board meeting of JJSEC.
October 1974: talks between Fumio Tanaka and Kuzmin in Moscow.
October/November 1974: official Soviet proposal at sixth meeting of JJSEC.
April 1975: talks concerning a second plant in Jeniseysk.

Results
None known.

Sources: Ogawa Kazuo, *Shiberia-kaihatsu to Nihon* (The Development of Siberia and Japan), Tokyo 1974; Bernhard Grossmann, 'Wirtschaftliche Zusammenarbeit zwischen Japan und der Sowjetunion' (Economic Cooperation between Japan and the Soviet Union), in *Europa Archiv*, vol. 30, no. 13 (July 1975), pp. 411-418; information from *Gaimusho*.

JAPAN'S TRADE WITH THE SOVIET UNION 1957–1990
(in thousands of US$)

	Exports	Imports	Total	Balance
1957	9.294	12.324	21.618	−3.030

6 Dec. 1957: Trade contract and payment agreement

	Exports	Imports	Total	Balance
1958	18.100	22.150	40.250	−4.050
1959	23.026	39.490	62.516	−16.464

2 March 1960: Trade and payment agreement (1960–2)

	Exports	Imports	Total	Balance
1960	59.976	87.025	147.001	−27.049
1961	65.380	145.409	210.789	−80.029
1962	149.390	147.309	296.699	2.081

4 Feb. 1963: Trade and payment agreement (1963–5)

	Exports	Imports	Total	Balance
1963	158.136	161.940	320.076	−3.084
1964	181.810	226.729	408.539	−44.919
1965	168.358	240.198	408.556	−71.840

21 Jan. 1966: Trade and payment agreement (1966–70)

	Exports	Imports	Total	Balance
1966	214.022	300.361	514.383	−86.339
1967	157.688	453.918	611.606	−296.230
1968	179.018	463.512	642.530	−284.494
1969	268.247	461.563	729.810	−193.316
1970	340.932	481.038	821.970	−140.106

22 Sept. 1971: Trade and payment agreement (1971–5)

	Exports	Imports	Total	Balance
1971	377.267	495.880	873.147	−118.613
1972	504.179	593.906	1,098.085	−89.727
1973	484.210	1,077.701	1,561.911	−593.491
1974	1,095.642	1,418.143	2,513.785	−322.501
1975	1,626.200	1,169.618	2,795.818	456.582

	Exports	Imports	Total	Balance
30 May 1977: Trade and payment agreement (1976–80)				
1976	2,251.894	1,167.441	3,419.335	1,084.453
1977	1,938.877	1,421.875	3,355.752	512.002
1978	2,502.195	1,441.723	3,943.918	1,060.472
1979	2,461.464	1910.681	4,372.145	550.783
1980	2,778.233	1,859.866	4,1638.099	918.367
22 May 1981: Trade and payment agreement (1981–5)				
1981	3,259.415	2,020.706	5,280.121	1,238.709
1982	3,898.841	1,682.017	5,580.858	2,216.824
1983	2,821.249	1,456.001	4,277.250	1,365.248
1984	2,518.314	1,393.987	3,912.301	1,124.327
1985	2,750.583	1,429.255	4,179.838	1,321.328
22 Jan. 1986: Trade and payment agreement (1986–90)				
1986	3,149.547	1,972.033	5,121.580	1,177.514
1987	2,562.855	2,345.163	4,908.018	217.692
1988	3,129.9	2,765.8	5,895.7	364.1
1989	3,081.7	3,004.5	6,086.2	77.2
1990	2,563.0	3,351.0	5,914.0	–788.0

Sources: Ministry of Finance Statistics, in Teruji Suzuki, 'Japanese-Soviet Trade: Past Trends and Future Prospects', in *Coexistence*, vol. 25, no. 3 (Sept. 1988), pp. 285–6; 'Summary Report on Trade of Japan', in Manfred Pohl (ed.), *Japan 1990/91. Politik und Wirtschaft*, Hamburg 1991, pp. 337–8.

D

OPINION POLLS

Views of Former Island Inhabitants (Results of a Survey in November 1989)

Question 1: Do you want the northern territories to be returned to Japan?

	%
Yes, very much	68.6
Tendency towards yes	16.0
Don't know	12.0
Tendency towards no	1.1
Am against return	1.1
No answer	1.1

Question 2: Do you believe that the northern territories will be returned to Japan in the future?

	%
Probably not	26.1
Perhaps returned in distant future.	39.5
Perhaps returned in near future	12.3
Don't know; no answer	22.2

Question 3: There are various ideas for methods of solving the territorial question. Please give your opinion of the individual ideas.

The aim should be to secure the return of all four islands – Kunashiri, Etorofu, Shikotan and the Habomai Islands:

	%
Agree	69.5
Don't know	17.4
Disagree	11.2
No answer	2.0

First the return of Shikotan and the Habomai Islands should be aimed for, then the return of Kunashiri and Etorofu should be considered:

	%
Agree	46.5
Don't know	23.5
Disagree	26.1
No answer	3.9

Japan should not cling to the exclusive idea of a return; Kunashiri, Etorofu, Shikotan and the Habomais could be placed under joint Japanese-Soviet rule, and it would be a good thing if Japanese could live there as well as Soviets:

	%
Agree	35.6
Don't know	23.0
Disagree	36.7
No answer	4.8

Question 4: Do you wish contact with Kunashiri, Etorofu, Shikotan and the Habomai Islands today?

	%
Yes, very much	40.1
Tendency towards yes	33.6
Don't know	15.4
Tendency towards no	5.6
Absolutely no desire	3.9
No answer	1.4

Subjects answering 'Strong desire' and 'Tendency towards yes' were asked about the type of contact. More than one answer could be given:

	%
Cultural and sporting activities	15.7
Sightseeing tours etc.	33.6
Economic activities	40.1
Other	4.2

Question 5: It appears that since General Secretary Gorbachev took office the political climate has been changing in the Soviet Union. What is your impression of this change?

	%
Positive impression	23.8
Tendency towards positive	25.8
Don't know	40.6
Tendency towards negative	2.8
Negative impression	0.8
No answer	6.2

Question 6: Does the political change in the Soviet Union give you feelings of hope?

	%
Have a feeling of hope	35.6
Tendency towards hope	23.8
Don't know	24.6
Tendency against hope	2.8
No feeling of hope	7.8
No answer	5.3

Source: *Tokyo Shimbun*, 12 Nov. 1989, in *DSJP*, 18–20 Nov. 1989, pp. 5–6.

Soviet Union-Japan: How We See Each Other (Results of a Joint Survey Conducted at the Beginning of 1990)

How do you rate your knowledge of Japan/the USSR?
1. I am well informed on politics, economics, history, geography, culture, art and other aspects of Japan/the USSR: 5.4% Russian, 3.6% Japanese.
2. I have a certain degree of knowledge about individual aspects of life in Japan/the USSR: 44.2% Russian, 21.7% Japanese.
3. I have a vague idea of individual aspects of life in the other country: 31.6% Russian, 39.6% Japanese.
4. I know almost nothing about Japan/the USSR: 14.1% Russian, 33.2% Japanese.
5. Don't know: 4.7% Russian, 1.7% Japanese.

What is your personal feeling towards the Japanese/Soviet people?
1. Positive feeling: 56.5% Russian, 9.8% Japanese.
2. Not positive, but not hostile: 35.1% Russian, 79.3% Japanese.
3. Extremely hostile: 1.1% Russian, 8.8% Japanese.
4. Don't know: 7.3% Russian, 2.1% Japanese.

You have probably formed a definite opinion of Japan/the USSR. What played the greatest role in shaping your opinion?
1. Newspapers and magazines: 43.1% Russian, 33.4% Japanese.
2. TV and radio: 67.1% Russian, 57.0% Japanese.
3. Books: 14.1% Russian, 1.8% Japanese.
4. Personal contact with Japanese/Russians who have been to the USSR/Japan: 3.0% Russian, 1.3% Japanese.
5. Personal experience of the country: 2.5% Russian, 1.4% Japanese.

6. Reports from people who have been to Japan/the USSR: 20.8% Russian, 2.2% Japanese.
7. Don't know: 5.4% Russian, 2.9% Japanese.

When news items about Japan/the USSR appear in the press, TV or radio, how much attention do you pay to them?
1. I pay attention to almost all news items: 31.8% Russian, 13.8% Japanese.
2. I pay attention to items on subjects which interest me: 32.0% Russian, 24.4% Japanese.
3. Depends on how important the events are: 20.4% Russian, 51.4% Japanese.
4. Hardly pay any attention: 10.6% Russian, 9.3% Japanese.
5. Don't know: 5.2% Russian, 1.0% Japanese.

In your opinion, which field of activity is furthest developed in Japan/the USSR today? (Select three areas)
1. Foreign affairs: 8.8% Russian, 33.0% Japanese.
2. Home affairs: 7.1% Russian, 25.0% Japanese.
3. Economy: 72.9% Russian, 19.2% Japanese.
4. Military: 5.8% Russian, 62.7% Japanese.
5. Education: 28.1% Russian, 6.3% Japanese.
6. Environmental conservation: 18.2% Russian, 5.7% Japanese.
7. Health care: 19.3% Russian, 4.3% Japanese.
8. Art and culture: 18.3% Russian, 27.3% Japanese.
9. Conquering space: 0.9% Russian, 51.3% Japanese.
10. Science and technology: 78.2% Russian, 22.0% Japanese.
11. Other: 0.7% Russian, 7.2% Japanese.
12. No answer: 5.0% Russian, 9.4% Japanese.

Which aspects of the life of the Japanese/Soviet people would you like to know more about?
1. History, geography: 11.0% Russian, 6.0% Japanese.
2. Home affairs: 6.4% Russian, 14.0% Japanese.
3. Foreign affairs: 4.4% Russian, 12.4% Japanese.
4. Industry, economy: 23.5% Russian, 7.1% Japanese.
5. Science and technology: 28.1% Russian, 6.1% Japanese.
6. Culture and art: 20.4% Russian, 5.5% Japanese.
7. Nature, ecology: 14.0% Russian, 8.6% Japanese.
8. Everyday life of the people: 47.2% Russian, 17.5% Japanese.
9. Sport: 6.1% Russian, 4.6% Japanese.
10. Young people's lives: 18.9% Russian, 3.7% Japanese.
11. Solutions to social problems: 33.0% Russian, 10.4% Japanese.
12. Don't know: 1.5% Russian, 4.1% Japanese.

Which of the characteristics listed apply the most accurately in your opinion to Soviets and Japanese? (Select three characteristics)

	Japanese on Russians (%)	Russians on themselves (%)	Russians on Japanese (%)	Japanese on themselves (%)
Energetic	20.1	12.7	51.1	15.5
Irritable	10.0	29.1	0.6	9.0
Conscientious, keen	12.6	4.9	72.9	61.2
Reliable	9.5	18.3	12.1	10.2
Egotistical	31.9	8.8	2.7	12.9
Democratic	6.6	11.1	5.9	19.5
Conservative	36.7	12.2	9.5	25.6
Arrogant	12.1	3.4	7.3	5.1
Optimistic	8.4	20.6	7.5	9.6
Emotional	15.0	15.1	6.5	12.4
Intellectual	9.8	3.3	33.8	6.6
Passive	7.1	25.3	0.6	20.2
Active	9.5	4.6	24.0	7.9
Peace-loving	7.0	53.2	11.3	29.8
Friendly	10.4	36.2	13.8	13.6
Aggressive	33.8	2.8	7.1	2.9
Honest, open	5.6	20.4	2.3	13.8

How in your opinion have Soviet-Japanese relations changed over the last five years?
1. Relations have improved: 40.0% Russian, 35.8% Japanese.
2. No clear-cut answer possible: 37.4% Russian, 35.3% Japanese.
3. No change: 10.9% Russian, 22.8% Japanese.
4. Relations have worsened: 1.1% Russian, 3.2% Japanese.
5. Don't know: 10.6% Russian, 2.9% Japanese.

Do you think Soviet-Japanese relations should become closer?
1. Must become closer: 83.7% Russian, 52.8% Japanese.
2. Can stay at present level: 6.7% Russian, 16.4% Japanese.
3. No necessity for closer relations: 1.6% Russian, 7.1% Japanese.
4. Impossible to say with certainty: 5.2% Russian, 22.2% Japanese.
5. Don't know: 2.8% Russian, 1.5% Japanese.

In your opinion, to what extent does the state of Soviet-Japanese relations affect the world situation?
1. Has a great effect: 12.1% Russian, 19.7% Japanese.
2. Has a noticeable effect: 29.7% Russian, 33.2% Japanese.
3. Has a certain effect: 38.6% Russian, 34.1% Japanese.
4. No particular effect: 6.0% Russian, 7.6% Japanese.
5. No effect: 1.5% Russian, 0.6% Japanese.
6. Don't know: 12.1% Russian, 4.8% Japanese.

In your opinion, is the problem of the northern territories (Japan's demand that the Soviet Union should return the islands of Kunashiri, Etorofu and the smaller Kurile chain) of an anti-Soviet character?
1. Yes: 25.2% Russian, 17.6% Japanese.
2. Yes, to a certain extent: 31.4% Russian, 38.5% Japanese.
3. No: 18.9% Russian, 40.4% Japanese.
4. Don't know: 24.5% Russian, 3.5% Japanese.

Do you believe that the fulfilment of the territorial demands which Japan is making of the Soviet Union is essential for relations between the two countries developing towards good neighbourliness and mutually profitable cooperation?
1. Is essential: 5.7% Russian, 44.7% Japanese.
2. To a certain extent: 16.8% Russian, 34.8% Japanese.
3. Impossible to say with certainty: 17.9% Russian, 14.5% Japanese.
4. Is not essential: 48.3% Russian, 4.3% Japanese.
5. Don't know: 11.3% Russian, 1.7% Japanese.

How could the USSR and Japan cooperate most effectively?
1. In the economic and social development of Siberia: 23.1% Russian, 17.0% Japanese.
2. In the export of raw materials from the USSR to Japan and to other countries: 5.3% Russian, 11.4% Japanese.
3. In joint development of technology, machinery and equipment: 55.7% Russian, 21.8% Japanese.
4. In the exchange of new technological developments: 35.8% Russian, 11.8% Japanese.
5. In fishing: 11.0% Russian, 32.2% Japanese.
6. Other areas: 0.9% Russian, 1.3% Japanese.
7. Don't know: 6.4% Russian, 4.5% Japanese.

If you were offered work in a joint Soviet-Japanese company, what would be your attitude to the offer?
1. Would accept unreservedly: 37.8% Russians, 4.9% Japanese.
2. Would accept, but with reservations: 21.4% Russian, 24.9% Japanese.

3. Would refuse: 7.4% Russian, 29.6% Japanese.
4. No clear-cut answer possible: 23.6% Russian, 37.6% Japanese.
5. Don't know: 9.7% Russian, 3.0% Japanese.

What is your opinion of the idea of special economic zones in which optimum conditions for cooperation and bartering between the USSR and Japan existed?
1. Agree: 71.1% Russian, 38.1% Japanese.
2. Object: 5.3% Russian, 5.2% Japanese.
3. No clear-cut answer possible: 17.6% Russian, 50.8% Japanese.
4. Don't know: 6.0% Russian, 5.9% Japanese.

Would you like to travel to Japan/the USSR if you were given the chance?
1. Would definitely go: 46.9% Russian, 24.4% Japanese.
2. Would go: 33.4% Russian, 40.9% Japanese.
3. Would not like to go: 4.7% Russian, 18.0% Japanese.
4. No clear-cut answer possible: 9.6% Russian, 16.0% Japanese.
5. Don't know: 5.4% Russian, 0.7% Japanese.

Are you familiar with any areas of Japanese/Soviet culture, art and sport? (Any number of areas may be selected)
1. Music: 14.3% Russian, 35.7% Japanese.
2. Fine arts: 17.5% Russian, 14.8% Japanese.
3. Dance: 8.0% Russian, 24.7% Japanese.
4. Literature: 15.4% Russian, 21.3% Japanese.
5. Film: 40.0% Russian, 32.1% Japanese.
6. Circus: 9.6% Russian, 36.2% Japanese.
7. Sports events: 32.2% Russian, 79.1% Japanese.
8. Other: 1.6% Russian, 3.7% Japanese.
9. Don't know: 22.5% Russian, 2.9% Japanese.

Do you believe that the Japanese/Soviet arms potential represents a threat to the Soviet Union/Japan?
1. Yes: 18.1% Russian, 62.1% Japanese.
2. No clear-cut answer possible: 40.8% Russian, 27.3% Japanese.
3. No: 25.6% Russian, 9.0% Japanese.
4. Don't know: 15.5% Russian, 1.6% Japanese.

Do you believe the aim of reaching an agreement to destroy all nuclear weapons is realistic?
1. Yes: 49.8% Russian, 16.5% Japanese.
2. No clear-cut answer possible: 25.0% Russian, 49.4% Japanese.
3. No: 18.3% Russian, 31.3% Japanese.
4. Don't know: 6.9% Russian, 2.8% Japanese.

Do you believe that the principle of adequate defence without nuclear weapons can be put into practice?
1: Yes, absolutely: 53.1% Russian, 20.4% Japanese.
2. Yes, but I am not completely sure: 22.3% Russian, 31.7% Japanese.
3. No clear-cut answer: 10.6% Russian, 27.5% Japanese.
4. No: 5.6% Russian, 17.5% Japanese.
5. Don't know: 8.4% Russian, 2.9% Japanese.

Of the two countries USSR and USA, which is more active in nuclear disarmament?
1. USSR: 62.5% Russian, 24.4% Japanese.
2. USA: 2.3% Russian, 17.3% Japanese.
3. Both countries equally: 16.2% Russian, 42.8% Japanese.
4. Neither one nor the other: 8.2% Russian, 10.5% Japanese.
5. Don't know: 10.8% Russian, 5.0% Japanese.

How much influence do you believe meetings of the leaders of the USSR and the USA have on the development of Soviet-Japanese relations?
1. Very great influence: 11.6% Russian, 20.3% Japanese.
2. Fairly great influence: 39.3% Russians, 36.0% Japanese.
3. Insignificant influence: 21.1% Russians, 34.0% Japanese.
4. No influence at all: 4.6% Russian, 5.4% Japanese.
5. Don't know: 23.4% Russian, 4.6% Japanese.

On December 7th 1988 in front of the United Nations M.S. Gorbachev announced a unilateral reduction in Soviet troops and arms, partly also in the Asiatic region of the USSR. How do you believe this reduction will affect Soviet-Japanese relations?
1. Will significantly improve relations: 10.5% Russian, 3.6% Japanese.
2. Will improve relations to some extent: 27.1% Russian, 20.6% Japanese.
3. Will improve them insignificantly: 25.6% Russian, 42.8% Japanese.
4. Will have little or no effect: 8.8% Russian, 14.8% Japanese.
5. No clear-cut answer possible: 15.5% Russian, 12.6% Japanese.
6. Don't know: 13.5% Russian, 5.6% Japanese.

M.S. Gorbachev is implementing a policy of perestroika. How strong is your interest in this?
1. Very strong: 22.9% Russian, 15.9% Japanese.
2. Fairly strong: 22.2% Russian, 16.4% Japanese.
3. A certain interest: 48.1% Russian, 42.1% Japanese.
4. Little interest: 7.4% Russian, 17.1% Japanese.
5. No interest: 2.1% Russian, 7.4% Japanese.
6. Don't know: 3.3% Russian, 1.1% Japanese.

Do you believe perestroika will be successful or unsuccessful?
1. Definitely successful: 10.6% Russian, 15.9% Japanese.
2. Probably successful: 22.9% Russian, (no figures) Japanese.
3. No clear-cut answer possible: 44.1% Russian, 74.5% Japanese.
4. Probably unsuccessful: 13.4% Russian, 2.9% Japanese.
5. Definitely unsuccessful: 2.8% Russian, (no figures) Japanese.
6. Don't know: 8.2% Russian, 6.7% Japanese.

Source: *Mirovaja Ekonomika i Meždunarodnye Otnošenija*, no. 3 (1990), pp. 134–8.

SELECT BIBLIOGRAPHY

Documents and Primary Material

Akademija Nauk SSSR (Academy of Sciences of the USSR) (ed.), *Japonija 19 . . , Ežegodnik* [Japan 19 . . , Yearbook], 1972–88 edns, Moscow 1973–89.

—— *Meždunarodnye otnošenija na Dal'nem Vostoke v poslevoennye gody* [International Relations in the Far East in the Period after the Second World War], vol. 2: *1958–1976*, Moscow 1978.

—— Institut Dal'nego Vostoka (Institute of Far Eastern Studies) (ed.), *Vnešnaja politika i meždunarodnye otnošenija Kitajskoj Narodnoj Respubliki* [Foreign Policy and International Relations of the People's Republic of China], vol. 2: *1963–1973*, Moscow 1974.

—— Institut Dal'nego Vostoka (Institute of Far Eastern Studies) (ed.), *Kitajskaja Narodnaja Respublika. Političeskoe i ekonomičeskoe razvitie v 1973 godu* (The People's Republic of China, its Political and Eeconomic Development, 1973), Moscow 1975.

—— Institut Vostokovedenija (Institute of Oriental Studies) (ed.), *Istorija Japonii* [History of Japan] *1945–1975*, Moscow 1978.

Bôeichô (Defence Agency) (ed.), *Nihon-no bôei* [Defence of Japan], 1970–91 edns, Tokyo 1970–91.

Defence Agency (ed.), *Defence of Japan*, Tokyo 1970–91.

Gaimushô (ed.), *Waga gaikô-no kinkyô, Shôwa 48 and 49* [The Current State of our Foreign Relations, 1973 and 1974], vols 17 and 18, Tokyo 1973 and 1974.

Greenville, J.A.S., *The Major International Treaties 1914–1973: A History and Guide with Texts*, London 1974.

Gromyko, A.A. et al. (ed.), *Diplomatičeski slovar'* (Lexicon of Diplomacy), 3 vols, 2nd–4th edns, Moscow 1960–4, 1970–3 and 1984–6.

International Institute for Strategic Studies (IISS) (ed.), *The Military Balance 1993–1994*, London 1993.

Keizai Koho Center – Japan Institute for Social and Economic Affairs (ed.), *Japan 19 . . : An International Comparison*, 1980–92 edns, Tokyo 1980–91.

Kissinger, Henry, *The White House Years*, London 1979.

Levchenko, Stanislav, *On The Wrong Side: My Life in the KGB*, Washington, DC 1988.

Meissner, Boris, *Die 'Breshnew-Doktrin'* (The 'Brezhnev Doctrine'), Cologne 1969.
Ministerstvo vnešnich ekonomičeskich svjazej SSSR (Ministry of Foreign Trade of the USSR) (ed.), *Vnešnaja torgovlja SSSR v 1987 g* (Foreign Trade of the USSR in 1987), Moscow 1988 and other years.
Northern Territories Issue Association (ed.), *A Border yet Unresolved — Japan's Northern Territories*, Tokyo 1981.
Research Institute for Peace and Security (ed.), *Asian Security 19...*, 1979–1990 edns, Tokyo 1980–91.
Shigeta, Hiroshi and Shôji Suezawa (eds), *Nisso-kihon-bunsho-shiryôshû* (Collection of Fundamental Documents of Japanese-Soviet Relations), Tokyo 1988.
Sôrifu kôhôshitsu (Information Service of the Prime Minister's Office) (ed.), *Yoron-chôsa, gekkan* [Opinion Surveys, Monthly], vols 4–23, 1972–91.
Sovetskij Sojuz, 'Japonija: kak my smotrim drug na druga' (The Soviet Union and Japan: How We See Each Other), in *Mirovaja Ekonomika i Meždunarodnie Otnošenija*, no. 3 (1990), pp. 134–41.
Stoecker, Helmut and Adolf Rüger, *Handbuch der Verträge 1871–1964. Verträge und andere Dokumente aus der Geschichte der internationalen Beziehungen* (Handbook of Treaties 1871–1964. Treaties and Other Documents in the History of International Relations), Berlin (East) 1968.

Monographs and Essays

Ahrens-Thiele, Dagmar, *Japans Rohstoffpolitik im Kräftefeld Moskau-Peking* (Japan's Raw Materials Policies within the Force-field of Moscow–Peking), Hamburg 1977.
Astafiev, G.W. and A.M. Dubinski (eds), *Aussenpolitik und internationale Beziehungen der Volksrepublik China* (Foreign Policy and International Relations in the People's Republic of China), Berlin 1976.
Avtorskij kollektiv (Authors' Collective), *SSSR–Japonija: Problemy torgovo-ekonomičeskich otnosenij* (The USSR and Japan: Problems of Trade and Economic Relations), Moscow 1984.
Berton, Peter, Paul F. Langer and George O. Totten, *The Russian Impact on Japan's Literature and Social Thought*, Los Angeles 1981.
Bunin, V., 'Koncepcija "kompleksnogo obespečenija nacional'noj bezopasnosti"' (The Concept of 'Comprehensive National Security'), in Akademija Nauk SSSR (Academy of Sciences of the USSR) (ed.), *Japonija 1982, Ežegodnik*, Moscow 1983, pp. 67–79.

Select Bibliography

Bunin, V., 'Tokyo – A Course toward Militarization', in *Far Eastern Affairs*, no. 2 (1983), pp. 61–71.

—— 'The Defeat of Japanese Militarism: Lessons for our Time', in *Far Eastern Affairs*, no. 3 (1985), pp. 25–35.

—— 'Japan and Washington's Asian Pacific Strategy', in *Far Eastern Affairs*, no. 3 (1987), pp. 32–42.

Campbell, Robert W., 'Prospects for Sibirian Economic Development', in Donald S. Zagoria (ed.), *Soviet Policy in East Asia*, New Haven, Conn./London 1982, pp. 229–54.

Clark, Gregory, 'Hoppô-ryôdo-wa tabû shisuru na' (Do not Place the Northern Territories under a Taboo), in *Voice*, Dec. 1986, pp. 96–105.

Clement, Hermann, 'Sibirien – Reserve oder Bürde?' (Siberia – Reserve or Burden?), in Bundesinstitut für Internationale und Ostwissenschaftliche Studien (German Federal Institute for International and Eastern Studies) (ed.), *Soviet Union 1984/85. Ereignisse, Probleme, Perspektiven*, Cologne 1985, pp. 190–201.

Furui, Yoshimi, 'Inside Story of Normalization of Sino-Japanese Diplomatic Relations', in *Summaries of Selected Japanese Magazines*, Tokyo, Jan. 1973, pp. 43–54.

Glaubitz, Joachim and Dieter Heinzig (eds), *Die Sowjetunion und Asien in den 80er Jahren* (The Soviet Union and Asia in the 1980s), Baden-Baden 1988.

Grossmann, Bernhard, 'Wirtschaftliche Zusammenarbeit zwischen Japan und der Sowjetunion' (Economic Cooperation between Japan and the Soviet Union), in *Europa-Archiv*, vol. 30, no. 13 (July 1975), pp. 411–18.

Hasegawa, Tsuyoshi, 'Japanese Perceptions of the Soviet Union 1960–1980', in Hasegawa (ed.), *The Soviet Union Faces Asia: Perceptions and Policies*, Sapporo 1987, pp. 37–70.

—— *Russia and Japan: An Unresolved Dilemma between Distant Neighbours*, Jonathan Haslum and Andrew Kuchins (eds), Berkeley, CA 1993.

Heinzig, Dieter, 'SS-20 in Asien (I) und (II)', Cologne, 5/6.2.1984 (Bundesinstitut für Internationale und Ostwissenschaftliche Studien, *Aktuelle Analysen*, 1984, nos 6/7).

Itô, Kenichi, 'Strategy for Return of Northern Territory', in *Summaries of Selected Japanese Magazines*, March 1986, pp. 18–28.

Ivanov, M.I., *Rost militarizma v Japonii* (The Growth of Militarism in Japan), Moscow 1982.

Jain, Rajendra Kumar, *The USSR and Japan 1945–1980*, Atlantic Highlands, NJ 1981.

Kaihara, Osamu, 'Migu 25 to Nihon-no bôei' (The MiG-25 and Japan's Defence), in *Sekai Shûhô*, 28 Sept. 1976, pp. 4–5.

Kamiya, Fuji, 'The Northern Territories: 130 Years of Japanese Talks with Czarist Russia and the Soviet Union', in Donald S. Zagoria (ed.), *Soviet Policy in East Asia*, New Haven, Conn./London 1982, pp. 121–51.

Kapitsa, M., 'Paths to Peace and Security in the Asia Pacific Region', in *International Affairs*, Moscow, no. 8 (1987), pp. 27–37.

Kazakov, I., 'Soviet-Japanese Economic Relations', in *Far Eastern Affairs*, no. 2 (1976), pp. 78–89.

Kim, Euikon, *Explaining Soviet-Japanese Relations, 1972–1985: Domestic Politics versus the Global Superpower Rivalry*, Ann Arbor, Mich. 1988.

Kimura, Hiroshi, *Hoppô-ryôdo – kiseki to henkan e no josô* (The Northern Territories – the Position and Approach to their Return), Tokyo 1989.

—— 'Chikara-kankei ga Nihon-yûri na no da kara seinak-subeki de aru' (Japan Should Observe Events Calmly, since the Balance of Power is in its Favour), in *Sekai Shûhô*, 10 March 1991, pp. 108–13.

—— (ed.), *Hoppô-ryôdo wo kangaeru* (On the Northern Territories), Tokyo 1981.

Kitahara, Kenichi, 'Shiberia-kaihatsu no tenbô' (Survey of Exploitation in Siberia), in *Seiji-keizai*, no. 3 (1975), pp. 28–38.

Knabe, Bernd, 'Her mit dem BAM-Programm' (Make Way for the BAM Programme), Cologne, 16 Oct. 1985 (Bundesinstitut für Internationale und Ostwissenschaftliche Studien, *Aktuelle Analysen*, 1985, no. 31).

Koloskov, B., *Vnešnaja politika Kitaja* [China's Foreign Policy] *1969–1976*, Moscow 1977.

Kôsaka, Masataka, 'Shingaikô-jidai-no kôsô' (Concept of a New Era in Foreign Policy), in *Shokun*, no. 12 (1971), pp. 23–44.

Kroncher, Allan, *Siberian Oil becomes a Problem*, Munich, 10 April 1984 (Radio Liberty Research, RL 147/84).

Krupinski, Kurt, *Russland und Japan. Ihre Beziehungen bis zum Frieden von Portsmouth* (Russia and Japan: Their Relations up to the Treaty of Portsmouth), Königsberg 1940.

Kuchins, Andrew, *Russia and Japan: An Unresolved Dilemma between Distant Neighbors*, Berkeley: International and Area Studies, University of California, 1993.

Kunadze, G.F., *Japono-kitajskie otnošenija na sovremennom etape, 1972–1982* (Japanese-Chinese Relations of the Present Day), Moscow 1983.

—— *Rossija i Japonija* (Russia and Japan), Moscow 1988.

Kutakov, L.N., *Moskva-Tokio, Očerki diplomatčeskich otnošenij 1956–1986* (Moscow–Tokyo: Compendium of diplomatic relations), Moscow 1988.

Langen, Benita, *Die Gehietsverluste Japans nach dem Zweiten Weltkrieg. Eine völkerrechtliche Studie* (Japan's Territorial Losses after the Second World War. A Study in International Law), Berlin 1971 (Schriften zum Völkerrecht, Vol. 19).

Lensen, George Alexander, *The Strange Neutrality: Soviet-Japanese Relations during the Second World War, 1941–1945*, Tallahassee, Fla. 1972.

Leške, V.G., *Japono-amerikanskij sojuz – itogi trech desjatiletij* (The Japanese-American Alliance – Results of Three Decades), Moscow 1983.

McGuire, Sumiye O., *Soviet-Japanese Economic Relations*, Santa Monica, Calif. 1990.

Maiya, Kenichirô (ed.), *Shû Onrai Nihon-wo kataru* (Zhou Enlai on Japan), Tokyo 1972.

Markov, A.P., *Japonija: Kurs na vooruženie* (Japan – On Course to Rearmament), Moscow 1970.

Matsumoto, Shunichi, 'Tenka-ni haji-wo sarasu Nihon gaikô' (Japan's Shameful Foreign Policy), in *Bungei Shunjû*, no. 12 (1971), pp. 124–32.

Mayer, Hans-Jürgen, *Der japanisch-sowjetische Territorialstreit. Aussen- und sicherheitspolitische Aspekte* [The Japanese-Soviet Territorial Conflict. Aspects of Foreign and Security Policy] *1975–1978*, Hamburg 1980 (Mitteilungen des Instituts für Asienkunde, Hamburg, no. 111).

Mazorov, S.T., *Voenno-ekonomičeskij potencial sovremennoj Japonii* (Japan's Military and Economic Potential), Moscow 1979.

Mazurov, V.M., *SSA – Kitaj – Japonija: perestroika mežgosudarstvennych otnošenij, 1969–1979* (The USA–China–Japan: Restructuring International Relations), Moscow 1980.

Mendl, Wolf, 'Stuck in a Mould: The Relationship between Japan and the Soviet Union', in *Millenium*, vol. 18, no. 3 (Winter 1989), pp. 455–78.

—— 'Japan and the Soviet Union: towards a Deal?', in *The World Today*, vol. 47, no. 11 (Nov. 1991), pp. 196–200.

Nakajima, Mineo, 'Hoppô-ryôdo "nitô-henkanron" wa tabû ka?' (Is the Discussion of 'the Return of Two Islands' of the Northern Territories Taboo?) in *Shokun*, March 1987.

Nakamura, Shintarô, *Nihonjin to Roshiyajin – Japontsy i Ruskije* (Japanese and Russians), Moscow 1983

Näth, Marie-Luise, *Die Entwicklung der amerikanisch-chinesischen Beziehungen seit 1972: Hintergründe, Probleme, Perspektiven* (The Development of American-Chinese Relations since 1972: Background, Problems, Perspectives), Cologne 1979 (Berichte des Bundesinstituts für Internationale und Ostwissenschaftliche Studien, no. 36).

Nikolayev, N., 'USSR–Japan: Fifty Years of Diplomatic Relations', in *Far Eastern Affairs*, no. 4 (1975), pp. 16–23

Nosov, M.G., *Japano-kitajskie otnošenija* (Japanese-Chinese Relations), Moscow 1978.

Ogawa, Kazuo, *Shiberia-kaihatsu to Nihon* (The Exploitation of Siberia and Japan), Tokyo 1974.

Ohira, Masayoshi, 'A New Foreign Policy for Japan', in *Pacific Community*, vol. 3, no. 3 (April 1972), pp. 405–18.

Okazaki, Hisahiko, *A Grand Strategy for Japanese Defense*, Lanham/New York/London 1986.

Panov, A.A. and L.P. Pinaev, 'Voenno-političeskie koncepcii pravjascich krugov Japonij' (Concepts of Military Policy of Japan's Ruling Circles), in Akademija Nauk SSSR (Academy of Sciences of the USSR) (ed.), *Japonija 1978, Ežegodnik*, Moscow 1979, pp. 94–108.

Pavlovski, V., 'Regionale Zusammenarbeit und kollektive Sicherheit für Asien' (Regional Cooperation and Collective Security for Asia), in *Neue Zeit*, no. 30 (July 1972), pp. 18–20.

Petrov, D., 'Japan in the Nuclear Strategy of the United States', in *Far Eastern Affairs*, no. 3 (1984), pp. 55–8.

Pohl, Manfred (ed.), *Japan 1990/91. Politik und Wirtschaft* (Politics and Economics), Hamburg 1991.

Pospelov, B., 'The Japanese Approach', in *Far Eastern Affairs*, no. 6 (1988), pp. 26–30.

Rees, David, *The Soviet Seizure of the Kuriles*, New York 1985.

Robertson, Myles L.C., *Soviet Policy towards Japan. An Analysis of Trends in the 1970s and 1980s*, Cambridge, Mass. 1988.

Saeki, Kiichi, 'Towards Japanese Cooperation in Siberian Development', in *Problems of Communism*, vol. 21, no. 3 (May/June 1972), pp. 1–11.

—— and Shigeki Hakamada, '91-nen Gorubachofu-shokichô no-Nichi hyômei-no Soren-zenryaku-wo-dô miru ka' (How Should the Soviet Strategy behind Gorbachev's Declaration of a Visit to Japan in 1991 be Evaluated?), in *Ajia-jihô*, no. 12 (1989), pp. 30–49.

Šapožnikov, B.G., 'Problemy "nacional'noj oborony" Japonii' (Problems of Japan's 'national defence'), in Akademija Nauk SSSR

Select Bibliography

(Academy of Sciences of the USSR) (ed.), *Japonija 1972, Ežegodnik*, Moscow 1973, pp. 102–7.

Sase, Masamori, 'Die militärische Dimension der sowjetischen Asienpolitik' (The Military Dimension of Soviet Policy on Asia), in Joachim Glaubitz and Dieter Heinzig (eds), *Die Sowjetunion und Asien in den 80er Jahren* (The Soviet Union and Asia in the 1980s), Baden-Baden 1988, pp. 31–54.

Sergienko, I., *Vozroždenie militarizma v Japonii* (Revival of Militarism in Japan), Moscow 1969.

Shigemitsu, Akira, '"Hoppô-ryôdo" to Soren gaikô' (The Northern Territories and Soviet Foreign Policy), Tokyo 1983.

Širyaev, H.P., 'Ekonomičeskie otnošenija SSSR i Japonii' (Economic Relations between the USSR and Japan), in *Problemy Dal'nego Vostoka*, no. 1 (1972), pp. 97–103.

Sladkovski, M.I., Kitajsko-japonskie otnošenija [uroki istorii, sovremennost'] (Sino-Japanese relations [Lessons from the past and the present], in: *Problemy Dal'nego Vostoka*, no. 1 (1972), pp. 60–76.

Solodovnik, Sergei, 'Is there Room for US in the APR?', in *International Affairs*, Moscow, no. 3 (1991), pp. 60–9.

Solomon, Richard H. and Masataka Kosaka (eds), *The Soviet Far East Military Buildup*, London, 1986.

Spandaryan, V.B., 'Perspektivy sovetsko-japonskich otnošenij' (Perspectives of Soviet-Japanese Economic Relations), in *Problemy Dal'nego Vostoka*, no. 2 (1972), pp. 28–43.

—— 'Major Landmark in Soviet-Japanese Trade', in *Far Eastern Affairs*, no. 2 (1978), pp. 90–100.

Stephan, John J., *The Kuril Islands: Russo-Japanese Frontiers in the Pacific*, Oxford 1974.

—— 'The Kuril Islands: Japan versus Russia', in *Pacific Community*, vol. 7, no. 3 (April 1976), pp. 311–30.

Swearingen, Roger, *The Soviet Union and Postwar Japan. Escalating Challenge and Response*, Stanford, Calif. 1978.

Timmermann, Heinz, 'Japans Kommunisten nach ihrem 17. Parteitag vom November 1985' (Japan's Communists after their 17th Party Conference of November 1985), Cologne, 22 Jan. 1986 (Bundesinstitut für Internationale und Ostwissenschaftliche Studien, *Aktuelle Analysen*, 1986, no. 2).

Ueno, Hideo, *Gendai Nitchû-kankei no tenkai* (Recent Developments in Sino-Japanese relations), Tokyo/Osaka 1974.

Wada, Haruki, 'Hoppô-ryôdo mondai-ni-tsuite no kôsatsu' (Observations on the Question of the Northern Territories), in *Seika*, Dec. 1986, pp. 150–61.

Wada, Haruki, *Hoppô ryôdo-mondai wo kangaeru* (On the Problem of the Northern Territories), Tokyo 1990.

—— 'Yontô-henkanron wa kakute kimerareta' (The Creation of a Concept for the Return of the Four Islands), in *Sekai Shûhô*, 15–22 Jan. 1991, pp. 18–21.

Whiting, Allen S., *Siberian Development and East Asia. Threat or Promise?*, Stanford, Calif. 1981.

Zanegin, B., 'US Strategy in the Asian Pacific Region', in *Far Eastern Affairs*, no. 6 (1988), pp. 17–25.

NAME INDEX

Abe, Shintaro 67, 75–8, 127, 205, 210, 211, 214
Afanasyev, V.G. 108, 109
Afanasyev, Yu. N. 208
Aichi, Kiichi 44
Akhromeyev, S.F. 214
Akihito, Emperor 217
Andropov, Yu. V. 216
Arai, Hirokazu 60
Arbatov, G.A. 189, 190
Arbatsumov 245

Baibakov, N.K. 57
Belenko 183
Bessmertnykh, A.A. 216, 217
Brezhnev, L.I. 6, 7, 45, 51, 52, 54, 57, 58–60, 64–6, 83, 91, 108, 140, 144, 145, 149, 150, 163, 164, 174–6, 184, 191
Brzezinski, Zbigniew 152, 155
Bush, George 208

Carter, Jimmy 152, 155, 182
Chen Chu 138
Chen Xiliang 158
Chiang Kai-shek 13
Chiao Guanhua 138, 139
Chun Doo Hwan 221

Deng Xiaoping 136, 146, 155, 159–61
Dulles, John Foster 42

Endo, Kazuyoshi 227

Falin, W.M. 75, 217

Fujiyama, Aiichiro 44
Fukuda, Takeo 17, 147, 149, 152, 155
Fukunaga, Kenji 44
Fyodorov, V. 236, 247

Gerasimov, G. 95, 213
Gorbachev, M.S. 43, 49, 61, 63, 70, 73–82, 84–6, 88–90, 93, 95, 96, 109, 110, 116, 122, 123, 132, 142, 163, 167, 174–8, 181, 196, 197, 205–14, 216, 217–20, 223–29, 231, 232, 234, 236, 244, 251
Gorbacheva, Raisa 217
Gromyko, A.A. 42, 45, 47, 49, 50, 57, 58, 65, 66, 68, 76, 137, 139, 148, 190
Gubenko, N.N. 217

Hatoyama, Iichiro 147
Hiraiwa, Gaishi 220
Hirazawa, Kazuhige 70–2, 74
Hirohito, Emperor 221
Hitler, A. 140
Honecker, E. 61
Hua Guofeng 160, 161

Ikeda, Hayato 27
Ishida, Hirohide 165
Ishikawa, Tadao 144
Ishkov, A.A. 57
Itoyama, Eitaro 79
Iwashima, Hisao 157–59

Jaruzelski, W. 110
Jiang Zemin 142, 176

301

Name Index

Kaifu, Toshiki 198, 217–19, 228, 238
Kaihara, Osamu 159
Kanemaru, Shin 73, 74, 208, 211
Kapitsa, M.S. 50, 179, 188
Kasantsev 95
Katushev, K.F. 217
Kawai, Ryoichi 99, 130
Keizo, Obuchi
Khasbulatov, R. 234–6
Khrushchev, N.S. 44
Kimura, Hiroshi 208, 209
Kimura, Takeo 138
Kissinger, Henry 4, 14, 18
Kobayashi, Sadao 119, 120
Kohl, Helmut 208
Koivisto, M. 245
Korolev, V. 111, 129
Kosygin, A.N. 8, 44, 45, 51, 57–9, 152
Kosyrev, A. 216, 217, 232, 236, 238
Kovalenko, I. 81
Kozyrevski 32
Kudryavtsev, V. 46, 54
Kunadze, G.F. 155, 156, 201, 233, 236
Kurihara, Yuko 162
Kurisu, Hiroomi 192

Latyshev, I. 235
Leonov, P. 68
Levchenko, S.A. 164, 165
Li Peng 142, 176, 229
Liao Chengzhi 105, 158
Lukin, V. 218

Makayama, Taro
Malkevich, V.L. 128, 130
Mao Zedong 5, 6, 9, 136, 137, 138, 168
Maruyama, Hiroyuki 187
Masurov, K.T. 58
Matsumoto, Shunichi 41, 42, 45

Matsuoka, K. 159
Matsushita, Konosuke 160
Mayevski, V. 49
Mazurov 156
Miki, Takeo 65, 71, 144, 145
Mitsuzuka, Hiroshi 214
Miyamoto, Kenji 91, 154
Miyazawa, Kiichi 64, 139–41, 145, 153, 156, 229, 238, 246
Miyoshi, H. 159
Muto 249

Nagai 159
Nagano, Shigeo 104, 126
Nakasone, Yasuhiro 61, 73, 78, 80, 110, 126, 160, 163, 170, 189–91, 206
Nakayama, Taro 142, 205, 212, 229, 232, 233, 235, 241, 242
Niizeki, Kinya 41, 50, 52, 53
Nikolayev 218
Nishimura, Kumao 40
Nixon, Richard 3, 4, 5, 14, 16, 17, 19, 47
Novozhilov, V. 193, 198

Obuchi, Keizo 205, 226
Ohira, Masayoshi 13, 27, 29, 49, 50, 51, 52, 55, 60, 160
Ovchinnikov, V. 214
Oyama, Ikuo 169
Ozawa, Ichiro 205, 208, 209, 211

Pankin, B. 232, 234, 236,
Patolichev, N.S. 57
Podgorny, N.V. 44, 59
Poltoranin 246
Polyanski, D.S. 145, 149, 184, 194
Primakov, Ye. M. 74, 75

Qian Qichen 142

Reagan, Ronald 122

Name Index

Reischauer, Edwin O. 173
Rogachov, I.A. 32, 40, 83, 231
Rogers, William P. 51
Roh Tae Woo 178, 209
Roosevelt, F.D. 37

Sadorozhny, G. 7
Saeki, Kiichi 206, 207
Saito, Kunichiko 231, 240, 249
Sakurauchi, Yoshio 213
Samyatin, L. 53, 54
Sasaki, Kozo 137
Sase, Masamori 82
Sato, Eisaku 14, 16, 17, 45, 47, 48, 171
Scheel, Walter 51
Schumann, Maurice 51
Sedov 99
Semichastnov, I.F. 99, 103, 104
Shashin, V. 104
Shevardnadze, E.A. 49, 61, 67, 75–7, 79, 81, 84, 127, 205, 214–16, 218
Shigemitsu, Mamoru 38, 41
Shiina, Etsusaburo 144
Shultz, George 189
Sihanouk, Norodom 9
Solodovnik, S. 180
Sonoda, Sunao 147–9, 152, 153, 156, 194
Stalin, J.W. 37, 38, 167, 168, 231, 238
Sun Pinghua 18, 158
Sushkov 122, 126
Suzuki, Zenko 88, 124

Takamoto, Masaichi 89

Takeiri, Yoshikatsu 51, 138
Takeshita, Noboru 82, 83, 129
Tan Chenlin 141
Tanaka, Kakuei 12–14, 17, 18, 22, 27, 42, 49, 50, 52, 53–6, 58–63, 66, 69, 82, 83, 97, 104, 105, 137–9, 148, 149
Tikhonov 126
Troyanovski, O. 60, 144

Uemura, Kogoro 104
Uno, Sosuke 75, 84

Wada, Tsutomu 53
Watanabe, Koji 111, 129
Watanabe, Michio 237, 238, 240, 246
Watanabe, Taizo 215
Wörner, Manfred 180
Wu Xiuquan 160

Yakovlev, B.P. 217
Yamaguchi, Tsuruo 227
Yamashita, Ganri 194
Yanayev, G.I. 213
Yasov, D.T. 177, 225
Yeltsin, B.N. 209, 212, 223, 225, 231, 232, 234–8, 240, 243–52,
Yoshida, Shigeru 39, 40, 41

Zhang Aiping 162
Zhang Caitian 160
Zhao Ziyang 189
Zhou Enlai 5, 8, 9, 13, 17–19, 22, 51, 137–9, 165, 169

SUBJECT INDEX

Abandonment of alliance with USA (opinion poll question) 199–200
Afghanistan, Soviet invasion of 30, 115, 118, 124
Aid, Japan's to Soviet Union/Russia 225, 233ff., 249, 251
Air force, Soviet 187f.
Alliance with USA 10f., 22, 23, 30, 43, 80, 84, 91f., 150, 158, 162, 167, 169, 171, 179, 180, 199, 200, 219, 223
Anti-hegemony clause 19, 136, 143, 145, 150–2, 155, 181
Anti-Soviet alliance 140
APEC (Asia Pacific Economic Cooperation) 175
Article 9 of Japanese constitution 167
ASEAN (Association of Southeast Asian Nations) 135, 172

Backfire bombers 165
Baikal-Amur-Magistrale (BAM) 103, 104, 107
Border patrols, on the islands 195
Brezhnev Doctrine 6

Cairo Declaration 36, 38
Cambodia 9
Cape Nosappu 138
China, views on territorial question 138–43, 229
Coal imports, Japan's 98, 99, 113, 124, 127
Collective security in Asia 7, 8, 20, 45, 57, 148, 150, 163, 176, 181
Comecon region 132
Communist Party of China 5
Communist Party of Japan 91, 92, 154, 227
Commonwealth of Independent States (CIS) 234, 241, 245
Conference for Security and Cooperation in Europe (CSCE) 65, 176, 218
Conference of Foreign Ministers (Shevardnadze's proposal) 218
Continental shelf of Sakhalin, prospecting on 100, 109, 116–19, 121–3, 130
Cooperation, Korea's willingness to engage in 228
Copper deposits 101
Cultural Revolution viii, 5, 8, 9
Czechoslovakia, Soviet invasion of 6, 7, 91, 142

Defence, Japan's efforts in 151–62
Democratic Socialist Party (DSP) 92, 190, 199
Diaoyütai *see* Senkaku Islands
Diplomatic Lexicon, various editions 68–70
Disinformation of KGB 164–5
Diversification, capability of 112–13
Doctrine of limited sovereignty of Soviet states *see* Brezhnev Doctrine
Dulles' threat 42

Eastern Treaties 65

Subject Index

Economic zone, 200 nautical miles 64
Eight-point proposal (S. Abe) 210
Equidistance, Concept of 29
European models for Asia 219
Export-Import Bank (Exim Bank) 105, 110, 121, 124, 125, 132, 225

Financial aid from Japan to Soviet Union 226, 233, 238
Fishing rights 59, 62, 63, 64, 87, 96, 110, 115, 147
Five powers conference, proposal of 218
Five principles of Japan against Soviet Union 232
Five-Phase Plan, Yeltsin's 212, 234, 235, 238

Germany and Japan, Stalin on 168
Germany, Reunification of 208
Glasnost in territorial question 84
Gorbachev's visit, opinions on 226–7
Gradual return of islands (*dankaiteki-henkan-ron*) 74
Graves, visiting 66–7

Hegemonism, Hegemony 135, 137, 143, 145, 154, 155, 156, 163
Helsinki Agreement *see* Conference for Security and Cooperation in Europe (CSCE)
Hokkaido, natural gas supply to 117

Indochina conflict 3, 9
INF question 189, 191
Inseparability of politics and economics, principle of 30, 96, 110, 126, 133, 177, 224–5, 227, 238–9
International security in Asian Pacific region 181
Internationalisation (*kokusaika*) 239

Japanese-American alliance 135, 160, 190, 191, 193
Japanese-American cooperation on defence issues 172
Japanese-American security pact *see* Alliance with USA
Japanese defence and security policy 181ff.
Japanese military technology for China 159, 160
Japanese prisoners of war 221, 250
Japanese-Russian security talks 248–9
Japanese threat from Soviet viewpoint 201
Joint Communiqué of 1991 58, 61, 77
Joint Declaration of 1956 43, 69, 70, 73, 74, 90, 193, 213, 214, 222, 223, 226, 236, 247, 255–7 (full text)
Joint Declaration of 1973 221, 225, 258–64 (full text)
Joint Japanese-Soviet Economic Committee (JJSEC) 55, 98, 99, 102, 116, 120, 122–3, 127–9, 184
Joint ventures 116, 127, 128, 130, 131

Kaliningrad 212
Keidanren 98, 105
KGB (Soviet secret service) 78, 164, 165
Komei Party 92, 199
Korea viii, 178, 209
Korea, double representation in United Nations 228
Korea, colonisation of 221

Korean Airlines, shooting down of passenger aircraft 115
Korean peninsula 167, 222, 229, 250
Korean war 168
Krasnoyarsk, speech in 75, 81, 174, 177, 218
Kurile Islands 32, 36–42, 137

Land lease in Shikotan 246, 252
Landing manoeuvres of Soviet troops 191, 195
Liberal Democratic Party 141, 144–5, 179, 189, 199, 208–9, 211, 234, 243
Loans, Soviet Union's need for 100, 124
Long-term governmental agreement 132

Major solution of territorial question 240
Manchuria viii
Martial law in Poland 125
Medium-range missiles in Asia 188–91
Memorandum, Soviet of 27 January 1960 43
MiG incident 115, 158, 183–5
Militarism in Japan, revival of 167, 170, 179
Militarisation of islands 68
Military cooperation of Japan and China 157, 159, 161
Military cooperation of Japan and USA 171
Military cooperation with China (Soviet accusation) 161, 162
Ministry for International Trade and Industry 120, 122
Minor solution of territorial question 241
Mongolia viii

Nakhodka, port of 99
Nationalities, problems of 216
NATO 135, 180, 181, 208
Natural gas 100, 117, 118, 120, 121
Natural gas and oil on Sakhalin *see* Sakhalin project
Natural gas in Yakutiya 102
Natural gas pipes deal 124
Natural gas project in Yamburg 124
Neutrality pact 82, 134
New Liberal Club 199
'New Thinking' in Soviet Union 75, 79, 127, 169, 181, 200, 206
Nixon Doctrine 3, 10
'Nixon Shock' 5
Normalization of Sino-Japanese relations 13, 14, 17, 21–3, 51, 52, 55
Normalization of Sino-Soviet relations 30
Northern territories 133, 139, 141, 142. 192
Day 88
Nuclear aggression, renunciation of 191
Nuclear arms in North Korea 222
Nuclear arms, Japan's renunciation of 170, 190
Nuclear waste 251
Nuclear weapons in Japan 173, 174, 190

Ogasawara 40
Oil and natural gas off Sakhalin *see* Sakhalin project
Oil diplomacy, China's 105, 106
Oil drilling: in Siberia 98
project in Tyumen 55, 98, 102, 106, 114, 219
Oil shock 97

Subject Index 307

Oil, crude from China 105, 106
Okhotsk, Sea of 171
Okinawa 10, 40, 42, 44, 47, 48, 71, 143, 190, 207, 246
Opinion polls 16, 17, 85–7, 93, 94, 198–201, 213, 227, 248,

Pacific Economic Cooperation Conference (PECC) 175, 226
Pacific fleet of Soviet Union 38, 161, 182, 185–7, 191, 197
Package solution to territorial question 70, 73, 74, 92, 244
Paper and pulp industry 100, 130
Parliamentary League for Japanese-Soviet Friendship 165
Peaceful coexistence, five principles of 7, 13
People's diplomacy 16
Post-war borders 45, 46, 51, 65, 83, 213
Potsdam Declaration 38
Prevention of incidents at sea, agreement on 234
Proletarian Internationalism 6
Property rights, island-dwellers' 237

Raw materials, demand for 97, 112, 113
Reduction of Soviet troops on islands 222, 225, 245
Referendum, March 213
Regional stability and Japan 180–1
Remilitarisation of Japan (opinion poll) 199–200
Residual sovereignty 47–8
Return of two islands 72, 74, 87
Revision of Japanese-American security pact 43
Russian national feeling 235
Russian nationalism 224, 245

Safeguard agreement 222
Sakhalin Oil Development Cooperation (SODECO) 116, 119, 122
Sakhalin project 100, 109, 116–19, 121–3, 130
Sanctions 115, 118, 123, 124, 125
Sea routes, control of 182
Security pact with USA, see Alliance with USA
Self-defence forces (SDF) 157, 158, 167, 169, 172, 173, 199
Senkaku Islands (Diaoyütai) 84, 143, 151,
Seven-point plan with Soviet Union 214
Siberia, development of 29, 52, 56, 80, 97–8, 107–108, 124–7, 133, 136, 176, 178, 207, 209, 229, 241
Sino-American détente 5, 20
Sino-Japanese normalisation see Normalisation of Sino-Japanese relations
Sino-Japanese *rapprochement* 11, 115, 154, 165
Sino-Japanese relations viii, ix, 12, 16, 29, 50, 105, 113, 114, 119, 123, 134, 138–9, 146, 161
Sino-Japanese treaty negotiations 29, 115, 135, 136, 141, 143–48, 152–5, 157, 181, 193
Sino-Soviet relations 4, 10, 12, 23, 30, 45, 106, 115, 137, 143, 154–7, 162, 181, 196, 229
Socialist Party of Japan (SPJ) 92, 137, 187, 189, 190
South Korea, Gorbachev's talks in 228
South Kuriles 40, 48
Soviet policies on Asia see Collective security in Asia

Soviet-Japanese economic cooperation *see* Joint Japanese-Soviet Economic Committee
Sovietisation of islands 67–8
Surveys *see* Opinion polls
Swing concept 182

Territorial demands, opinion poll on 94
Theory of differentiation of the three worlds 136
Threat to Japan by Soviet Union 181, 198, 200–1
Three principles of the renunciation of nuclear weapons 173, 178, 191
Timber: imports 113; resources 98, 124
Toshiba Affair 78, 129
Trade between China and Soviet Union 115
Treaty of friendship, alliance and mutual support (Soviet Union-China) 146, 167
Treaty of good neighbourliness and cooperation (Soviet Union-Japan) 144, 148–50, 269ff. (full text); (Soviet Union-South Korea) 228
Treaty of peace and friendship between Japan and China *see* Sino-Japanese treaty negotiations
Treaty of St Petersburg 32, 36
Treaty of Portsmouth 32, 36
Treaty of Shimoda 32, 88

Treaty, peace, between Japan and the Soviet Union/Russia 42–4, 50, 52, 53, 58, 59, 65, 69, 70, 72, 76, 83, 92, 139, 143–4, 192, 215, 221, 231–3, 235, 238, 246
Treaty, peace, of San Francisco 39, 46, 92, 225
Triangle Japan-China-Soviet Union 11
Trilateral consultations 219
Trustee system for islands 237
Tyumen *see* Oil drilling project in Tyumen

United front, anti-Soviet 155
United Nations 138, 169
Unity of politics and economics *see* Inseparability of . . .

Visit of Pres. Nixon to People's Republic of China 5
Vladivostok: Gorbachev's speech in 75, 79, 109, 174, 176, 218; opening of city 130
Vostochny, port of 99, 101, 110, 127, 220

White Paper on defence, Japanese (1970) 170
Williamsburg, G7 conference 191
Wrangel Bay, port in 99, 273

Yalta Agreement 37, 91
Yeltsin's visit 243, 245